"Men's lives are complicated, despite stereotypes to the contrary. Recognizing and making sense of the challenges faced by male survivors of sexual abuse requires even more complex thinking. We're very fortunate that Richard Gartner and a who's who of experts have shared their insights – and the voices of many men they've worked with – in order to help professionals better understand and serve these men. This book is a must-read for therapists, lawyers, clergy, and anyone who spends time with male survivors." – **Andrew P. Smiler**, Ph.D., Board President, MaleSurvivor: National Organization against Male Sexual Victimization; Past President, Society for the Psychological Study of Men and Masculinity, Division 51, American Psychological Association; author, *Dating and Sex: A Guide for the 21st Century Teen Boy.*

"*Understanding the Sexual Betrayal of Boys and Men* is a chorus of voices, coming from a range of perspectives, on the oft-misunderstood topic of men who have been sexually abused. Covering neurobiological, medical, psychological, empirical, diversity and first person perspectives, it offers practical and evidence-based information that will be a lifesaver for men who have survived abuse. This book is a 'must read' for every therapist working with such men." – **Ronald F. Levant**, Ed.D., M.B.A., A.B.P.P., Professor of Psychology, University of Akron; Former President, American Psychological Association; co-editor, *The Psychology of Men and Masculinities, A New Psychology of Men*, and *New Psychotherapy for Men.*

"*Understanding the Sexual Betrayal of Boys and Men* is a treasure trove of illuminating essays on the devastating effects of childhood sexual abuse on boys, and on the men they become. Approximately one in six men in our culture have been sexually abused as children. Authors from a variety of fields of expertise describe the effects of childhood sexual abuse on brain chemistry and structure, interpersonal distrust, distorted and fearful feelings about the body, issues of gender and sexual identity confusion on boys, and more. All of this is in the context of straitjacketing stereotypes that instruct men not to be vulnerable. Also exposed is the surrounding dark side our culture that has implicitly allowed abuse of boys, whether in the church, in sports, or as aspects of high-ranking privileged men's customs. This book is a must-read for anyone interested in the lives of men.

The editor, Richard Gartner, PhD, was the first major mental health expert to document, and describe in detail, the high prevalence of sexual abuse of boys and its effects on them. His specialized treatment approaches are described in earlier books: Betrayed as Boys: Psychodynamic Treatment of Men Abused as Boys and Beyond Betrayal: Taking Charge of Your Life after Boyhood Sexual Abuse." – **Elizabeth Howell**, Ph.D., author, *Understanding and Treating Dissociative Identity Disorder: A Relational Approach* and *The Dissociative Mind*; co-editor, *The Dissociative Mind in Psychoanalysis: Understanding and Working with Trauma.*

"*Understanding the Sexual Betrayal of Boys and Men* is an essential and incisive compendium. Integrating multiple perspectives, this book addresses the full implications of male sexual abuse: its emotional, physiological, and legal aftermath. The contributing authors achieve this with depth, wisdom, and compassion. We must thank Gartner for continuing to awaken us to this trauma, and for releasing these men from the shadows." – **Sue Grand**, Ph.D., author, *The Reproduction of Evil: A Clinical and Cultural Perspective* and *The Hero in the Mirror: From Fear to Fortitude.*

"Public and professional recognition of male sexual abuse did not come into view until the 1980s. Dr. Gartner changed that and continues to do so. He has written a number of books on male sexual abuse and now, by means of this book and its cohort volume (*Healing Sexually Betrayed Men and Boys*), we have a much better understanding of male sexual victimization.

Gartner does a masterful job of gathering mental health professionals of various backgrounds, plus academics, survivors, attorneys, and a physician to contribute to this edited book. The chapters provide clinical examples and personal vignettes. Together, these give a wide-ranging picture of male sexual victimization. A broad range of topics is considered: historical, biological, medical, institutional and cultural effects and issues related to exploitation and sexuality (including trafficking in adolescent boys), sexual interests and compulsions, and sexual dysfunctions.

Understanding the Sexual Betrayal of Boys and Men will impact how male sexual victimization is socially and personally understood and clinically and legally addressed. This book is a compulsory read for all those who want to understand the sexual victimization of boys and men." – **Judith L. Alpert**, Ph.D., Professor of Applied Psychology and Former Co-Director, Trauma and Violence Transdisciplinary Studies Program, New York University; Professor and Consultant, New York University Postdoctoral Program in Psychotherapy and Psychoanalysis.

Understanding the Sexual Betrayal of Boys and Men

Understanding the Sexual Betrayal of Boys and Men: The Trauma of Sexual Abuse is an indispensable go-to book for understanding male sexual victimization. It has become increasingly clear since the 1980s that men and boys, like women and girls, are sexually abused and assaulted in alarming numbers. Yet there have been few resources available to victims, their loved ones, or those trying to help them.

Richard B. Gartner has been in the vanguard of clinicians treating male sexual victimization and has written extensively about it, initially in professional papers, then in his landmark 1999 book for clinicians *Betrayed as Boys: Psychodynamic Treatment of Sexually Abused Men*, continuing with his 2005 work *Beyond Betrayal: Taking Charge of Your Life after Boyhood Sexual Abuse*. He has been a tireless teacher, clinician, and advocate for male victims of sexual abuse in the classroom, the lecture hall, and of course the consulting room as well as in newspaper, television, radio, and online interviews.

Dr. Gartner has gathered together expert colleagues from the trauma, psychoanalytic, medical, and survivor treatment fields. Together, they have created a comprehensive guide to what was once thought to be a rarity but now is clearly an all-too-common occurrence. *Understanding the Sexual Betrayal of Boys and Men* looks at the realities of male sexual victimization, guiding clinicians and lay people alike to understand the complexities of the devastation it causes in victimized boys and men. It considers topics as diverse as:

- sexual assault in institutions like the military, sports teams, schools, universities, and religious organizations;
- sex trafficking of boys and adolescents;
- neurobiology and brain chemistry of male survivors of sexual abuse;
- gender and sexual dysfunctions and confusions resulting from sexual exploitation and trauma;
- physicians' treatment of sexually abused men's medical problems;
- socio-cultural influences on processing and treating men's and boys' sexual victimization.

Understanding the Sexual Betrayal of Boys and Men is required reading for anyone working with male victims of sexual abuse and assault at any level – psychotherapists, rape counselors, attorneys, journalists, guidance counselors, physicians, clergy, graduate students, and lawmakers – and helpful to lay people interested in this often-unrecognized problem.

Richard B. Gartner is Training and Supervising Analyst, Faculty, and Founding Director of the Sexual Abuse Service at the William Alanson White Psychoanalytic Institute in New York City; author of *Betrayed as Boys: Psychodynamic Treatment of Sexually Abused Men* (1999) and *Beyond Betrayal: Taking Charge of Your Life after Boyhood Sexual Abuse* (2005); and editor of *Trauma and Countertrauma, Resilience and Counterresilience: Insights from Psychoanalysts and Trauma Experts* (2017) and *Memories of Sexual Betrayal: Truth, Fantasy, Repression, and Dissociation* (1997) as well as the companion volume to this one, *Healing Sexually Betrayed Men and Boys: Treatment for Sexual Abuse, Assault, and Trauma*. Co-Founder and Past President of MaleSurvivor.org, he is a pioneer in treating sexually abused men and is quoted widely in the media on the subject.

PSYCHOANALYSIS IN A NEW KEY BOOK SERIES

DONNEL STERN
Series Editor

When music is played in a new key, the melody does not change, but the notes that make up the composition do: change in the context of continuity, continuity that perseveres through change. Psychoanalysis in a New Key publishes books that share the aims psychoanalysts have always had, but that approach them differently. The books in the series are not expected to advance any particular theoretical agenda, although to this date most have been written by analysts from the Interpersonal and Relational orientations.

The most important contribution of a psychoanalytic book is the communication of something that nudges the reader's grasp of clinical theory and practice in an unexpected direction. Psychoanalysis in a New Key creates a deliberate focus on innovative and unsettling clinical thinking. Because that kind of thinking is encouraged by exploration of the sometimes surprising contributions to psychoanalysis of ideas and findings from other fields, Psychoanalysis in a New Key particularly encourages interdisciplinary studies. Books in the series have married psychoanalysis with dissociation, trauma theory, sociology, and criminology. The series is open to the consideration of studies examining the relationship between psychoanalysis and any other field—for instance, biology, literary and art criticism, philosophy, systems theory, anthropology, and political theory.

But innovation also takes place within the boundaries of psychoanalysis, and Psychoanalysis in a New Key therefore also presents work that reformulates thought and practice without leaving the precincts of the field. Books in the series focus, for example, on the significance of personal values in psychoanalytic practice, on the complex interrelationship between the analyst's clinical work and personal life, on the consequences for the clinical situation when patient and analyst are from different cultures, and on the need for psychoanalysts to accept the degree to which they knowingly satisfy their own wishes during treatment hours, often to the patient's detriment. A full list of all titles in this series is available at: https://www.routledge.com/series/LEAPNKBS

RECENT TITLES IN THIS SERIES:

Vol. 41 *Understanding the Sexual Betrayal of Boys and Men: The Trauma of Sexual Abuse* Edited by Richard B. Gartner

Vol. 40 *Healing Sexually Betrayed Men and Boys: Treatment for Sexual Abuse, Assault, and Trauma* Edited by Richard B. Gartner

Understanding the Sexual Betrayal of Boys and Men

The Trauma of Sexual Abuse

Edited by Richard B. Gartner

Routledge
Taylor & Francis Group
LONDON AND NEW YORK

First published 2018
by Routledge
2 Park Square, Milton Park, Abingdon, Oxon OX14 4RN

and by Routledge
711 Third Avenue, New York, NY 10017

Routledge is an imprint of the Taylor & Francis Group, an informa business

British Library Cataloguing in Publication Data
A catalogue record for this book is available from the British Library

Library of Congress Cataloging in Publication Data
Names: Gartner, Richard B., editor.
Title: Understanding the sexual betrayal of boys and men : the trauma of sexual abuse / edited by Richard B. Gartner.
Description: New York : Routledge, [2017] | Series: Psychoanalysis in a new key book series ; 41 | Includes bibliographical references and index.
Identifiers: LCCN 2017009592| ISBN 9781138942219 (hardback : alk. paper) | ISBN 9781138942226 (pbk. : alk. paper) | ISBN 9781315673240 (master e-ISBN) | ISBN 9781317375586 (web pdf) | ISBN 9781317375579 (epub) | ISBN 9781317375562 (mobipocket/kindle)
Subjects: LCSH: Adult child sexual abuse victims. | Male sexual abuse victims. | Psychodynamic psychotherapy. | Psychotherapist and patient.
Classification: LCC RC569.5.A28 U53 2017 | DDC 616.85/8369—dc23
LC record available at https://lccn.loc.gov/2017009592

ISBN: 978-1-138-94221-9 (hbk)
ISBN: 978-1-138-94222-6 (pbk)
ISBN: 978-1-315-67324-0 (ebk)

Typeset in Times New Roman
by Swales & Willis Ltd, Exeter, Devon, UK

In memory of
David L. Zucker
1947–2016
cherished friend,
witty, droll, and loving,
we said goodbye too soon

Contents

Acknowledgments

I am grateful to many colleagues, friends, and family who offered help, support, and encouragement as I prepared the manuscripts for this book and its companion volume, *Healing Sexually Betrayed Men and Boys: Treatment for Sexual Abuse, Assault, and Trauma*. I am especially appreciative of my colleagues at MaleSurvivor: National Organization against Male Sexual Victimization and the William Alanson White Psychoanalytic Institute's Sexual Abuse Service; my personal cohort of peer supervisors with whom I have met weekly for over 30 years; my publisher and editors; the contributors to this volume; and my closest family and friends. You all know who you are. Thank you.

But I want most to acknowledge the candor, courage, and generosity of the men I have met over the years who taught me what it means for a man to be sexually abused. My patients, numerous members of MaleSurvivor, colleagues who are openly both survivors and professionals, and prominent men who bravely revealed their histories to the world, thus encouraging others to seek help: You are the people I acknowledge as being central to the success of this book. You deserve compassion, admiration, and a welcome place at life's table.

Contributors

Lee Beckstead, Ph.D., is a psychologist in private practice in Salt Lake City, Utah. His research focused on understanding the benefits and harms of trying to change sexual orientation. His clinical work has focused on helping others resolve sexual orientation, religious, and social conflicts. He was part of on the American Psychological Association's Task Force to evaluate research on changing sexual orientation and make therapeutic recommendations. He has been a member of the International Academy of Sex Research since 2004 and feels privileged to be involved with the MaleSurvivor Weekend of Recovery program since 2005.

Grant H. Brenner, M.D., is a psychoanalytically-trained psychiatrist known for enabling his clients to overcome stubborn obstacles and build resilience, bringing nearly two decades of consultation, workshops, speaking engagements, teaching, therapy, and coaching to his clients. He is a co-founder of Neighborhood Psychiatric Associates of Manhattan, PLLC, is on faculty at Mount Sinai Beth Israel, is Director of the Trauma Service of the William Alanson White Institute where he studied psychoanalysis and organizational psychodynamics, and serves on the board of Disaster Psychiatry Outreach, a non-profit. He is co-author of *Irrelationship: How We Use Dysfunctional Relationships to Hide from Intimacy* and the forthcoming sequel *Relationship Sanity* (anticipated CRP, 2018) and published *Creating Spiritual and Psychological Resilience: Integrating Care in Disaster Relief Work*.

William Burmester, M.A., MFT, has been a licensed marriage and family therapist in private practice in California since 1994, with training and experience in the treatment of sexual abuse and other relational trauma, dissociative disorders and PTSD, using EMDR, sensorimotor psychotherapy, modern and relational psychoanalytic psychotherapy, and mindfulness practices. Since 1990, he has facilitated groups for men healing from sexual abuse and since 2002 has been a facilitator with MaleSurvivor's Weekends of Recovery. He served for many years on the board of the East Bay intern training organization, GHHTC, and has presented at various conferences on the process of psychotherapy with male survivors as well as on the portrayal of male sexual abuse survivors in film.

Scott D. Easton, Ph.D., ACSW, LMSW, is an associate professor at the Boston College School of Social Work and chair of the Department of Mental Health. Dr. Easton's program of research has focused on identifying risk and protection factors for mental health outcomes of adults who experienced traumatic experiences in childhood. In 2010 he partnered with national survivor organizations in conducting the largest study to date on adult male survivors of child sexual abuse. This study resulted in numerous peer-reviewed publications in leading academic journals on topics such as disclosure patterns, trauma processing, suicidality, and post-traumatic growth. His scholarly endeavors have been supported by the John A. Hartford Foundation, Boston College Office of the Provost, and the National Institutes of Health. Most recently, he received an R03 Award from the National Institute on Aging (R03AG048768) for a project entitled "Population Analysis of Male Survivors of Child Sexual Abuse at Mid and Late Life." Dr. Easton serves on the Archdiocese Review Board for the Catholic Church of Boston and editorial boards of the *Journal of Loss and Trauma* and *Psychology of Men and Masculinity*. He regularly presents his research on men with histories of sexual abuse at local, national, and international conferences.

Howard Fradkin, Ph.D., LICDC-CS, has counseled male and female survivors of sexual victimization in individual, couples, and group psychotherapy, as well as weekend workshops, in his 34-year career as a psychologist, and trained over 2,500 professional colleagues. He authored *Joining Forces: Empowering Male Survivors to Thrive*, published by Hay House in 2012. One of Dr. Fradkin's proudest achievements was appearing as an expert on Oprah Winfrey's "200 Men" shows in 2010. He was a founding board member of MaleSurvivor and an Advisory Board Member. As Chair and Co-Chair of the Weekends of Recovery program from 2001 to 2016, he directed over 50 Weekends of Recovery. He founded Affirmations: A Center for Psychotherapy and Growth, in Columbus, Ohio, in 1984, and is currently Partner Emeritus, where he provides psychotherapy in the areas of trauma recovery, depression and anxiety, alcoholism and drug addiction, sex addiction, sexual orientation confusion and acceptance, and HIV and AIDS.

Richard B. Gartner, Ph.D., is Training and Supervising Analyst, faculty, and Founding Director of the Sexual Abuse Service at the William Alanson White Psychoanalytic Institute in New York City, which has honored him with its Director's Award for his contributions to the psychoanalytic understanding of trauma. A pioneer in treating sexually abused men, Dr. Gartner has written and spoken widely about the subject and has been quoted in media throughout the world. He is the editor of this book's companion volume, *Healing Sexually Betrayed Men and Boys: Treatment for Sexual Abuse, Assault, and Trauma*. In addition, he is the author of *Betrayed as Boys: Psychodynamic Treatment of Sexually Abused Men* (1999), runner up for the Gradiva Award for Best Book on a Clinical Subject given by the National Association for the Advancement of Psychoanalysis (NAAP), as well as *Beyond Betrayal: Taking Charge of Your Life after Boyhood Sexual Abuse* (2005). He most recently edited *Trauma and Countertrauma, Resilience and Counterresilience: Insights from Psychoanalysts and Trauma Experts* (2017), and also edited *Memories of Sexual Betrayal: Truth, Fantasy, Repression, and Dissociation* (1997). He is a founder and past president of MaleSurvivor: National Organization against Male Sexual Victimization (malesurvivor.org), which honored him by establishing an award in his name, the Richard Gartner Award for Clinical Contributions, and is a fellow of the Psychoanalysis and Trauma Divisions of the American Psychological Association. www.richardgartner.com

James W. Hopper, Ph.D., is an independent consultant and Teaching Associate in Psychology at Harvard Medical School. For over 25 years his research, clinical and consulting work has focused on the psychological and biological effects of child abuse, sexual assault, and other traumatic experiences. He has conducted research on male victims of sexual abuse, the nature of traumatic memories, the biological bases of dissociation, and dysfunction of the brain's reward circuitry in PTSD. As a clinician Dr. Hopper works with adults who have experienced abuse or assault as children or adults. In his forensic work he testifies on short- and long-term impacts of child abuse and sexual assault. Dr. Hopper was a founding board member of 1in6, a non-profit organization that serves men with histories of childhood sexual abuse, and served on the Peace Corps Sexual Assault Advisory Council. He consults and teaches nationally and internationally to clinicians, military and civilian investigators, prosecutors, victim advocates, commanders, and higher education administrators.

Joe Kort, Ph.D., MSW, is a psychotherapist and author who started his practice in 1985. He specializes in Gay Affirmative Psychotherapy, emphasizing how being knowledgeable about LGBT issues informs the therapeutic process, IMAGO Relationship Therapy, a specific program to help couples and singles learn to improve their communication and relationship skills. He also specializes in sex therapy and sexual identity issues, including Out-Of-Control Sexual Behavior; responsible non-monogamy/monogamy; childhood sexual, physical and emotional abuse; mixed-orientation relationships coming out; and depression and anxiety disorders. Dr. Kort graduated from Michigan State University with dual majors in Psychology and Social Work. At Wayne State University, he earned his Master's in Social Work (MSW), then a Master's (MA) in Psychology, and has received his Doctorate (Ph.D.) in Clinical Sexology from the American Academy of Clinical Sexologists (AACS).

David Lisak, Ph.D., is a researcher and forensic consultant who for 25 years has studied the causes and consequences of interpersonal violence. His work has focused on the long-term effects of sexual abuse in men, the relationship between child abuse and violence, and the motives and characteristics of rapists. Dr. Lisak has served as a consultant to judicial, prosecutor, and law enforcement education programs across the country, and has conducted workshops in all 50 states. He consults widely with universities, the four services of the US Military, the Department of Defense, and other institutions regarding sexual assault prevention and policies, and frequently serves as an expert witness in homicide and sexual assault cases. Dr. Lisak is a founding member of 1in6, a non-profit agency that serves men who were sexually abused as children.

Ernesto Mujica, Ph.D., is a supervisor of psychotherapy at the William Alanson White Institute, where he is an associate editor of the Institute's journal, *Contemporary Psychoanalysis*. He is also a supervisor of psychotherapy at the Doctoral Programs in Clinical Psychology of Teachers College/Columbia University and at the City University of New York. Dr. Mujica was the Clinical Co-Chair for the 2012 and 2014 International Conferences, and he is a member of the MaleSurvivor Facilitator Team for its Weekends of Recovery program. In 2010 Dr. Mujica was President of the Division of Psychoanalysis for the New York State Psychological Association, and he has served on the Board of the Division of Psychoanalysis of the American Psychological Association.

Steven L. Procopio, ACSW, LICSW, is a consultant whose expertise is working with males and complex trauma with an emphasis on commercially sexually exploited boys, adolescent males and young men. Steven brings extensive experience in the area of public health, with a focus on HIV, homelessness, youth services and service coordination. He has been a program director, service coordinator, trainer, educator, and project developer. He is a graduate of the University of Connecticut School of Social Work. Steven's work in the area of homelessness has involved managing a multi-disciplinary team of providers for a federal health disparities project with a focus on homeless persons with chronic disease. Steven has taught and presented on issues of male victimization on a local and national level, consulting with various groups on the effects of the commercial exploitation of boys and young men.

Frank Spinelli, M.D., FACP, is a licensed and board certified internist. He is an Associate Clinical Professor at New York Medical College and a fellow of the American College of Physicians. He is the author of *Advocate Guide to Gay Men's Health and Wellness*, published in 2008 by Alyson Books and *Pee-Shy: A Memoir*, published by Kensington Books in 2014. In 2012, he was featured in two documentaries, *Positive Youth* and the Emmy-nominated *30 Years from Here*. Currently, he is a contributor to Dr. Oz's Sharecare website.

Jim Struve, LCSW, has been a clinical social worker since 1976, currently in private practice in Salt Lake City. With special attention to mindful presence in the healing relationship, Jim provides psychotherapy services to individuals, couples, and groups. He works with a wide range of client issues: trauma (including male survivors of sexual trauma), relationship enhancement (including intimacy, assertiveness, identity, gender, self-esteem, and sexuality), and dissociative disorders (including Dissociative Identity Spectrum). Jim is a founding member of MaleSurvivor.org. He was the recipient of the Richard Gartner Outstanding Clinical Services Award at the 2010 International MaleSurvivor Conference. He is also a founding member and Coordinator (since 2004) for the LGBTQ-Affirmative Psychotherapist Guild of Utah. Jim is the author of "Dancing With The Patriarchy: The Politics of Sexual Abuse," in *The Sexually Abused Male, Volume 1: Prevalence, Impact, & Treatment*, edited by Mic Hunter (1990) and co-author, with Mic Hunter, of *The Ethical Use of Touch in Psychotherapy* (1997).

Introduction

Richard B. Gartner

When I began speaking in public about the sexual victimization of men and boys in the early 1990s, I frequently met with blank stares from both lay people and colleagues. The subject was rarely mentioned in either the literature or the media, and many doubted such behavior ever happened.

When speaking to professional audiences, I began by asking how many among them were treating male patients who had been sexually victimized. In a group of 100 therapists, perhaps two or three would raise their hands. I then asked, "How many of you have ever asked a man about a history of sexual victimization?" Virtually no one ever raised a hand. Professionals had simply not been trained to inquire about male sexual victimization. Indeed, they were generally not trained to inquire about childhood sexual abuse at all.

I never had that training either, and I also never asked about male sexual victimization when I began practicing. Early in my career some men did reveal boyhood sexual abuse, but in my ignorance I never addressed it at any length and never knew how to understand their disclosures or deal with the aftereffects of their sexual trauma. The little I'd heard about childhood sexual abuse suggested accounts of it should be approached cautiously, as they were likely to be expressions of sexual fantasy or wish fulfillment rather than reports of real events. This was the legacy of early battles in the psychoanalytic world about the origins of hysteria and whether patients who reported being sexually abused as children could be believed.[1]

1 See Gartner (1997) for a discussion of how Freud recanted his early reports about treating sexually abused young women, later insisting that Ferenczi's discussions of his own work with sexually abused patients should be silenced.

But in the 1980s a patient of mine slowly began to recall boyhood sexual abuse by his father and brother. Memory fragments emerged slowly over a period of months, with neither of us initially understanding the portent of the unnerving flashes and partial images he recalled. There was partial confirmation of his abuse when he confided in a sister who disclosed she had been abused as well. Then other pieces of his history began to fall into place as his sexual abuse became clearer.[2] I could no longer deny what we were dealing with.

I looked into the professional literature for help in understanding how to treat this man. I was surprised to discover that other than a few articles (e.g., Nasjleti, 1980; Finkelhor, 1981; Johnson & Shrier, 1985), virtually nothing had been written about male sexual victimization.

There were articles and books about female victims of sexual abuse and incest, though not many (Herman, 1981, is one example). These usually acknowledged the existence of male victims, but included no discussion, leaving the reader to believe either that boys and men were rarely abused or that the impact on them was not different than on female victims. Neither, as it turns out, is true.

By the time I wrote *Betrayed as Boys: Psychodynamic Treatment of Sexually Abused Men* (Gartner, 1999), more articles and some books had been published about male sexual victimization in the professional literature (e.g., Briere, Evans, Runtz, & Wall, 1988; Bolton, Morris, & MacEachron, 1989; Singer, 1989; Mezey & King, 1992; Gonsiorek, Bera, & LeTourneau, 1994; Friedrich, 1995; Lisak, Hopper, & Song, 1996; Holmes & Slap, 1998). Additionally, there were now books on the subject written for sexually abused men themselves (e.g., Lew, 1988; Hunter, 1990). The field had gained a certain amount of professional recognition, although it was not yet part of the public discourse.

This changed in 2002, when an increasingly public series of scandals emerged involving sexual abuse of boys by Roman Catholic priests and its subsequent cover-up by the Church hierarchy.[3] At that point, whether or not any individual accusation was thought to have merit, it was undeniable that the sexual victimization of young boys by adults could and did take place.

2 See the case of Patrick in Gartner (1999) for descriptions of this treatment.

3 See Chapter 8 in this volume by Burmester on institutional dissociation and Chapter 9 by Gartner on abuse by priests for further discussion.

By now, as demonstrated by the contributors to this book and its companion volume, *Healing Sexually Betrayed Men and Boys: Treatment for Sexual Abuse, Assault, and Trauma*, we know much more about male sexual victimization than we did in 1999. Rather than write, as I did in *Betrayed as Boys*, in a single voice, sharing my own expertise, I have invited individuals experienced with diverse aspects of male sexual victimization to write about their areas of knowledge.[4] They are a varied group, including mental health professionals of distinct backgrounds, academics, survivors, survivor-professionals, attorneys, and a physician. Each has written about a topic in which he or she is experienced and authoritative. In this volume the focus is on understanding how a boy or man processes sexual victimization, using clinical examples. The companion volume focuses on the healing process for sexually traumatized boys and men.

This book introduces the reader to sexually abused men and their experience, first through clinical and personal vignettes (Gartner, Lisak), then through understanding a male survivor's reaction to somatic problems (Spinelli), research about male sexual victimization (Easton), and brain chemistry after trauma (Brenner, Hopper). Next the emphasis is on the cultural and institutional settings of male sexual victimization (Mujica, Burmester, Gartner), and finally on various aspects of sexuality, from trafficking in adolescent boys (Procopio) to gender and/or sexually diverse men (Struve, Fradkin, and Beckstead) to orientation confusion, sexual interests and compulsions, kinks, and sexual dysfunctions (Kort).

The breadth of points of view is astounding. I invite you to partake.

References

Bolton, F., Morris, L., & MacEachron, A. (1989). *Males at risk: The other side of child sexual abuse*. Newbury Park, CA: Sage.

Briere, J., Evans, D., Runtz, M., & Wall, T. (1988). Symptomatology in men who were molested as children: A comparison study. *American Journal of Orthopsychiatry, 58*, 457–451.

4 I have written elsewhere about a number of topics not covered extensively in this book. See Gartner (1999) for discussions of encoding sexual abuse as sexual initiation, female abusers, boundary violations, dissociation, intimate relatedness, therapist-patients dyads, transference and countertransference considerations, and group therapy for men with histories of sexual abuse.

Finkelhor, D. (1981). The sexual abuse of boys. *Victimology, 6*, 76–84.
Friedrich, W. (1995). *Psychotherapy with sexually abused boys: An integrated approach*. Thousand Oaks, CA: Sage.
Gartner, R. B. (1997). The controversy in context. In R. B. Gartner (Ed.), *Memories of sexual betrayal: Truth, fantasy, repression, and dissociation* (pp. 13–27). Northvale, NJ: Jason Aronson.
Gartner, R. B. (1999). *Betrayed as boys: Psychodynamic treatment of sexually abused men*. New York, NY: Guilford.
Gonsiorek, J., Bera, W., & LeTourneau, D. (1994). *Male sexual abuse: A trilogy of intervention strategies*. Thousand Oaks, CA: Sage.
Herman, J. L. (1981). *Father–daughter incest*. Cambridge, MA: Harvard University Press.
Holmes, W., & Slap, G. (1998). Sexual abuse of boys: Definition, prevalence, correlates, sequelae, and management. *Journal of the American Medical Association, 280*, 1855–1862.
Hunter, M. (1990). *Abused boys: The neglected victims of sexual abuse*. Lexington, MA: Lexington Books
Johnson, R., & Shrier, D. (1985). Sexual victimization of boys: Experience at an adolescent medicine clinic. *Journal of Adolescent Health Care, 6*, 372–376.
Lew, M. (1988). *Victims no longer: Men recovering from incest and other sexual child abuse*. New York, NY: Harper & Row.
Lisak, D., Hopper, J., & Song, P. (1996). Factors in the cycle of violence: Gender rigidity and emotional constriction. *Journal of Traumatic Stress, 9*, 721–743.
Mezey, G., & King, M. (Eds.). (1992). *Male victims of sexual assault*. Oxford: Oxford University Press.
Nasjleti, M. (1980). Suffering in silence: The male incest victim. *Child Welfare, 49*, 269–275.
Singer, K. (1989). Group work with men who experienced incest in childhood. *American Journal of Orthopsychiatry, 59*, 468–472.

Part I

Sexually abused men and their challenges

Chapter 1

Effects of sexual abuse and assault on boys and men

Richard B. Gartner

What have we learned about understanding boys and men with histories of sexual victimization and trauma?

When teaching about the subject, I often start by talking about overt and covert abuse; memories that have always been present and shadowy memories that remain forever elusive although persistent; sexualized attachment that never becomes physical; prevalent feelings of responsibility for abuse that happened even in early boyhood; and violent assault versus skilled grooming that makes a boy accede to ensuing sex acts.

I then tell my students and colleagues there are three themes I want them to recognize in order to understand how male victims of sexual abuse and assault differ from their female counterparts. These are: masculine gender socialization; feelings and worries about homosexuality; and fears of becoming predators themselves.

Masculine gender socialization informs how boys and men think of masculinity and therefore how they measure up as men. As I have said elsewhere, for many men this means believing that:

> "[R]eal" men are in charge of themselves and therefore cannot be victimized . . . masculine men don't express emotions, are "independent" rather than "needy," are competitive and resilient, and welcome sexuality whenever it is offered, particularly from women.
>
> (Gartner, 1999, pp. 67–68)

According to these traditional masculine stereotypes, "ideal" men must suppress many of the very characteristics needed to heal from sexual abuse, most importantly, the capacity to experience themselves as victims without sacrificing their inner sense of being men. Therefore, an important part of psychotherapeutic treatment may involve actively challenging and critiquing these stereotypes (Lisak, 1995).[1] As Kia-Keating, Grossman, Sorsoli, and Epstein (2005) put it:

> Therapists can take on the role of helping men to see their experiences in the context of traditional expectations of masculinity, to critically assess gender roles, and to learn how to reformulate traditional codes based on their own provisions. It is important for therapists to acknowledge and support the process of gender deconstruction, with the understanding that it is necessary to inform the process of amending patterns of abuse and violence.
>
> (p. 183)

While stereotyped ideas about manhood continue to prevail in many parts of society, new ideas have started to take their place in others (cf. Messerschmidt, 2015; Hammarén, Haywood, Herz, Johansson, & Ottemo, 2017). In an op-ed in the *New York Times*, journalist Charles Blow (2016) eloquently describes these changes and the complications they bring:

> Today, both men and women are called upon to live up to the traditional ideals of both genders. So the ideal man, at least in polite society, gracefully achieves a series of balances. He is steady and strong, but also verbal and vulnerable. He is emotionally open and willing to cry, but also restrained and resilient. He is physical, and also intellectual . . . [He] honors the women in his life in whatever they want to do. He treats them with respect in the workplace and romance in the bedroom. He is successful in the competitive world of the marketplace but enthusiastic in the kitchen and gentle during kids' bath time. This new masculine ideal is an unalloyed improvement on all the earlier masculine ideals. It's a great achievement of our culture. But it is demanding and involves reconciling a difficult series of tensions.

1 For extended discussions of traditional masculine ideals and the problems they present for men's emotional lives, see Levant and Pollack (1995), Lisak (1995), Pollack (1998), Gartner (1999), and Pollack and Levant (2008).

My second focus about male sexual victimization involves fears and concerns about homosexuality. Most male sexual predators and victims self-identify as heterosexual, yet male-on-male sexual abuse is often perceived as a sign of homosexuality in one or the other, or both. The impact on a boy – whether straight or gay – of sexual abuse by a man or boy can be considerable. Boys growing up with a predominantly straight identification often feel their sexual identity is undermined at an age when it is just forming. Such a boy may wonder why he was chosen by a man as a sexual victim; whether the abuser knew something about his sexual identity he himself didn't know; or whether he was "really" gay because he "allowed" abuse to occur. Boys growing up with a predominantly gay identification, on the other hand, may feel hurried into recognition of their sexual preferences. Or, they may associate gay sex with secrecy, exploitation, and betrayal. Most destructively, they may decide the abuse "turned them gay," thus making it far more complicated to develop a positive sense of themselves as gay men, since they may feel that being gay means the abuser "won."[2]

Finally, male survivors of sexual abuse and assault frequently worry they themselves will become abusers, even if they have never experienced desires to be sexual with a child. Or, aware of the commonly believed myth that sexually abused boys almost inevitably grow up to become sexually abusing men, they may fear disclosing their history, thinking others will perceive them as potential abusers and be afraid to allow them near children. One man who disclosed sexual abuse in his 60s, first to his wife, then to a therapist, was terrified to tell his grown sons about it, fearful his daughters-in-law would no longer allow him near his grandchildren.

Particularly challenging is helping a man who in later childhood or adolescence was reactively but inappropriately sexual with a vulnerable, usually younger, child. I am not talking about habitual predators or pedophiles here. I have not worked with such individuals. Rather, I am referring to men who reacted before they had matured enough to fully comprehend that what was done to them was wrong (Johnson, 2009). As boys, they may have assumed it was all right to repeat it with others, or perhaps had the sense that such actions were inappropriate but had not yet developed sufficient judgment and

2 For further discussion of issues involving men's sexual orientation and histories of sexual abuse, see Chapter 11 in this volume by Struve, Fradkin, and Beckstead and Chapter 12 by Kort (see also Tremblay & Turcotte, 2005).

self-control to stop themselves. Working with such a man involves helping him acknowledge that he did something very wrong, experience remorse and make amends if appropriate, but also move beyond his guilt in order to heal from the hurt done to him.

These are the underpinnings that often inform the psychology of sexually victimized boys and men. Following are stories of how lives of actual men in treatment unfolded following sexual betrayal. First is Nels,[3] a victim of brutal incest. Second, Jozef, an athlete trapped by the coach who could bring him stardom. Third, Tucker, "lucky" enough to be seduced by his female educator. And, finally, Brandon, whose creepy relationship with his father subverted his emerging sexuality.

Nels: good boys serve others

Nels grew up on a farm in a strait-laced rural area. His parents, while not religious themselves, came from repressive religious and cultural backgrounds. Growing up, there was little tolerance for questioning, "whining," or discussion of negative or sexual experiences.

Living far from the small town where he attended school, Nels had little opportunity to play with children other than his siblings. In any case, there were always chores to be done on the farm, so playtime was considered a foolish luxury.

Residing on the farm with Nels's family was his mother's younger brother, Uncle Henrik. Henrik was a dwarf, a man regarded with great sympathy in the community because of the misfortune of his birth. That he had overcome his disabilities enough to earn a living and even volunteer for various charities was considered an admirable example of how adversity can be overcome.

But when Nels was 4 years old Uncle Henrik grabbed him one day and brutally raped him. From that day forward sexual attacks by Uncle Henrik were nearly a daily part of Nels's young life. With time, Henrik also assaulted Nels's younger brother and one of his sisters, sometimes coercing Nels into participating with them as well.

There was never a pretense that these assaults arose from affection for the children. They were always painful, fierce, and vicious. Nevertheless, Nels devised an internal narrative that he was nobly sacrificing himself to

3 Names and identifying information including ethnicity have been changed.

help his worthy uncle maintain his sanity while living the harsh life his body sentenced him to. After all, as his mother was fond of saying, if anyone had any grievances about life, all they had to do was look at Henrik to see how fortunate they were. So who was Nels to complain? Self-sacrifice was a great virtue in Nels's family and culture, and Nels tried hard to be a virtuous boy.

Nels and his siblings never discussed these rapes. Their family frowned on talking about life's travails and in any case they had no language with which to discuss these terrible things. For that matter, the attacks began so early in their lives, and their lives were so isolated from other children's, that they barely knew the assaults were unusual.

So the three children adapted to their trauma alone. When they discussed things much later in life, Nels's sister acknowledged that Henrik had "tried" to assault her but maintained she had successfully resisted him; this despite Nels's total recall of seeing her assaulted and in pain on multiple occasions. This denial (or dissociation) was his sister's pervasive style of dealing with anxiety. On the other hand, quite possibly as an aftereffect of these childhood assaults, Nels's brother became a drug addict and male prostitute, dying of a drug overdose in his 40s.

Nels's own adaptation was both positive and negative. He left the farm and was successful in university and then in an arts career. But he developed a severe alcohol problem, eventually experiencing blackouts. In addition, he found himself unexpectedly (and disturbingly) attracted to some men, though he never acted on this attraction and never truly questioned his heterosexual orientation. He was also highly ambivalent about the attention he got in his career: feeling vulnerable to attack if highly visible, he grew more anxious the more successful he became.

Nels never revealed to anyone what happened with Uncle Henrik, trying hard not to think about it himself. By now he lived far from his extended family, although he maintained close ties to it. Then Henrik suddenly died. Sitting through the glowing eulogies at his uncle's funeral was agonizing to Nels. He remained silent but later went on a severe bender. He could no longer bear his life.

To the astonishment of all who knew him, Nels precipitously switched from his burgeoning arts career to one in business that required skill and intelligence but where it was easy to stay under the radar and not be noticed. At this point he attended a few AA meetings, started long-term therapy, and over time maintained consistent sobriety on his own.

Nels eventually told some family members he had been sexually abused as a boy, but only named his abuser to one or two. After all, Henrik remained a saint in many people's eyes and Nels could not bring himself to face the anger and disbelief he felt sure people would express if he disclosed what his uncle had done. His widowed mother was exhibiting signs of dementia and he saw no purpose in confronting her with how she had not protected him from Henrik.

Once he stopped drinking, his severe depression became more apparent; he started psychotherapy in his late 30s. His characteristic self-sacrificing became increasingly apparent. His extended family continued to turn to him for help, and he was unfailingly available no matter what they asked of him. His wife and children also made many demands, often appropriately but sometimes well beyond what Nels could reasonably accomplish. Yet he never said no. Similarly, at work he was asked to work beyond the hours others did, and he could never set limits on these demands.

Only with time did he realize how angry he was about his role as constant rescuer. And he noticed again and again that when he asked for help it was rarely forthcoming either within his family or at work.

For example, Nels's mother eventually had to be put in a nursing home. Although competent members of the family lived nearby, it fell upon Nels, who lived ten states away, to decide on the placement, manage the move, and get rid of the detritus of a lifetime. It was a major shift on his part to agree to my suggestion that he hire movers and an estate liquidator. At first he demurred, saying that in his town it would be considered scandalous not to do everything by himself. But when he thought about it Nels realized his extended family and neighbors had no real hold on him regarding how he handled things. He was stretched to his limit because of work responsibilities and the care his wife now required because of a chronic illness. Since no one else stepped up to the plate, he decided he could deal with the move as he chose. He did so, dismissing relatives' complaints about the money he was spending from his mother's estate and ignoring gossip about his "spendthrift ways." This was extraordinarily liberating for him.

With time, Nels found ways to make mild requests of others, and often when he was politely firm people did their part. By the same token, through a series of changes at work and mild modifications of his attitude, his work situation improved. As he ended treatment, he began to re-engage as an amateur in the creative field he'd pursued earlier in life, rediscovering the tremendous satisfaction he had once felt expressing himself through his medium.

Jozef: the price of athletic stardom

Jozef has come a long way from his impoverished beginning in a small city in another country. The illegitimate son of a salesclerk and a married man, he only met his father three times by age 18; when they did meet his father was aloof and formal. He extended little child support to Jozef's mother, who later had two children by other men. The father himself was a "shady character," according to Jozef, a profligate womanizer who fathered several children by other women, showing little interest in any of them.

A bright boy, Jozef used his athletic prowess to gain admission to an elite private school where he excelled in his sport, eventually getting chosen for his country's national team. While his family was never considered quite respectable in his hometown, Jozef became something of a celebrity due to his athletic triumphs.

Jozef developed a close relationship with his coach, Axel, also a national hero because of the winning streaks of the nationally prominent teams he coached. Having no other father figure in his life, Jozef gravitated to Axel. Three afternoons a week, Jozef went home with Axel between school and practice. They played video games or watched sports, and Axel bought groceries and made Jozef lunches. These lunches were a major source of nourishment for Jozef, as his slatternly mother was often absent, leaving her children to fend for themselves regarding meals.

One afternoon, when Jozef was 14, Axel casually mentioned there were porn videos in the VHS player and Jozef should feel free to watch them while Axel was out. Although sexually rather naive, Jozef was eager to watch these X-rated videos. As he watched, aroused, Jozef began to masturbate, feeling a combination of stimulation, shame, and guilt that he was doing this on his coach's couch. Over three years he was aroused by increasingly strange, kinky, and/or homoerotic content.

Then Jozef stumbled upon a set of videotapes in Axel's apartment and to his horror saw they were videos of Jozef masturbating. Axel had set up elaborate videotaping systems timed for the period Jozef was left alone with the pornography. Appalled, alarmed, and angry, Jozef stopped the masturbation sessions and managed to extricate himself from the by-now time-honored visits to Axel's home.

Although enraged, Jozef had a dilemma. A national figure for his sports accomplishments, he was currently competing internationally. Axel was also a public figure as the national team's coach. Jozef was afraid that if he disclosed what Axel did, Axel would throw him off the team and he'd lose his one exit out of poverty. Having no responsible adult to turn to for advice, Jozef remained silent for seven years, putting mounting feelings of anger and betrayal into an internal deep freeze while continuing to compete on the national team under Axel's direction.

His secret ate away at him despite his attempts to ignore it. Eventually, Jozef discovered through a casual remark by a teammate that Axel had similarly abused several young men on the current team. Jozef had a panic attack, and then the fury he had frozen for seven years re-emerged. He convinced one of his abused teammates to go with him to the police, who raided Axel's home, confiscating hundreds of videos of young athletes masturbating or otherwise in sexually compromised situations.

Axel was arrested and imprisoned after a lengthy, sensationalistic trial during which Jozef and his teammate testified against him. But Axel was a beloved figure in the sports world, and the backlash against Jozef was swift and devastating. As happened in the United States at Penn State after Jerry Sandusky plunged the university into disgrace after an ugly set of revelations about sexual abuse of adolescent boys, Axel's many supporters reviled Jozef for "causing trouble" by going public about his abuse. Teammates shunned Jozef, and he eventually quit the team and came to the United States to complete his education.

There, Jozef started psychotherapy. In a long, painful process, he sorted out his anger, shame, guilt, and humiliation about both his sexual abuse and the national outcry when Axel was prosecuted. This led to uncovering his feelings about the lack of good parenting that set the stage for Axel to groom him for abuse. In turn, he had to face his ambivalence about the coach who'd helped Jozef in many real ways through his adolescence. Jozef got himself to a point where he could return to his native country for visits without getting triggered. He even re-established some acquaintanceships with former teammates. Likewise, he began to develop close relationships with friends in the United States who knew nothing of the baggage he carried in his own country. He began having romantic relationships as well. The scars from his childhood remained, but they were much faded and rarely painful. Intelligent, eager to learn and succeed, he excelled at a major elite university and launched himself into a challenging and potentially lucrative career having nothing to do with sports.

Tucker: the lucky duck

At age 42, Tucker sadly reviewed the wreck of his life as he looked back on his adolescent "affair" with his 42-year-old female high school assistant principal. A former athlete, he was now overweight, twice-divorced, and a recovering alcoholic and porn addict.

Born in the western United States, Tucker's early life was chaotic with little nurturing. His parents never married or even lived together. He described his mother as a "good-time girl," physically and emotionally abusive and likely alcoholic. His father won custody of Tucker after she left Tucker unattended overnight when he 6.

But Tucker's father, Bud, also had limitations as a parent. He was always broke and unable to provide much structure for his son. Yet he was warm and loving, and Tucker considered his dad his best friend. They moved a number of times before settling in a suburban town when Tucker was 12.

Mrs. S., a divorcée they met in church, at first seemed to be a great help to Tucker and his father, who was working two jobs. Bud was delighted when she reached out to Tucker since he himself was so unavailable. She eventually persuaded Bud to allow Tucker to live with her and her family: she would be more available than Bud could be; there would be greater stability in her house than his; it would even be easier for Tucker to attend high school since she lived nearby; and as she was the assistant principal she could be a further positive influence on Tucker.

Tucker saw in her the generous, interested, and emotionally available mother he'd never had. Her sexual advances about a month after he moved in therefore shocked him. He initially told her he was uncomfortable. She was relaxed about this, saying nothing had to happen. Yet she persisted, and a week later they began sexual relations. Tucker says he was confused at first, not sure why this was happening but not questioning it either. "At first I didn't enjoy it, but then I got into it." Eventually, he was more than willing, describing their sexual relations as frequent and passionate. They never used a condom, nor did they discuss birth control. He believed at the time that he and Mrs. S. were in love and would soon marry.

Mrs. S. was twice married; her first husband was a former student who fathered her son while he was still in high school and the second was also much younger, apparently someone she'd tutored in high school.

At first, Tucker saw this as a "win-win" situation, since he enjoyed Mrs. S.'s maternal attention as well as her sexual favors: "I had a mother figure. I wasn't talking to my mom at the time. She fed and clothed me and then I had sex whenever I wanted it. That's how I saw it then. I was a lucky duck."

Tucker soon noticed Mrs. S. kept him away from family and friends. Extremely jealous about his phone contact with them, she limited family visits. She was particularly threatened by any contact with Bud and referred to him in negative and degrading ways.

She also severely restricted time Tucker could spend with friends, especially girls. She shouted at him if he spent time with female friends. After looking up the school record of a girl he liked, she referred to it to during arguments, screaming "Go stay with that stupid slut." Because of her jealous rages Tucker learned not to spend time away from her. He says, "I stayed away from my friends. They were doing what kids are supposed to do. I should have been experimenting with girls, not having sex all the time with her. I lost my friends." Looking back, Tucker says it was "pretty sick," but that was not clear to him at the time.

Tucker was a mediocre student, partially because he had changed schools frequently, but Mrs. S. engineered a transfer into classes he could cut easily, and he spent much of his first two high school years in her office. Despite his missing many classes, his grades improved considerably, but he believes Mrs. S. tampered with his records, arranging for him to get good grades. But, Tucker says, "I didn't learn much."

Then Bud received several anonymous notes warning him about his son's "relationship" with Mrs. S. Tucker denied there was any improper behavior. But a friend's parents got alarmed when they overheard Tucker talking intimately to her on the phone. They taped these phone conversations, which eventually led to her arrest.

Tucker then went through a period of guilt and rage. He felt responsible for her arrest and guilty he had "ruined her life." At school, some of his former friends would not talk to him, angry he had "gotten her into trouble." His social life remained constricted: "I didn't go out much in high school."

Eventually, however, he came to see her as having used him for sex. As Tucker began to see the "relationship" as abusive, he got angry with Bud, blaming Bud for having left him with Mrs. S. and not protecting him by monitoring the situation. His temper was sometimes uncontrollable, and remained so into adulthood. His rage frightens him: "I feel out of control. My fists clench, I throw stuff, I break things, I boil up."

In addition, Tucker has trouble relating to women. He never dated in high school after the "relationship" with Mrs. S. ended. Despite all his sexual experience with her, Tucker has little idea about how to relate to a woman. Interactions are filled with suspicion, anger, and a need to isolate, especially if she is affectionate.

Sex is also problematic: perfunctory, passionless, and infrequent. He does get excited if there is "a chance of being caught." So he tries to convince women to have sex in public places, or with a door ajar. "When sex is easy, it's not that important to me." Likewise, he sometimes masturbates when a woman is nearby, finding the risk she might discover him thrilling. His pornography addiction, fueled by alcohol, always involves older women.

Otherwise he often feels lethargic, doesn't want to get up in the morning, and has lost jobs because of spotty attendance. Tucker is angry that he has no real career and worries he may end up like Bud, financially insecure and dependent on others. Miserable, with low self-esteem, little pleasure in life, a pattern of excessive sleep, and lack of interest in the world, he suffers from major depression, which medication has helped to some extent.

When Tucker started to put his life together he said in despair that Mrs. S. was the first adult he had faith in. He was proud to be her "lover," but was now ashamed he was duped. "I trusted her, relied on her, had sex with her. I felt she loved me. But how could she possibly have cared about me? Now I see it was a sick fetish."[4]

Brandon: was it abuse? He never touched me

Brandon thought he did not "qualify" as having been sexually abused. After all, his father never laid a hand on him, never exposed himself to

4 For a discussion of boys sexually abused by female perpetrators, see Gartner (1999, pp. 42–58) on encoding sexual abuse as sexual initiation.

Brandon, never showed him pornography, at least not directly. His father's abuse, although undermining and unnerving, was of a far more subtle nature.

Born into a middle-class family in a small Midwestern town, Brandon had two sisters, both more than ten years his senior. His parents were mid-level medical professionals, both ambitious to provide themselves and their children more comfortable lives than they had known. His father, Pat, was popular and active in community activities. His mother, serene and competent, was careful to make sure the family showed a proper, "decent" face to the community.

His parents often worked different shifts, and as a young child Brandon frequently accompanied the non-working parent on various errands and excursions. An early recurrent memory is going with Pat to visit his friend Larry. Telling Brandon to play quietly in Larry's living room, Pat would go with Larry into another room, closing the door for an hour or more. Occasionally Brandon would hear noises he later identified as the sounds of sex. He found these noises disturbing yet strangely exciting.

Occasionally Brandon, Larry, and Pat would go on an outing together, to a state fair or country auction. Brandon did not really like Larry, who nonetheless tried hard to extend himself to Brandon. When Brandon was 8, Pat gave him a beautiful new shirt and baseball hat, both in distinctive colors. Brandon wore them on their next jaunt with Larry. When they picked Larry up, he saw Larry was wearing an identical shirt and cap, also gifts from Brandon's dad. Pat was delighted at the surprise he'd engineered and immediately wanted to take a photograph of Larry and Brandon in these matching outfits. Brandon could not explain to himself why he felt sickened by this, but he never wore the shirt and cap again.

When Brandon was about 10, he accidentally pushed over a box stored on a shelf in his bedroom closet. He discovered a trove of gay pornography there. Already dimly aware of his attraction to men, Brandon looked at the pornography night after night. As he began to self-identify as a gay pre-adolescent, these images became his first masturbatory fantasies. He never mentioned the pornography to either parent.

"Why," Brandon asked me, tearfully, "would my father leave his pornography in my closet? We had a big house. Why there? Did he want me to find it and get turned on? And how could my mother not have known it was there? She was a meticulous housekeeper – she thought nothing of rearranging my drawers and closet. Did she not know what those magazines and videos were and where they came from? Did she not care?"

Brandon felt close to his mother, his childhood confidante about most things other than the covert erotic interplay with Pat. It pains him to realize that even though he tried to hide his sexual awakening from her – especially disturbing because of Pat's role in it – she had many clues about it and was either in extraordinary denial or covert collusion about it.

By the time Brandon was 14, the last child at home, he discovered Internet chatrooms. He began to chat with older men interested in teenage boys, having erotic conversations he could barely understand with men who flattered him, seemed interested in him, and made suggestive remarks he could not altogether follow. Several of them wanted to meet, but it took a while before he got up the courage to accept an invitation. They met in the parking lot of a fast food restaurant; the man drove him to his apartment, offered him beer, chatted intimately with him, showed him pornography, undressed him, and gave him oral sex. Brandon was very aroused and excited. But afterward this man hurried Brandon out of the house, dropping him off near home. Brandon was confused by this haste and the man's brusque goodbye, so different from the seemingly intimate heart-to-heart that preceded sex. It made him feel bad about trusting this man, even as he recalled with longing his sexual arousal and feeling of being cared for before being abandoned. He never saw this man again.

But he went on visiting chatrooms. This filled more and more of his time, ultimately becoming compulsive. Brandon continued to meet men in seedy and potentially dangerous places. At one point he had unprotected receptive anal sex and panicked that he had contracted HIV. He called a man he'd met previously, one who seemed more genuinely interested in him than the others. This man was sympathetic and reassuring but almost immediately asked him to come over again for sex. Brandon quickly hung up.

Brandon was underage during this whole period, and so by definition all these encounters constituted sexual abuse. Yet he never thought of them as sexually abusive, since he'd been a willing and eager participant. It was not until two decades later, when I talked to him about how even sexually interested and aroused teenagers are not fully capable of making informed decisions about sexual situations with adults, that he began to see his culpability as less than he'd assumed.

One day, due to some confusion in a conversation with a man with whom he had been chatting over time, Brandon discovered his father was tracking his chatroom visits. Pat took a screen name one letter different from Brandon's own screen name. Then, assuming Brandon's identity, he went into these same chatrooms, impersonating Brandon as he chatted with men there, often men who had chatted with Brandon. On one occasion Pat confronted a man who'd actually met Brandon for sex, telling him to stop all contact with his son. While superficially this seems like a protective act on his Pat's part, he followed it up by asking this man if he wanted to meet him for sex instead. Brandon felt nauseated and frightened when he understood what happened. He confronted Pat for the first time – the only time as a teenager – about the sexual undertones in their relationship. Brandon ordered him to stop impersonating him. Pat apparently complied.

Evidently Pat ended his relationship with Larry, but he soon met another man, Jonathan. He brought Jonathan into the house – always when Brandon's mother was at work but often when Brandon was at home – ostensibly because Jonathan, a computer expert, was working on the father's computer. "I never actually heard them having sex, but there was a sense of sex in the air. I felt I was babysitting them, stopping them from having sex, doing that somehow for my Mom." Pat sometimes asked Brandon to join them in the computer room. "I was a sexually curious, horny gay adolescent, so I was fascinated by them even though I didn't want them to have sex. I inserted myself somehow between them and was very attracted to Jonathan." In adulthood Brandon is sometimes drawn to men who physically resemble Jonathan.

Then Pat put ads in a local paper offering free erotic massages to attractive men. Brandon discovered these ads, since Pat's identity was barely disguised. The massages were given in the family home, again when Brandon's mother was at work but sometimes when Brandon was present.

> I longed for a connection with my father and asked him once to massage me. It was a way to feel close to him. And I did feel close to him until he said he would "get the oil." Suddenly everything felt erotic and dangerous and I had to break free. I got up and left.

By this time Brandon was spending as much time as he could away from home.

Brandon's goal was to leave home and never live near his parents again. He was intelligent and motivated in school. Despite his compulsive pornography viewing and sexual trysts, his ongoing confusion, and his paralyzing fear, he maintained very good grades and excelled in a team sport, thereby gaining admission to a top university in a distant state. He developed a more positive identity as a gay man there, but his compulsive activities continued. In addition, he was recurrently attracted to older men who used him sexually but, even when seeming to offer him a relationship, were insensitive, emotionally absent, and/or uninterested in any real personal tie to him. This remained his pattern throughout his 20s and early 30s.

Brandon's therapy involved working with him, first, on recognizing that the furtive, surreptitious experiences and interactions amounted to severe sexual abuse by his father despite their never having direct sexual contact. This sexual mistreatment totally undermined Brandon's natural development as a gay man. It furthermore precipitated Brandon's premature entry into a sexual underworld he did not understand, but where he was subject to overt and possibly dangerous sexual encounters with men he met in chatrooms while underage.

Despite what he thought at the time, these meetings traumatized Brandon. The men often lied to him and treated him poorly. He came to believe men are uncaring and untrustworthy and sex is dirty, frightening, sleazy, and divorced from emotion. This reinforced expectations about men and sex derived from observing how Pat conducted his life.

Brandon himself was looking for love in his relationships with men. But, as the song goes, he was looking in all the wrong places, finding men who seemed intensely involved with him for a week, then disappeared, cheated on him, or dropped him without warning or explanation.

Brandon finally found Reuben, a solid man who clearly cared about him. They entered a committed relationship. But while he felt safe and secure with Reuben, he also felt stultified and eventually bored. "We're like a couple in late middle age watching TV together, sitting on opposite ends of a couch, going to bed after the ten o'clock news." They stayed together for two years, then Brandon broke off from Reuben, feeling guilty but relieved. "Safety itself isn't enough for me."

The more Brandon talked about his relationships with men and saw them in the context of his relationship with his father, the angrier he grew at both parents. When he opened up to his older sisters about Pat's behavior he discovered they, too, had sat in Larry's living room listening to the sounds emanating from the bedroom. He confronted his mother about his father's behavior, and she tearfully denied any knowledge of his father's secret life. In despair, Brandon began to see his parents' entire marriage as a fraud: Pat hid behind a "respectable" marriage while having foolishly daring and public trysts with men. Brandon had stopped speaking to his father a few years earlier, although Pat continued to try to communicate with Brandon, telling him how much he loved him and how bewildered he was by Brandon's "callousness."

His mother was desperate to maintain her sense of public propriety as well as the economic benefits of maintaining her marriage. She asked Brandon to come to her therapist with her, where she attempted to explain herself, promising to confront Pat and leave him if she could not get him to acknowledge and change his behavior. But little came of these promises. Brandon demanded of both parents that they pay for his therapy, payments he could no longer manage. His mother agreed to this. Pat also acceded to Brandon's demand, although with great self-pity and denial of culpability.

At this point, Brandon began to consider what sex had meant in his life. There were extensive periods in his adulthood when he had sex with multiple men in anonymous or semi-anonymous situations or watched pornography incessantly on his computer.

> Looking back, I feel the computer room was a locus of evil in our house. I wanted that computer out of my life, out of our lives. I see it now as a symbol of our powerlessness, mine and my Dad's. I had such low self-esteem! I was a sexual object to be given to men. I felt worthless, felt such shame to be a product of such shitty stuff.

Brandon began to view himself and Pat as sex addicts. He began to attend a 12-step meeting for sexual addiction and gradually gained control over his compulsive sexuality. He had not talked to his father in several years but now started to consider what his father's life had been like. "I'm sure he was sexually assaulted as a boy, then became a compulsively sexual closeted man taking bigger and bigger risks."

At this point Brandon started to consider confronting his father and, equally important, forgiving him:

> It's such a weight off my shoulders to think of him as a man who neglected and mistreated his son, yes, but who himself faced terrible demons. He compulsively stashed pornography all over the house, any hiding place he could find. I see that now. If I forgive him, and tell him so, I can let go of the whole burden I've carried around all these years!

From there Brandon moved forward, trying to find a healthier life, wanting to relate to a man other than in a latter-day version of his exploitative connection to Pat. But neither did he not want a repetition of his parents' relationship, as he now saw his connection with Reuben to have been.

Brandon still has work to do as he tries to lead a more satisfying life, but at last he has some lucidity about all the obscurities of his childhood, adolescence, and young adulthood.

Conclusions

What do we learn from these men's stories? Each was asked to handle life experiences he was in no way ready to understand or manage. Each did his best to handle premature sexual and/or sexualized experiences. Each managed to develop areas of strength despite enduring pain, shame, trauma, and humiliation. But each had relational deficits based on early sexual betrayal. I ask readers to remember them as they explore the rest of this book.

References

Blow, C. (2016, March 29). The sexual politics of 2016. *New York Times*. Retrieved from www.nytimes.com/2016/03/29/opinion/the-sexual-politics-of-2016.html?action=click&contentCollection=Politics&module=Trending&version=Full&region=Marginalia&pgtype=article&_r=0.

Gartner, R. B. (1999). *Betrayed as boys: Psychodynamic treatment of sexually abused men*. New York, NY: Guilford.

Hammarén, N., Haywood, C., Herz, M., Johansson, T., & Ottemo, A. (2017). *The conundrum of masculinity: Hegemony, homosociality, homophobia and heteronormativity*. New York, NY: Routledge

Johnson, T. C., (2009). *Helping children with sexual behavior problems: A guidebook for professionals and caregivers* (4th Ed.). San Diego, CA: IVAT.

Kia-Keating, M., Grossman, F. K., Sorsoli, L., & Epstein, M. (2005). Containing and resisting masculinity: Narratives of renegotiation among resilient male survivors of childhood sexual abuse. *Psychology of Men & Masculinity, 6*(3), 169–185.

Levant, R. F., & Pollack, W. S. (Eds.). (1995). *A new psychology of men*. New York, NY: Basic Books.

Lisak, D. (1995). Integrating a critique of gender in the treatment of male survivors of childhood abuse. *Psychotherapy, 32*, 258–269.

Messerschmidt, J. W. (2015). *Masculinities in the making: From the local to the global*. Lanham, MD: Rowman & Littlefield.

Pollack, W. S. (1998). *Real boys: Rescuing our sons from the myths of boyhood*. New York, NY: Random House.

Pollack, W. S., & Levant, R. F. (2008). *New psychotherapy for men*. New York, NY: Wiley.

Tremblay, G., & Turcotte, P. (2005). Gender identity construction and sexual orientation in sexually abused males. *International Journal of Men's Health, 4*(2), 131–147.

Chapter 2

The Bristlecone Project

Portraits of courage

David Lisak

He is one of the more than 120 men who have so far volunteered to sit in front of the camera and tell the entire world his story of sexual abuse and healing. His eyes are wet with tears. His openness, his vulnerability, is exquisitely palpable. In fact, you want to put your hand on his shoulder. You want to reassure him. Because at this moment he is describing the grinding doubts about his strength, his courage, his masculinity, doubts that have haunted and plagued him his entire life. And you, his witness, see and feel with sublime clarity exactly the opposite as you listen to these tormenting inner thoughts. You see and feel his courage, the courage to reveal his vulnerability to the entire world, to tell his story, to lend his face and full name to that story, so other survivors might be strengthened by his strength, might find courage in his courage.

You are a witness to a paradox so stark it is difficult to comprehend. How can a man be so riven by self-doubts and self-condemnation when he is so obviously displaying such strength and courage?

This is one of the many profound questions and insights that have emerged from the Bristlecone Project,[1] an outreach and awareness campaign of 1in6.org. The Project was launched in 2013 with a simple premise:

- The stigma surrounding the sexual abuse of males remains so pervasive and so negating that it condemns the vast majority of survivors to decades of utter silence.
- That silence often stifles healing, and it allows society to ignore the reality that millions of men have suffered sexual victimization.
- Therefore, we must break through that silence. And who will do that if not male survivors themselves?

1 The Bristlecone Project is named after the Bristlecone pine tree, an extremely resilient tree that grows at high altitudes in the Southern Rocky Mountains.

So, beginning in the winter of 2012–13 I began contacting some of the male survivors I knew from the many years I spent as a clinician and researcher who focused my work the effects of sexual abuse on men. A survivor myself, I had a good understanding of how most survivors feel about talking publicly about their experiences, about openly confronting the stigma.

The men I initially approached were, for the most part, already open about their experiences, at least to some degree. And these first volunteers were almost without exception unreserved in their support for the project and their willingness to participate.

Although I have been an avid photographer for many decades, I did not view Bristlecone as primarily an artistic endeavor. I wanted the men's portraits to be vivid and professionally rendered, and I wanted their stories to be well captured. But Bristlecone is primarily a vehicle by which brave men confront the stigma that has for far too long silenced all of us. So, I wanted each man's portrait to be an unambiguous confrontation with that stigma, eyes directly into the camera lens and therefore into the eyes of every viewer who would thereafter gaze at the portrait, whether in a physical exhibition or on the Bristlecone website (www.bristleconeproject.org).

The Bristlecone Project is also, by design, very labor-intensive. I meet with each volunteer individually, usually at his home. We get to know each other a little, and then we proceed to the interview, which is an unstructured opportunity for the man to tell his story.

During the first year, the interviews were audiotaped. Thereafter, the interviews have been videotaped, a medium that has amplified both the seriousness of the commitment made by each survivor, and the impact of his participation. The edited videos of the men's testimonies provide powerful windows into each man's journey, an evocative way for fellow survivors to connect with their brethren. But the videos also amplify the commitment needed from each Bristlecone volunteer. As the videos are edited and added to the Bristlecone website, each volunteer will be seen and heard in an entirely new and vivid way.

In May, 2013, the Bristlecone Project website went live with the first handful of volunteers. Soon, I began receiving emails from survivors who viewed it: thank-yous, inquiries, and often enthusiastic commitments to participate themselves. The number of men presented on the website increased steadily, and soon the limiting factor was not the availability of volunteers, but rather my capacity to travel and meet with them.

Still, there were periodic reminders of what I was asking of these survivors. With some survivors, initial email contact evolved into a months-long correspondence about the pros and cons of going public, about their fears of such public exposure. On a few occasions, a man's ambivalence surfaced in its greatest intensity only in the hours before his scheduled interview and portrait session. A last-minute phone call or text message would tell me the time was not right for him.

After one such last-minute cancelation I called my wife from the hotel room where I had been waiting, my portable portrait studio set up but unused. I told her simply, "I feel like I'm recruiting for the French Resistance." I was not, of course, but I was sitting at the very cutting-edge of our collective effort to break the stigma that has for too long silenced male survivors of sexual violence. The Bristlecone volunteers were facing down that stigma.

The individual stories that emerge from the Bristlecone interviews reveal two truths, simultaneously. One, there are clearly discernible common themes in the testimonies of male survivors, and they are recognizable to anyone who is familiar with the relevant psychological literature. The men talk about rigid masculine norms that very often hinder their efforts to heal themselves. They talk about persistent difficulties with trust that very often hinder their intimate relationships. They talk about deeply held negative beliefs about themselves, in essence, their internalization of the abuse they suffered. They talk about the turning points, sometimes the specific moments that opened the door to healing.

One repeated theme that surprised me was the importance of spirituality to the process of healing. For many men, spiritual beliefs and particular spiritual experiences were critical – and even the cornerstones – in their healing from their childhood traumas.

The second truth to emerge from the interviews seems, on the surface, to contradict the first: each man's story is so beautifully unique, so one-of-a-kind. Each man's story, its telling enriched and textured by profound emotion, is like a hand-woven tapestry created with unique dyes and the weaver's personal method of knotting each individual thread. As witness and photo-chronicler, I have been the honored witness to the revelation of these unique tapestries.

Below are the stories of three of the Bristlecone men, told in greater detail than the brief biographies that appear on the website.

Lee Jones[2]

Lee was a hellion as a child, and neither Lee nor his British career military parents could fathom why this was so. Growing up in Hong Kong, where his parents were based during three childhood years, Lee was a child-combatant. By the age of 6 he was part of a gang of British kids who fought endless battles with rival gangs of Chinese kids.

After one such battle, in which a Chinese boy was injured, Lee's father frog-marched Lee to the local jail to teach him there were consequences for his wild behavior. But the engine that drove Lee's wild, rebellious behavior remained a mystery. Finally, his parents shipped Lee off at the age of eight to a boarding school back in England. Said Lee: "Think Harry Potter, but without the magic."

The boarding school's strict structure helped contain Lee's behavior, but with a profound tradeoff: he grew up largely without his parents. The separation has affected Lee's relationship with his parents to the present day.

After a decade at the boarding school, at age 17, Lee graduated. His parents moved back to England and he lived with them in York and worked in the British library at Boston Spa. One day he was photocopying something when a woman walked past him wearing a strong, distinctive perfume. With absolutely no warning, the scent triggered a storm of memories. Suddenly, he remembered everything his female babysitter had done to him when he was 6 years old.

Sexual abuse was not something one talked about, and so the 6-year-old Lee buried the memories. Raised as he was in a British military family, he already knew at the age of 6 that whatever happens to you, you suck it up and take it on the chin. You don't talk about it. And so memories of the abuse receded into a room to which Lee no longer had access. Until that day in the library.

Less than two years later, at age 19, Lee joined the British army. He needed to put distance between himself and his past. He told himself, "It's okay, it was a girl that did that to me. It's no big deal."

2 https://bristleconeproject.org/men/lee-jones/.

By his early thirties, Lee had shifted from a military career to civilian police work. He emigrated to Canada and joined the Saskatoon Police Service. His patrol district included a hospital where many sexual assault victims were taken for exams, so Lee was soon being dispatched to talk to them. "I realized that I could use my own experience to connect with these victims."

It took years, but eventually Lee became a detective with the sex crimes and child abuse unit. His empathy not only improved his ability to uncover the evidence needed to successfully prosecute cases, but it also enabled him to provide a measure of solace to victims. "I was able to tell them that I get it, I get what they're going through. But I could also tell them that it doesn't have to ruin their life."

But the investigative success came with a price, an emotional cost. Lee at last broke through the injunction that had been bred into him and he sought help from a counselor. The counseling enabled him to find the balance he needed between his work and his family, and also helped Lee accomplish another crucial life goal – to have a genuinely intimate relationship with his wife and children.

It was a bitingly-cold February evening in Saskatoon when Lee and I sat together in his home. After telling me his story, Lee looked at me through tear-rimmed eyes and focused his empathy toward me. He commented that interviewing fellow survivors must have a cost for me, hearing stories that must resonate with my own experiences of abuse. His comment reminded me why I refer to the Bristlecone men as brothers.

Lee was very grateful to have the opportunity to participate in the Bristlecone Project, he said, because it is "breaking down barriers and people are understanding that it isn't just women who get affected by this, that get targeted by this. It's men as well. And they come from all walks of life."

Tony Rodgers[3]

It has been a long – decades long – process for Tony to relinquish a bone-deep sense of responsibility, a persistent feeling that there was something he could have, or should have, done to somehow prevent the rape from happening. It is remarkable persistence given that Tony was raped when he was 9 years old.

3 https://bristleconeproject.org/men/tony-rodgers/.

A milestone in that long process came when Tony the adult went to a courthouse in St. Louis to claim a copy of the court record of the trial of the man who raped him. He had called ahead, so the courthouse staff had gathered the documents, and when Tony, a tall black man, entered the office it was clear they were waiting for him. He approached the woman behind the counter and told her why he was there. From her response, it was clear she assumed he was the rapist, not the victim. She told him they were obliged to protect the confidentiality of the victim in the case.

"I informed them, 'If you look through the records and you see the record of a 9 year old boy, whose name is Anthony, with the last initial R, they couldn't put my name fully in there because I was 9. I am that child. So I have a right to these files.'"

The woman responded by asking Tony, "Did he take it, or did you give it away?"

Thus was Tony assaulted at the courthouse, once for being black, and once for being a man. To the courthouse staff, what could a black man be other than the rapist?

There was an all but undetectable hitch in Tony's voice when he recounted the clerk's abominable words. Myself, I felt a molten mixture of rage, sadness, and despair.

Tony's response to the woman vividly illustrates the type of human being he is.

"I just said to her, 'I was 9 years old. Imagine any boy that you love at 9 being sexually harmed by someone else. Would you ask the same question, and would you ask it in that way?'"

The clerk looked down, and Tony walked out of the courthouse. And as he walked away, Tony felt good he had stood up for himself, that he had protected the 9-year-old boy. But there was still a voice in him that whispered, "Was there something I could have done to stop it?"

In the wake of the rape, Tony's maternal grandmother took him from his parents and took care of him for two months. She didn't use a lot of words. They didn't talk about the rape. She limited the number of people that came around. She nurtured him. She gave him the opportunity to gather himself. Said Tony, "She saved my life."

During those protected months, Tony had brief visits with some of his many cousins, but only through a car window. And when he recalls the look of pain on their faces, when he remembers how much the pain inflicted on him was also inflicted on them, he begins to cry for the first time during the interview. Such is Tony's exquisite capacity for empathy born of suffering.

The rape at age 9 was not the end of Tony's childhood challenges. His parents split up shortly after the trial in which Tony's rapist was convicted. In the years following, Tony was sexually abused by an older cousin.

But there lives in Tony a powerful, immovable center, and its gravity drew the pained and damaged parts of himself, inexorably, back to his core. That immovable center is a resident source of wisdom. At a point in his life when he was suffering, Tony understood something crucial: "I knew that something had to give. And I knew that it was me that had to give."

And so Tony has been open to change, inner change, which has yielded inner growth. Growth through an African healer, therapists, group therapy, meditation, a peer support group.

After the end of that support group, Tony went to Santa Cruz and sat on the beach.

> I visualized little Tony sitting next to me. I really did. And I talked with him, and I said, "I'm sorry about all the times that I forgot about you, and didn't do the work to help you heal. And I love you. I've always loved you. And I am your father. I'm your protector, and I will keep you dear and you will always be a part of me and I will not abandon you."

Jason Lee[4]

The phone call came out of nowhere during Jason's first year away at college. No warning. The police from his hometown in Alabama called and said to him: "We have some questions about Don Corley." With those seven words Jason's carefully reconstructed world shifted on its axis. The town, the people, the experiences he had worked so hard to put behind him all came roaring back like a flash flood. Recounting it many years later, Jason is still awash in intense emotions. He remembers a clear, distinct instant during the phone call when he decided, "I'm going to talk."

He had much to tell the police. At the age of 12 Jason's parents got divorced and his mother relocated to Alabama, where she had family. Knowing she would need the community's support, his mother got them

4 https://bristleconeproject.org/men/jason-lee/.

involved in the church, and she enrolled Jason in the Boy Scouts. Unbeknownst to her or anyone else, a predator lurked there.

Don Corley was an assistant scoutmaster and was also involved in the church's youth program. He had placed himself perfectly to target young boys, and, missing his father, Jason was uniquely vulnerable. He needed a father figure, and Corley preyed on his need. After several months of intensive grooming,[5] having Jason over to his house to do chores, giving him a lot of extra attention, Corley began sexually abusing Jason.

He abused Jason from the age of 12 until 17. His psychological control over Jason was so pervasive and complete that Jason describes it as brainwashing. His formative years were distorted by Corley, and this produced some of the most difficult legacies for Jason to undo.

During the summer between his junior and senior year of high school, something shifted in Jason. He ran for senior class president and was elected. "They elected me president and I don't know why." Simultaneously, Jason stopped Corley's predation. Corley tried hard to keep his talons in him, but Jason held firm and finally broke the control that bound him for five years.

Having set himself free from Corley, Jason chose a college as far away from his hometown as was possible while remaining close enough to get back within a day if his mother needed him. In going off to college, Jason made a conscious and determined decision to leave Alabama and Corley behind. To start anew.

And then, in his second semester at college, came the phone call from the Alabama police.

After deciding to talk to the detective, Jason authentically opened up and disclosed – for the first time, ever – what he had suffered for so long at the hands of a sexual predator. Corley had been reported to the police by the parents of another boy whom he targeted. An investigation was opened, leading to Jason and eventually other boys Corley sexually abused over many years.

"They found more and more and more boys," Jason recalls through tears. Like so many survivors, Jason struggles with self-blame and a distorted sense of responsibility. In his case, he still holds himself responsible

5 Editor's note: See Chapter 13 by Clemente and Hakes in the companion volume, *Healing Sexually Betrayed Men and Boys: Treatment for Sexual Abuse, Assault, and Trauma*, for a discussion of grooming.

for not himself reporting Corley to the police. The pain caused by this self-blame is vividly evident in the tears he sheds as he describes the phone call with the police.

Of the more than 40 boys who were sexually abused by Corley, only Jason and three others agreed to cooperate in the prosecution, and one of the others had to be excluded because of the statute of limitation. I had to prod Jason to acknowledge that choosing to testify, to confront the painful past, to openly confront the stigma, was an act of supreme courage. Like most survivors, self-condemnation is far more accessible to him than acknowledging courage.

Corley was convicted and sentenced to 30 years in prison. The trial over, Jason returned to college, determined to focus on his education and his future. But he still grappled with the legacies. For example, feeling "less than": less worthy than his peers; less capable. He worked, and still does work, extra hard at everything he does. "I want to be good enough. Loyalty to my company, and loyalty to my family and friends, are incredibly important to me. Those things are really sacred."

Years passed. Jason graduated from college, moved to Atlanta, found a job, got married, bought a house. One day his wife revealed to him that Corley's lawyer had contacted her, angling to get Jason to acquiesce to Corley's request for parole after serving less than half his sentence. Enraged, Jason told the lawyer to stop all contact with his family. And he went into action.

With the help of friends and colleagues, Jason established 30is30 (http://30is30.com), an organization devoted to holding Corley to his 30-year sentence while simultaneously educating the community about childhood sexual abuse and its impact.

In the lead-up to Corley's parole hearing, the efforts of 30is30 produced significant media coverage and widespread participation. The state attorney general appeared in person to ask that Corley be denied parole. The hearing became a teaching moment, for the community and beyond. And then the result: Corley was denied parole.

As with all survivors, Jason's path to healing has been a mixture of triumphs and struggles. Through his activism he has found his voice, literally and figuratively. He has confronted and overcome the stigma that haunts and binds all male survivors. And Jason is married and raising a family.

But some struggles have been more difficult. While in college, still tormented by his self-condemnation for not reporting Corley to the police when he was a child, Jason became acutely suicidal. He bought over-the-counter sleeping pills, climbed up onto his bunk bed, and swallowed dozens of them. He felt his body begin to shut down, and he waited for death. And then suddenly there was a voice next to his left ear, a female voice, and it said: "I forgive you." As he speaks these words, Jason is consumed by profound and overwhelming emotions. He weeps without restraint. "It was the first time I had ever heard something like that. I had therapy before, I had so much, and I don't know who it was or what it was, but I needed that. 'I forgive you.'"

Like many of his fellow Bristlecone participants, Jason's path toward healing was nurtured by a profound spiritual experience. He received help from a powerful, unknown source at a moment when he needed it most.

Lee Jones, Tony Rodgers, and Jason Lee are three of the 71 men who grace the Bristlecone website as of this writing. And that number keeps growing. An additional 80 men are on the Bristlecone volunteer list, awaiting their turn, and that number too keeps growing. Each volunteer has a unique story but also shares many common threads with his brethren. One of those common threads is a profound courage – the courage to openly stand up to and defy the negating stigma that has for so long attached itself to male survivors of sexual victimization.

And woven together with that thread is a profound resistance to seeing just how courageous they are.

Part II

Research, biology, and medical treatment

Chapter 3

The sexually abused man's relationship with his physician

Frank Spinelli

This chapter is the result of my work as a physician, a survivor of sexual abuse, and an advocate for sexually abused men. It is written especially for healthcare providers and focuses on key aspects of healthcare that pose a problem for sexual abuse survivors, particularly oral, genital, and anal care, and consulting with a urologist, a dentist or a gastroenterologist. Within this chapter, I will discuss some of the most common obstacles male sexual abuse survivors[1] face and what healthcare professionals can do to, first, recognize the clues suggesting their patient may have a history of sexual abuse and, second, specific ways to help them deal with their fears.

Sexual betrayal

Lewis

Lewis avoided going to the doctor nearly his entire adult life. At 42, he seemed like an overgrown child, impishly smiling when asked why. Molested for years by his older brother, Lewis was unable to gain any real insight as to why this happened. He internalized his confusion and pretended the abuse never took place. In his early twenties, he was hit by a car and taken to the emergency room. As the male physician examined his leg, Lewis developed an erection. This involuntary reaction forced him to consider that the encounters he

1 Throughout this chapter, for ease of expression I will use masculine pronouns, since my focus is on male patients.

had with his older brother might have made him gay, and Lewis did not want to be. To avoid this prospect, he retreated from medical care for decades and adopted an asexual existence. After a recent visit to an urgent care center for a sinus infection, Lewis was found to have high blood pressure.

At our initial visit, he explained his reluctance for comprehensive medical care, prefacing the upcoming physical exam by saying, "I sometimes get erections but I can't help it. I'm not gay!"

"One in six men are survivors of childhood sexual abuse" (Felitti & Anda, 2010, p. 78). Furthermore, "In the United States, 1 in 71 men reports having been raped, with 27.8% of these men indicating their first experience of rape by age 10 years or younger" (Black et al., 2010, p. 1). There is mounting evidence that childhood sexual abuse can lead to greater susceptibility to lifelong physical and mental heath problems, including cardiovascular disease, hypertension, diabetes, anxiety disorders, depression, substance abuse, and perpetration of future violence (Leeb, Paulozzi, Melanson, Simon, & Arias, 2008).

And finally,

> Childhood maltreatment is defined as any act or series of acts of commission or omission by a parent or other caregiver, in the context of a relationship of responsibility, trust, or power, that results in harm, potential for harm, or threat of harm to a child's health, survival, development, or dignity.
>
> (Seeman, Singer, Rowe, Horwitz, & McEwen, 1997, p. 58)

Childhood maltreatment poses a substantial risk for long-term health for many reasons. First, frequent exposure to the stress associated with maltreatment can lead to potentially irreversible changes in the interrelated brain circuits and hormonal systems that regulate stress (Repetti, Taylor, & Seeman, 2002). Changes in these brain systems can lead to a premature physiological aging of the body that increases vulnerability to disease over time (Williams & Collins, 1995). Childhood maltreatment increases the risk of behavioral problems such as smoking, substance abuse, obesity, and sexual promiscuity. A related body of evidence indicates that early adverse childhood experiences have a profound effect on a range of cognitive, social, and emotional competencies that lay the foundation for successful learning, coping, and subsequent economic productivity.

While many studies and reviews have concluded that survivors of childhood sexual abuse are highly likely to experience several adverse effects, strongly implying a causal relationship between child sexual abuse and the later development of psychopathology, others have been more cautious, arguing that outcomes are variable, rather than being consistently and intensely negative (Paolucci, Genuis, & Violato, 2001; Sharpe & Faye, 2006; Smolak & Murnen, 2002).

The *New York Times* published an article entitled "Let's (Not) Get Physicals" (Rosenthal, 2012), in which Elizabeth Rosenthal listed the pointless and dangerous reasons why a routine physical exam – and many of the screening tests that routinely accompany them – are useless. I wrote a rebuttal for *The Huffington Post* entitled, "In Support of the Annual Physical Exam" (Spinelli, 2012), emphasizing the need to focus on preventative healthcare.

Many healthcare providers utilize the annual physical exam as a time to delve deeper into psychosocial issues. Beyond the textbook questions about smoking, alcohol consumption, and recreational drug use, this is an opportunity to review a patient's mood and family interactions as well as have a thorough discussion about sexual practices and childhood traumas. No healthcare provider could be expected to cover the breadth of this information in a routine 15-minute visit. I have always encouraged patients to schedule an annual physical exam around their birthday. I allot 45 minutes to have a discussion before performing the exam.

But most patients are reluctant or ashamed to talk about sexuality and sexual traumas. The question, then, is how do you broach the topic of sexual abuse without asking the question directly? My advice is to ask your patient about his childhood. "Did anything traumatic happen to you when you were a child?" This question could be interpreted many different ways and initiates a conversation. I would avoid asking, "Did you have a normal childhood?" "Normal" is hard to define, and who, really, has had a "normal" childhood? Even the best childhood experiences are interpreted as having abnormal periods at some point during those formative years.

Lewis may not have divulged his history of sexual abuse had it not been for his full physical. It was in the context of a longer appointment and after careful probing that I was able to gain this information. It is amazing how responsive patients can be once their healthcare provider encourages them to speak freely, filling in those uncomfortable silences while the provider waits for the patient to respond. As a result of our conversation, Lewis agreed to enter talk therapy and was encouraged to attend a support group for male sexual abuse survivors.

Dental health

Adam

> Adam is a 30-year-old gay male who hadn't been to a dentist in over ten years. When asked why, he shook his head and shrugged. Since most people avoid the dentist out of fear, Adam was referred to a dentist who had received sensitivity training to deal with anxious patients.
>
> Following Adam's appointment, the dentist reported to the healthcare provider that while in the dentist's chair, Adam experienced symptoms of acute anxiety: sweating, labored breathing, and involuntary retching at the onset of the exam. The dentist thought Adam was having a seizure because he was staring blankly into space, appearing suddenly startled and unable to explain what he was feeling. After several minutes, Adam calmed down. He was able to sit up, drink water, and verbalize that he did not know what was happening to him. The dentist began to ask Adam about his childhood, and it was then that Adam revealed he had been sexually abused as a boy.

A number of aspects of dental treatment symbolically represent sexual abuse for many male survivors:

- being alone with a male or, if the abuser was female, a woman;
- being placed in a horizontal position;
- feeling restrained;
- having someone touch him;
- having someone put objects in his mouth;
- being unable to talk or swallow;
- experiencing or anticipating pain.

Given the high numbers of boys affected by sexual abuse, it seems likely that many are unaware of the long-term consequences of abuse and consequently fail to associate difficulties in receiving dental treatment with their abuse. As a result, dental treatment is avoided without a clear understanding of why. Even if they are aware, they may not disclose the information readily.

Also, adult survivors can find it difficult to tolerate dental treatments and may repeatedly cancel appointments. Many avoid dental treatment entirely. Multiple factors play a role in the establishment and maintenance of dental fear, but a history of childhood sexual trauma is often associated with elevated dental fear (Stalker, Russell, Teram, & Schachter, 2005).

As noted, there are parallels between some aspects of childhood sexual abuse experiences and dental care. Patients are expected to lie in a chair while someone touches them and penetrates their mouth. Patients are supposed to trust the dentist, who may assure them that while the experience may be uncomfortable in the end, it is for their good. But this is similar to how abusers often groom victims, beginning initially with harmless activities and reassurances that the discomfort is minor and/or the experience is for the child's own good. In addition, sexual abuse frequently involves the child's mouth (Leeners et al., 2006).

Adult survivors often do not disclose their history of abuse to their dentist. Instead, they may just tell their dentist they are anxious. It's vital that healthcare providers probe further into why their patient feels anxious. If a history of child sexual abuse is uncovered, it is important for the dentist to address this issue directly.

Survivors report that having an empathic and understanding dentist who was patient and willing to listen to their concerns was critical in reducing their anxiety. Before the initial dental exam, the examiner should describe to the patient what is about to take place so the patient can feel he is involved in the process instead of being a reluctant participant. Agreeing on non-verbal cues to indicate increasing anxiety may alleviate some of that anxiety. When patients feel they have some control, it tends to put them more at ease. Often, listening to relaxing music via headphones during a procedure can soothe the patient. If possible, allow a friend or family member to stay in the room during the appointment. During the procedure, offer to let the patient hold the suction device and provide regular reassurance and explanations throughout the procedure, particularly when the procedure is nearly complete, to give your patient a sense that the light at the end of the tunnel is nearing.

Adult survivors are likely to communicate poorly, especially when anxious or when trying to talk – or trying *not* to talk – about their needs based on their trauma and triggers. It is important for the dentist to pay close attention and to recognize non-verbal signs of anxiety: cringing at your touch, gagging when instruments are inserted into their mouths, and/or lying still and silently screaming.

In addition, survivors of sexual abuse often exhibit avoidance of stimuli associated with eliciting such intense emotional reactions. Many studies (e.g., Felitti & Andra, 2010) report that survivors will deliberately avoid healthcare services where some aspect of the treatment has previously resulted or is likely to result, in the abrupt emergence of fear, anger, terror, or grief. Common triggers include:

- body position discomfort;
- sense or loss of control;
- latex gloves;
- cologne or aftershave;
- instruments in the mouth.

Reclining, in particular, has been reported as being most threatening to survivors of sexual abuse. Strategies to avoid triggering patients include offering them a sheet or cover, such as a blanket, so they feel less exposed. If possible, allow the patient to have one foot on the floor to provide him with a sense of control. Control can also be gained by allowing him to hold a mirror so he can see what the dentist is doing inside his mouth.

The smell of latex gloves can remind survivors of condoms, which may have been used during the abuse. Vinyl gloves are an alternative. Moreover, the smell of cologne or aftershave by healthcare providers may also trigger memories of the past perpetrator. Try to avoid wearing cologne or aftershave, or ask your patient if the scent bothers him. And, whenever possible, patients should be encouraged to invite chaperones to escort or accompany them to their appointment (Willumsen, 2004).

Survivors note that when the dental assistant is empathically engaged the experience is further enhanced. It is therefore important that dental assistants be familiar with the patient's history so they too can look for signs the patient is experiencing anxiety and offer comfort. Of course, the healthcare provider needs to get the patient's permission first before disclosing sensitive information to the assistant. A simple gesture like offering to hold the patient's hand, placing a hand on the patient's shoulder, or speaking in a soft, reassuring voice, can be very soothing for a male survivor of sexual abuse. But make sure you check in with the patient and ask their permission first. Remember even a gentle touch or a soft reassuring voice may act as a trigger for sexual abuse survivors. Words of encouragement like, "You're doing great," and "We're nearly done," are helpful, and routinely check in with the patient throughout the procedure, "Are you okay?"

Prostate and colorectal care

John

John was a 60-year-old male who had moved to New York recently from Los Angeles. During an initial visit, he complained of having to get up from bed several times during the night to urinate. When the physician asked if he could perform a digital rectal exam, John adamantly refused.

As a 60-year-old man, John should have had had a rectal exam, a PSA, and a colonoscopy. When asked why he wouldn't allow the physician to perform a rectal exam, John immediately said, "I wasn't molested or anything if that's what you're insinuating."

Since this was his first visit, the physician deferred the rectal exam but drew a PSA and encouraged John to consult with a gastroenterologist for a screening colonoscopy. When his blood work came back, John's PSA was 12 ng/mL, or three times the upper limit of normal. At his follow-up visit, the physician explained the results could be due to an inflammation of the prostate called prostatitis, which is often caused by a bacterial infection, but firmly expressed concern that the elevated PSA could be a sign that something more serious could be going on. At this point, the physician again asked John to allow him to perform a digital rectal exam. Again, John refused. As a result, they agreed that John should see a urologist as part of a workup to rule out prostate cancer. John agreed, but he never went to the urologist or the gastroenterologist and canceled his follow-up appointment with the primary care physician. When the receptionist finally got in touch with John, he explained that he had returned to Los Angeles and would follow up with a physician there.

Three years later, John returned to New York. He said he went to a urologist in Los Angeles, but the experience was awful. "After I explained the results of my PSA," said John, "the urologist told me to stand up and assume the position, meaning I had to bend over the exam table. Then, as he examined my prostate, my anus began clenching involuntarily. The doctor joked, 'Hey, I'm going to need that finger back.' I was so humiliated that I left right then and there."

The primary care physician strongly suspected that John may have been sexually violated as a child even though, unasked, John volunteered at his first visit that he had never been abused. Still, the primary care doctor brought up the topic again. This time, John admitted that he was molested for years by his father, who spoke to him almost the same way the urologist had, ordering him around like a child and mocking him. The primary care doctor explained that it was his choice whether to get examined again, but that there was a sense of urgency, particularly since three years had passed. The physician recommended a female urologist and a psychologist. John agreed with this plan. Unfortunately, he was diagnosed with stage III prostate cancer. John underwent surgery to remove his prostate followed by radiation therapy. Although the likelihood of his surviving for at least five years is over 90%, he has issues with urinary incontinence and impotence.

Richard

In contrast to John's experience, Richard was referred to a gastroenterologist for a colonoscopy because he complained of blood in his stool. Before the procedure, Richard told the doctor he was an incest survivor.

The doctor explained that a scope was going to be inserted into his anus but that Richard would be sedated. Later, Richard told the referring physician that initially he refused the colonoscopy. "I couldn't imagine letting anyone put something inside me," but the gastroenterologist explained it was completely Richard's decision and promised he would not feel any discomfort during the procedure. So Richard agreed. Afterward, Richard said that the gastroenterologist asked him how he felt and that he was brave for allowing him to perform the procedure.

The rectal exam is performed for multiple reasons. It is part of the annual physical exam in both men and women. The rectal exam provides information about the physical state of the rectum, but in men, the prostate is palpable through the rectal wall.

Typically, the prostate feels firm, smooth, and about the size of the base of your thumb. During a digital rectal exam, the examiner also collects a minuscule amount of stool to test for fecal occult blood used to screen for colon cancer called the guaiac test for all men and women beginning at age 50.

Reasons to perform a rectal exam:

- palpate the rectum;
- palpate the prostate in men;
- perform a fecal occult blood test or guaiac test.

In 1994, the Food and Drug Administration (FDA) approved the use of the prostate-specific antigen (PSA) test in conjunction with a digital rectal exam to test asymptomatic men for prostate cancer. Currently, the American Cancer Society recommends screening men for colon cancer and prostate cancer at age 50 with a colonoscopy and a testing of the man's PSA, a protein produced by cells of the prostate gland. This test measures the level of PSA in a man's blood. It requires a blood sample, which is sent to a laboratory for analysis. Most healthcare providers consider PSA levels of 4.0 ng/mL and lower as normal.

Although (PSA) screening has improved the detection of prostate cancer, the precise mortality benefit of early detection is unclear. This is in part due to a discrepancy between the two large randomized controlled trials comparing PSA screening to usual care. The European Randomized Study of Screening for Prostate Cancer (ERSPC) found a survival benefit to screening, while the United States Prostate, Lung, Colorectal, and Ovarian (PLCO) Cancer Screening Trial did not (Kim & Andriole, 2015).

Sexual abuse history disclosure and physician empathy

The significant difference between John's and Richard's experiences was that one chose to disclose his history while the other did not. Disclosure altered the relationship between Richard and his gastroenterologist.

The decision to reveal a history of sexual abuse relates to "triggering" discomfort/distress caused by intensified sensitivity to stimuli in the examination setting. The success of the changed relationship requires an empathic physician who recognizes the importance of the shared information for the patient and the patient's distress (Petronio, Reeder, Hecht, & Ros-Mendoza, 1996).

Unfortunately, it would be incorrect to assume that disclosing a history of abuse to a healthcare provider always results in a positive outcome. I have known many healthcare providers who would rather not engage in such a discussion, concerned it would take up too much time, leave the patient feeling emotionally unstable, or because they themselves are uncomfortable discussing sexual trauma. Still, if healthcare providers ignore the warning signs or refuse to educate themselves to identify signs of abuse, they are indirectly reinforcing a survivor's unwillingness to seek appropriate medical help.

My suggestion is to ask about a patient's history in an empathic way to encourage disclosure. Realize that once he admits to being sexually abused, it is not your responsibility to resolve it at that moment. Make a plan with the patient to bring up this topic again at your next visit, suggest a therapist if he is not already seeing one, and probe him about where he is emotionally regarding his history of sexual abuse. Just because you've uncovered something big doesn't mean you have to unpack it all upon discovery. Your patient will appreciate your concern and respect you as a healthcare provider for including it in his plan along with his other medical issues.

Dermatologic care

Rodney

> Rodney is a 23-year-old male of Jamaican descent who presents with darkening of his cheeks, forehead, and neck. His primary care physician referred him to a dermatologist. On exam, the dermatologist noted the hyperpigmentation but also that Rodney's facial complexion was significantly lighter than the skin on his arms. Rodney admitted to using various skin bleaching products to lighten his skin. When the dermatologist asked Rodney to disrobe for a complete skin assessment, he adamantly refused. The dermatologist

> did not push Rodney. He warned him to stop using the bleaching products immediately. Otherwise, the hyperpigmented areas would become permanent, and he could develop long-term health issues. Rodney was given an appointment in one month and referred to his primary care physician. After reviewing the dermatologist's consultation, the primary care physician asked Rodney why he refused the full skin assessment. Rodney stated that he doesn't like to see himself nude or have anyone see him without any clothes. When asked if he had been abused as a child, Rodney disclosed that his mother's boyfriend sexually abused him from age 10 to 13. After he told his mother, she accused him of seducing her boyfriend because Rodney was gay. Rodney was sent to live with his aunt in New York City. He began bleaching his skin in high school, thinking people with lighter skin were given more opportunities in life. The primary care physician concurred with the dermatologist's plan, and Rodney was referred to a psychiatrist.

Skin depigmentation/bleaching, the practice of using toxic cosmetic chemical agents to lighten the complexion of one's skin, poses grave health consequences including but not limited to irreversible skin damage, skin cancer, and kidney failure (Boonchai, Desomchoke, & Iamtharachai, 2011). The hyperpigmented areas on Rodney's face and neck were diagnosed as exogenous ochronosis. The condition is most often associated with alkaptonuria but can occur after the topical application of hydroquinone and is limited to sites of application. The hyperpigmentation may fade slightly after discontinuing the agent, but the discoloration is usually permanent. Exogenous ochronosis is an avoidable dermatitis that can be caused by the topical application of compounds such as hydroquinone or phenols, though mercury, picric acid, and antimalarials have also been implicated (Charlin et al., 2008).

A majority of the explanations that seek to describe the root causes of skin bleaching predominantly fall within a psychosocial paradigm, where having lighter skin (a proxy for European ideals of beauty) is equated with greater attraction (James et al., 2016; Thompson & Keith, 2001) or higher social status (Hunter, 2011). This theory, however, does not explain the desire to engage in skin bleaching despite its harmful effects. The experience of negative physical health outcomes of skin bleaching and its continued use implies that self-preservation may be in question, leaving researchers to hypothesize that the underlying motivation must be related to self-hate, as measured by low self-esteem (Hunter, 2011).

The presence of trauma symptoms and childhood physical and sexual abuse may increase the likelihood of skin bleaching (James et al., 2016). Skin bleaching can be considered similar to other forms of harmful body modification behaviors like Body Dysmorphic Disorder (Castle & Phillips, 2006) and Eating Disorders (Murray, Macdonald, & Fox, 2008). Childhood trauma historically has been linked to extreme self-harm behaviors such as self-mutilation (van der Kolk & Fisler, 1995).

But it was Rodney's refusal to disrobe that piqued his primary care physician's curiosity. Had he not asked about childhood trauma, Rodney might not have disclosed his history of childhood sexual abuse. Research has shown that although only a small fraction of physicians routinely inquire about historical traumatic incidents, most patients report that they would actually favor such inquiries (Friedman, Samet, Roberts, Hudlin, & Hans, 1992). Nevertheless, the power differential between Rodney and the dermatologist once he was asked to disrobe triggered feelings of powerlessness. The only way for Rodney to cope with these feelings was to refuse to get undressed.

Because of the obvious intimate nature of medical care, any number of triggers exists, among them the request to undress, physical contact, and positioning the patient's body (Gallo-Silver & Weiner, 2006). A patient's refusal to undress should prompt the physician to inquire why. The decision to disclose by a male survivor of childhood sexual abuse relates to the "triggering" discomfort/distress caused by the increased sensitivity/reactivity to stimuli. The success of the changed relationship requires an empathic physician response that recognizes the importance of the shared information for the patient and the patient's distress (Lewis, Matheson, & Brimacombe, 2011).

If your patient indicates he is fearful, ask him how to increase his feelings of safety. For a full skin assessment, review the evaluation with your patient before he undresses and ask for permission before you touch him. Taking off all your clothes can make anyone feel vulnerable. If you sense your patient is uncomfortable, perform the skin assessment in stages so that the patient can remain partially clothed. This will allow him to retain a sense of control. During the exam, look for signs of self-mutilation: scars from cutting, burning, or skin picking.

Best clinical practices with male survivors of childhood sexual abuse include physicians considering changes in the way they initially identify this patient population, communicate, respond, listen to, involve, examine, and plan for effective and empowering interactions with them (Gallo-Silver, Anderson, & Romo, 2014).

Substance abuse, smoking, high-risk sexual behavior, and STDs

Michael

> Michael is a 20-year-old unemployed actor with a long history of substance abuse. Upon being discharged for the third time from an in-patient drug rehabilitation program for crystal methamphetamine use, he was referred to a primary care physician. At the initial visit, Michael was overly friendly, making jokes about his addiction failures and lack of career. "This time things are different," he said, cheerfully, but when asked what made this time around different, he got quiet, staring down at the floor. Upon further questioning, Michael readily admitted that while in rehab he engaged in condom-less sex with some of the other patients, and that they often used drugs. "It's very common," he said. "Put a bunch of gay guys in a group and, believe me, they'll find ways to have sex and do drugs."

The US Department of Veterans Affairs (2016) states on its website:

> Men who have been sexually assaulted have a high incidence of alcohol and drug use. The probability for alcohol problems in adulthood is about 80% for men who have experienced sexual abuse, as compared to 11% for men who have never been sexually abused.

Similarly, survivors of child sexual abuse are more likely to engage in many harmful activities. Therefore, adult survivors are at increased risk of abusing alcohol and drugs, of smoking, and of risky sexual behavior.

In the Adverse Childhood Experiences (ACE) study, subjects who had experienced four or more adverse childhood events (psychological, physical, or sexual abuse; violence against mother; or living with household members who were substance abusers, mentally ill or suicidal, or ever imprisoned), compared to those who had experienced none, had four- to 12-fold increased health risks for alcoholism, drug abuse, depression, and suicide attempts (Felitti et al., 1998). In another primary-care sample, those with a history of victimization were more likely to use recreational and intravenous drugs (Kendall-Tackett, Marshall, & Ness, 2000). Similarly, in a study of gay and bisexual men, sexual abuse survivors were more likely to use psychoactive drugs (Hubbard, Craddock, Flynn, Anderson, & Etheridge, 1997).

Healthcare providers play an important role in screening patients for substance abuse, providing interventions, referring them for treatment, and providing ongoing monitoring. Screening and assessment to detect drug use can be administered during the annual routine visit by asking direct questions (Skinner, 1982; Smith, Schmidt, Allensworth-Davies, & Saitz, 2010; Yudko, Lozhkina, & Fouts, 2007):

1 How many times in the past year have you used an illegal drug or used a prescription medication for nonmedical reasons?
2 Have you ever had blackouts or flashbacks as a result of drug use?
3 Do you ever feel bad or guilty about your drug use?
4 Does your partner, spouse, or family ever complain about your involvement with drugs?
5 Have you engaged in illegal activities to obtain drugs?

Patients who report using drugs can be counseled to reduce their drug use and other risky behaviors. Specifically, they should be educated about how continued drug use may harm their brains, their overall health, and other areas of their life, including family relationships and work. Screening and interventions do not have to be time-consuming and can be integrated into general medical settings. In patients with positive screening results, substance use should be categorized into hazardous use, substance abuse, or substance dependence. For most substances, even infrequent use is considered hazardous because of potential health consequences, the risk of dependence, and the risk of legal repercussions. However, not all substance use is equally hazardous. Evidence suggests that the use of heroin, methamphetamine, and crack cocaine is associated with an intrinsically high risk of harm to self and others (Nutt, King, & Phillips, 2010).

Brief counseling is indicated for patients with hazardous substance use or substance abuse. Patients with substance dependence require more intensive treatment. Physician judgment is important in determining the appropriate intervention or advice regarding hazardous substance use. Patients with substance abuse issues should be referred for substance abuse treatment, and for those patients in treatment, healthcare providers can provide ongoing support to stay in treatment and abstain from drugs during their follow-up appointments. Closely monitor your patients and if you suspect a relapse or if they show signs of continued drug use, refer them back to treatment.

Cigarette smoking is another common addictive behavior, and a leading cause of mortality and morbidity in the United States (Baker, Brandon, & Chassin, 2004). Sexual abuse among men and women that occurred by 14 years of age and antedated age of smoking initiation was associated with a four-fold increase in smoking initiation (Anda et al., 1999). Moreover, survivors who are also formerly drug or alcohol dependent may continue to smoke tobacco to alleviate anxiety even though some studies suggest that nicotine use and withdrawal can actually increase anxiety (Morissette, Tull, Gulliver, Kamholz, & Zimering, 2007).

Although there is a vast literature suggesting that smoking is linked to heart disease and stroke, smoking remains the last vestige of control for many survivors. “All I have is my cigarette,” said Michael, stuffing it behind his ear. “And it’s my choice when to smoke it.” Having this small sense of control feels comforting for the survivor but does not circumvent the deleterious and atrocious effects of cigarettes. Still, it is important for healthcare professionals to monitor and provide treatment interventions for those patients who are most at risk for nicotine dependence.

Risky sexual behavior is the most highly documented form of harmful behavior in abuse survivors. This finding holds true for males and females and is consistent across the range of sexual orientations (Kendall-Tackett, 2002). And, of course, risky sexual behavior leads to a greater likelihood of contracting a sexually transmitted disease (STD).

In one study, gay and bisexual men with a history of childhood sexual abuse were more likely to have unprotected anal intercourse and had a two-fold increase in the prevalence of HIV infection compared with gay and bisexual men who had not been sexually abused. Those who had been sexually abused before age 13 were more likely to participate in anal intercourse without protection compared with men in their sample who had not been sexually abused by that age (Bartholow et al., 1994).

A history of child abuse or neglect can increase the risk for STDs in adulthood, according to a study partly funded by the National Institute of Mental Health. The researchers found that people who experienced abuse or neglect 30 years before the study were more likely than controls to have had an STD. In some cases, abuse survivors were three times more likely to have had more than one type of STD. Childhood sexual abuse appeared to increase the risk for STDs in women even more than in men, and in white participants more than in participants of color. Overall, however, survivors of sexual abuse are clearly at greater risk for sexually transmitted diseases (Wilson & Widom, 2009).

Screening adult survivors for STDs is one of the most important things you can do for any patient, but especially for survivors of sexual abuse. These are the STD testing recommendations for men by the Centers for Disease Control and Prevention:

- All adults and adolescents from ages 13 to 64 should be tested at least once for HIV.
- Screening at least once a year for syphilis, chlamydia, and gonorrhea for all sexually active gay, bisexual, and other men who have sex with men (MSM). MSM who have multiple or anonymous partners should be screened more frequently for STDs (i.e., at three- to six-month intervals).
- Anyone who has unsafe sex or shares injection drug equipment should get tested for HIV at least once a year. Sexually active gay and bisexual men may benefit from more frequent testing (e.g., every three to six months).

For more information, including guidelines for screening sexually active women for STDS, see www.cdc.gov/std/prevention/screeningreccs.htm.

Obesity and eating disorders

Jamie

Jamie is a 33-year-old male with Type II Diabetes. His Body Mass Index (BMI) is 39.5. Body mass index is a measure of body fat based on height and weight. Obesity equals having a BMI greater than 29. Being very self-conscious of his size, Jamie repeatedly apologizes as he maneuvers his way through the waiting room. Once inside the exam room, he sits on the table, wringing his hands. His blood sugar that day is over 200, and his hemoglobin A1C is 9.

A fasting blood sugar level less than 100 mg/dL is normal. A fasting blood sugar level from 100 to 125 is considered prediabetes. Having a blood sugar of 126 mg/dL or higher on two separate occasions meets the definition of diabetes. A random blood sugar level or non-fasting blood sugar of greater than 200 mg/mL is highly suggestive of diabetes. Glycated hemoglobin or hemoglobin A1C is a blood test that indicates your average blood sugar level for the past two to three months. It measures the percentage of blood sugar attached to hemoglobin. An A1C above 6.5% on two separate occasions indicates diabetes. Normal levels are below 5.7%.

Jamie is a known diabetic and is currently on oral medication to help control his diabetes, but he is non-compliant with a low sugar diet. As a result, his A1C is higher than it should be. If he lost weight, he could lower his A1C, but instead his healthcare provider has to increase the dose of his current diabetic regimen. When asked why it's so hard for him to control the amount of sugar he eats, Jamie becomes flushed, wringing his hands so that his knuckles blanch.

Over the course of several months, Jamie reveals that his uncle and older brother sexually abused him as a child. Worse still, Jamie suspects his parents knew about it but did nothing to prevent it. As a teenager, Jamie gained weight, finding comfort in food, and perhaps in some subconscious way he wore his obesity as an armor to protect him from further abuse.

Obesity is quite common among adult survivors of childhood abuse. In a study of 131 patients with a history of incest, 60% of these patients were more than 50 lbs overweight, compared with 28% of the control group. Twenty-five percent were more than 100 lbs overweight, compared with 6% of the control group (Felitti, 1991). Many survivors are prone to binge eating while others put on weight to desexualize themselves, trying to avoid future abuse.

Men with a history of sexual abuse may not fully recover from an eating disorder, or may experience chronic relapses, if they don't address the underlying trauma. Identifying patients with an eating disorder is the first step.

Knowing there is a strong correlation between early childhood sexual trauma and eating disorders, it's important to ask your patients about their childhood if they haven't already disclosed a history of childhood sexual abuse. Treatment often involves an integrative approach. Some suggestions include cognitive-behavioral therapy, a nutritional consultation, support groups, and exercising. In addition to cognitive-behavioral therapy there are several other interventions, including:

1 Eye Movement Desensitization and Reprocessing (EMDR)
2 Somatic Experiencing
3 Coping Skills Training
4 Movement or Art Therapy.

Sleep disorders

Jacob

> Jacob is a 48-year-old stockbroker who began having nightmares when he was notified his father was admitted to a hospice for terminal cancer. Jacob's wife accompanied him to his doctor's appointment and described episodes in which Jacob appeared to be choking or trying to scream while still asleep. Several times she was awakened by these awful sounds and had to wake Jacob up.
>
> His father began molesting Jacob by age 9. It wasn't until Jacob attempted suicide in his early twenties that he entered therapy and was able to move past this traumatic event by confronting it. The recent news of his father's failing health triggered the nightmares. Memory fragments that Jacob had filed into a closed container somewhere in his mind returned to him while asleep, and, even though Jacob's father was no longer a threat to him, the news about his father's health brought back memories of events when he was 9. During the day, he could fend off anxiety, but at night he found it difficult to fall asleep. When he did, he dreamt of his father breaking into his room.

Adequate sleep is essential for good health. Sleep occurs in every animal species and is necessary for survival. During childhood and adolescence, sleep is vital for brain maturation. The consequences of insufficient sleep have particular implications for the cognitive and emotional functioning of adolescents.

Lack of sufficient sleep affects health in various ways. People who are chronically short on sleep are more prone to infections and illnesses and are more likely to have accidents (Greenfield, Lee, Friedman, & Springer, 2011).

Safety promotes sleep; sleep naturally occurs in times and places that feel safe. Therefore, threats to safety – as is often the case with child sexual abuse – frequently result in extended periods of sleep disruption. Post-traumatic stress disorder resulting from sexual abuse may be characterized by sleep disturbances and nightmares. Also, poor sleep quality has been linked to depression (Harvey, Jones, & Schmidt, 2003).

In addition to accessing adult mental and physical health status, clinicians should be aware that there are a variety of other pathways through which childhood abuse might impair an adult's sleep:

1 chronic stress
2 depression
3 post-traumatic stress disorder (PTSD).

Overall health perception

Sexual abuse survivors often express less overall satisfaction with their health than non-survivors. In a study of primary-care patients, only 80% of patients who had been sexually abused described themselves as healthy, compared with 97% of the non-abused control group who were matched for age and sex (Kendall-Tackett, 2002).

Overall health is a complex interplay of psychosocial, physiologic, and mental wellbeing, which influence each other. Abuse influences these interconnections, and the outcomes vary for each. To improve health outcomes for adult survivors, healthcare providers first must identify patients as survivors of sexual abuse. Only when survivors confront their past are they able to move forward as active participants in their overall health.

Second, discuss a healthcare plan appropriate for your patient's age and family history, paying close attention to preventative healthcare measures as well as reducing modifiable risk factors with suggestions like smoking cessation, monitoring alcohol intake, and avoiding recreational drugs.

Remember, simply counseling a survivor to "quit smoking" or "lose weight" will not be helpful if the survivor does not believe that anything he does can make a difference in his life. Healthcare providers must acknowledge the complex forces that lead to good health, and help their patients confront the years of negative influences – the shame and guilt – with which their past history of sexual abuse has left them. Only then, by recognizing and addressing all these underlying influences, can we hope to improve the health of an adult survivor.

Best clinical practice for providing healthcare to male survivors of childhood sexual abuse cluster around issues of communication, control, and permission (Edwards, Dube, Felitti, & Anda, 2007).

The *communication cluster* focuses on disclosure of sexual abuse to the healthcare provider. Most survivors will not disclose a history of abuse at the initial visit, but if and when they do, they will view this as a test. How will my healthcare provider respond? Survivors use this as an opportunity to see how open and willing their healthcare provider is to listening. But the disclosure equally offers opportunities for providers to begin conversations about possible triggers.

The *control cluster* involves the triggering aspects of the medical exam, tests, and treatments. Clinicians must not disregard the hubris involved in asking a patient to disrobe and disclose personal information after a brief introduction. We ask a lot from our patients. Respect their trust. Allow them to share the responsibility of control. Adopting these practices will help alleviate their stress. By employing your patient as a partner in his healthcare, you lay the foundation for a relationship as opposed to being an adult telling a child what to do. You reinforce that the two of you are now in an adult relationship based on mutual trust.

The *permission cluster* is the exchange between the healthcare provider and the patient before the actual intimate aspect of medical care begins. Consider this scenario: you meet a patient for the first time. He is sitting on the exam room table wearing only a paper gown and underwear. The average person feels quite vulnerable in this position. Imagine this person is a survivor of sexual abuse. How much more difficult would it be for him? Instead, what would it be like if you allowed your patients to remain fully dressed during the initial intake? If you explained the events that are to take place before having them undress for the physical exam?

Sometimes these events may have to take place in stages. For sexual abuse survivors, it might be prudent to take a history and then allow them to decide if they want to proceed with the exam, offering the option to come back in a week.

The typical busy medical practice poses a challenge to optimal communication. Now, with electronic medical records becoming the standard of care, templates can be very useful to keep your patients up to date with their preventative healthcare in an efficient manner. A potential downside to the electronic medical record, however, is that it's easier for a physician to gaze at the computer screen or the keyboard rather than facing and interacting with the patient. The physician must be aware of this in order to accomplish a crucial goal, an empathic response to the disclosure of a history of childhood sexual abuse (Edwards et al., 2007). If your response doesn't meet with your patient's satisfaction, you may never see him again.

It is typical for male survivors of childhood sexual abuse to feel overwhelmed or intimidated during an interaction with their healthcare provider. For most survivors, healthcare providers represent authority figures. Often, the abuser was someone in a position of authority. It is critical for healthcare providers to remember that, even though their patient has agreed to an exam, procedure, or treatment, the patient may not feel empowered if he feels threatened. As a result, he may acquiesce even though he may have changed his mind. A good healthcare provider needs to reassess the patient regularly and look for visual cues that the patient may be uncomfortable. Maintain an ongoing dialogue with the patient about his experience and assess his coping ability at that moment.

Healthcare providers should be particularly careful to ask permission for invasive procedures like the digital rectal exam, testicular exam, or the retraction of the foreskin. Often healthcare providers assume patients have granted them permission to examine them fully because it's understood once they've made the appointment that an exam is part of the routine visit. By not specifically asking for permission, however, you imply the patient has no choice. This unfortunately replicates for some survivors their history of sexual abuse, in which the survivor's body ceased to be his own, with the abuser using it in various ways for the abuser's needs without regard for the needs of the survivor. If the survivor feels you are like his abuser, he is likely to flee from your medical care.

Conclusion

Childhood sexual abuse affects a significant number of men, making it necessary for healthcare providers who treat male health issues to alter their practice to meet the needs of these men. There is voluminous data to show that childhood sexual abuse has long-term effects on the overall physical and mental wellbeing of adult survivors. Since most perpetrators of abuse were authority figures, childhood sexual abuse survivors often develop intense feelings of mistrust, fear, and suspiciousness of later authority figures. Having a history of abuse can result in fear and avoidance of medical care, since many survivors see their healthcare providers as authority figures to be dreaded and avoided.

Healthcare providers must first learn to identify survivors of childhood sexual abuse, because most will not divulge this information readily. Once a history of abuse has been established, it is imperative for physicians to alter their clinical practice to accommodate survivors so their patients feel safe, empowered, and heard. When adults betray a relationship with a child, they destroy that child's future sense of trust. Since gaining survivors' trust can therefore take a long time, healthcare providers must remain patient and consistent.

Throughout their later lives, abused children will struggle to understand why abuse happened to them. Having a non-abusive relationship with a healthcare provider fosters mutual trust and promotes long-term health success by allowing a survivor to feel taken care of in an adult relationship with his physician, based on that trust.

References

Anda, R. F., Croft, J. B., Felitti, F. J., Nordenberg, D., Giles, W. H., Williamson, D. F., & Giovino, G. A. (1999). Adverse childhood experiences and smoking during adolescence and adulthood. *JAMA, 282*(17), 1652–1658. Retrieved from http://jama.jamanetwork.com/article.aspx?articleid=192056&resultclick=1.

Baker, T. B., Brandon, T. H., & Chassin, L. (2004). Motivational influences on cigarette smoking. *Annual Review of Psychology, 55*(1), 463–491.

Bartholow, B., Doll, L., Joy, D., Douglas, J., Bolan, G., Harrison, J., & McKirnan, D. (1994). Emotional, behavioral, and HIV risks associated with sexual abuse among adult homosexual and bisexual men. *Child Abuse & Neglect, 18*, 747–761.

Black, M. C., Brasile, K. C., Breiding, M. J., Smith, S. G., Walters, M. L., Merrick, T. M., Chen, J., & Stevens, M. R. (2010). National intimate partner and sexual violence survey (NISVS). Atlanta, GA: National Center for Injury Prevention and Control, Division of Violence Prevention, Centers for Disease Control and Prevention. Retrieved from www.cdc.gov/violenceprevention/pdf/nisvs_report2010-a.pdf.

Boonchai, W., Desomchoke, R., & Iamtharachai, P. (2011). Trend of contact allergy to cosmetic ingredients in Thais over a period of 10 years. *Contact Dermatitis, 65*, 311–316.

Castle, D. J., & Phillips, K. A. (2006). Obsessive-compulsive spectrum of disorders: A defensible construct? *Australian and New Zealand Journal of Psychiatry, 40*, 114–120.

Charlin, R., Barcaui, C. B., Kac, B. K., Soares, D. B., Rabello-Fonseca, R., & Azulay-Abulafia, L. (2008). Hydroquinone-induced exogenous ochronosis: A report of four cases and usefulness of dermoscopy. *International Journal of Dermatology, 47*, 19–23.

Edwards, V. J., Dube, S. R., Felitti, V. J., & Anda, R. F. (2007). It's ok to ask about past abuse. *American Psychologist, 62*(4), 327–328. Retrieved from www.ncbi.nlm.nih.gov/pubmed/17516786.

Felitti, V. J. (1991). Long-term medical consequences of incest, rape, and molestation. *Southern Medical Journal, 84*(3), 328–331.

Felitti, V. J., & Anda, R. F. (2010). The relationship of adverse childhood experiences to adult medical disease, psychiatric disorders, and sexual behavior: Implications for healthcare. In R. Lanius & E. Vermetten (Eds.), *The hidden epidemic: The impact of early life trauma on health and disease* (pp. 77–87). Cambridge: Cambridge University Press.

Felitti, V. J., Anda, R. F., Nordenberg, D., Williamson, D. F., Spitz, A. M., Edwards, V., Koss, M. P., & Marks, J. S. (1998). The relationship of adult health status to childhood abuse and household dysfunction. *American Journal of Preventive Medicine, 14*, 245–258.

Friedman, L. S., Samet, J. H., Roberts, M. S., Hudlin, M., & Hans, P. (1992). Inquiry about victimization experiences: A survey of patient preferences and physician practices. *Archives of Internal Medicine, 152*(6), 1186–1190. Retrieved from http://dx.doi.org/10.1001/archinte.1992.00400180056008.

Gallo-Silver, L., Anderson, C. M., & Romo, J. (2014). Best clinical practices for male adult survivors of childhood sexual abuse: "Do no harm." *Permanente Journal, 18*(3), 82–87. Retrieved from www.ncbi.nlm.nih.gov/pubmed/25106042.

Gallo-Silver, L., & Weiner, M. (2006). Survivors of childhood sexual abuse diagnosed with cancer: Managing the impact of early trauma on cancer treatment. *Journal of Psychosocial Oncology, 24*(1), 107–134. Retrieved from http://dx.doi.org/10.1300/J077v24n01_08.

Greenfield, E. A., Lee, C., Friedman, E., & Springer, K. W. (2011). Childhood abuse as a risk factor for sleep problems in adulthood: Evidence from a U.S. national study. *Annals of Behavioral Medicine, 42*, 245. Retrieved from www.ncbi.nlm.nih.gov/pmc/articles/PMC3211065/.

Harvey, A., Jones, C., & Schmidt, D. (2003). Sleep and posttraumatic stress disorder: A review. *Clinical Psychology Review, 23*, 377–407.

Hubbard, R. L., Craddock, S. G., Flynn, P. M., Anderson, J., & Etheridge, R. M. (1997). Overview of 1-year follow-up outcomes in the Drug Abuse Treatment Outcome Study (DATOS). *Psychology of Addictive Behaviors, 11*(4), 261–278.

Hunter, L. M. (2011). Buying racial capital: Skin-bleaching and cosmetic surgery in a globalized world. *Journal of Pan African Studies, 4*, 143–164.

James, C., Seizas, A., Harrison, A., Girardin, J. L., Butler, M., Zizi, F., & Samuels, A. (2016). Childhood physical and sexual abuse in Caribbean young adults and its association with depression, post-traumatic stress, and skin bleaching. *Journal of Depression and Anxiety, 5*, 214. Retrieved from www.ncbi.nlm.nih.gov/pmc/articles/PMC4807863/#R31.

Kendall-Tackett, K. A. (2002). The health effects of childhood abuse: Four pathways by which abuse can influence health. *Child Abuse & Neglect, 26*, 715–729.

Kendall-Tackett, K. A., Marshall, R., & Ness, K. E. (2000). Victimization, health-care use, and health maintenance. *Family Violence & Sexual Assault Bulletin, 16*, 18–21.

Kim, E. H., & Andriole, G. L. (2015). Prostate-specific antigen-based screening: Controversy and guidelines. *BMC Medicine, 13*, 61. Retrieved from www.ncbi.nlm.nih.gov/pmc/articles/PMC4371717/.

Leeb, R. T., Paulozzi, L., Melanson, C., Simon, T., & Arias, I. (2008). Child maltreatment surveillance: Uniform definitions for public health and recommended data elements, Version 1.0. Atlanta, GA: National Center for Injury Prevention and Control, Centers for Disease Control and Prevention. Retrieved from www.cdc.gov/violenceprevention/pdf/cm_surveillance-a.pdf.

Leeners, B., Stiller, R., Block, E., Görres, G., Imthurn, B., & Rath, W. (2006). Consequences of childhood sexual abuse experiences on dental care. *Journal of Psychosomatic Research, 62*(5), 581–588. Retrieved from www.ncbi.nlm.nih.gov/pmc/articles/PMC4309219/#B30.

Lewis, C. C., Matheson, D. H., & Brimacombe, C. A. (2011). Factors influencing patient disclosure to physicians in birth control clinics: An application of the communication privacy management theory. *Health Communication, 26*(6), 502–511. Retrieved from http://dx.doi.org/10.1080/10410236.2011.556081.

Morissette, S. B., Tull, M. T., Gulliver, S. B., Kamholz, B. W., & Zimering, R. T. (2007). Anxiety, anxiety disorders, tobacco use, and nicotine: A critical review of interrelationships. *Psychological Bulletin, 133*, 245–272.

Murray, C. D., Macdonald, S., & Fox, J. (2008). Body satisfaction, eating disorders and suicide ideation in an Internet sample of self-harmers reporting and not reporting childhood sexual abuse. *Psychology, Health, & Medicine, 13*, 29–42.

Nutt, D. J., King, L. A., & Phillips, L. D. (on behalf of the Independent Scientific Committee on Drugs) (2010). Drug harms in the UK: A multicriteria decision analysis. *Lancet, 376*(9752), 1558–1565.

Paolucci, E. O., Genuis, M. L., & Violato, C. (2001). A meta-analysis of the published research on the effects of child sexual abuse. *Journal of Psychology, 135*, 17–36.

Petronio, S., Reeder, H. M., Hecht, M. L., & Ros-Mendoza, T. M. (1996). Disclosure of sexual abuse by children and adolescents. *Journal of Applied Communication Research, 24*(3), 181–199. Retrieved from www.ncbi.nlm.nih.gov/pmc/articles/PMC4116270/.

Repetti, R. L., Taylor, S. E., & Seeman, T. E. (2002). Risky families: Family social environments and the mental and physical health of offspring. *Psychological Bulletin, 128*(2), 330–366.

Rosenthal, E. (2012, June 2). Let's (not) get physicals. *New York Times*. Retrieved from www.nytimes.com/2012/06/03/sunday-review/lets-not-get-physicals.html.

Seeman, T. E., Singer, B. H., Rowe, J. W., Horwitz, R. I., & McEwen, B. S. (1997). Price of adaptation—allostatic load and its health consequences: MacArthur studies of successful aging. *Archives of Internal Medicine, 157*(19), 2259–2268.

Sharpe, D., & Faye, C. (2006). Non-epileptic seizures and child sexual abuse: A critical review of the literature. *Clinical Psychology Review, 26*, 1020–1040.

Skinner, H. A. (1982). The drug abuse screening test. *Addictive Behaviors, 7*(4), 363–371.

Smith, P. C., Schmidt, S. M., Allensworth-Davies, D., & Saitz, R. (2010). A single-question screening test for drug use in primary care. *Archives of Internal Medicine, 170*(13), 1155–1160.

Smolak, L., & Murnen, S. K. (2002). A meta-analytic examination of the relationship between child sexual abuse and eating disorders. *International Journal of Eating Disorders, 31*, 136–150.

Spinelli, F. (2012, June 8). In support of the annual physical exam. *The Huffington Post*. Retrieved from www.huffingtonpost.com/dr-frank-spinelli/annual-physical_b_1582423.html.

Stalker, C. A., Russell, B. D., Teram, E., & Schachter, C. L. (2005). Providing dental care to survivors of childhood sexual abuse: Treatment considerations for the practitioner. *Journal of the American Dental Association, 136*, 1277–1281.

Thompson, M. S., & Keith, V. M. (2001). The blacker the berry: Gender, skin tone, self-esteem, and self-efficacy. *Gender & Society, 15*, 336–357.

US Department of Veterans Affairs (updated 2016). Men and sexual trauma. Retrieved July 6, 2016 from www.ptsd.va.gov/public/types/violence/men-sexual-trauma.asp.

van der Kolk, B. A., & Fisler, R. (1995). Dissociation and the fragmentary nature of traumatic memories: Overview and exploratory study. *Journal of Traumatic Stress, 8*, 505–525.

Williams, D. R., & Collins, C. (1995). U.S. socioeconomic and racial differences in health: Patterns and explanations. *Annual Review of Sociology, 21*, 348–386.

Willumsen, T. (2004). The impact of childhood sexual abuse on dental fear. *Community Dentistry and Oral Epidemiology, 32*, 73–79.

Wilson, H. W., & Widom, C. S. (2009). Sexually transmitted diseases among adults who had been abused and neglected as children: A 30-year prospective study. *American Journal of Public Health, 99 Suppl 1*, S197–203. PMID: 19218173. Retrieved from www.nimh.nih.gov/news/science-news/2009/child-abuse-survivors-have-higher-risk-for-stds-in-adulthood-than-non-abused-adults.shtml.

Yudko, E., Lozhkina, O., & Fouts, A. (2007). A comprehensive review of the psychometric properties of the Drug Abuse Screening Test. *Journal of Substance Abuse Treatment, 32*(2), 189–198.

Chapter 4

Building knowledge for recovery

Contemporary research on the long-term effects of child sexual abuse on men

Scott D. Easton

Introduction

Child sexual abuse (CSA) is increasingly recognized as a pernicious public health problem that threatens the healthy development of boys. Prevalence estimates vary, but one study found that 5% of boys experience penetrative sexual abuse and that the rates of other forms of sexual abuse are up to three times higher (Gilbert et al., 2009). Several studies provide evidence that approximately 15% of men report being sexually abused in childhood (Briere & Elliott, 2003; Dube et al., 2005; Lisak, Hopper, & Song, 1996).

Beyond epidemiological studies, other indicators of public recognition of the problem include: celebrity disclosures (actor Tyler Perry, Senator Scott Brown, CNN anchor Thomas Roberts, professional athletes Greg LeMond and Theo Fleury), mainstream movies (*Spotlight*, *Mystic River*, *The Prince of Tides*), and pervasive media coverage of institutional scandals involving CSA (e.g., Catholic Church, Penn State University, Boy Scouts of America). National organizations have emerged that are dedicated to advocacy, education, and support for adult survivors of CSA (e.g., MaleSurvivor.org, Survivors Network of those Abused by Priests). Finally, self-help literature has developed through the pioneering efforts of therapists and organizers such as Dr. Mic Hunter (1990), Dr. Stephen Grubman-Black (1990), Hank Estrada (1994), Dr. Richard Gartner (1999; 2005), Mike Lew (2004), and Dr. Howard Fradkin (2012).

The focus of this chapter is on the long-term effects of sexual abuse during childhood on men. An important, related topic, the sexual assault of men during adulthood, is beyond the current scope but deserves scholarly attention.

Despite these encouraging signs, the state of empirical research on the long-term effects of CSA on men (that is, scholarly, peer-reviewed studies that advance our understanding of the phenomenon through scientific observation or experimentation) lags behind. Men with histories of sexual abuse remain stigmatized, marginalized, and under-researched. This is highly problematic because results from well-designed empirical studies inform prevention programs, clinical treatment protocols, and policy decisions. Rather than merely filling scholarly journals, research can ideally be translated into efforts to alleviate suffering and enhance the well-being of men who endured CSA. In other words, it can help change lives.

This chapter highlights contemporary research (2000–present) with men who were sexually abused in childhood by reviewing one program of research on the long-term effects of CSA. The goal is to simultaneously summarize empirical knowledge while also encouraging other researchers to investigate topics pertinent to recovery and healing for male survivors. Organized into five sections, the chapter first discusses the rationale and methods of a recent large-scale study on male survivors of CSA. Next, existing research in three critical topic areas (predictors of mental distress, disclosure barriers, and factors that influence post-traumatic growth) is covered. The chapter concludes with a discussion of future directions for research.

2010 project: rationale, design, and participants

Rationale for the project

Previous scholarly articles have integrated and reviewed research studies on CSA and boys/men that were conducted in the 1980s and 1990s (Dhaliwal, Gauzas, Antonowicz, & Ross, 1996; Holmes & Slap, 1998; Putnam, 2003; Spataro, Moss, & Wells, 2001). Since 2000, many studies (both qualitative and quantitative) have been published on this population. Some of the topics include: gender identity (Kia-Keating, Grossman, Sorsoli, & Epstein, 2005), meaning-making (Grossman, Sorsoli, & Kia-Keating, 2006), physical health (Irish, Kobayashi, & Delahanty, 2009), psychiatric disorders (Cutajar, Mullen, Ogloff, Wells, & Spataro, 2010; Fater & Mullaney, 2000; Isely, Isely, Freiburger, & McMackin, 2008; Molnar, Buka, & Kessler, 2001), self-identity (Easton, Leone, & O'Leary, 2016; Krayer, Seddon, Robinson, & Gwilym, 2015), sexual behavior problems and risk-taking (Homma, Wang, Saewyc, & Kishor, 2012; Vaillancourt-Morel et al., 2015); social functioning (Fater & Mullaney, 2000; Isely et al., 2008), suicidality (Easton, Renner, & O'Leary, 2013; O'Leary & Gould, 2009), substance abuse (DiIorio, Hartwell, & Hansen, 2002; Molnar et al., 2001; Nelson et al., 2002), and trauma symptoms (Briere & Elliot, 2003). These valuable studies constitute noteworthy progress in understanding the experiences and needs of men who experienced CSA.

Although these recent studies have made important contributions to the knowledge base, scholarship has been limited by several factors. Many existing studies on the long-term effects of CSA on men have limitations in sampling (e.g., small size, drawn from clinical population, narrow age range) or measurement (e.g., non-standardized measures). In terms of the broader topic of CSA and mental health, most studies have focused on short-term effects (i.e., later childhood/adolescence) or were based on predominantly/exclusively female samples.

Merrill, Thomsen, Sinclair, Gold, and Milner (2001) proposed a useful typology to classify studies of CSA. The first type of study focuses on associations. This includes, for example, research that evaluates links between CSA and mental health outcomes. Studies in the second category focus on predictors of outcomes or problems; they attempt to explain why some male survivors experience depression, for example, while others do not. The third category of research includes process models. These studies seek to understand the mechanisms and pathways (i.e., "how") that connect CSA to outcomes. Most existing studies fall in the first category; more research is needed on predictors of problems and process models. Overall, relatively little is known—in research terms—about the effects of CSA on men over the life course.

Survey background

Given the dearth of data sources on men with histories of CSA, I decided to collect original data in 2010 during my doctoral program in social work at the University of Iowa. Prior to that, I had worked with mentors (most notably, Dr. Carol Coohey, University of Iowa) and content experts (such as Dr. Patrick O'Leary, Griffith University) to develop an anonymous survey that could be administered online, a useful strategy for reaching hidden, stigmatized populations. The instrument was titled the

2010 Health and Well-being Survey and consisted of approximately 150 items grouped into six sections: mental health, sexual abuse characteristics and disclosure history, cognitive processing of the abuse, gender norms, post-traumatic growth, and demographic/background information (Easton, 2011). The majority of items were drawn from standardized instruments that required permission to use (e.g., Conformity to Masculine Norms; Mahalik et al., 2003b). For concepts that did not have existing instruments (e.g., response to disclosure, account-making), we used project-created measures. Additionally, five survey items were open-ended questions designed to elicit valuable qualitative data by allowing participants to provide unlimited narrative responses. Before implementation, the survey underwent elaborate pre-testing over a two-year period with input from national sexual abuse and trauma experts, clinicians, and graduate students in social work.

The largest challenge to the project was gaining access to and recruiting participants from this hidden population. After considering a range of options, we pursued collaborations with a few national organizations dedicated to supporting survivors of sexual abuse: the Survivors Network of those Abused by Priests (SNAP), MaleSurvivor.org, and 1in6.org. We contacted leaders within these organizations to explore possibilities for forming research partnerships. Each organization had a different protocol. One group required submission of a formal proposal for review, discussion, and modification within their internal research and executive leadership committees. Another group requested a series of phone conversations and interviews with board members. Two organizations insisted on changes to the survey, including the elimination of questions related to sensitive topics (e.g., sexual orientation, religious affiliation, substance use) that they deemed could cause distress for survivors in recovery. All of the organizations required multiple mechanisms to safeguard the privacy of survey participants and protect them in case of an adverse reaction while taking the survey. These mechanisms included support resources such as an online therapist locator, a suicide prevention hotline, and a list of community mental health centers. The project was also reviewed, revised, and ultimately approved by the Institutional Review Board at the University of Iowa. In the end, two organizations agreed to post study announcements on their website (www.SNAPnetwork.org; www.malesurvivor.org). The third organization (1in6) was undergoing a major web redesign project. As an alternative, one of its board members agreed to post the announcement on his website (www.jimhopper.com), which contains a resource page on the sexual abuse of boys.

The study announcement provided a link to a separate survey website that displayed a welcome message, consent letter, and eligibility screening questions. To be included in the study, potential participants had to self-identify as being male, 18 years of age or older, and sexually abused before the age of 18. Interested, eligible men then completed the anonymous, internet-based survey during an eight-week period from April to June, 2010.

Summary of participants

Given the labyrinth of obstacles to recruitment, especially social stigma, and difficulties previous scholars experienced trying to conduct research with men who were sexually abused in childhood, we were anxious when the online survey initially went "live." Several weeks later, we were extremely gratified as nearly 500 men at various stages of recovery generously took time to participate in the study. Based on our reviews of the literature, this sample constituted the largest dataset collected to date on men with histories of CSA. By completing the survey, some participants disclosed for the first time that they had been sexually abused. At the other end of the spectrum, some participants were dedicated activists against sexual abuse whose survivor status was part of their public identity. Regardless, we were struck by the number of supportive responses from participants who completed the survey. Here are some examples:

- "Thank you for this survey, and your work."
- "Simply a sincere thanks for doing research in this area."
- "Thank you for bringing attention to the specific issue of male survivors of sexual abuse. There are many of us, and many of us remain silent."
- "Bless you for what you are doing. I hope others can find help and a place of peace in their lives through your work."

The overall profile of the 487 participants in the dataset is presented elsewhere (Easton, 2011; 2014). To summarize, participants ranged from 18 to 84 years of age (the average age was 50 years), the largest age range in studies of male sexual abuse survivors. This range was noteworthy, as it allowed for subsequent analyses of how age impacts outcomes such as mental health among survivors and how mental health varies across life stages. Most of the men were White (90.9%), were living with a spouse or partner (69.9%), held a bachelor's degree or higher (58.1%), and were members of either SNAP or MaleSurvivor.org (80.3%). On average, participants had between two and three children.

In terms of sexual abuse histories, the average age at the time of first being sexually abused was 10 years. For the majority of participants, the sexual abuse lasted more than six months (67.8%), involved penetration (54.2%), and was perpetrated by a male adult (94.6%). In more than one-third of the cases, the abuser used physical force (36.1%). Almost one-fourth of the men reported that they were physically injured by the sexual abuse (23.8%).

Perhaps the most striking characteristic of the sample was how long it took participants to disclose their sexual abuse to another person. Responses to this question ranged from zero to 63 years. Incredibly, the mean was 21 years. Thus, on average, men kept the abuse a secret for more than two decades. The length of time it took men to have an *in-depth discussion* of the sexual abuse was even longer (28 years). These disclosure characteristics, along with others such as quality of responses to disclosure, would later prove to be critical determinants of mental health in subsequent studies.

Next we will highlight studies that emerged from the dataset on three important topics: predictors of mental health, barriers to disclosure, and factors related to post-traumatic growth. For each topic, we will first present a summary of previous literature (including relevant theory) and then present the featured study's purpose, hypotheses, and major findings.

Study #1: predictors of mental distress

Despite the growing body of evidence of the harmful effects of CSA on men's long-term mental health, not all CSA survivors develop severe psychopathology or interpersonal dysfunction (Hunter, 2006; Putnam, 2003). This fact raises critical questions including "Why do some survivors do well psychologically and others struggle?", "Which factors explain resilience among adult survivors of CSA?", and "Which topics should be assessed and addressed in clinical intervention plans with this population?"

Studies that seek answers to these questions constitute the essence of second and third generation research (Merrill et al., 2001). Although this facet of the knowledge base is at a nascent stage with male survivors, we will review existing research before presenting results from a recent study based on the 2010 dataset (Easton, 2014).

Recent literature

CSA severity. Clinicians and scholars suggest that characteristics of the sexual abuse experience, namely indicators of abuse severity, may heighten the risk of mental health problems for survivors (Andrews, Corry, Slade, Issakidis, & Swanston, 2004; Lew, 2004). More severe forms of sexual abuse may inflict a deeper wound by reinforcing helplessness, powerlessness, and self-blame for survivors. Some research has established, for example, that contact sexual abuse (compared to non-contact forms such as pornography, voyeurism, and flashing) is associated with higher levels of depression and other psychological problems in adulthood (Andrews et al., 2004; Nelson et al., 2002). Other studies have found that penetration (Briere & Elliott, 2003; Cutajar et al., 2010; Dube et al., 2005; O'Leary & Gould, 2009), duration or frequency (Briere & Elliott, 2003; Molnar et al., 2001; Steel, Sanna, Hammond, Whipple, & Cross, 2004), coercion or force (Boudewyn & Liem, 1995; Molnar et al., 2001), and close relation to the abuser (Molnar et al., 2001; O'Leary, Coohey, & Easton, 2010) are linked to more mental health problems. However, not all studies found that severity variables predict long-term psychopathology (e.g., Cutajar et al., 2010) or contained male survivors. It is unclear whether indicators of CSA severity exert a similar effect for men.

Childhood environment. Acknowledging that "sexual abuse does not occur in a vacuum" (Finkelhor, 1998, p. 1865), studies have examined how childhood environment can compound long-term effects of CSA on survivors' mental health. Finkelhor and colleagues proposed a model called poly-victimization that encompasses multiple forms of maltreatment and victimization (Finkelhor, Omrod, Turner, & Holt, 2009). One study found that poly-victimization, defined as exposure to four or more types of adversities in the past year, was highly predictive of trauma symptoms (Finkelhor, Omrod, & Turner, 2007). Another pioneering study examined a range of childhood stressors (e.g., physical or sexual abuse, parental mental illness, domestic violence) labeled Adverse Childhood Experiences (ACE). Felitti et al. (1998) found a graded relationship between the number of ACE categories and numerous health risk behaviors and diseases (e.g., smoking, obesity, heart disease) in adulthood. Numerous subsequent studies have confirmed that ACE categories are related to long-term mental health problems and leading causes of death (e.g., Dube et al., 2001).

Disclosure. The interpersonal process of telling another person about having been sexually abused (i.e., disclosure) has been identified as a critical component in several theoretical frameworks on trauma processing (e.g., account-making; Harvey, Orbuch, & Weber, 1990) and recovery from CSA (Arias & Johnson, 2013; Chouliara, Karatzias, & Gullone, 2014; Draucker et al., 2011). In terms of disclosure timing, the empirical research is underdeveloped. Some studies have found that delayed disclosure is related to more symptoms of post-traumatic stress disorder (PTSD) in adulthood (Ruggiero et al., 2004; Ullman, 2007). However, O'Leary et al. (2010) found that early disclosure was related to *more* mental health problems; Ullman and Filipas (2005) found no relationship between the length of time until disclosure and PTSD symptom severity. In terms of reaction to disclosure, receiving a supportive response (e.g., emotional, instrumental, informational) may promote health and recovery for survivors by reducing problems associated with shame, self-blame, isolation, and the burden of maintaining a secret. Although a substantial body of research has demonstrated a positive relationship between parental support following disclosure and short-term mental health (for a review, see Elliott & Carnes, 2001), there is very little research on the effect of responses to disclosure on the long-term mental health of survivors (Easton, 2013). Ullman and Filipas (2005) found that negative social reactions to disclosure of CSA were related to more PTSD symptoms for adult survivors. Another study found that maternal support during childhood protects against mental health symptoms in adulthood for male survivors (Easton, 2013). Overall, more research is needed with men, as most existing studies on disclosure have been conducted with female survivors of sexual assault.

Gender norms. Mahalik's model of gender socialization proposes that standards and expectations of masculinity are shaped by dominant groups in society and transmitted through descriptive, cohesive norms. In Western societies, traditional masculinity consists of norms such as winning, self-reliance, emotional control, a dislike of homosexuality, and pursuit of status (Mahalik et al., 2003b). Many men with histories of CSA face gender role conflicts (Lew, 2004). For example, survivors often feel victimization is un-masculine, especially in cases of sexual violence (Spataro et al., 2001). Because many abusers are men, male survivors often struggle with heightened issues of homophobia, shame, and stigma (Lew, 2004; Spataro et al., 2001) and concerns about sexual orientation (Walker, Hernandez, & Davey, 2012). To cope with feelings of inadequacy, some male survivors adopt a hyper-masculine or hegemonic persona replete with exaggerated masculine attitudes and norms such as aggression (Dorais, 2002; Kia-Keating et al., 2005).

A growing body of research has found that some masculine scripts are associated with psychological and physical health problems for men generally (Mahalik, Good, & Englar-Carlson, 2003a; Mahalik et al., 2003b) and in sub-populations such as Asian men (Liu & Iwamoto, 2007) or men who identify as gay (Kimmel & Mahalik, 2005). However, only a few studies, such as one by Lisak et al. (1996), have examined gender rigidity among male survivors of CSA or the possible effects of gender conformity on their long-term mental health. One study found that resilience among male survivors of CSA depends, in part, on being able to contain, resist, and renegotiate masculine roles (Kia-Keating et al., 2005). Another clinical article encouraged treatment providers to critique traditional notions of masculinity in psychotherapy with men who were sexually abused (Lisak, 1995). As a possible explanation for variation in health status among male survivors, more research should examine whether conformity to masculine norms inhibits recovery and healing from CSA.

Purpose and hypotheses

The purpose of the study by Easton (2014) was to identify risk and protective factors related to long-term mental distress for male survivors using a large, non-clinical sample of men with self-reported histories of CSA. Mental distress was measured using an adapted, 25-item version of the General Mental Health Distress Scale (GMDS; Dennis, White, Titus, & Unsicker, 2008) that asked participants whether they had experienced symptoms in the past 12 months related to internalizing disorders including depression, anxiety, somatization, and suicidality. Based on previous research, theory, and clinical knowledge, we predicted that four indicators of CSA severity (i.e., duration, penetration, use of force, and) and number of childhood adversities (in addition to CSA) would be positively related to mental distress. In terms of disclosure, we predicted that the length of time to tell someone about the CSA (and the support received upon disclosure) would protect against mental health problems. Finally, we posited that higher conformity to masculine norms would contribute to mental health problems in the sample.

C. Major results

The results of the study indicated that five of the eight hypotheses were supported. Although all four severity variables were significant in bivariate analysis, only one (the abuser used physical force) was related to mental distress in multivariate models. This suggests that the use of physical force by an abuser may increase feelings of helplessness and powerlessness in the survivor that persist into adulthood, thus contributing to mental distress. Despite the negative effects of the use of physical force by abusers, therapists can help survivors reclaim their sense of control and boost self-efficacy. Consistent with the growing body of literature on adverse childhood experiences (e.g., Dube et al., 2001; Felitti et al., 1998), this study found that the number of stressors in childhood (in addition to CSA) was associated with more mental health symptoms in adulthood. Because child maltreatment (e.g., physical abuse) and deprivation (e.g., parental criminality) commonly co-occur with CSA for boys (Andrews et al., 2004), mental health practitioners should include ACE in clinical assessments and help male survivors untangle the residual effects of environmental stressors that occurred early in the lifespan.

Both variables related to disclosure predicted mental distress in the final model. The longer one waited to tell someone about the abuse (which ranged from 0 to 63 years in the sample), the more mental health problems were evident. Conversely, the level of helpfulness of confidants' responses was negatively related to (i.e., protected against) mental distress. Based on this data, public health campaigns should promote understanding of CSA and boys, including guidance to family and friends on how to be helpful to sexual assault survivors following disclosure (e.g., believing the survivor, providing emotional support). CSA prevention programs should include information on the sexual abuse of boys. Sexual assault centers should evaluate their procedures and resources to make them more inclusive and welcoming to men. These efforts may help reduce the length of time that male survivors keep the toxic secret of CSA and increase their access to support resources.

Finally, masculine norms were positively related to mental distress. In this sample, higher adherence or conformity to traditional masculine norms was linked to more symptoms of depression, anxiety, somatization, and suicidality. Some of the norms measured included emotional control, disdain for homosexuality, and self-reliance, all factors that could potentially inhibit help-seeking and processing of sexual abuse experiences for men. Therapists working with male survivors should assess adherence to masculine norms and, if necessary, help survivors develop alternate scripts of masculinity (Kia-Keating et al., 2005; Lisak, 1995) that might promote or enhance recovery.

One of the strengths of this study was the elaborate set of control variables that were included in the statistical models. Most of these variables were not significant predictors of mental distress. However, three variables—current age, income, and membership in a survivor organization—were protective factors. Conversely, poverty and other social-economic disadvantages likely add additional obstacles to recovery for male survivors. Future public health campaigns should make concerted efforts to reach men in communities that face social disadvantage and improve their access to quality recovery resources.

Study #2: barriers to disclosure

Recent literature

In the aftermath of sexual victimization, children often use avoidance coping strategies and delay disclosure (Alaggia, 2005; Hershkowitz, Lanes, & Lamb, 2007; Ullman & Filipas, 2005). Many children deny being abused or recant their stories following disclosure (Malloy, Lyon, & Quas, 2007). Some research suggests gender differences, as boys disclose sexual abuse less frequently than girls (O'Leary & Barber, 2008). Another study (Easton, 2013) found that only one-fourth of adult male survivors (25.7%) told anyone in childhood about being abused; most waited until adulthood to first disclose. Low rates of early disclosure for sexually abused boys (10–33%) were confirmed in a review of literature (Holmes & Slap, 1998).

To better understand the low rates of disclosure, some studies have examined obstacles to reporting, telling, or disclosing sexual abuse among children. Some factors that impede disclosure in children include: older age at the time of the abuse, close relationship to the abuser (i.e., incest), feelings of responsibility for the abuse, and anticipation of negative repercussions following disclosure (Goodman-Brown, Edelstein, Goodman, Jones & Gordon, 2003; Hershkowitz et al., 2007). Environmental factors that deter disclosure include rigid gender roles and closed communication patterns in the family, violence or physical abuse, and social isolation (Alaggia & Kirshenbaum, 2005). In a review, Paine and Hansen (2002) identified barriers to childhood disclosure of CSA related to the self (e.g., feelings of shame, self-blame), family and loved ones (e.g., disruption of family), and the abuser (e.g., desire to protect). Paine and Hansen (2002) concluded that despite the growing clinical literature on disclosure barriers, more empirical research is needed.

The empirical literature on disclosure of CSA in adolescence or adulthood is even less developed than that on childhood disclosure (Ullman, 2003). A few studies have identified barriers such as shame, self-blame, and anticipation of unsupportive responses (Gilligan & Akhtar, 2006; Jonzon & Lindblad, 2004, 2005; Ruggiero et al., 2004; Staller & Nelson-Gardell, 2005). However, most of these studies were based on female samples. Although some obstacles may deter disclosure for either male or female survivors, it is likely that other factors uniquely obstruct the telling process for men (Roberts, Watlington, Nett, & Batten, 2010).

Within the context of social psychology, theorists posit that men's gendered identity can impede prospects for well-being (Courtenay, 2000). The experience of CSA violates gender norms and expectations for boys and men in Western culture; both victimhood and homosexuality are often denigrated in the male socialization process (Mahalik et al., 2003a; 2003b; Spataro et al., 2001). Given that boys are often sexually abused by another male (Holmes & Slap, 1998), many survivors have a compounded sense of shame due to homophobia (Holmes, Offen, & Waller, 1997) and fear being stigmatized as a homosexual, a victim, or a future sexual offender following disclosure (Alaggia, 2005). Another barrier is the naming process associated with abuse experiences. Many men who meet objective criteria for CSA do not label the experience as sexual abuse (Fondacaro, Holt, &

Powell, 1999; Holmes, 2008; Widom & Morris, 1997; Vaillancourt-Morel et al., 2016), possibly due to unfamiliarity with legal definitions, feelings of complicity, or minimization (Sorsoli, Kia-Keating, & Grossman, 2008; Vaillancourt-Morel et al., 2016). External barriers impede disclosure as well. Child protection and law enforcement professionals are less inclined to substantiate sexual abuse cases involving boys compared to girls (Dersch & Munsch, 1999). Clinicians often have biases that undermine the identification, assessment, and treatment of CSA in men (Holmes & Offen, 1996; Holmes et al., 1997; Lab, Feigenbaum, & De Silva, 2000). Also, crisis centers and other sexual assault treatment services are often designed primarily for female survivors (Hooper & Warwick, 2006).

In one of the only studies that examined the challenges of disclosure for male survivors of CSA, Sorsoli et al. (2008) conducted semi-structured interviews with a small sample of men and identified barriers to disclosure in three domains: personal (e.g., shame), relational (e.g., fears of negative repercussions), and sociocultural (e.g., myths surrounding masculinity). They concluded that in addition to barriers faced by all CSA survivors, men often face additional obstacles. However, due to their sample composition (most participants were highly educated, survivors of incest, and self-identified as gay or bisexual), Sorsoli and colleagues (2008) called for more research with larger, more representative samples of male survivors.

Because disclosure is often a part of help-seeking and clinical treatment for survivors, it is important to understand the full range of barriers to disclosure of CSA for men.

Major findings

The purpose of the qualitative study by Easton, Saltzman, and Willis (2014) was to examine barriers to disclosure of CSA by listening to the voices of a large, non-clinical sample of male survivors ($N = 487$). Men provided narrative responses to an open-ended prompt: *Some men take many years to tell someone that they were sexually abused. Others choose to never tell. Please describe why it may be difficult for men to tell someone about/discuss the sexual abuse.* Our research team analyzed responses, which ranged in length from a few words to a full page, over a one year period. The analysis found that the barriers reflect a complex, multi-level interaction between the person and environment. The primary barriers that deter, obstruct and impair men from disclosing CSA were grouped into three domains: (a) socio-political, (b) interpersonal, and (c) personal (see Figure 4.1). Within each domain, several categories emerged (see Table 4.1). Importantly, more than half (54.9%) of men identified multiple categories of barriers. Additionally, the domains overlapped, which reflects the multitude of forces that simultaneously impact men's decision-making process of whether to disclose.

The first domain was socio-political barriers and consisted of widely embraced social values (i.e., gender norms) and limited resources. One participant explained that "[sexual abuse] is deeply shameful, makes us look weak, damaged, inferior, unworthy, unmanly" (p. 463). Another participant wrote: "In Western culture, men are taught to be the tough ones: they're not to cry, they're supposed to have the answers, be the providers, and above all it's not okay to show emotion. Would you tell under circumstances like that?" (p. 464). Finally, men discussed the fact that support and recovery resources (e.g., counseling agencies, sexual assault centers) are primarily geared toward serving female clients, which deters men from services for discussion and recovery from CSA.

The second domain was interpersonal barriers, mentioned by half the participants. The domain emerged primarily through social interactions or relationships and centered on potential negative consequences of disclosing. The domain consisted of five categories: mistrust of others,

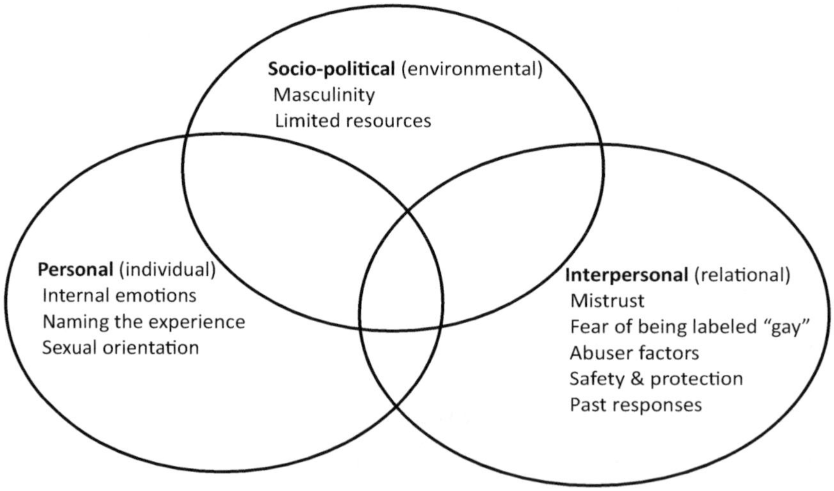

Figure 4.1 Visual representation of domains and categories of disclosure barriers (adapted from Easton, Saltzman, and Willis, 2014, p. 463)

Table 4.1 Frequency of disclosure barrier domains and categories ($N = 460$)

Domain and categories	*N*	*% of total sample*
Socio-political domain	174	37.8
1 Masculinity	173	37.6
2 Limited resources	14	3.0
Interpersonal domain	232	50.4
1 Mistrust of others	149	32.4
2 Fear of being labeled as gay	59	12.8
3 Abuser factors	47	10.2
4 Safety and protection issues	53	11.5
5 Past negative responses from others	34	7.4
Personal domain	309	67.2
1 Internal emotions	246	53.5
2 Naming the experience as "sexual abuse"	89	19.3
3 Concerns related to sexual orientation/identity	39	8.5
Number of categories (referenced by participants)		
One	208	45.2
Two	130	28.3
Three	78	17.0
More than three	44	9.6

Source: adapted from Easton, Saltzman, and Willis (2014, p. 464)

Note: Because participant responses often included barriers that are classified within more than one category within the same domain, the category counts within the same domain do not sum to the total count for the domain.

fear of being labeled gay, abuser factors, safety and protection issues, and past negative responses to previous disclosures. Many men reported thinking they were the only one sexually abused and feared others would not believe them. Another manifestation of mistrust was in men's fears that disclosure could result in being judged, blamed, criticized, or even ostracized. Participants said: "the social stigma of men letting it out is HUGE," talking about CSA "leaves a stigma of being damaged and screwed up beyond repair," and "many men who were abused by men assume that people will think that they are gay, even when they are not" (p. 464). Another participant summarized: "There are many reasons why men find it difficult to talk about their abuse and choose to never speak about it at all: shame, guilt, doubt, denial, fear of not being believed, loved, cared for, fear of being judged, abandoned, and alienated" (p. 464). For some men, previous attempts to disclose were unsuccessful, thus deterring future disclosures. In fact, one participant expressed a desire to protect other people from the discomfort of hearing about sexual assaults on boys/men: "We are soldiers of an unpopular war and no one wants to see us on parade. We remind them of something that makes them uncomfortable" (p. 465).

The third domain, personal, was the most frequently endorsed set of barriers; it was cited by two-thirds of participants. One commonly mentioned barrier was negative emotions such as shame, embarrassment, self-blame, humiliation, generalized fear, guilt, low self-esteem, confusion, and anger/rage. One survivor eloquently stated:

> Because the pain is so intense you don't think anyone will understand it. As a man you're not supposed to feel that level of pain, that level of loneliness, that deep, deep, deep feeling of being utterly and completely alone. Of being lost in a darkness so complete there's no hope of light.
>
> (p. 466)

The results indicated that some men do not name the experience as sexual abuse due to lack of knowledge, minimization, avoidance, repression of memories, and denial. Finally, some participants mentioned that the experience was so deeply traumatic that it caused them to question their own identity and sexual orientation. Taken together, these findings enhanced our understanding of the range and depth of barriers to disclosure of CSA for men and provided valuable information to guide interventions aimed at reducing such barriers.

Study #3: factors related to post-traumatic growth

Recent literature

Although early trauma has been associated with a variety of negative long-term outcomes, severely stressful experiences may provide an opportunity for individuals to reflect on the meaning and direction of their lives that, over time, may result in perceived benefits (Calhoun & Tedeschi, 1998; Janoff-Bulman, 1992; Park & Fenster, 2004). A great deal of research has documented that people can actually derive positive benefits through the process of coping with a traumatic event (e.g., death of a partner/spouse, life-threatening illness, a natural disaster; for reviews, see Helgeson, Reynolds, & Tomich, 2006; Linley & Joseph, 2004). Some positive changes include an increased appreciation for life, a greater sense of personal strength and an improved understanding of relationships with others. These perceived positive changes are dimensions of what is known as *post-traumatic growth* (PTG; Tedeschi & Calhoun, 2004).

Emerging evidence suggests adult survivors of CSA experience levels of PTG at rates comparable to survivors of other types of trauma (Lev-Wiesel, Amir, & Besser, 2005; Shakespeare-Finch & de Dassel, 2009). Although not all survivors experience PTG, many have noted benefits such as strengthened personality, increased knowledge of CSA, improved ability to protect children, spiritual development, reduced social isolation, and improved marital satisfaction (McMillen, Zuravin, & Rideout, 1995; Wright, Crawford, & Sebastian, 2007). Overall, though, the research base on PTG among adults with histories of CSA is sparse and has been based almost entirely on female samples (e.g., Lev-Wiesel et al., 2005; McMillen et al., 1995; Shakespeare-Finch & de Dassel, 2009; Wright et al., 2007). Furthermore, women report higher levels of growth in the general population than men (Linley & Joseph, 2004). Because of the possibility of gender-specific factors that could influence PTG, research is clearly needed with men with histories of CSA.

Purpose and hypotheses

The purpose of the study by Easton, Coohey, Rhodes, and Moorthy (2013) was to examine factors related to PTG among a large, non-clinical sample of men with histories of CSA. Based on research, theory, and clinical knowledge, we developed an additive model and considered the cumulative contribution of six factors to growth. First, we hypothesized that survivors' level of understanding of the sexual abuse experience (i.e., placing blame/responsibility on the perpetrator, acceptance of the response to CSA, recognition of the impact of CSA on emotions and behavior) would be related to more growth. This hypothesis is based on evidence that thinking about a traumatic event predicts growth (Helgeson et al., 2006; Linley & Joseph, 2004; Stockton, Hunt, & Joseph, 2011). Even intrusive thoughts about a trauma may motivate survivors to make meaning of the experience and reconstruct their thoughts about the trauma, themselves, and others (Calhoun & Tedeschi, 1998; Janoff-Bulman, 1992; Park & Fenster, 2004). A second proposed factor was based on the association (both direct and indirect) between social support and growth (Prati & Piertrantoni, 2009; Shaefer & Moos, 1998; Tedeschi & Calhoun, 2004). We predicted that a specific form of social support for CSA survivors—positive response to disclosure—would enhance growth. We also hypothesized that survivors who endorse a hyper-masculine persona (a possible response to cope with the gender conflict, shame, and stigma of surviving CSA for boys/men [Dorais, 2002; Lisak, 1994]) would experience lower rates of growth.

During the course of recovery, some survivors experience a turning point, a key component of life course theory (Hutchison, 2011) that involves an awakening or change in long-term trajectories. We predicted that turning points would be positively related to growth. Next, we considered the role of time following trauma, as researchers have found an inconsistent relationship between age and growth (Linley & Joseph, 2004). We proposed that the passage of time from the experience of CSA would promote growth. More time since the abuse might allow survivors opportunities to discuss and process their abuse with a trusted, empathetic partner/spouse, family member, friend, or mental health professional. Finally, spirituality and religious beliefs and practice are potential sources of support in recovery from traumatic events. Although any form of CSA may be harmful, clergy abuse may be particularly menacing because it often undermines sources of resilience. It is also related to spiritual rage against God, the church, and religious authorities (Fater & Mullaney, 2000). Thus, our last prediction was that being abused by a clergy member (compared to other types of perpetrators) undermines growth.

Results

We found evidence to support three of the six hypotheses. Men's level of understanding of the sexual abuse was positively related to growth following trauma. To promote growth, support resources (e.g., mental health counseling, survivor groups, public awareness campaigns) should help men make sense of their trauma history and its perceived impact on their lives. These efforts should help survivors place the blame on the perpetrator, understand responses to the abuse, and make connections between the abuse and subsequent mental health problems. Results also indicated that holding rigid, hyper-masculine norms is counterproductive for growth. Clinical interventions should help men identify, evaluate, and possibly adjust notions of gender norms, thereby increasing opportunities for self-expression and processing that could allow survivors to realize positive benefits during recovery. Last, data indicated that turning points were conducive to PTG. Subsequent research has identified numerous types of turning points (Easton, Leone, Sophis, & Willis, 2015) for men with histories of CSA, including influential relationships (personal and professional), insights and realizations (about the sexual abuse, necessity to change, and spirituality), and action-oriented communication such as disclosure and pursuit of justice through advocacy, reporting, or judicial procedures.

Future directions for research

The 2010 Health and Well-being Survey collected valuable information and represents the most comprehensive dataset to date on men with histories of CSA. Studies based on the dataset (such as the three highlighted in this chapter) have advanced our empirical and theoretical knowledge of this population, informed policy development and clinical practice, and provided guidelines for future research. Nonetheless, several limitations should be kept in mind when interpreting the results of these studies. Next we will review the strengths and limitations of the studies with respect to future directions for scholarship.

First, the models for mental distress and PTG (within studies #1 and #3) included innovative concepts and domains seldom explored with this population (e.g., masculine norms, disclosure history, and understanding of CSA). They also included elaborate control variables that reduced the chances of spurious findings. These characteristics represent tangible progress in research with this population. However, the use of a cross-sectional design limits the ability to infer causal relationships between variables. Future studies are needed that utilize a longitudinal design, which would allow us to understand how factors such as mental health change over time for men with histories of CSA and increase our ability to understand key relationships between variables.

Second, national survivor organizations provided instrumental assistance in recruiting the large sample from a hidden, stigmatized population, an extremely difficult task that limited prior studies. Nonetheless, most participants in the 2010 Health and Well-being Study were White, members of a survivor organization, and were abused by a member of the clergy. Thus, the sample did not necessarily reflect all male survivors in the general population. For example, clergy abuse survivors were over-represented and survivors abused by female perpetrators were under-represented. Moving forward, studies with population-based, probability sampling are needed. We know very little about similarities and differences between male survivors based on race, ethnicity, socio-economic status, country of origin, and religious affiliation, to name a few. Certainly factors such as poverty or educational disparities can obstruct recovery; cultural norms may also interact to either augment or suppress social support following sexual abuse disclosure. More research is needed to understand the experience of (and healing from) CSA from the perspective of men of diverse backgrounds.

Third, in an effort to protect its members from distress, the national survivor organizations did not authorize survey questions on topics they perceived to be highly sensitive (e.g., sexual orientation, substance use, religious affiliation, perpetration of CSA or offending behaviors) in the 2010 survey. These topics, however, may be critical to more fully understand the challenges faced by men with histories of CSA. Few studies, for example, have explored how the experience of being sexually abused may affect survivors' experiences of later becoming a parent. We need to expand the lens of our research with this population to enhance assessment and treatment services.

Finally, the use of an anonymous, one-time internet survey simultaneously promoted privacy and reduced administrative burden on participants. Nonetheless, the use of a single source, self-report technique of data collection is subject to retrospective recall bias and may have reduced the accuracy of the data. In addition to research directly with survivors, studies that gather information from additional sources (e.g., therapists, spouses/partners, administrative records) would help us more fully understand the phenomenon of CSA, its effects, and the healing process for men.

Additionally, scholarly efforts are needed in other areas to strengthen the knowledge base on men with histories of CSA. A systematic, comprehensive review of the literature is needed to critically access what is "empirically known" at all three levels of scholarship outlined by Merrill et al. (2001). Some valuable reviews have helped to consolidate empirical studies (e.g., Holmes & Slap, 1998; Spataro et al., 2001), but most were conducted years ago and did not employ techniques such as meta-analysis. Similarly, studies that evaluate treatment services for this clinical population are desperately needed. Some important studies have provided valuable recommendations for evidence-informed policies and practices with men who experienced CSA (Foster, Boyd, & O'Leary, 2012; Hovey, Stalker, Schachter, Teram, & Lasiuk, 2011; Teram, Stalker, Hovey, Schachter, & Lasiuk, 2006). However, very few studies have evaluated intervention strategies with this population (e.g., Romano & De Luca, 2006). Treatment studies that employ experimental designs could greatly advance the quality of clinical practice with male survivors.

Furthermore, important theoretical models are emerging on recovery and healing from traumatic experiences such as CSA (e.g., Arias & Johnson, 2013; Chouliara et al., 2014; Draucker et al., 2011). However, many of these theories do not adequately incorporate unique issues that arise for male survivors. As such, scholarly efforts are needed to test, evaluate, and refine theories to more accurately explain phenomena related to CSA and men.

The purpose of this chapter was to review contemporary research in selected areas with men who were sexually abused in childhood. As such, it is apparent that considerable progress has been made in building the foundation of an empirical knowledge base. Nonetheless, we are still at the beginning stages of developing a fully coherent, well-established body of knowledge that can direct prevention, treatment, and policy efforts. Many questions remain unanswered, especially in the second and third categories of scholarship (Merrill et al., 2001). The population remains stigmatized and under-studied.

A secondary purpose of the chapter was to encourage and challenge new researchers to further advance the knowledge base. By highlighting one program of research, I attempted to illustrate that it is possible to conduct research with this relatively hidden, marginalized population. Hopefully emerging scholars will read this and realize they can make important, much-needed contributions to the field that could help alleviate suffering and promote healing for male survivors. Because of the dire consequences that CSA too often has on men's lives, there is urgency to such endeavors. But there are also personal rewards: knowledge that the research process (and outcomes) can assist in the sacred healing journey. This was eloquently expressed in the words of a survivor who completed the 2010 survey:

> Thank you for taking on this subject and doing this research. One of my group therapy partners asked the group, "What is the purpose of experiencing these horrors and all the suffering?" The answer was that there was no purpose. However, we could give purpose to it, by becoming the truth tellers to those who should know, and to impart to others the wisdom we have learned from our terrible experiences. Completing this survey is one small step in telling the truth about sexual abuse of children. I have given you this information so you can find wisdom in these data that will help the victims, and help the people who provide healing and recovery.

Acknowledgments

Parts of this chapter were based on a plenary address delivered at the 2014 Social Work Conference on Men, Fathers, and Mental Health held at Brigham Young University, Provo, UT. Several organizations and individuals provided instrumental support during the design, recruitment, and analysis phases of the 2010 Health and Well-being Survey: the Survivors Network of those Abused by Priests (SNAP), MaleSurvivor.org, 1in6.org, Dr. Carol Coohey, Dr. Patrick O'Leary, Dr. Rob Baller, and Dr. Jim Hopper. Financial support for the three studies highlighted in this chapter was received from the John A. Hartford Foundation (Geriatric Social Work Initiative) and the Boston College Center on Aging (Aging Research Incentive Grant). The author appreciated the assistance of Dr. Jooyoung Kong, Robert Hasson, and Manuel Cano, who helped with preparation of the chapter. Finally, the author is grateful for the generosity and courage of the men who participated in the original survey. By doing so, they selflessly helped advance the knowledge base on male survivors and improved evidence-informed treatment of survivors who still suffer from the effects of sexual abuse.

References

Alaggia, R. (2005). Disclosing the trauma of child sexual abuse: A gender analysis. *Journal of Loss and Trauma, 10*, 453–470. doi: http://dx.doi.org/10.1080/15325020500193895

Alaggia, R., & Kirshenbaum, S. (2005). Speaking the unspeakable: Examining the impact of family dynamics on child sexual abuse disclosure. *Families in Society, 86*(2), 227–234.

Andrews, G., Corry, J., Slade, T., Issakidis, C., & Swanston, H. (2004). *Child sexual abuse: Comparative quantification of health risks*. Geneva: WHO.

Arias, B. J., & Johnson, C. V. (2013). Voices of healing and recovery from childhood sexual abuse. *Journal of Child Sexual Abuse, 22*(7), 822–841. doi: 10.1080/10538712.2013.830669

Boudewyn, A., & Liem, J. (1995). Childhood sexual abuse as a precursor to depression and self-destructive behavior in adulthood. *Journal of Traumatic Stress, 8*, 445–459. doi: 10.1002/jts.2490080307

Briere, J., & Elliott, D. M. (2003). Prevalence and psychological sequelae of self-reported childhood physical and sexual abuse in a general population sample of men and women. *Child Abuse & Neglect, 27*, 1205–1222. doi: 10.1016/j.chiabu.2003.09.008

Calhoun, L. G., & Tedeschi, R. G. (1998). Posttraumatic growth: Future directions. In R. G. Tedeschi, C. L. Park, & L. G. Calhoun (Eds.), *Posttraumatic growth: Positive changes in the aftermath of crisis* (pp. 215–238). Mahwah, NJ: Erlbaum.

Chouliara, Z., Karatzias, T., & Gullone, A. (2014). Recovering from childhood sexual abuse: A theoretical framework for practice and research. *Journal of Psychiatric and Mental Health Nursing, 21*(1), 69–78. doi: 10.1111/jpm.12048

Courtenay, W. H. (2000). Constructions of masculinity and their influence on men's well-being: A theory of gender and health. *Social Science & Medicine, 50*, 1385–1401. doi: http://dx.doi.org/10.1016/S0277-9536(99)00390-1

Cutajar, M. C., Mullen, P. E., Ogloff, J. R., Wells, D. L., & Spataro, J. (2010). Psychopathology in a large cohort of sexually abused children followed up to 43 years. *Child Abuse & Neglect, 34*, 813–822. doi: 10.1016/j.chiabu.2010.04.004

Dennis, M. L., White, M. K., Titus, J. C., & Unsicker, J. I. (2008). *Global Appraisal of Individual Needs (GAIN): Administration guide (Version 5)*. Bloomington, IL: Chestnut Health Systems.

Dersch, C. A., & Munsch, J. (1999). Male victims of sexual abuse: An analysis of substantiation of child protective services reports. *Journal of Child Sexual Abuse, 8*(1), 27–48. doi: http://dx.doi.org.proxy.bc.edu/10.1300/J070v08n01_03; doi: 10.1606/1044-3894.2457

Dhaliwal, G. K., Gauzas, L., Antonowicz, D. H., & Ross, R. R. (1996). Adult male survivors of childhood sexual abuse: Prevalence, sexual abuse characteristics, and long-term effects. *Clinical Psychology Review, 16*, 619–639.

DiIorio, C., Hartwell, T., & Hansen, N. (2002). Childhood sexual abuse and risk behaviors among men at high risk for HIV infection. *American Journal of Public Health, 92*(2), 214–219. doi: 10.2105/AJPH.92.2.214

Dorais, M. (2002). *Don't tell: The sexual abuse of boys* (D. Meyer, Trans.). Quebec City: McGill-Queens.

Draucker, C. B., Martsolf, D. S., Roller, C., Knapik, G., Ross, R., & Stidham, A. W. (2011). Healing from child sexual abuse: A theoretical model. *Journal of Child Sexual Abuse, 20*, 435–466. doi: 10.1080/10538712.2011.588188

Dube, S. R., Anda, R. F., Felitti, V. J., Chapman, D., Williamson, D. F., & Giles, W. H. (2001). Childhood abuse, household dysfunction and the risk of attempted suicide throughout the life span: Findings from Adverse Childhood Experiences Study. *JAMA, 286*, 3089–3096. doi: 10.1001/jama.286.24.3089

Dube, S. R., Anda, R. F., Whitfield, C. L., Brown, D. W., Felitti, V. J., Dong, M., & Giles, W. H. (2005). Long-term consequences of childhood sexual abuse by gender of victim. *American Journal of Preventive Medicine, 28*, 430–438. doi: 10.1016/j.amepre.2005.01.015

Easton, S. D. (2011). *Men who were sexually abused during childhood: An examination of factors that influence long-term mental health* (Doctoral dissertation). Retrieved from ProQuest Dissertations and Theses (Order No. 3461121).

Easton, S. D. (2013). Disclosure of child sexual abuse among adult male survivors. *Clinical Social Work Journal, 41*(4), 344–355. doi: 10.1007/s10615-012-0420-3

Easton, S. D. (2014). Masculine norms, disclosure, and childhood adversities predict long-term mental distress among men with histories of child sexual abuse. *Child Abuse & Neglect, 38*(2), 243–251. doi: 10.1016/j.chiabu.2013.08.020

Easton, S. D., Coohey, C., Rhodes, A. M., & Moorthy, M. V. (2013). Posttraumatic growth among men with histories of child sexual abuse. *Child Maltreatment, 18*, 211–220. doi: 10.1177/1077559513503037

Easton, S. D., Leone, D., & O'Leary, P. J. (2016). "I will never know the person who I could have become"; Perceived changes in self-identity among adult survivors of clergy-perpetrated sexual abuse. *Journal of Interpersonal Violence*, 1–24. doi: 10.1177/0886260516650966

Easton, S. D., Leone, D. M., Sophis, E. J., & Willis, D. G. (2015). "From that moment on my life changed": Turning points in the healing process for men recovering from childhood sexual abuse. *Journal of Child Sexual Abuse, 24*(2), 152–173. doi: 10.1080/10538712.2015.997413

Easton, S. D., Renner, L. M., & O'Leary, P. (2013). Suicide attempts among men with histories of child sexual abuse: Examining abuse severity, mental health, and masculine norms. *Child Abuse and Neglect, 37*(6), 380–387. doi: 10.1016/j.chiabu.2012.11.007

Easton, S. D., Saltzman, L. & Willis, D. (2014). "Would you tell under circumstances like that?": Barriers to disclosure for men who were sexually abused during childhood. *Psychology of Men and Masculinity, 15*(4), 460–469. doi: 10.1037/a0034223

Elliott, A. N., & Carnes, C. N. (2001). Reactions of non-offending parents to the sexual abuse of their child: A review of the literature. *Child Maltreatment, 6*, 314–331. doi: 10.1177/1077559501006004005

Estrada, H. (1994). *Recovery for male victims of child sexual abuse.* Santa Fe, NM: Red Rabbit Press.

Fater, K., & Mullaney, J. A. (2000). The lived experience of adult male survivors who allege childhood sexual abuse by clergy. *Issues in Mental Health Nursing, 21*, 281–295. doi: 10.1080/016128400248095

Felitti, V. J., Anda, R. F., Nordenberg, D., Williamson, D. F., Spitz, A. M., & Marks, J. S. (1998). Relationship of childhood abuse and household dysfunction to many leading causes of death in adults. *American Journal of Preventive Medicine, 14*, 245–258. doi: 10.1016/S0749-3797(98)00017-8

Finkelhor, D. (1998). Improving research, policy, and practice to understand child sexual abuse. *Journal of the American Medical Association, 280*, 1864–1865. doi: 10.1001/jama.280.21.1864

Finkelhor, D., Ormrod, R. K., & Turner, H. A. (2007). Poly-victimization: A neglected component in child victimization. *Child Abuse & Neglect, 31*, 7–26. doi: 10.1016/j.chiabu.2013.08.020

Finkelhor, D., Ormrod, R. K., Turner, H. A., & Holt, M. (2009). Pathways to polyvictimization. *Child Maltreatment, 14*, 316–329. doi: 10.1177/1077559509347012

Fondacaro, K. M., Holt, J. C., & Powell, T. A. (1999). Psychological impact of childhood sexual abuse on male inmates: The importance of perception of child abuse & neglect. *Child Abuse & Neglect, 23*(4), 361–369. doi: http://search.proquest.com/docview/ 619418648?accountid=9673

Foster, G., Boyd, C., & O'Leary, P. (2012). Improving policy and practice responses for men sexually abused in childhood. Australian Centre for the Study of Sexual Assault, Australian Institute of Family Studies. Vol. 12, 1–20. Retrieved from www98.griffith.edu.au/dspace/handle/10072/51507.

Fradkin, H. (2012). *Joining forces: Empowering male survivors to thrive.* Carlsbad, CA: House Hay.

Gartner, R. B. (1999). *Betrayed as boys: Psychodynamic treatment of sexually abused men.* New York, NY: Guildford Press.

Gartner, R. B. (2005). *Beyond betrayal: Taking charge of your life after boyhood sexual abuse.* New York, NY: Wiley.

Gilbert, R., Widom, C. S., Browne, K., Fergusson, D., Webb, E., & Janson, S. (2009). Burden and consequences of child maltreatment in high income countries. *The Lancet, 373*, 68–81. doi: 10.1016/S0140-6736(08)61706-7

Gilligan, P., & Akhtar, S. (2006). Cultural barriers to the disclosure of child sexual abuse in Asian communities: Listening to what women say. *British Journal of Social Work, 36*(8), 1361–1377. doi: http://dx.doi.org/10.1093/bjsw/bch309

Goodman-Brown, T. B., Edelstein, R. S., Goodman, G. S., Jones, D. P. H., & Gordon, D. S. (2003). Why children tell: A model of children's disclosure of sexual abuse. *Child Abuse & Neglect, 27*, 525–540. doi: http://dx.doi.org/10.1016/S0145-2134(03)00037-1

Grossman, F. K., Sorsoli, L., & Kia-Keating, M. (2006). A gale force wind: Meaning making by male survivors of childhood sexual abuse. *American Journal of Orthopsychiatry, 76*(4), 434–443. doi: 10.1037/0002-9432.76.4.434

Grubman-Black, S. D. (1990). *Broken boys, mending men: Recovering from childhood sexual abuse*. New York, NY: Ivy Books.

Harvey, J. H., Orbuch, T. L., & Weber, A. L. (1990). A social psychological model of account-making in response to severe stress. *Journal of Language and Social Psychology, 9*, 191–207. doi: 10.1177/0261927X9093002

Helgeson, V. S., Reynolds, K. A., & Tomich, P. L. (2006). A meta-analytic review of benefit finding and growth. *Journal of Consulting and Clinical Psychology, 74*(5), 797. doi: 10.1037/0022-006X.74.5.797

Hershkowitz, I., Lanes, O., & Lamb, M. E. (2007). Exploring the disclosure of child sexual abuse with alleged victims and their parents. *Child Abuse & Neglect, 31*, 111–123. doi: http://dx.doi.org/10.1016/j.chiabu.2006.09.004

Holmes, G., & Offen, L. (1996). Clinicians' hypotheses regarding clients' problems: Are they less likely to hypothesize sexual abuse in male compared to female clients? *Child Abuse & Neglect, 20*(6), 493–501. doi: http://search.proquest.com/docview/618859288?accountid=9673

Holmes, G. R., Offen, L., & Waller, G. (1997). See no evil, hear no evil, speak no evil: Why do relatively few male victims of childhood sexual abuse receive help for abuse-related issues in adulthood? *Clinical Psychology Review, 17*, 69–88. doi: http://search.proquest.com/docview/619055911?accountid=9673

Holmes, W. C. (2008). Men's self-definitions of abusive childhood sexual experiences, and potentially related risky behavioral and psychiatric outcomes. *Child Abuse & Neglect, 32*, 83–97. doi: http://dx.doi.org/10.1016/j.chiabu.2007.09.005.

Holmes, W. C., & Slap, G. B. (1998). Sexual abuse of boys: Definition, prevalence, correlates, sequelae, and management. *Journal of the American Medical Association, 280*, 1855–1862. doi: http://search.proquest.com/docview/619368221?accountid=9673

Homma, Y., Wang, N., Saewyc, E., & Kishor, N. (2012). The relationship between sexual abuse and risky sexual behavior among adolescent boys: A meta-analysis. *Journal of Adolescent Health, 51*(1), 18–24. doi: 10.1016/j.jadohealth.2011.12.032

Hooper, C. A., & Warwick, I. (2006). Gender and the politics of service provision for adults with a history of childhood sexual abuse. *Critical Social Policy, 26*, 467–479. doi: 10.1177/0261018306062596

Hovey, A., Stalker, C. A., Schachter, C. L., Teram, E., & Lasiuk, G. (2011). Practical ways psychotherapy can support physical healthcare experiences for male survivors of childhood sexual abuse. *Journal of Child Sexual Abuse, 20*(1), 37–57. doi: 10.1080/10538712.2011.539963

Hunter, M. (1990). *Abused boys: The neglected victims of sexual abuse*. New York, NY: Fawcett Books.

Hunter, S. V. (2006). Understanding the complexity of child sexual abuse: A review of the literature with implications for family counseling. *The Family Journal: Counseling and Therapy for Couples and Families, 14*, 349–358. doi: 10.1177/1066480706291092

Hutchison, E. D. (2011). A life course perspective. In E. D. Hutchison (Ed.), *Dimensions of human behavior: The changing life course* (pp. 1–38). Thousand Oaks, CA: Sage.

Irish, L., Kobayashi, I., & Delahanty, D. L. (2009). Long-term physical health consequences of childhood sexual abuse: A meta-analytic review. *Journal of Pediatric Psychology, 35*(5), 450–461. doi: 10.1093/jpepsy/jsp118

Isely, P. J., Isely, P., Freiburger, J., & McMackin, R. (2008). In their own voices: A qualitative study of men abused as children by Catholic clergy. *Journal of Child Sexual Abuse, 17*(3–4), 201–215. doi: 10.1080/10538710802329668

Janoff-Bulman, R. (1992). *Shattered assumptions: Towards a new psychology of trauma*. New York, NY: Free Press.

Jonzon, E., & Lindblad, F. (2004). Disclosure, reactions, and social support: Findings from a sample of adult victims of child sexual abuse. *Child Maltreatment, 9*, 190–200. doi: http://dx.doi.org/10.1177/1077559504264263

Jonzon, E., & Lindblad, F. (2005). Adult female victims of child sexual abuse multitype maltreatment and disclosure characteristics related to subjective health. *Journal of Interpersonal Violence, 20*(6), 651–666. doi: http://dx.doi.org/10.1177/0886260504272427

Kia-Keating, M., Grossman, F. K., Sorsoli, L., & Epstein, M. (2005). Containing and resisting masculinity: Narratives of renegotiation among resilient male survivors of childhood sexual abuse. *Psychology of Men and Masculinity, 6*, 169–185. doi: 10.1037/1524-9220.6.3.169

Kimmel, S. B., & Mahalik, J. R. (2005). Body image concerns of gay men: The roles of minority stress and conformity to masculine norms. *Journal of Consulting and Clinical Psychology, 73*, 1185. doi: 10.1037/0022-006X.73.6.1185

Krayer, A, Seddon, D., Robinson, C. A., & Gwilym, H. (2015). The influence of child sexual abuse on the self from adult narrative perspectives. *Journal of Child Sexual Abuse, 24*(2), 135–151. doi: 10.1080/10538712.2015.1001473

Lab, D., Feigenbaum, J., & De Silva, P. (2000). Mental health professionals' attitudes and practices towards male childhood sexual abuse. *Child Abuse & Neglect, 24*, 391–409. doi: http://dx.doi.org/10.1016/S0145-2134(99)00152-0

Lev-Wiesel, R., Amir, M., & Besser, A. (2005). Posttraumatic growth among female survivors of childhood sexual abuse in relation to the perpetrator identity. *Journal of Loss and Trauma, 10*(1), 7–17. doi: 10.1080/15325020490890606

Lew, M. (2004). *Victims no longer: The classic guide for men recovering from sexual child abuse* (2nd Ed.). New York, NY: Harper Perennial.

Linley, P. A., & Joseph, S. (2004). Positive change following trauma and adversity: A review. *Journal of Traumatic Stress, 17*(1), 11–21. doi: 10.1023/B:JOTS.0000014671.27856.7e

Lisak, D. (1994). The psychological impact of sexual abuse: Content analysis of interviews with male survivors. *Journal of Traumatic Stress, 7*(4), 525–548. doi: 10.1002/jts.2490070403

Lisak, D. (1995). Integrating a critique of gender in the treatment of male survivors of childhood abuse. *Psychotherapy: Theory, Research, Practice, Training, 32*(2), 258–269. doi: http://dx.doi.org/10.1037/0033-3204.32.2.258

Lisak, D., Hopper, J., & Song, P. (1996). Factors in the cycle of violence: Gender rigidity and emotional constriction. *Journal of Traumatic Stress, 9*, 721–743. doi: 10.1002/jts.2490090405

Liu, W. M., & Iwamoto, D. K. (2007). Conformity to masculine norms, Asian values, coping strategies, peer group influences and substance use among Asian American men. *Psychology of Men & Masculinity, 8*(1), 25–39. doi: http://dx.doi.org/10.1037/1524-9220.8.1.25

Mahalik, J. R., Good, G. E., & Englar-Carlson, M. (2003a). Masculinity scripts, presenting concerns, and help seeking: Implications for practice and training. *Professional Psychology: Research and Practice, 34*, 123–131. doi: http://dx.doi.org/10.1037/0735-7028.34.2.123

Mahalik, J. R., Locke, B. D., Ludlow, L. H., Diemer, M. A., Scott, R. P. J., Gottfried, M., & Freitas, G. (2003b). Development of the Conformity to Masculine Norms Inventory. *Psychology of Men and Masculinity, 4*(1), 3–25. doi: http://dx.doi.org/10.1037/1524-9220.4.1.3

Malloy, L. C., Lyon, T. D., & Quas, J. A. (2007). Filial dependency and recantation of child sexual abuse allegations. *Journal of the American Academy of Child and Adolescent Psychiatry, 46*, 162–170. doi: 10.1097/01.chi.0000246067.77953.f7

McMillen, C., Zuravin, S., & Rideout, G. (1995). Perceived benefit from child sexual abuse. *Journal of Consulting and Clinical Psychology, 63*(6), 1037–1043. doi: 10.1037/0022-006X.63.6.1037

Merrill, L. L., Thomsen, C. J., Sinclair, B. B., Gold, S. R., & Milner, J. S. (2001). Predicting the impact of child sexual abuse on women: The role of abuse severity, parental support and coping strategies. *Journal of Consulting and Clinical Psychology, 69*(6), 992–1006. doi: 10.1037/0022-006X.69.6.992

Molnar, B. E., Buka, S. L., & Kessler, R. C. (2001). Child sexual abuse and subsequent psychopathology: Results from the national comorbidity study. *American Journal of Public Health, 91*, 753–760. doi: 10.2105/AJPH.91.5.753

Nelson, E., Heath, A. C., Madden, P. A. F., Cooper, M. L., Dinwiddie, S. H., Bucholz, K. K., & Martin, N. G. (2002). Association between self-reported childhood sexual abuse and adverse psychosocial outcomes: Results from a twin study. *Archives of General Psychiatry, 59*, 139–145. doi: 10.1001/archpsyc.59.2.139

O'Leary, P. J., & Barber, J. G. (2008). Gender differences in silencing following childhood sexual abuse. *Journal of Child Sexual Abuse, 17*(1), 133–143. doi: http://dx.doi.org/10.1080/10538710801916416

O'Leary, P. J., Coohey, C., & Easton, S. D. (2010). The effect of severe child sexual abuse and disclosure on mental health in adulthood. *Journal of Child Sexual Abuse, 19*, 275–289. doi: 10.1080/10538711003781251

O'Leary, P. J., & Gould, N. (2009). Men who were sexually abused in childhood and subsequent suicidal ideation: Community comparison, explanations, and practice implications. *British Journal of Social Work, 39*, 950–968. doi: 10.1093/bjsw/bcn130

Paine, M. L., & Hansen, D. J. (2002). Factors influencing children to self-disclose sexual abuse. *Clinical Psychology Review, 22*(2), 271–295. doi: 10.1016/S0272-7358(01)00091-5

Park, C. L., & Fenster, J. R. (2004). Stress-related growth: Predictors of occurrence and correlates with psychological adjustment. *Journal of Social & Clinical Psychology, 23*(2), 195–215. doi: 10.1521/jscp.23.2.195.31019

Prati, G., & Pietrantoni, L. (2009). Optimism, social support, and coping strategies as factors contributing to posttraumatic growth: A meta-analysis. *Journal of Loss and Trauma, 14* (5), 364–388. doi: 10.1080/15325020902724271

Putnam, F. W. (2003). Ten-year research update review: Child sexual abuse. *Journal of the American Academy of Child and Adolescent Psychiatry, 42*, 269–278. doi: 10.1097/00004583-200303000-00006

Roberts, S. T., Watlington, C. G., Nett, S. D., & Batten, S. V. (2010). Sexual trauma disclosure in clinical settings: Addressing diversity. *Journal of Trauma and Dissociation, 11*, 244–259. doi: http://dx.doi.org/10.1080/15299730903502961

Romano, E., & De Luca, R. V. (2006). Evaluation of a treatment program for sexually abused adult males. *Journal of Family Violence, 21*(1), 75–88. doi: 10.1007/s10896-005-9006-y

Ruggiero, K. J., Smith, D. W., Hanson, R. F., Resnick, H. S., Saunders, B. E., Kilpatrick, D. G., & Best, C. L. (2004). Is disclosure of childhood rape associated with mental health outcome? Results from the National Women's Study. *Child Maltreatment, 9*, 62–77. doi: 10.1177/1077559503260309

Shaefer, J., & Moos, R. (1998). The context for posttraumatic growth: Life crises, individual and social resources, and coping. In R. Tedeschi, C. Park, & L. Calhoun (Eds.), *Posttraumatic growth: Positive changes in the aftermath of crisis* (pp. 99–126). Mahway, NJ: Erlbaum.

Shakespeare-Finch, J. E., & de Dassel, T. (2009). The impact of child sexual abuse on victims/survivors: Exploring posttraumatic outcomes as a function of childhood sexual abuse. *Journal of Child Sexual Abuse, 18*(6), 623–640. doi: 10.1080/10538710903317224

Sorsoli, L., Kia-Keating, M., & Grossman, F. K. (2008). "I keep that hush-hush": Male survivors of sexual abuse and the challenges of disclosure. *Journal of Consulting Psychology, 55*(3), 333–345. doi: http://dx.doi.org/10.1037/0022-0167.55.3.333

Spataro, J., Moss, S. A., & Wells, D. L. (2001). Child sexual abuse: A reality for both sexes. *Australian Psychologist, 36*(3), 177–183. doi: 10.1080/00050060108259653

Staller, K. M., & Nelson-Gardell, D. (2005). "A burden in your heart": Lessons of disclosure from female preadolescent and adolescent survivors of sexual abuse. *Child Abuse & Neglect, 29*(12), 1415–1432. doi: http://dx.doi.org/10.1016/j.chiabu.2005.06.007

Steel, J., Sanna, L., Hammond, B., Whipple, J., & Cross, H. (2004). Psychological sequelae of childhood sexual abuse: Abuse-related characteristics, coping strategies, and attributional style. *Child Abuse & Neglect, 28*, 785–801. doi: 10.1016/j.chiabu.2003.12.004

Stockton, H., Hunt, N., & Joseph, S. (2011). Cognitive processing, rumination, and posttraumatic growth. *Journal of Traumatic Stress, 24*(1), 85–92. doi: 10.1002/jts.20606

Tedeschi, R. G., & Calhoun, L. G. (2004). Posttraumatic growth: Conceptual foundations and empirical evidence. *Psychological Inquiry, 15*, 1–18. doi: 10.1207/s15327965pli1501_01

Teram, E., Stalker, C., Hovey, A., Schachter, C., & Lasiuk, G. (2006). Towards malecentric communication: Sensitizing health professionals to the realities of male childhood sexual abuse survivors. *Issues in Mental Health Nursing, 27*(5), 499–517. doi: 10.1080/01612840600599994

Ullman, S. E. (2003). Social reactions to child sexual abuse disclosures: A critical review. *Journal of Child Sexual Abuse, 12*, 89–121. doi: http://dx.doi.org/10.1300/J070v12n01_05

Ullman, S. E. (2007). Relationship to perpetrator, disclosure, social reactions, and PTSD symptoms in child sexual abuse survivors. *Journal of Child Sexual Abuse, 16*, 19–35. doi: 10.1300/J070v16n01_02

Ullman, S. E., & Filipas, H. H. (2005). Gender differences in social reactions to abuse disclosures, post-abuse coping, and PTSD of child sexual abuse survivors. *Child Abuse & Neglect, 29*, 767–782. doi: 10.1016/j.chiabu.2005.01.005

Vaillancourt-Morel, M., Godbout, N., Labadie, C., Runtz, M., Lussier, Y., & Sabourin, S. (2015). Avoidant and compulsive sexual behaviors in male and female survivors of childhood sexual abuse. *Child Abuse & Neglect, 40*, 48–59. doi: http://dx.doi.org.proxy.bc.edu/10.1016/j.chiabu.2014.10.024

Vaillancourt-Morel, M. P., Godbout, N., Bédard, M. G., Charest, É., Briere, J., & Sabourin, S. (2016). Emotional and sexual correlates of child sexual abuse as a function of self-definition status. *Child Maltreatment,* 1–11. doi: 1077 559516656069

Walker, M. D., Hernandez, A. M., & Davey, M. (2012). Childhood sexual abuse and adult sexual identity formation: Intersection of gender, race, and sexual orientation. *The American Journal of Family Therapy, 40*(5), 385–398. doi: 10.1080/01926187.2011.627318

Widom, C. P., & Morris, S. (1997). Accuracy of adult recollections of childhood victimization: Part 2. Childhood sexual abuse. *Psychological Assessment, 9*(1), 34–46. doi: http://dx.doi.org/10.1037/1040-3590.9.1.34

Wright, M. O., Crawford, E., & Sebastian, K. (2007). Positive resolution of childhood sexual abuse experiences: The role of coping, benefit-finding, and meaning making. *Journal of Family Violence, 22*, 597–608. doi: 10.1007/s10896-007-9111-1

Chapter 5

Neurobiology, trauma, and dissociation

From basic science to clinical relevance

Grant H. Brenner

Introduction

Neuroscience is a field of increasing relevance for therapists and patients, daunting due to the proliferation of technical material and research. A working knowledge of clinical neuroscience is important because patients are better though inconsistently informed as a result of the Internet. Patients come looking for information and guidance about emerging treatments, seeking treatments on their own without consulting us, wondering if what we are telling them is trustworthy, and fundamentally wishing for rapidly effective and painless treatments. With up-to-date information, we are best prepared to meet their needs.

Treating complex trauma is usually thought to take a long time, be arduous as well as rewarding, and have often unclear goals and efficacy. Naturally, all involved desire treatments that provide enduring relief, bolster resilience, and enhance therapeutic progress. Given an expanding array of options, some more proven than others, and treatment selection often at best an educated guess, more is not necessarily better. It is important for clinicians to have a grasp of available treatment options in order to best advise patients.

Finally, contrasting with psychiatric medications, emerging neuromodulation options offer different mechanisms of action, a lower burden of adverse events, and the possibility of targeted treatments. Neuromodulation approaches fill a gap in the biological treatment armamentarium by approaching clinical problems differently from medications.

Research with survivors of male sexual abuse is sparse given the scope of the problem. The field would benefit from well-designed research protocols looking at male survivors, with the understanding that treating trauma and dissociation in general remains under-researched. According to Bagley and Thurston (1996), it is estimated that 10–15% of males will experience at least one instance of sexual abuse before the age of 16. The denial of male sexual abuse has been identified as an endemic problem (Urquiza & Keating, 1990; Holmes and Slap, 1998). Several additional factors, addressed in greater detail elsewhere in this volume, impede progress: the false blaming of homosexuality, the misperception that sexual abuse is consensual or experimental for similar aged boys, and the idea that seduction of an adolescent or a boy by an older woman is desirable. Such attitudes are profoundly problematic and strengthen denial and avoidance, impede research and treatment, and hamper social change.

Treating male survivors of early sexual abuse is complicated because of systemic issues fostering traumatogenic and dissociogenic environments, leading to betrayal on not just familial but broad institutional and societal levels (Smith & Freyd, 2014).[1] It is not unusual for the abuser to also be an important and beloved figure in the male survivor's early life, even an attachment oasis in a deficient family and social context (Gartner, 1999). Such factors lead to delays in treatment and potentially poorer outcomes. Therefore, it is even more imperative to have additional tools to assess and treat developmental trauma and its adult co-morbidities, including depression, complex posttraumatic stress, dissociative disorders, and related conditions such as substance and alcohol abuse, sexual addiction, eating disorders, characterological issues and negative repercussions of repeating dysfunctional patterns in adult relationships.

In brief, the embodied brain is an unfathomably complex organ, serving as an instrument for basic and higher behavior, including social and relational functioning. We are born not with a blank slate, but with a network of information-processing tissue poised to enter into a complex physical and relational world. The brain is equipped with many abilities from the moment of birth, which aside from basic functions required specifically include capacities to relate with others – to recognize familiar faces, to accept care, to read non-verbal cues, and to develop more sophisticated abilities to communicate with others and develop reciprocal relationships based on giving and receiving various forms of care. For

1 Editor's note: See Chapter 8 by Burmester in this volume for discussion of institutional betrayal.

relational beings with a prolonged maturation period, survival requires offspring to attentively care for caregivers, a greater challenge when caregivers themselves are impaired.

The embodied brain is a resilient organ, the cornerstone of broader forms of resilience. For most of us, bumps in the road of development do not significantly derail the course of our lives. Children are resistant to failures on the part of their parents, using inner and outer resources to serve as developmental shock absorbers for most distress. Most of us are quite resilient, requiring higher levels of earlier distress to result in longer-term negative consequences.

The nature of the distress is important. When trauma strikes at the very core relational functions of the developing person, often originating within the family, even healthy and adaptive coping can strain, deform, and collapse.

Neurobiology of trauma

Discussion of the neurobiology of trauma with consideration for male sexual abuse is important for understanding clinical approaches directly modifying brain activity. Treatment planning must be thoughtful, informed, and clearly communicated, given the important role of ethics and trust with survivors of abuse and neglect. The rule is that the primary therapist is an active collaborative partner in care, an especially important consideration when contemplating newer treatment approaches. This chapter will provide background on several emerging treatments so psychotherapists will gain a greater understanding of both treatments and referral options. While some of the discussion is technical, it is offered for those seeking a finer understanding. Taking time to absorb this material will enhance clinical capacity.

Basic brain anatomy and function[2]

The human brain is elegant and stunningly beautiful. There are approximately 100 billion neurons in the human brain, and 100 trillion or more synapses. Far from static, while the gross anatomy of the brain generally

2 For a 3D illustration of brain anatomy, interested readers are referred to the app on the American Association for the Advancement of Science website at http://sciencenetlinks.com/tools/3d-brain/.

changes only very slowly, on closer view it is revealed to be constantly remodeling itself on a cellular level over shorter time frames (Nestler, Hyman, & Malenka, 2009). The brain exhibits this "neuroplasticity" throughout adulthood. The balance between a relatively stable pattern and the ability to change responsively creates a flexible system.

Note that the brain is composed of oscillatory units (Buzsáki, 2006) on the level of individual neurons and discrete functional clusters of neurons on the level of interconnected areas of the brain. Brain function, including conscious experience, may be based on synchronized bursts of different brain areas firing together. We will discuss viewing the brain as sets of networks, a key framework for understanding individual and relational experience.

The brain may be divided into cortical and subcortical regions. The cortex is a thin layer on the brain's surface, and is folded into gyri and sulci (ridges and furrows, respectively), giving the brain its iconic corrugated appearance. Neuron cell bodies exist in higher numbers in grey matter. Cell processes leading away from the cell body, called axons, make up the white matter, which connects together different nuclei, which are functionally discrete collections of cell bodies. The cortex is evolutionarily newer than deeper subcortical regions, and the neocortex is a thin layer of cortex that appears crucial to making the human experience unique.

On a gross level, the cerebral cortex is divided into left and right hemispheres, connected by a few pathways; the largest is the corpus callosum. Each hemisphere has frontal, parietal, temporal, cingulate, and occipital lobes. They have complex functions, some of which are still being better understood, but for the purposes of discussion we will look at basic functions. The frontal cortex is generally associated with various aspects of executive function, including attention, memory, planning, and decision-making; the occipital cortex with visual processing; the parietal lobe with multiple sensory modalities, spatial sense and navigation, and aspects of language function; and the temporal lobe with meaning, language comprehension, and aspects of emotion and memory. The cingulate lobe is folded into the midline of the hemispheres, and is involved with regulation of emotions and states of conflict.

In addition to the cortex and brain lobes, important deeper structures include the midbrain, brainstem, and cerebellum, which are involved with many important functions ranging from basic life support to integrating and timing information coming from other areas of the brain and body. The general concept of limbic system is used to indicate the emotional function of the brain, rather than a particular distinct anatomic region, and the limbic system includes elements from many different parts of the brain.

Readers wishing to have a basic breakdown of more specific functions by brain sub-region will find the following section on basic brain areas useful in providing a more detailed contact to frame the discussion of neuromodulation-based interventions. Readers who want to move past more technical material can go to the next section, and refer back to this section.

Note that patients who have experienced abuse may have brain injuries that appear psychological in origin but are neuropsychiatric, requiring evaluation by an appropriate specialist.

Frontal lobe

These are some areas of particular interest in the frontal cortex, generally associated with *executive function*.

Dorsolateral prefrontal cortex (DLPFC)

The DLPFC is an important part of the frontal cortex involved with directing attentional and working memory resources and managing awareness of emotional states. Along with many other brain regions, the DLPFC has top-down effects on structures in the limbic system, and so is involved with regulating emotional reactions. A loss of frontal inhibition of the limbic system would lead to difficulty suppressing negative emotions. This area is a common target for transcranial magnetic stimulation (TMS), neurofeedback (NF), and transcranial direct current stimulation (tDCS).

Dorsomedial prefrontal cortex (DMPFC)

The DMPFC is involved with self-reflection and self-awareness including regulation of perceptions of oneself in the eyes of others, and has effects on areas of the brain involved with habitual behaviors and conflict. The DMPFC may be a useful target for interventions, and has been shown to have potential use for treatment of obsessive-compulsive disorder with TMS (Downar et al., 2013) as well as in binge eating disorders (see below), by restoring connectivity between DMPFC and areas of the brain that regulate habitual, automatic behaviors.

Orbitofrontal cortex (OFC)

The OFC is involved with making fast judgments about threats, and integrates information from the amygdala into the frontal cortex. Poor OFC functioning is associated with impaired impulse control and socially inappropriate behavior, including aggression and sociopathy. Notably, patients with Orbitofrontal Syndrome exhibit these problems to an extreme as a result of bilateral damage, and have been misdiagnosed at times with Bipolar mania (Murad, 1999).

Ventromedial prefrontal cortex (VMPFC)

The VMPFC is involved with the embodied sense of self, in conjunction with other areas of the brain (e.g., the insular cortex, see below). This area may be functioning poorly in states where one is cut off from experiences of the body, and may be involved with one's relationship with one's body as well as with having a coherent embodied sense of self.

Temporal lobe

Cingulate cortex

The cingulate runs from front to back folded into the midline of the brain, and has multiple functions. The ACC (anterior cingulate cortex) is involved with autonomic regulation, for example heart activity, as well as decision-making and reward processing, conflict-resolution and error-processing, aspects of emotion regulation, and impulse control (Tolomeo et al., 2016). ACC activity is implicated in many clinical conditions including PTSD (see below) and OCD. The function of the PCC (posterior cingulate cortex) is less clear, but it is thought to be involved in directing cognitive resources involved in internally focused thought processes (Leech & Sharp, 2013).

Insular cortex

This region of the brain governs "interoception"[3] – integrating sensory information from the body regarding body movement and condition, sensory information from the body, and homeostatic functions, emotional

3 This is the sensory awareness of the internal state of the body, typically referring to visceral and physiological processes, used to represent the body from inside.

states, self-perception, and interpersonal experience. The insula has been implicated in disorders related to body image, for example in body dysmorphic disorder and anorexia, where a loss of functional connectivity involving the insula and face recognition areas has been observed (Moody et al., 2015). Areas within the insula are likely to be active when people experience a sense of self-disgust (Schiepek et al., 2013).

Limbic system

The term "limbic system" refers to a collection of cortical and subcortical regions that function together to govern emotional activity. The term "limbic system" can be understood as a conceptual tool, as the various regions involved are not necessarily anatomically related to one another. Cortical areas included in the limbic system include the insular cortex, OFC, cingulate, and hippocampus, among others. Subcortical components of the limbic system include the olfactory bulb, hypothalamus, amygdala, and areas of the thalamus.

Hypothalamus

The hypothalamus has multiple functional areas involved in autonomic control, sexual function, endocrine function, and behavioral functions. It receives inputs from the hippocampus and amygdala; its outputs regulate many areas, including levels of alertness. It is important because of its role in regulating basic functions, including autonomic activity. Many physical symptoms of mental and emotional problems are regulated via the hypothalamus.

Hippocampus

This complex area of the brain is involved with declarative memory functions, understanding spatial relations in the environment, and corticosteroid production, and is part of the temporal lobe. It is densely and reciprocally interconnected with many other areas of the brain, including the frontal cortex, amygdala, and structures involved with learning and conditioned responses (e.g., the ventral striatum), and involved with formation and retrieval of memories in proper context.

Amygdala

The amygdala is involved in behavior, autonomic, and endocrine function connected with emotional activation. It has a special role in regulating survival responses. Excessive activation of the amygdala is associated with states of heightened anxiety and rage. It is located in the anterior temporal lobe, and connects with multiple brain areas including the hippocampus, thalamus, hypothalamus, orbitofrontal cortex, cingulate cortex, brainstem, and other areas.

Autonomic nervous system (ANS)

The ANS regulates basic essential physiologic processes, without the need for conscious control, and innervates the entire body. In states of health, the ANS functions to keep the system in balance between activation by the sympathetic part of the ANS and repose by the parasympathetic part of the ANS. The sympathetic nervous system is catabolic, increasing energy utilization and governing fight–flight and stress responses, while the parasympathic nervous system is anabolic, conserving energy and ideally fostering recovery. Generally speaking, excessive sympathetic tone is associated with mental and physical hyperarousal symptoms, while excessive parasympathic tone is associated with dissociative and shutting down responses.

Examples of sympathetic system effects include increasing heart activity, improving oxygen flow to the lungs, increasing how fast the body burns energy, getting more blood to muscles to prepare for action, and shunting blood away from areas non-essential in a crisis, and so on. Examples of parasympathetic effects include increasing digestive activity to absorb and store energy, resting heart function, and moving the body toward recuperation after high activity.

The HPA (hypothalamic-pituitary-adrenal) axis has a key role in regulation of the sympathetic nervous system, as the hypothalamus secretes many hormones, such as corticotropin-releasing hormone (CRH) and adrenocorticotrophic hormone (ACTH). Such signaling hormones are part of a complex system of endocrine checks and balances, acting loosely like the thermostat in a home's heating and cooling system. In health, it keeps things running smoothly, but with trauma and dissociation the system gets stuck, for instance in crisis states of activation and deactivation, and can get burned-out and unresponsive to normal stressors, or jump suddenly between activation and deactivation, from being pushed past its limits for too long.

Dysregulation of this system therefore is commonly considered to be a hallmark of trauma-related and dissociative disorders. The exact physiology varies and is still not well-understood, and the clinical presentation and approach also varies.

Neuroimaging findings and functional brain networks

Brain science is undergoing a significant paradigm shift with the integration of complexity theory into models of brain function. This has allowed us to conceptualize brain function in terms of brain networks as a cohesive organizing concept, integrating earlier models. From this point of view, the target of therapeutics are brain networks, in addition to traditional targets (e.g., neurotransmitter levels in specific regions). To illustrate, let's see how PTSD manifests in three key brain networks: the central executive network, the default mode network, and the salience network (Reiter, Andersen, & Carlsson, 2016).

The default mode network is the brain's "idle" state, generating activity when nothing in particular is going on externally. It focuses on internal activity and experience. The salience and central executive networks, by contrast, are directed toward managing the external world. The salience network is involved with monitoring the environment, giving weight to some stimuli over others, while the central executive network manages attention and working memory. There are many other relevant networks, beyond the scope of this review.

Compare PTSD networks with non-PTSD networks. The default mode network in PTSD is active in ways that likely subjectively correspond to intrusive thoughts. For example, the mind of someone with PTSD who experienced sexual assault may at rest generate unwanted traumatic memories, rather than focusing on present needs. The brain appears to be stuck in past traumatic states, as well as anticipating a repetition of trauma. Tragically, such distracting brain activity leaves such a person more vulnerable to immediate threats.

The salience network is similar in terms of being biased toward threat, but different with respect to being geared toward the external environment. For instance, while walking down the street the person may give more perceptual weight, and have an emotional response to, people who remind them of an assailant, or they may be more vigilant in some situations, or to some threats over others. A classic example of this is the combat veteran suffering from PTSD who returns home after multiple deployments during which he learned to drive an armored vehicle in an environment rich in IEDs (Improvised Explosive Devices), which are typically disguised to look like ordinary objects such as roadside debris, or are otherwise hidden. That person's salience network tends to become "wired" to see the world in a different way. This learning becomes both deeply ingrained and generalized. Upon returning home, this veteran driving down the once-familiar roads of home will involuntarily perceive harmless objects by the side of the road as potentially deadly bombs. In the best-case scenario, he will be very tense and distracted while driving. This often has a negative effect on others in the car due to irritability, stress, and detachment: an illustration of how PTSD can hurt relationships and break families apart. If things go poorly, he might take evasive action to avoid a harmless object or miss a more ordinary threat, and cause an accident . . . leading to additional trauma.

Likewise, with someone who experienced sexual abuse, such perceptual bias will likely have a detrimental effect on interpersonal relations. Such perceptual changes often play out in the transference-countertransference matrix in familiar ways, giving a taste of traumatic reality. For instance, the patient may evade what his vigilance tells him is a dangerous relationship, but which is actually benign, thereby leaving himself lonely, deprived, and vulnerable.

Research has looked at brain imaging to examine differences in traumatized groups compared with unaffected groups. It is hard to tease apart multiple factors from one another in different forms of maltreatment, and to differentiate the effects of co-morbid conditions such as PTSD, depression, and substance abuse from one another. To make matters even more complicated, it can be difficult to tell whether observed differences are truly caused by maltreatment, or if they are simply correlated, connected by an underlying causal factor, or reciprocally inter-related. In spite of those caveats, it is informative to review the literature. Hanson et al. (2012), for example, studied children with early life stress and found a correlation with reduced prefrontal volumes encompassing the anterior cingulate and frontal cortices. This was associated with diminished executive function, and reduced working memory. In a study of adult women with sexual versus emotional abuse, researchers (Heim, Mayberg, Mletzko, Nemeroff, & Pruessner, 2013) found cortical thinning in somatosensory areas related to genital sensation in sexual abuse survivors, by contrast with thinning in areas related to self-awareness and self-evaluation in emotional abuse survivors.

Several studies have shown decreased hippocampal volume in childhood trauma survivors (reviewed in Opel et al., 2014, and more recently by Nemeroff, 2016) which were able to show that reduced hippocampal volume in depressed patients was likely independent of depression and related to early life distress. Finally, the amygdala has been shown to be consistently hyperactive in people with high levels of childhood trauma (Nemeroff, 2016), replicated in multiple research studies. Taken together, we see consistent findings of distress connected with decreased hippocampal activity and increased amygdala activity, in addition to trauma-specific findings in other brain areas. Identifying whether specific patterns are present in male survivors could provide future regions for targeted interventions and help refine current approaches.

Researchers use network analysis of brain activity to provide insight into the nature of abuse, providing a global picture of what is going on. In a recent paper (Kärgel et al., 2015) examining brain network activity in pedophiles who either perpetrated or did not perpetrate, versus healthy controls, researchers demonstrated that functional connectivity at rest was diminished in perpetrators in default mode and limbic networks. They saw decreased functional connectivity between the left amygdala and orbitofrontal as well as anterior prefrontal regions, brain regions involved in broad motivational and socio-emotional processes. The loss or lack of functional connectivity correlates with, for example, the inability to appropriately inhibit negative behaviors.

Furthermore, Teicher, Anderson, Ohashi, and Polcari (2014) used high resolution MRI scans to compare over 100 non-medicated young adults who were classified as "mistreated," according to careful and comprehensive interviews and clinical measures, with a control group. Researchers employed a complex mathematical analysis to calculate cortical morphometric network characteristics between the two groups, allowing them to measure difference in brain network structure as a result of maltreatment. Using graph theory (a branch of mathematics that studies networks) they sought to determine whether maltreatment results in "altered network centrality" for different brain regions for the mistreated people than those without maltreatment. Centrality is a measure of how important a given brain region is in overall brain network activity. We would expect people who had experienced maltreatment to process information differently, reflective of how developmental trauma skews perceptions of reality.

Different kinds of centrality determine whether a brain region may be a focal point for communication, may control communication channels, may rapidly spread information around the brain, or may have a high level of global influence on the whole network.

In this landmark study, Teicher et al. found a consistent pattern of differences in network centrality associated with childhood maltreatment versus controls. Regions with the greatest changes included the left anterior cingulate gyrus and sulcus and related areas having to do with self-referential processing, social cognition, emotional regulation, and interpersonal function. This is a major finding, as it shows distinctly different and pervasive patterns of brain activity in individuals with and without childhood maltreatment, affecting brain regions that are key to the construction of social and physical reality. The anterior cingulate is of particular clinical relevance because it is involved with conflict resolution and affect regulation, linking prefrontal "cognitive" areas with limbic "emotional" areas (Stevens, Hurley, & Taber, 2011). Presumably, with successful treatment conflict is managed more effectively and causes less distress and dysfunction.

Teicher et al.'s findings make progress toward mapping out abnormal brain activity and associated anatomic areas, which could be both therapeutic targets and provide the means to measure the efficacy of therapeutic change, track progress, and guide treatment. Individualized imaging, while not in widespread use, could be an effective tool to help patients thrive.Therapeutic efforts may be thought of as "normalizing" activity in brain networks. We may look at changes in networks in addition to changes in specific regions, enriching our ability to understand and modify brain activity to get better outcomes.

The network organization of the brain is adaptive because it creates resilience. Insults to one region can be compensated for by other brain regions, and unaffected brain regions can help with damage control. For example, in patients with limited tissue damage, such as following a smaller stroke, another brain region can pick up those functions, another manifestation of neuroplasticity, while yet another brain region can inhibit activity around the stroke to contain the damage by reducing "excitoxicity." These mechanisms are limited, but might be enhanced through various therapeutic interventions.

It is important to underscore that trauma causes *physical* changes in the brain, not just *functional* disturbances – in fact, they are interconnected.

Observations of brain alterations from traumatic experience persuade us that trauma causes damage to the brain on gross and subtle levels. We exercise caution in interpreting neuroanatomic and neurofunctional findings, however, because it is difficult to separate causality from correlation and because research methodologies, as sophisticated as they appear, are limited and developing. We may learn that some findings are not replicated, and others are the result of artifacts related to computer algorithms, for example. Furthermore, it is difficult to conduct experiments that test causality due to ethical considerations, since it is not permissible to deliberately expose a group to trauma and see what it causes compared to a non-exposed group, and it is very laborious to study unavoidable trauma in human cultures. Regardless, we hope that the growing literature will enable us to better help suffering patients.

Endocrine factors

HPA axis

In distressed and posttraumatic states, the HPA (hypothalamic-pituitary-adrenal) axis shows variable patterns of dysregulation combined with consistent abnormalities. People with early life stress (ELS) have been shown to have hyperactive stress reactions in response to a social stress test (Trier Social Stress Test), with elevated adrenocorticotrophic hormone (ACTH) and cortisol responses in both men and women with depression.

Traumatized stress response systems often have exaggerated reactions to challenge with externally administered stress hormones (Heim et al., 2013). Parallel results have been demonstrated in combat veterans' offspring (Pesonen et al., 2010), in patients with depression and borderline personality disorder, and in those with a history of trauma (Rinne et al., 2002). By contrast, victims of bullying show blunted HPA responses upon provocative testing (Ouellet-Morin et al., 2011). It is important clinically to assess where patients are hyper-reactive, and where they show blunted responses to stress, given differing histories and clinical presentations, and incorporate this into collaborative treatment planning.

Why different populations have hyperactive responses versus blunted responses is still being understood. It is likely related to several factors, including the nature of the stress, the degree of psychosocial support, the addition of adult traumatic experiences, family history of psychiatric disorders, and genetic and epigenetic factors (Nemeroff, 2016). The focus of much research is on elucidating a "two-pathway model" given the dichotomized pattern of hyper-activation and blunting of response.

For clinicians conducting psychotherapy these findings suggest the need for both careful attention to multiple factors, as well as recognition that different patients may present with variable patterns of stress response and different phase of treatment, requiring responsive and variable approaches. Given the general picture dysregulated stress response, a focus on optimizing regulation and supporting resilience is a clear priority from the very beginning of treatment and an opportunity to provide psychoeducation and interactively engage patients in their own care.

Oxytocin

Attachment is highly disrupted in individuals who have experienced early childhood sexual abuse and other forms of trauma and neglect, which typically co-occur and feed off one another. Given that 80% of maltreatment is from one or both parents (Child Maltreatment, 2012), understanding the effect on the brain systems involved in attachment is of crucial importance. Relational trauma and dissociative activity typically present early and ongoing challenges to the therapeutic relationship and alliance. Oxytocin, a neuropeptide produced in the posterior pituitary gland, is being studied in growing detail. It is often labeled the "bonding hormone," but this term is misleading given its complex effects on the brain. Nevertheless, oxytocin is involved in mediating social relationships, attachment, maternal behavior, intimacy, and trust, and plays a crucial role in breast-feeding. Abnormalities in oxytocin levels have been observed in groups with various forms of early distress. Heim et al. (2013) found that healthy adult women with histories of mistreatment in childhood had lower levels of oxytocin in cerebrospinal fluid, correlated with higher levels of mistreatment. Subsequent work has identified a genetic role for variations in oxytocin genotype, where individuals with specific gene mutations showed greater adult pathology (Myers et al., 2014). We may be able to test patients for the presence or absence of genotypes in order to predict treatment outcomes, manage expectations, and guide treatment planning.

Other neuroendocrine systems are certainly affected, but there is minimal research at this time. Systems possibly involved include: hypothalamic-pituitary-gonadal axis (which speculatively may relate to changes in sexual behavior in adult males who experienced childhood sexual abuse), including specifically testosterone, progesterone, and estrogen; the hypothalamic-pituitary-thyroid axis (which may affect factors such as energy levels and metabolism in addition to mood); and growth hormone and prolactin (Nemeroff, 2016). It is also likely that neuron-specific factors are involved, including brain derived growth factor (BDNF), and other neuropeptides, such as neuropeptide Y, involved with plasticity, learning and development, and resilience.

Epigenetic factors

Until relatively recently, the prevailing paradigm for understanding what influences human development has been nature *versus* nurture – nature of course being genetic influences and nurture being environmental factors. Epigenetic factors represent the interaction between nature and nurture, and how that gets passed biologically from one generation to the next. Recently, an increasing role for epigenetic factors has been identified in many different areas, including the study of stress and trauma (Kundakovic & Champagne, 2014; Provençal & Binder, 2015).

While, conceptually speaking, epigenetic factors are where nature and nurture interact, formally epigenetics is the study of how the genomic code is read and expressed, and how this may be altered without changing the underlying genetic code. For example, an individual with identical genetic make-up may express those genes in radically different ways based on (1) experiences of ancestors (extending to the level of grandparents in human and animal studies); (2) intra-uterine effects; and (3) post-natal effects. ELS has been shown to interact with epigenetic factors to influence future pathological outcomes via specific pathways (see below). In addition, transgenerational transmission of trauma is likely to be mediated in significant part by epigenetic effects (see below) that not only affect the individual's response to stress, but also partially govern the way the individual engages in child-rearing. Epigenetic effects may be inherited, without a change to the underlying genome itself.

Epigenetic effects, while demonstrable directly in brain tissue, are easier to study outside of the central nervous system, such as via blood samples. Post-mortem studies of brain tissue have been conducted, for example, in suicide victims with and without ELS. In these two groups, differences were discovered in how glucocorticoid receptors are expressed (Suderman et al., 2014). Studies of epigenetic profiles contrasting adults with PTSD with and without childhood mistreatment also show differences in DNA methylation patterns (see below) in 12 different genetic locations (Mehta et al., 2013).

Recall that genes are "written" in DNA, and then are "read" into RNA by transcription machinery in the cell. The RNA is then translated into proteins, which undergo modification to become the final product. Epigenetic changes have a far-reaching impact, among others affecting neurotransmitter function, endocrine function, stress response, neuroplasticity, and inflammatory activity. A number of general mechanisms for epigenetic effects have been identified. This field is new so caution is required in interpreting findings, but epigenetics is poised to explode in the next decades. For the purposes of this chapter, we will discuss basics of epigenetics and give a few illustrations relevant to ELS.

Three major mechanisms for epigenetic effects include: (1) DNA methylation, (2) histone modification, and (3) non-coding RNA. DNA methylation is a process by which methyl chemical groups bind to, and block, regions of DNA. DNA methylation modifies gene expression via promoter regions, which are akin to dimmer switches, increasing or decreasing the activity of the genes they regulate depending on how much of the promotor region is exposed or covered. Histones mediate the way genes are packed together, and unavailable for transcription, or unpacked, and available for translation into RNA. Non-coding RNA refers to usually small fragments of RNA ("micro-RNA") and other forms of RNA that are not directly translated into proteins, but which themselves modify DNA transcription in a variety of ways, for example by acting as messengers.

Epigenetic factors are important in early mistreatment and neglect, carrying over from prior generations and passed on to future generations. A growing body of literature (reviewed in Zhang et al., 2013) is demonstrating epigenetic effects with the HPA axis, correlated with developmental and adult behavioral effects in animals and humans. Early caregiving, richness of attachment, and presence of neglect in addition to the presence of actively distressing factors, modify gene expression and adult behavior. Some modifications appear partly reversible via epigenetic manipulations. While such approaches are years from direct applications in human beings, they hold promise for a new avenue to address intractable posttraumatic sequelae. It is also important to see if conventional therapeutics have epigenetic effects, which may be more effectively leveraged, particularly for groups who appear to respond less vigorously to treatment.

Therapeutic approaches

Psychopharmacology

PTSD prevention

It is of obvious importance to determine what, if any, interventions have potential for preventing PTSD and other traumatic sequelae. Most of the research has been done with adults, though there are some studies of children in intensive medical care environments, for example burn units, which look at causes and prevention of PTSD. Few interventions mitigate the subsequent development of PTSD, and decision-making regarding the use of such interventions remains unclear. According to a definitive review of the literature (Qi, Gevonden, & Shalev, 2016), hydrocortisone and CBT show promise for prevention of PTSD. Hydrocortisone, a corticosteroid hormone that hypothetically facilitates extinction learning as well as enhances synaptic plasticity, significantly reduced rates of PTSD in trauma survivors at a level I trauma center (Delahanty et al., 2013). In some but not all studies, CBT with prolonged exposure reduced PTSD symptoms following traumatic experience. In terms of timing and patient selection, a meta-analysis of early interventions (Roberts, Kitchiner, Kenardy, & Bisson, 2010) suggests CBT is effective when PTSD is diagnosable at the beginning of treatment. Other potentially promising approaches, for example medications that may interfere with traumatic memory formation such as beta adrenergic blockers (e.g., propranolol), and opiate medications (e.g., morphine), which have been associated with lower rates of PTSD in burn units, have not been shown to be effective for prevention of PTSD. Importantly, in addition to being ineffective in prevention, benzodiazepines, specifically clonazepam and alprazolam, have been shown to have PTSD-enhancing effects in patients (Gelpin et al., 1996) and in animal models (Matar, Zohar, Kaplan, & Cohen, 2009), putatively due to impeding fear extinction. Promising approaches are being investigated, involving neuropeptide targets including oxytocin, involved in fear and social behavior, and neuropeptide Y, involved in stress-regulation and resilience. In the future, such approaches may prevent PTSD, attenuate re-traumatizing experiences, and augment talk therapy.

PTSD treatment

Research investigating the psychopharmacologic treatment of PTSD is limited, and developing. There are to date no large multicenter trials systematically examining the efficacy of medications for PTSD, although there are a handful of randomized controlled trials, a larger number of open label studies, and numerous case reports. PTSD treatment is challenging to systematically study due to the diversity of presentations and etiologies. In the absence of clear guidelines, clinicians tend to try different medications, without a systematic approach, making it impossible to make sense of data or draw conclusions regarding treatment guidelines. Many patients with PTSD avoid the most effective psychotherapeutic approaches available, such as prolonged exposure, leading clinicians to use variety of poorly substantiated treatments. In addition, researchers use inconsistent inclusion criteria for studies (e.g., duration of prior medication treatment before calling a medication trial a failure, lack of specificity regarding the duration, and kind of psychotherapy) as well as inconsistent outcome assessment tools. PTSD is often co-morbid with other disorders, including substance use and mood disorders, making investigation additionally difficult. These factors make it premature to offer definitive treatment guidelines, and current recommendations are a work-in-progress.

Pharmacotherapy and related treatment considerations

In a recent systematic review and meta-analysis in the *British Journal of Psychiatry*, in which Hoskins et al. (2015) used state-of-the-art statistical methods, findings were clear: only the selective serotonin reuptake inhibitors/serotonin-norepinephrine reuptake inhibitors (SSRI/SNRI) fluoxetine, paroxetine, and venlafaxine were found to have strong evidence for efficacy in PTSD treatment. Expert recommendations vary – in some cases, these medications are recommended as first line treatments along with psychotherapy, and in other cases are considered second line treatments if psychotherapy is ineffective. This is because the effect sizes versus placebo are lower than for psychological treatments; but it is much simpler to administer medication than therapy, making access to care easier. Other medications were shown in randomized controlled trials to lack efficacy. Hoskins et al. noted that in single randomized controlled studies, four drugs showed efficacy – amitriptyline (a tricyclic antidepressant), GR205171 (a neurokinin-1 antagonist), mirtazapine (an atypical antidepressant), and phenelzine (an MAOI antidepressant).

There is insufficient evidence for other antidepressants and medication classes, including anticonvulsants, antipsychotics, and a variety of novel approaches, including ketamine, baclofen, MDMA, cannabinoids, and others.

Treatment resistant PTSD (TRPTSD) presents a different situation, in which chronic, severe, and unremitting PTSD may justify the use of less-well studied treatment approaches if the potential benefits outweigh the risks. TRPTSD is an important framework because it is characteristic of the treatment refractory presentation clinicians encounter in the aftermath of severe, early abuse. Koek et al. (2016) conducted a comprehensive review and meta-analysis of the literature pertaining to TRPTSD. They reviewed all trials of PTSD treatment, and divided them by several criteria related to how well-designed the studies had been. They then examined reports on treatment efforts in populations where mainstay treatments had already failed, looking at a wide array of therapeutic approaches. Combat-related PTSD was most commonly identified; generalizing recommendations for survivors of childhood sexual and other abuse and neglect therefore must be done with caution.

The researchers reviewed treatment with: antidepressants, anticonvulsants, antipsychotics, antiadrenergic agents, glutamate/NMDA regulatory agents, MDMA (ecstasy), cannabinoids, stimulant medications, and others. They attempted to identify the criteria for "treatment failure" to ensure findings are truly "treatment resistant," although there is no standard definition yet. There were few randomized controlled trials, a greater number of open label studies, and many optimistic case reports of unclear significance. Placebo responses can be very powerful, and other factors are often not described in reports; however, it is compelling to read reports of people who have had severe PTSD for many years, who have tried many, many different medications, when they show a large and sustained improvement coinciding with a specific medication change. In many cases, it seems to make sense to try a variety of treatments, as long as their risk is not high. However, it is equally important to be thoughtful and avoid creating a situation in which patients are jumping from one treatment of limited or unclear efficacy to the next, potentially interfering with acceptance and accommodation. The clinical relevance of research in this area is limited due to inconsistent definitions of treatment response and failure, as well as by study designs that do not always reflect real-world treatment settings. Therefore, greater consensus on working definitions of treatment response and failure, as well as design of research protocols that accurately reflect common treatment settings, would increase the clinical utility of research on treatment-refractory PTSD.

Major recommendations from Hoskins et al.'s review are as follows:

For antidepressants, a trial with another antidepressant may help, perhaps from a different class than the SSRIs/SNRIs, possibly with mirtazepine, duloxetine, or nefazodone, based on open-label trials. They note that tianeptine, a tricyclic antidepressant with unique properties developed in the 1960s and not widely available, may have promise for TRPTSD but requires more investigation, as with large-scale trials for depression (e.g., STAR-D).

Antipsychotics have the clearest indication for use in PTSD with co-occurring psychotic symptoms, in only open-label trials. Risperidone was the best-studied antipsychotic, and they concluded there is insufficient evidence to recommend it. In open-label trials with limited data, olanzapine, quetiapine, and aripiprazole showed a non-significant trend toward efficacy. Other second-generation antipsychotics have not been studied, and Koek et al. recommend systematic investigation with these medications because, while they carry a higher risk of medically-significant adverse events, they could be useful in TRPTSD.

With anticonvulsants, research is less conclusive. The authors identified no high-quality prospective trials for TRPTSD, but findings for PTSD suggest that topiramate may be helpful in some cases; divalproex may be helpful in some cases of civilian PTSD only; tiagabine is not likely effective; and the myriad other anticonvulsants should be carefully studied. Carbamazepine, gabapentin, and lamotrigine in particular have shown positive results in less well-designed research protocols, and may prove to be useful.

Among antiadrenergic agents, only prazosin was shown to be clearly useful, especially for improvement in sleep and nightmares. Some experts consider prazosin to be a first-line medication, before antidepressants. Clonidine may have utility but requires more study. Beta blockers (e.g., propranolol) and guanfacine do not appear to be effective. Interestingly, a class of blood pressure medications called "ACE inhibitors" (angiotensin converting enzyme) was associated with reductions in PTSD in a clinical population.

Among the other pharmacologic and non-pharmacologic agents reviewed, a few are notable. Lithium, while not effective for PTSD, may be a useful medication, as it reduced suicidality, frequently a significant and treatment-refractory problem in PTSD. A synthetic opiate, tramadol, may be useful some PTSD sufferers, and stimulant medications may be of benefit to address cognitive and mood disturbances. D-cycloserine, an anti-tuberculosis agent shown to enhance fear-based learning in simple phobias, may turn out to have utility in enhancing CBT for PTSD, though current research is non-conclusive. Ketamine may produce short-term improvement, but has not been associated with long-term gains and may exacerbate PTSD symptoms, notably dissociative symptoms. MDMA, the drug commonly known as ecstasy, was not clearly effective in two research studies of whether it would augment psychotherapy, but also showed benefit it one treatment group. Corticosteroid administration did not appear effective.[4]

Cannabinoids, such as marijuana, bind to receptors in the endocannabinoid system, influencing emotional states. Medical cannabinoid use remains controversial, though there is greater acceptance of recreational and medicinal use; research to determine when cannabinoids may be useful and when harmful is developing. Zer-Aviv, Segev, and Akirav (2016) reviewed cannabinoids and PTSD, noting people with PTSD use cannabis more often and report it helps them cope with symptoms. Likewise, people using cannabis are more likely to have PTSD. Studies in humans suggest cannabis may improve PTSD symptoms, including poor sleep, nightmares, and hyper-arousal. Animal studies suggest cannabis may play a role in reducing stress and possibly anxiety, and facilitating fear extinction.

4 Interested readers may obtain a copy of the Koek et al. review for full detail about other agents beyond the scope of this chapter (e.g., medical foods, inflammatory modulators, and investigational medications).

They conclude it may have a role in PTSD treatment and prevention, but there are no large, well-designed studies; more research is required. Because cannabis may cause adverse reactions, and remains illegal in many areas, it can be difficult for clinicians to recommend cannabis even if they support its use for patients.

Pharmacogenomic testing (El-Mallakh, Roberts, El-Mallakh, Findlay, & Reynolds, 2016) is an emerging component of personalized medicine already in use in clinical psychiatric practice. It can help, among other things, to guide medication decision-making. This kind of testing, using a simple cheek swab to collect a DNA sample, involves assaying for individual liver enzyme profiles related to drug metabolism, known variations in neurotransmitter mechanism related to symptomatology, and other relevant factors such as folic acid metabolism status. This information is then cross-referenced with a pharmacogenomic database, a list of medications is generated with guidelines regarding use, and this information is used to inform clinical decision-making. When useful, pharmacogenomic testing enables selecting treatments that are more likely to work, less likely to have adverse reactions, and provide a better understanding of aspects of treatment such as drug–drug interactions and whether augmentation strategies are worth using in specific individuals. Favorable reports, often industry-sponsored, suggest that the effect of such testing is useful enough to warrant the expense. More conservative critics suggest the information and technology is too new to be in routine use.

A limitation of pharmacogenomic testing is that it does not measure real-time physiologic activity. Testing of blood and salivary levels of various indicators may be useful in guiding treatment. Current data is inconclusive for psychiatric application, although there are established medical applications in other disciplines (Javaid, Ahmed, Durand, & Tran, 2016). Clearly, clinicians would welcome personalized testing that helps make accurate predictions about effective treatment selection.

Psychotherapeutic considerations

Eye Movement Desensitization and Reprocessing (EMDR) and Trauma Focused Cognitive Behavioral Therapy (TFCBT) are statistically equivalent in the reference Cochrane Database of Systematic Reviews. The most recent Cochrane report (Bisson, Roberts, Andrew, Cooper, & Lewis, 2013) for psychotherapy treatment of PTSD found EMDR and

TFCBT to be the most effective treatment options. Proponents describe a bi-hemispheric processing component unique to EMDR; no definitive difference has been elucidated. EMDR includes the key elements of TFCBT, notably prolonged exposure and desensitization. Eye movements in EMDR are hypothesized to increase access to episodic memory via bilateral stimulation, reducing the negative affect associated with traumatic memories and improving ability to reprocess such memories (Jeffries & Davis, 2013), although these hypotheses are unproven.

A meta-analysis by Cusack et al. (2016) found multiple psychotherapeutic approaches effective in severe PTSD, noting:

> Evidence supports efficacy of exposure therapy (high SOE [strength of evidence]) including the manualized version Prolonged Exposure (PE); cognitive therapy (CT), cognitive processing therapy (CPT), cognitive behavioral therapy (CBT)-mixed therapies (moderate SOE); eye movement desensitization and reprocessing (EMDR) and narrative exposure therapy (low-moderate SOE).

Effect sizes were generally high for various approaches, and none were clearly superior to any other. A systematic review and meta-analysis by Lee et al. (2016) compared psychotherapy versus pharmacotherapy for PTSD, finding trauma-focused psychotherapies, as a whole, were more effective than medication management and had more sustained benefits, consistent with advocates recommending evidence-based psychotherapy as a first line treatment in PTSD.

Pharmacotherapy for dissociation

There is limited research on medication management for dissociative disorders. Pilot studies have found naltrexone to have efficacy for dissociative symptoms, presumably because it blocks opioid activity connected with dissociation. Anecdotally, patients often report a sense of self-generated anesthesia prior to dissociation, either a numbing and/or pleasurable feeling. Most recently, naltrexone was shown to be effective in reducing dissociative symptoms in borderline personality disorder (Schmahl et al., 2012) in small randomized, placebo-controlled double-blind trials. It is worth noting again that some pharmacologic approaches worsen dissociative symptoms, including ketamine, MDMA, and other psychotropics, and are not recommended in the presence of a dissociative disorder.

Transcranial magnetic stimulation (TMS)

TMS is a non-invasive research and intervention tool first approved in 2008 for clinical use in the United States for the treatment of major depressive disorder failing to respond to medications. TMS was originally investigated in the UK in the 1980s, with a clinical rationale based on the oft-cited observation that patients with right frontal cerebrovascular accidents tend to become happier, whereas patients with left frontal damage tend to become depressed, suggesting that bi-hemispheric L-R balance has a component in mood regulation. Specific guidelines for TMS may be found in the American Psychiatric Association's Practice Guidelines (Gelenberg et al., 2010), with broader applications that are expanding as new research emerges.

TMS uses an electromagnet to generate strong magnetic pulses (about 1.5 Tesla magnetic pulses; compare with 3 Tesla for a standard imaging MRI), which can be delivered to any area of the cerebral cortex by passing through superficial layers of skin, bone, other tissues, and cerebrospinal fluid to stimulate neural tissue. The way TMS interacts with neural tissue is by causing electrical charge to move in tissue element perpendicular to the magnetic field orientation, according to Faraday's Law, which says that a changing magnetic field will induce an electrical current in a conductive material. This is how a basic electrical generator works: rotating magnetic elements cause electrons to flow in coil of wire, and the resultant electrical current can be used to run other things – lightbulbs, cellphone chargers, hydroelectric power generation from turbines, and so on.

In the brain, depending on the strength of the magnetic field, TMS will either cause neurons to depolarize (fire), causing an "action potential," or will affect the probability of them firing if below action potential threshold. This is of clinical significance based on the observation that high frequency TMS leads to sustained increase in activity, whereas low frequency TMS tends to suppress brain activity. This allows for design and testing of specific protocols involving activation and suppression of different functional regions, leading to alterations in local and network activity.

Thus, the standard treatment for depression involves stimulation of the left frontal cortex (specifically the dorsolateral prefrontal cortex), and in patients who respond to treatment and maintain the response after treatment is completed, there is not only sustained activity in the left frontal cortex, but also are associated changes in limbic and para-limbic regions

(Kito, Fujita, & Koga, 2008). By contrast, investigational approaches that appear to have clinical utility (Machado et al., 2012; Clark, Cole, Winter, Williams, & Grammer, 2015) for anxiety and some PTSD symptom domains use low frequency TMS to suppress activity in the right frontal cortex. Interestingly, suppression of the right frontal cortex, which is "contralateral" to left frontal cortex, alleviates symptoms of depression and anxiety. There is a noteworthy study (Dunlop et al., 2015) demonstrating that high frequency TMS to the dorsomedial prefrontal cortex can rapidly produce a cessation of binge eating in humans, but only when there is a lack of connectivity between the cortex and deeper brain areas governing compulsive behaviors. This is a good example of how TMS may restore a lack of connectivity between higher brain areas and deeper brain areas to restore normal function. Regulating connectivity may be a therapeutic target for TMS, highlighting the need for research clarifying network dysfunction in PTSD and related conditions.

Case illustration

> Mr. S, a 43-year-old single man working in tech support, presented for initial consultation with a long history of complaints of depression and posttraumatic symptoms. He noted he did not think his depression had been treated adequately despite requests to his former psychiatrist to do so, and the patient had been averse to addressing posttraumatic issues. This had affected their treatment alliance to the point of precipitating withdrawal from care. After a period of evaluation and development of a therapeutic alliance with a new psychiatrist, who agreed to provisionally focus on the patient's main concern of depression, a course of TMS therapy allowed the patient to have a moderately effective and sustained treatment response, giving him relief required to address other issues. With depression stabilized, and trust partially established, he more productively engaged in treatment for complex PTSD and dissociation.

TMS treatment: Essential considerations. Depending on the power and design of the magnet, the pulses can penetrate from 2–4 centimeters into the cortex. Magnetic pulses can be delivered with variable frequency, waveform, and timing, to produce either simple and repetitive patterns or more complicated patterns with variations over time. There are infinite possibilities and understanding of how neural tissue responds to different protocols is an expanding area of research. Neural engineers work with different forms and patterns of stimulation, studying which may yield better clinical results, or even be used for performance enhancement. Research techniques have been developed that allow direct observation of the effect of TMS on neural function by mounting thin slices of living neural tissue on an apparatus and testing how it responds to stimulation. For example, *theta burst stimulation*, which uses one frequency of bursts superimposed on another frequency, like a big ocean wave with smaller waves on top of it, may be more effective in treating depression than standard approaches.

The literature on the efficacy of TMS for depression is the most robust, while data for other conditions are less developed. Initial studies of TMS (O'Reardon et al., 2007) showed smaller effect sizes in depression, and gained FDA clearance. Because of the good safety profile of TMS, and the lack of effective treatments for many conditions, practitioners often use TMS "off-label," as with pharmacological treatment.

Since then, as the result of efficacy shown in large multi-center clinical trials, the indication has been extended to include failure to adequately respond to one or more antidepressant medications. Access to TMS therapy has also increased as health insurance companies provide better coverage. A typical TMS policy might require failure of at least four medications and CBT.

For uncomplicated depression, patients treated with TMS show statistically significant changes in measures of both symptomatic and functional outcomes (Janicak et al., 2013; Solvason et al., 2014). The standard protocol for treating depression involves delivery of 3000 pulses per treatment session (about 40 minutes). Patients receive an average of 25 sessions of TMS for depression, five days per week, for a total of five weeks of treatment, though this can vary greatly from patient to patient. Most responders sustain an antidepressant response for six months to a year (Dunner et al., 2014) or longer, based on observations of patients who have remained in remission for years following successful treatment. Of those who relapse following treatment, a short course of re-treatment will often restore the response. Some patients benefit from maintenance treatments, usually a few sessions a month. Guidelines are being developed as clinical experience and research accumulate.

TMS devices. World-wide, there are many TMS machines available for research and clinical application. In the United States, as of this writing, there are three FDA-cleared devices available – Neuronetics, Brainsway, and MagVenture. A key difference among different machines is in the "coil geometry," meaning the design of the electromagnet used. Some systems use a simple linear electromagnet, others use a circle or figure-eight shape, while others use designs such as the "H coil," intended to deliver magnetic pulses to deeper cortical layers ("deep TMS"). It is unclear based on existing data whether clinical efficacy is better with any particular design for different conditions, though this is likely to change in the future as understanding improves. TMS can be paired with "neuro-navigation" systems, which typically use a stereoscopic camera coupled with a computer and a 3D MRI to localize treatment. Such systems were pioneered for neurosurgical applications. Lastly, it is worth noting that TMS holds promise for treating neurological conditions, such as Parkinson's disease and symptoms of dementia, and may be useful for improving rehabilitation outcomes in patients with brain injury.

TMS for PTSD and dissociative disorders. There are many small studies looking at the utility of TMS for treating different symptom areas in PTSD, predominantly small pilot studies with a small number of treatment sessions. Meta-analyses of TMS for PTSD (Karsen, Watts, & Holtzheimer, 2014; Trevizol et al., 2016) may guide off-label use along with clinical experience. For PTSD, the best evidence to date is for low frequency R dorsolateral prefrontal cortex treatment for hyperarousal symptoms, a protocol similar to that used to treat generalized anxiety disorder.

TMS protocols involving other frequencies and patterns of pulse delivery may show promise as well. For example, researchers (Philip, Ridout, Albright, Sanchez, & Carpenter, 2016) reported that TMS delivered at five cycles per second to the L dorsolateral prefrontal cortex showed efficacy for treatment of co-morbid Major Depressive Disorder and PTSD in a population of VA patients. More research is required to determine which treatment protocols are most effective with which patients and variations of PTSD. Researchers are also investigating whether entraining TMS to patients' electroencephalogram (EEG) frequencies (dubbed "Magnetic Resonance Therapy" [MTR]) is a useful approach. For example, Taghva et al. (2015), in a brief report of an open-label trial, found that patients showed trends toward normalization of EEG and clinical improvement on standardized rating scales measuring PTSD symptoms. There are essentially no published studies looking at TMS for the treatment of dissociative disorders, though there are clinical trials under way, for example using

TMS to treat Depersonalization Disorder, and studies of dissociation using TMS as a research probe (Spitzer et al., 2004).

EEG biofeedback/neurofeedback is a form of biofeedback. Biofeedback trains people to regulate physiological functions using real-time information about what their bodies are doing. For example, an individual can learn to lower heart rate by listening to a tone changing from higher to lower pitch as pulse falls. A progressively more pleasing tone is paired with the desired outcome. Biofeedback uses classical and operant conditioning to train the brain to regulate parameters such as heart rate, galvanic skin response, and other physiologic targets.

EEG biofeedback, often referred to as *neurofeedback*, measures EEG waveforms over different parts of the cortex the individual is learning to control. Training can target amplitude of one waveform over another in a given region, increase synchronization of brainwaves in different areas, or address delays in processing between different areas (Fisher, 2014). Neurofeedback may be based on other measures of brain activity as well, such as fMRI activity (see below). Such approaches offer promise because they can track greater resolution of real-time brain activity and key anatomically deep areas, such as the amygdala, where EEG cannot reach. Neurofeedback is generally well-tolerated. QEEG stands for Quantitative EEG, and is a computer-analytic method for examining digitized EEGs to help guide treatment, sometimes called *brain mapping*. QEEG is used for many applications, from predicting medication response, to assessing neurocognitive function and evaluating traumatic brain injury, to guiding neurofeedback treatment. QEEG is controversial due to a lack of clarity regarding utility and standardization, but may become more widely and carefully used as the field evolves.

Case illustration

> A 32-year-old single male, employed as a successful professional, was referred for neurofeedback treatment by his therapist due to high levels of debilitating anxiety about intimacy and interpersonal relationships. He was raised in an emotionally deprived and rejecting home environment and was chronically bullied and teased by peers. He had learned to survive by suppressing needs and feelings, pretending to be someone he was not. While ongoing therapy was useful, he was stuck, and the therapy as reported by the therapist had reached an

> impasse, especially around relatedness and authenticity. He refused to participate in recommended treatments including group therapy, did not want to take psychiatric medications, and found meditation unpleasant due to intrusive thoughts. The patient was treated with 25 sessions of neurofeedback and showed early signs of improvement. His therapist reported three months following cessation of treatment that the patient had continued to show improvement and was making progress both in therapy and in his social life. He noted that the patient had lower levels of anxiety, appeared less narcissistic and obsessional, and had large improvements in cognitive flexibility.

Reiter et al. (2016) provide a review of well-designed studies using neurofeedback to treat posttraumatic stress disorder and related symptoms. They reviewed five studies that targeted increasing theta wave frequency, in some cases seeking to train an increased ratio of theta waves to alpha waves. The total number of subjects was relatively low in each study. Nevertheless, positive findings were noted. Groups studied included cohorts with PTSD from combat, individuals with developmental trauma, and subjects with co-morbid conditions including alcohol and substance use disorders as well as depression and anxiety disorders. Theta waves are associated with deep states of meditation and calmness. One of the studies focused on Sensory Motor Rhythm (SMR) as well, which is associated with decreased thalamic activation, and facilitates attention and decreased physical (motor) activity; it is used in treating ADHD and epilepsy.

In all five studies, PTSD symptoms were significantly reduced, and in the two studies that looked at participants on long-term follow-up the majority of participants sustained improvement for over two years following training. Furthermore, using fMRI, which indirectly measures brain metabolic activity by anatomic area, three of the reports studied brainwave activity and/or network connectivity. While overall symptom changes were not observed, in one study a significant correlation was found between network connectivity and calmness. An increase in alpha waves post-training reflected increased alpha synchronization, with correlated changes in salience and default mode network-associated regions.

A more recent development in neurofeedback involves the use of functional neuroimaging, typically fMRI. With fMRI-guided neurofeedback, users can look at images of their own brain activity in real-time, and focus on changing that brain activity directly. There are few if any clinical studies using fMRI-guided neurofeedback for PTSD, but Cisler, Bush, James, Smitherman, and Kilts (2015) conducted a study aimed at identifying targets for fMRI-guided neurofeedback in patients with PTSD. They analyzed brain activity during traumatic memory recall, and found that heightened activity in the L hippocampus, associated with L amygdala activation, discriminated traumatic from non-traumatic memory recall correlated with severity of symptoms. These areas are putative targets for real-time neurofeedback. In a small pilot study of patients with OCD, real-time fMRI feedback was used to down-regulate excessive insular activity, reducing feelings of disgust and improving behavioral outcomes (Buyukturkoglu et al., 2015). Hypothetically, regulating insular activity would also be helpful for many patients with developmental trauma, who experience intense self-disgust affecting both self-image and interpersonal decision-making.

While neurofeedback has been investigated and applied clinically for decades now, there is a generally lower level of research available about it compared to other modalities (e.g., psychopharmacology). Given the promising clinical results, relative lack of adverse associated effects, and comparatively low costs involved, neurofeedback is a potentially valuable treatment for patients suffering from PTSD and related conditions.

Transcranial Direct Current Stimulation (tDCS). tDCS is a brain-stimulation technique using direct current to deliver a continuous low level of electricity via electrodes placed on the surface of the skull. The typically "montage" (the term conventionally used to describe the layout of electrodes in tDCS) uses two electrodes, which may simply be sponges soaked in salt water; these are the positive (anode) and negative (cathode) electrodes. Electrical current flows through the intervening substances, including skin, connective tissue, bone, cerebrospinal fluid (CSF), and neural tissue, in a complex path due to differences in conductivity among different tissues.

Because of the low current, tDCS does not cause neurons to depolarize, rather influencing the probability they will fire. In the most simplistic model, the anode is viewed as excitatory, and the cathode inhibitory, to underlying brain tissue. Targeting is dependent on individual anatomy. In principle, it is possible to reach deep brain structures, which is of potential clinical use. tDCS is generally safe and well-tolerated with minimal risk of skin irritation or electrical burns when administered properly.

There are refinements of tDCS that have been developed to keep current target to a local region on the cortex, called high-definition tDCS or HD-tDCS. With this technology, there is a central electrode immediately surrounded by several electrodes in close proximity. The current, rather than flowing through deep brain structures, flows through the tissue immediately under the central electrode, and back out via the closely placed peripheral electrodes, keeping it local and focused. Another refinement uses a 3D scan of the brain, loading it into a current density simulation software program, which creates a personalized electrical flow simulation allowing placement of electrodes to affect specific targets.

In terms of clinical use, tDCS has shown limited efficacy, primarily in smaller studies and meta-analyses, for treating psychiatric conditions such as depression (Brunoni et al., 2016), pain (Vaseghi, Zoghi, & Jaberzadeh, 2015) from various sources, during various stages of rehabilitation post-stroke (Kang, Summers, & Cauraugh, 2015), and in other neurological conditions. There is also much interest in augmenting various areas of normal function (Bennabi et al., 2014; Hill, Fitzgerald, & Hoy, 2016). There is little research on PTSD, though a small study showed tDCS may improve working memory in patients with PTSD (Saunders et al., 2015), and the potential to use tDCS to augment fear-extinction in PTSD (Marin, Camprodon, Dougherty, & Milad, 2014). There is little or no research on tDCS in dissociative disorders, though in theory it could be used to address connectivity issues present in those conditions.

Cranial Electrical Stimulation (CES). In Cranial Electrical Stimulation, a small alternating current is applied to the head, for instance across both earlobes. It can be easily administered at home under the direction of a healthcare provider. CES has been in use in Europe and the United States for several decades, and received FDA clearance in the United States for anxiety, depression, and sleep difficulties. There is limited controlled data on efficacy, though many clinician and patient reports find it helpful. Regarding PTSD, there are small studies showing CES efficacy for anxiety (Novakovic et al., 2011), suggestive of possible future use for PTSD. Given CES is safe and well tolerated, it may be a useful tool for patients with difficulty controlling anxiety.

Electroconvulsive Therapy (ECT). ECT applies electrical stimulation to the brain while the patient is anaesthetized, and produces a generalized tonic-clonic seizure. It can be applied unilaterally or bilaterally, and is best known for its use in treatment-resistant depression, where remission rates of up to 80% are reported (Petrides et al., 2001), with relapse rates up to 50% within the first six months after acute treatment (Bourgon & Kellner, 2000). Adverse reactions stem from risks of anesthesia; memory loss is characteristically limited to the day of the procedure. There are several case reports, and more recently one prospective open study, of ECT used to treat PTSD, as well as a retrospective analysis of a large number of patients treated for PTSD and depression. These studies show independent and sustained efficacy for both PTSD and depression symptoms, and reduction in co-morbid medical conditions with greater overall survival rates (Margoob, Ali, & Andrade, 2010; Ahmadi, Moss, Simon, Nemeroff, & Atre-Vaidya, 2015). Given these findings, ECT may be useful for severe, chronic, treatment-resistant PTSD, especially in the presence of co-morbid major depressive disorder.

Deep Brain Stimulation (DBS). In DBS, an electrode is surgically implanted into the brain to stimulate a target region of interest. DBS has been used for neurological applications such as in the treatment of Parkinson's disease and other movement disorders, as well as in the treatment of refractory OCD and depression (Novakovic et al., 2011). There is no clinical research available for DBS in the treatment of PTSD, though animal models suggest that interfering with brain regions involved in PTSD, notably disrupting function in areas of the amygdala, improves extinction and lessens anxiety in fear-conditioned rodents (Reznikov, Binko, Nobrega, & Hamani, 2016), and a treatment protocol using DBS for combat veterans with severe PTSD and functional disturbance targeting the amygdala has been approved and subjects are being recruited (Koek et al., 2014).

Vagal Nerve Stimulation (VNS). This approach uses an implanted device to provide electrical stimulation to the vagus nerve. VNS was approved in 1997 for epilepsy and in 2005 for treatment resistant depression. There is theoretical reason to hypothesize that VNS may have a role in PTSD treatment, as stimulation of the vagus nerve can cause activation of the amygdala resulting in enhanced extinction of conditioned responses and hippocampal activation resulting from amygdala activation, which improves memory consolidation (Marin et al., 2014). Indeed, Childs, Alvarez-Dieppa, Mcintyre, and Kroener (2015) demonstrated that VNS can enhance extinction learning in rats.

Conclusion

This chapter is intended to provide an overview of how the brain and related physiological systems in the body are altered in trauma and dissociation; a sufficient understanding to follow developments and applications for brain-based interventions; and a review of pharmacotherapy. There is problematically scant research specific to male survivors. Additional research to map out how the brain is affected in this population would be advantageous in developing targeted and effective therapeutic strategies. Similarly, there is little information regarding dissociative disorders, in terms of understanding the neuroscience and regarding treatment efficacy of different interventions. Dissociative symptoms are often under-recognized and under-treated. Hopefully, investigators focusing on dissociative disorders will continue to conduct and encourage research in this important area, and the inclusion of a dissociative subtype of PTSD in the DSM 5 is a positive development in this regard. In spite of the less-than-ideal evidence-base, and in keeping with standard clinical practice when evidence is lacking, lower risk clinical approaches on the frontiers of neuroscience may be safely used on a provisional basis if conducted by careful practitioners for properly selected patients in the context of an overall thoughtful and collaborative treatment plan.

References

Ahmadi, N., Moss, L., Simon, E., Nemeroff, C. B., & Atre-Vaidya, N. (2015). Efficacy and long-term clinical outcome of comorbid post traumatic stress disorder and major depressive disorder after electroconvulsive therapy. *Depression and Anxiety, 33*, 640–647. doi: 10.1002/da.22451

Bagley, C., & Thurston, W. E. (1996). *The understanding and prevention of child sexual abuse. Volume II: Male victims, adolescents, adult outcomes, and offender treatment*. Hampshire, England: Ashgate.

Bennabi, D., Pedron, S., Haffen, E., Monnin, J., Peterschmitt, Y., & Waes, V. V. (2014). Transcranial direct current stimulation for memory enhancement: From clinical research to animal models. *Frontiers in Systems Neuroscience, 8*. doi:10.3389/fnsys.2014.00159

Bisson, J. I., Roberts, N. P., Andrew, M., Cooper, R., & Lewis, C. (2013). Psychological therapies for chronic post-traumatic stress disorder (PTSD) in adults. *Cochrane Database of Systematic Reviews, 12*, CD003388

Bourgon, L. N., & Kellner, C. H. (2000). Relapse of depression after ECT: A review. *Journal of ECT, 16*(1), 19–31.

Brunoni, A. R., Moffa, A. H., Fregni, F., Palm, U., Padberg, F., Blumberger, D. M., . . . Loo, C. K. (2016). Transcranial direct current stimulation for acute major depressive episodes: Meta-analysis of individual patient data. *British Journal of Psychiatry, 208*(6), 522–531. doi: 10.1192/bjp.bp.115.164715

Buyukturkoglu, K., Roettgers, H., Sommer, J., Rana, M., Dietzsch, L., Arikan, E. B., & Ruiz, S. (2015). Self-regulation of anterior insula with real-time fmri and its behavioral effects in obsessive-compulsive disorder: A feasibility study. *PLOS ONE, 10*(12). doi: 10.1371/journal.pone.0145027

Buzsáki, G. (2006). *Rhythms of the brain.* Oxford: Oxford University Press.

Child Maltreatment (2012). Children's Bureau (Administration on Children, Youth and Families, Administration for Children and Families) of the U.S. Department of Health and Human Services. Retrieved from www.acf.hhs.gov/sites/default/files/cb/cm2012.pdf.

Childs, J. E., Alvarez-Dieppa, A. C., Mcintyre, C. K., & Kroener, S. (2015). Vagus nerve stimulation as a tool to induce plasticity in pathways relevant for extinction learning. *Journal of Visualized Experiments, 102.* doi: 10.3791/53032

Cisler, J. M., Bush, K., James, G. A., Smitherman, S., & Kilts, C. D. (2015). Decoding the traumatic memory among women with PTSD: Implications for neurocircuitry models of PTSD and real-time fMRI neurofeedback. *PLOS ONE, 10*(8).

Clark, C., Cole, J., Winter, C., Williams, K., & Grammer, G. (2015). A review of transcranial magnetic stimulation as a treatment for post-traumatic stress disorder. *Current Psychiatry Reports, 17*(10), 83.

Cusack, K., Jonas, D. E., Forneris, C. A., Wines, C., Sonis, J., . . . Gaynes, B. N. (2016). Psychological treatments for adults with posttraumatic stress disorder: A systematic review and meta-analysis. *Clinical Psychology Review, 43,* 128–141. doi: 10.1016/j.cpr.2015.10.003

Delahanty, D. L., Gabert-Quillen, C., Ostrowski, S. A., Nugent, N. R., Fischer, B., Morris, A., & Fallon, W. (2013). The efficacy of initial hydrocortisone administration at preventing posttraumatic distress in adult trauma patients: A randomized trial. *CNS Spectrums, 18*(2), 103–111.

Downar, J., Bakker, N., Dunlop, K., Salomons, T., Geraci, J., Giacobbe, P., & Woodside, B. (2013). 1343 – RTMS of the dorsomedial prefrontal cortex achieves robust and durable improvements in refractory obsessive-compulsive disorder. *European Psychiatry, 28,* 1.

Dunlop, K., Woodside, B., Lam, E., Olmsted, M., Colton, P., Giacobbe, P., & Downar, J. (2015). Increases in frontostriatal connectivity are associated with response to dorsomedial repetitive transcranial magnetic stimulation in refractory binge/purge behaviors. *Neuroimage Clinical, 8,* 611–618.

Dunner, D. L., Aaronson, S. T., Sackeim, H. A., Janicak, P. G., Carpenter, L. L., Boyadjis, T., . . . Demitrack, M. A. (2014). A multisite, naturalistic, observational study of transcranial magnetic stimulation for patients with pharmacoresistant major depressive disorder: Durability of benefit over a 1-year follow-up period. *Journal of Clinical Psychiatry, 75*(12), 1394–1401. doi: 10.4088/JCP.13m08977

El-Mallakh, R. S., Roberts, R. J., El-Mallakh, P. L., Findlay, L. J., & Reynolds, K. K. (2016). Pharmacogenomics in psychiatric practice. *Clinics in Laboratory Medicine, 36*(3), 507–523. doi: 10.1016/j.cll.2016.05.001

Fisher, S. F. (2014). *Neurofeedback in the treatment of developmental trauma: Calming the fear-driven brain*. New York, NY: Norton.

Gartner, R. B. (1999). *Betrayed as boys: Psychodynamic treatment of sexually abused men*. New York, NY: Guilford.

Gelenberg, A. J., Freeman, M. P., Markowitz, J. C., Rosenbaum, J. F., Thase, M. E., Trivedi, M. H., & Van Rhoads, R. S. (2010). Work group on major depressive disorder. *Practice Guideline for the Treatment of Patients with Major Depressive Disorder* (3rd Ed.). American Psychiatric Association. Retrieved from http://psychiatryonline.org/pb/assets/raw/sitewide/practice_guidelines/guidelines/mdd.pdf.

Gelpin, E., Bonne, O., Peri, T., Brandes, D., & Shalev, A. Y. (1996). Treatment of recent trauma survivors with benzodiazepines: A prospective study. *Journal of Clinical Psychiatry, 57*(9), 390–394.

Hanson, J. L., Chung, M. K., Avants, B. B., Rudolph, K. D., Shirtcliff, E. A., Gee, J. C., & Pollak, S. D. (2012). Structural variations in prefrontal cortex mediate the relationship between early childhood stress and spatial working memory. *Journal of Neuroscience, 32*(23), 7917–7925.

Heim, C. M., Mayberg, H. S., Mletzko, T., Nemeroff, C. B., & Pruessner, J. C. (2013). Decreased cortical representation of genital somatosensory field after childhood sexual abuse. *American Journal of Psychiatry, 170*(6), 616–623.

Hill, A. T., Fitzgerald, P. B., & Hoy, K. E. (2016). Effects of anodal transcranial direct current stimulation on working and recognition memory: A systematic review and meta-analysis of findings from healthy and neuropsychiatric populations. *Brain Stimulation, 8*(2), 331. doi: 10.1016/j.brs.2015.01.072

Holmes W. C., & Slap, G. B. (1998). Sexual abuse of boys: Definition, prevalence, correlates, sequelae, and management. *JAMA, 280*(21), 1855–1862.

Hoskins, M., Pearce, J., Bethell, A., Dankova, L., Barbui, C., Tol, W. A., & Bisson, J. I. (2015). Pharmacotherapy for post-traumatic stress disorder: Systematic review and meta-analysis. *British Journal of Psychiatry, 206*(2), 93–100.

Janicak, P. G., Dunner, D. L., Aaronson, S. T., Carpenter, L. L., Boyadjis, T. A., Brock, D. G., . . . Demitrack, M. A. (2013). Transcranial magnetic stimulation (TMS) for major depression: A multisite, naturalistic, observational study of quality of life outcome measures in clinical practice. *CNS Spectrums, 18*(6), 322–332. doi: 10.1017/S1092852913000357

Javaid, M. A., Ahmed, A. S., Durand, R., & Tran, S. D. (2016). Saliva as a diagnostic tool for oral and systemic diseases. *Journal of Oral Biology and Craniofacial Research, 6*(1), 67–76.

Jeffries, F. W., & Davis, P. (2013). What is the role of eye movements in eye movement desensitization and reprocessing (EMDR) for post-traumatic stress disorder (PTSD)? A review. *Behavioural and Cognitive Psychotherapy, 41*(3), 290–300.

Kang, N., Summers, J. J., & Cauraugh, J. H. (2015). Transcranial direct current stimulation facilitates motor learning post-stroke: A systematic review and meta-analysis. *Journal of Neurology, Neurosurgery & Psychiatry, 87*(4), 345–355. doi: 10.1136/jnnp-2015-311242

Kärgel, C., Massau, C., Weiß, S., Walter, M., Kruger, T. H., & Schiffer, B. (2015). Diminished functional connectivity on the road to child sexual abuse in pedophilia. *Journal of Sexual Medicine, 12*(3), 783–795.

Karsen, E. F., Watts, B. V., & Holtzheimer, P. E. (2014). Review of the effectiveness of transcranial magnetic stimulation for post-traumatic stress disorder. *Brain Stimulation, 7*(2), 151–157.

Kito, S., Fujita, K., & Koga, Y. (2008). Changes in regional cerebral blood flow after repetitive transcranial magnetic stimulation of the left dorsolateral prefrontal cortex in treatment-resistant depression. *Journal of Neuropsychiatry and Clinical Neurosciences, 20*(1), 74–80.

Koek, R. J., Langevin, J., Krahl, S. E., Kosoyan, H. J., Schwartz, H. N., Chen, J. W., . . . Sultzer, D. (2014). Deep brain stimulation of the basolateral amygdala for treatment-refractory combat post-traumatic stress disorder (PTSD): Study protocol for a pilot randomized controlled trial with blinded, staggered onset of stimulation. *Trials, 15*(1), 356.

Koek, R. J., Schwartz, H. N., Scully, S., Langevin, J. P., Spangler, S., Korotinsky, A, . . . Leuchter, A. (2016). Treatment-refractory posttraumatic stress disorder (TRPTSD): A review and framework for the future. *Progress in Neuropsychopharmacology and Biological Psychiatry, 70*, 170–218. doi: 10.1016/j.pnpbp.2016.01.015

Kundakovic, M., & Champagne, F. A. (2014). Early-life experience, epigenetics, and the developing brain. *Neuropsychopharmacology, 40*(1), 141–153.

Lee, D. J., Schnitzlein, C. W., Wolf, J. P., Vythilingam, M., Rasmusson, A. M., & Hoge, C. W. (2016). Psychotherapy versus pharmacotherapy for posttraumatic stress disorder: Systemic review and meta-analyses to determine first-line treatments. *Depression and Anxiety, 33*, 792–806.

Leech, R., & Sharp, D. J. (2013). The role of the posterior cingulate cortex in cognition and disease. *Brain, 137*(1), 12–32.

Machado, S., Paes, F., Velasques, B., Teixeira, S., Piedade, R., Ribeiro, P., . . . Arias-Carrión, O. (2012). Is rTMS an effective therapeutic strategy that can be used to treat anxiety disorder? *Neuropharmacology, 62*(1),125–134.

Margoob, M. A., Ali, Z., & Andrade, C. (2010). Efficacy of ECT in chronic, severe, antidepressant- and CBT-refractory PTSD: An open, prospective study. *Brain Stimulation, 3*(1), 28–35. doi: 10.1016/j.brs.2009.04.005

Marin, M., Camprodon, J. A., Dougherty, D. D., & Milad, M. R. (2014). Device-based brain stimulation to augment fear extinction: Implications for PTSD treatment and beyond. *Depression and Anxiety, 31*(4), 269–278. doi: 10.1002/da.22252

Matar, M. A., Zohar, J., Kaplan, Z., & Cohen, H. (2009). Alprazolam treatment immediately after stress exposure interferes with the normal HPA-stress response and increases vulnerability to subsequent stress in an animal model of PTSD. *European Neuropsychopharmacology, 19*(4), 283–295.

Mehta, D., Klengel, T., Conneely, K. N., Smith, A. K., Altmann, A., Pace, T. W., & Binder, E. B. (2013). Childhood maltreatment is associated with distinct genomic and epigenetic profiles in posttraumatic stress disorder. *Proceedings of the National Academy of Sciences, 110*(20), 8302–8307. doi: 10.1073/pnas.1217750110

Moody, T. D., Sasaki, M. A., Bohon, C., Strober, M. A., Bookheimer, S. Y., Sheen, C. L., & Feusner, J. D. (2015). Functional connectivity for face processing in individuals with body dysmorphic disorder and anorexia nervosa. *Psychological Medicine, 45*(16), 3491–3503. doi: 10.1017/s0033291715001397

Murad, A. (1999). Orbitofrontal syndrome in psychiatry. *Encephale, 25*(6), 634–637.

Myers, A. J., Williams, L., Gatt, J. M., McAuley-Clark, E. Z., Dobson-Stone, C., Schofield, P. R., & Nemeroff, C. B. (2014). Variation in the oxytocin receptor gene is associated with increased risk for anxiety, stress and depression in individuals with a history of exposure to early life stress. *Journal of Psychiatric Research, 59*, 93–100. doi: 10.1016/j.jpsychires.2014.08.021

Nemeroff, C. (2016). Paradise lost: The neurobiological and clinical consequences of child abuse and neglect. *Neuron, 89*(5), 892–909. doi: 10.1016/j.neuron.2016.01.019

Nestler, E. J., Hyman, S. E., & Malenka, R. C. (2009). *Molecular neuropharmacology: A foundation for clinical neuroscience* (2nd Ed.). New York, NY: McGraw-Hill.

Novakovic, V., Sher, L., Lapidus, K. A., Mindes, J., Golier, J. A., & Yehuda, R. (2011). Brain stimulation in posttraumatic stress disorder. *European Journal of Psychotraumatology, 2*, 5609. doi: 10.3402/ejpt.v2i0.5609

Opel, N., Redlich, R., Zwanzger, P., Grotegerd, D., Arolt, V., Heindel, W., & Dannlowski, U. (2014). Hippocampal atrophy in major depression: A function of childhood maltreatment rather than diagnosis? *Neuropsychopharmacology, 39*(12), 2723–2731. doi:10.1038/npp.2014.145

O'Reardon, J. P., Solvason, H. B., Janicak, P. G., Sampson, S., Isenberg, K. E., Nahas, Z., . . . Sackeim, H. A. (2007). Efficacy and safety of transcranial magnetic stimulation in the acute treatment of major depression: A multisite randomized controlled trial. *Biological Psychiatry, 62*(11), 1208–1216.

Ouellet-Morin, I., Odgers, C. L., Danese, A., Bowes, L., Shakoor, S., Papadopoulos, A. S., . . . Arseneault, L. (2011). Blunted cortisol responses to stress signal social and behavioral problems among maltreated/bullied 12-year-old children. *Biological Psychiatry, 70*(11), 1016–1023.

Pesonen, A. K., Räikkönen, K., Feldt, K., Heinonen, K., Osmond, C., Phillips, D. I., . . . Kajantie, E. (2010). Childhood separation experience predicts HPA axis hormonal responses in late adulthood: A natural experiment of World War II. *Psychoneuroendocrinology, 35*(5), 758–767. doi: 10.1016/j.psyneuen.2009.10.017

Petrides, G., Fink, M., Husain, M. M., Knapp, R. G., Rush, A. J., Mueller, M., . . . Kellner, C. H. (2001). ECT remission rates in psychotic versus non-psychotic depressed patients: A report from CORE. *Journal of ECT, 17*, 244–253.

Philip, N. S., Ridout, S. J., Albright, S. E., Sanchez, G., & Carpenter, L. L. (2016). 5-Hz transcranial magnetic stimulation for comorbid posttraumatic stress disorder and major depression. *Journal of Traumatic Stress, 29*(1), 93–96. doi: 10.1002/jts.22065

Provençal, N., & Binder, E. B. (2015). The effects of early life stress on the epigenome: From the womb to adulthood and even before. *Experimental Neurology, 268*, 10–20.

Qi, W., Gevonden, M., & Shalev, A. (2016). Prevention of post-traumatic stress disorder after trauma: Current evidence and future directions. *Current Psychiatry Reports, 18*, 20.

Reiter, K., Andersen, S. B., & Carlsson, J. (2016). Neurofeedback treatment and posttraumatic stress disorder. *Journal of Nervous and Mental Disease, 204*, 69–77.

Reznikov, R., Binko, M., Nobrega, J. N., & Hamani, C. (2016). Deep brain stimulation in animal models of fear, anxiety, and posttraumatic stress disorder. *Neuropsychopharmacology, 41*(12), 2810–2817. doi: 10.1038/npp.2016.34

Rinne, T., de Kloet, E. R., Wouters, L., Goekoop, J. G., DeRijk, R. H., & van den Brink, W. (2002). Hyperresponsiveness of hypothalamic-pituitary-adrenal axis to combined dexamethasone/corticotropin-releasing hormone challenge in female borderline personality disorder subjects with a history of sustained childhood abuse. *Biological Psychiatry, 52*, 1102–1112.

Roberts, N. P., Kitchiner, N. J., Kenardy, J., & Bisson, J. I. (2010). Early psychological interventions to treat acute traumatic stress symptoms. *Cochrane Database of Systematic Reviews, 3*, CD007944.

Saunders, N., Downham, R., Turman, B., Kropotov, J., Clark, R., Yumash, R., & Szatmary, A. (2015). Working memory training with tDCS improves behavioral and neurophysiological symptoms in pilot group with post-traumatic stress disorder (PTSD) and with poor working memory. *Neurocase, 21*, 271–278. doi: 10.1080/13554794.2014.890727

Schiepek, G., Tominschek, I., Heinzel, S., Aigner, M., Dold, M., Unger, A., . . . Karch, S. (2013). Discontinuous patterns of brain activation in the psychotherapy process of obsessive-compulsive disorder: Converging results from repeated fMRI and daily self-reports. *PLoS ONE, 8*(8), e71863.

Schmahl, C., Kleindienst, N., Limberger, M., Ludäscher, P., Mauchnik, J., Deibler, P., & Bohus, M. (2012). Evaluation of naltrexone for dissociative symptoms in borderline personality disorder. *International Clinical Psychopharmacology, 27*, 61–68.

Smith, C. P., & Freyd, J. J. (2014). Institutional betrayal. *American Psychologist, 69*, 575–587.

Solvason, H. B., Husain, M., Fitzgerald, P. B., Rosenquist, P., McCall, W. V., Kimball, J., . . . Lisanby, S. H. (2014). Improvement in quality of life with left prefrontal transcranial magnetic stimulation in patients with pharmacoresistant major depression: Acute and six month outcomes. *Brain Stimulation, 7*, 219–225. doi: 10.1016/j.brs.2013.10.008

Spitzer, C., Willert, C., Grabe, H., Rizos, T., Möller, B., & Freyberger, H. J. (2004). Dissociation, hemispheric asymmetry, and dysfunction of hemispheric interaction: A transcranial magnetic stimulation approach. *Journal of Neuropsychiatry and Clinical Neurosciences, 16*, 163–169. doi: 10.1176/jnp.16.2.163

Stevens, F. L., Hurley, R. A., & Taber, K. H. (2011). Anterior cingulate cortex: Unique role in cognition and emotion. *Journal of Neuropsychiatry and Clinical Neuroscience, 23*, 121–125.

Suderman, M., Borghol, N., Pappas, J., Pereira, S., Pembrey, M., Hertzman, C., & Szyf, M. (2014). Childhood abuse is associated with methylation of multiple loci in adult DNA. *BMC Medical Genomics, 7*, 13. doi: 10.1186/1755-8794-7-13

Taghva, A., Silvetz, R., Ring, A., Kim, K. A., Murphy, K. T., Liu, C. Y., & Jin, Y. (2015). Magnetic resonance therapy improves clinical phenotype and EEG alpha power in posttraumatic stress disorder. *Trauma Monthly, 20*, e27360. doi: 10.5812/traumamon.27360

Teicher, M. H., Anderson, C. M., Ohashi, K., & Polcari, A. (2014). Childhood maltreatment: Altered network centrality of cingulate, precuneus, temporal pole and insula. *Biological Psychiatry, 76*, 297–305.

Tolomeo, S., Christmas, D., Jentzsch, I., Johnston, B., Sprengelmeyer, R., Matthews, K., & Steele, J. D. (2016). A causal role for the anterior mid-cingulate cortex in negative affect and cognitive control. *Brain, 139*, 1844–1854.

Trevizol, A. P., Barros, M. D., Silva, P. O., Osuch, E., Cordeiro, Q., & Shiozawa, P. (2016). Transcranial magnetic stimulation for posttraumatic stress disorder: An updated systematic review and meta-analysis. *Trends in Psychiatry and Psychotherapy, 38*, 50–55. doi: 10.1590/2237-6089-2015-0072

Urquiza, A., & Keating, L. M. (1990). The presence of sexual victimization of males. In Hunter, M. (Ed.), *The sexually abused male, Vol. 1* (pp. 89–103). Lexington, MA: Lexington Books

Vaseghi, B., Zoghi, M., & Jaberzadeh, S. (2015). A meta-analysis of site-specific effects of cathodal transcranial direct current stimulation on sensory perception and pain. *PLOS ONE, 10*. doi: 10.1371/journal.pone.0123873

Zer-Aviv, T. M., Segev, A., & Akirav, I (2016). Cannabinoids and post-traumatic stress disorder: Clinical and preclinical evidence for treatment and prevention. *Behavioral Pharmacology, 27*, 561–569. doi: 10.1097/FBP.0000000000000253

Zhang, T. Y., Labonté, B., Wen, X. L., Turecki, G., & Meaney, J. M. (2013). *Neuropsychopharmacology Reviews, 38*, 111–123. doi: 10.1038/npp.2012.149

Chapter 6

Brain circuitries, brain apps, cultural software, and the inner worlds of sexually abused males

A new framework for understanding, healing, and happiness

James W. Hopper

There are many ways of understanding and treating men who suffer from the consequences of childhood sexual abuse. Here I offer a framework that is focused on men's inner worlds and bridges neuroscience and Internal Family Systems (IFS). Also fundamental to the framework are Buddhist and other contemplative psychologies and the sociology and psychology of masculine gender socialization.

Central to this framework is a metaphor of "apps" running on "circuitries" of our brains. I begin by discussing some key brain circuitries that undergird human experiences and motivations, and then some fundamental cycles of suffering, healing, and happiness. Next I summarize some key concepts of IFS and introduce the metaphor of the "parts" described by IFS as apps running on our brains and briefly explain how masculine gender socialization shapes those apps. Finally, I discuss how accessing universal capacities for love and wisdom can transform inner families of parts, and the key circuitries on which they run, to bring healing and happiness to traumatized people and specifically men with histories of child sexual abuse.

Brain hardware: key circuitries

The human brain is incredibly complex, consisting of many interconnected circuitries that perform many functions. ("Circuitry" simply means a collection of brain areas that work together to perform certain functions.) But some circuitries and functions are more fundamental than others, and some of those can be subjectively experienced, understood, and deliberately influenced by us. Those fundamental, accessible, and workable circuitries are the ones I teach about, in ways consistent with perennial teachings of contemplatives and "psychologists" from humanity's philosophical, religious, and spiritual traditions.

These fundamental circuitries and their most important interactions are described in more depth elsewhere (Hopper, 2014) and only summarized here. Two of the most important are the brain circuitries involved in *fear and aversion*, on the one hand, and *wanting and seeking*, on the other. These are among the best studied circuitries in neuroscience, and the bases of what Buddhist psychology and other contemplative traditions have long taught are two fundamental sources of suffering: aversion and craving. Critically, the activities of these two circuitries can be objects of not only attention and investigation (What am I fearing? What am I seeking?), but conscious and deliberate influence – in therapy offices, on meditation cushions, and in the passing moments of our daily lives.

Fear and aversion circuitry. The fear and aversion circuitry includes not only the amygdala, but also hypothalamic and brain stem regions (LeDoux, 2000, 2012). It is always on, monitoring the external and internal worlds for signs of danger or attack, or even just indications that things aren't going as expected, which could be a harbinger of something unwanted, threatening, or dangerous. Anything that's aversive at all – an unpleasantly tense neck muscle, a twinge of embarrassment – triggers the activation of this circuitry. For anyone experiencing suffering, including from long-term effects of childhood trauma, the circuitry of fear and aversion is continually triggered by unpleasant and unwanted memories, feelings and bodily sensations.

Seeking circuitry. The seeking circuitry is always on too. Indeed, it's fundamental to survival and engaging with life. We wouldn't get out of bed in the morning, drink water, or eat meals without this circuitry propelling us forward to do and get what we need. We wouldn't seek out conversations or get our work done. Anything we want and seek triggers and channels the activity of this circuitry (Alcaro & Panksepp, 2011). Importantly, and consistent with research on this dopaminergic seeking circuitry (e.g., Salamone & Correa, 2012), seeking can be deliberate and effortful, or automatic and habitual (including compulsive). And while the seeking circuitry is mostly studied for its involvement in addiction, it also enables us to pursue our highest values and goals, and supports our deepest longings. However, as addressed below, the circuitry of wanting and seeking is often driven by fear and aversion, dominated by attempts to avoid and escape suffering, especially in traumatized people.

Satisfaction circuitry. Most clinicians, especially those working with addictions, have heard of the "reward circuitry." But few understand that the reward circuitry can parsed into two interconnected circuitries, those of seeking and satisfaction. While the seeking circuitry is a dopaminergic circuitry involved in wanting, seeking, craving, and clinging to what is wanted, the *satisfaction circuitry* is an opioid circuitry that is activated by the satisfaction of getting what we were seeking, and by experiences of contentment or fulfillment, including in safe and loving connection with another person (e.g., Nelson & Panksepp, 1998). (The term "seeking circuitry" was coined by the influential neuroscientist Jaak Panksepp; "satisfaction circuitry" by me.) Extensive research indicates that, depending on the state of the organism, activation of the opioid satisfaction circuitry is associated with comfort or joy (Loseth, Ellingsen, & Leknes, 2014). Comfort is a calm state that may be elicited by connecting with someone in a soothing way; joy an excited state often experienced by connecting with others in playful ways. Not surprisingly, given how good comfort and joy feel in our bodies, some people, including traumatized men who lack supportive and enjoyable relationships, seek opiate pain pills or heroin to pharmacologically induce such states.

The seeking and satisfaction circuitries are distinct but also intertwined (or partly "co-localized" as neuroscientists say). Indeed, the circuitries of seeking and satisfaction are continually activated in small and potentially large ways, and continually activated in cycles of alternation, on timescales from very brief (e.g. noticing an itch, scratching it, and feeling relief) to very long (e.g. longing for a life partner, finding one, and finally getting married). We repeatedly seek things we need or want, and repeatedly have experiences of satisfying (or not), to some degree or another, the needs and wants we have sought to fulfill. As the Buddha and other sages have always pointed out, the typical human condition entails an underlying sense of dissatisfaction (or quiet desperation, as Thoreau put it), which drives habitual and compulsive seeking of things and experiences that, alas, cannot satisfy our deepest needs and longings. Traumatized people – including men struggling with severe child abuse-related symptoms such as anxiety, depression, dissociation, and anger – experience very little satisfaction in their lives and relationships.

Embodiment circuitry. I use the term *embodiment circuitry* to refer to the circuitry that allows us to know how it feels to be in our bodies, in the present moment, as sensations and emotions arise and pass away. Neuroscientists have intensively studied this circuitry over the past 15 years, and typically call it the "interoceptive" circuitry (e.g., Craig, 2002; Singer, Critchley, & Preuschoff, 2009). But for many people, especially clinicians and their clients, that Latinate term is too abstract and doesn't convey the visceral nature and immediacy of how it feels to be an embodied consciousness.

So much of human suffering comes down to unpleasant, unwanted, and painful sensations of embodiment. So many of our efforts to be free of suffering involve seeking to avoid and escape unwanted experiences of embodiment; seeking out bodily sensations that we find pleasurable; or seeking experiences that push away or obliterate unwanted sensations. Embodied experiences of vulnerability – for example sadness, shame, and fear – are intolerable for many people, especially men who have not yet healed from childhood abuse. Many men are unable even to recognize, let alone admit, such feelings and sensations within themselves, and go to great lengths to avoid and escape them. But feeling strong and powerful in their bodies – in angry, aggressive, or other dominant states, whether in intimate relationships, at work, driving car, or firing a gun – *those* are experiences of embodiment that feel safe and "right" to most males.

Default mode circuitry. Like the embodiment circuitry, the brain's "default mode" circuitry has been a subject of intensive study over the past 15 years (e.g., Buckner & Vincent, 2007; Gusnard & Raichle, 2001). This circuitry (sometimes with support from other circuitries, e.g., Fox, Spreng, Ellamil, Andrews-Hanna, & Christoff, 2015) is responsible for what our minds do, by default, when we're not highly engaged with the external environment or attempting to solve some immediate problem. Our minds wander through thoughts, memories, fantasies, and plans about things that are relevant to us – what's "on our minds," things we fear, need, and want (Smallwood & Schooler, 2015). It's the inner chatter and imagery that we slip right into with little or no reflective awareness, whenever our attention and thinking aren't demanded by some other activity – and even when we are trying to focus on something else (McKiernan, D'Angelo, Kaufman, & Binder, 2006). Anyone who has meditated knows just how incessant and ingrained such default mode thought processes are.

The default mode circuitry is the core group of brain areas on which such thought processes "run," like software apps on a computer processor. For men with histories of childhood sexual abuse, this circuitry is often occupied by thoughts of others' betrayals and their own failures; by memories of shame and compensatory fantasies of masculine power, control, and domination; and finally by typical human plans and hopes for success, acceptance, recognition, and perhaps even love – although such thoughts often lead right back to memories and fears of failing to get them.

Executive circuitry. By now some readers will have noticed the absence of any discussion of the brain's prefrontal cortex or "executive" circuitry. Certainly that is a very important circuitry responsible for rational thought; deliberate regulation of attention, emotions, and impulses; interpersonal empathy and attunement; self-observation and insight. Daniel Siegel (e.g., 2010) has written extensively about this circuitry, its functions, and how its capacities can be cultivated for healing and fulfilling relationships. Thanks to him, most clinicians interested in the brain need no introduction to the executive circuitry.

My work is focused on brain circuitries – especially seeking, satisfaction, and embodiment – that play central roles in motivated thoughts and behaviors, including habitual ones with no executive circuitry involvement. Those circuitries can be accessed and harnessed by therapeutic and contemplative practices to transform suffering and foster healing, happiness, and fulfillment. While such accessing and harnessing can be facilitated by the prefrontal cortex, in my framework it is *the dynamic relationships among those circuitries* that is most fundamental to suffering, healing, and happiness – not the executive circuitry and whatever it may or may not be doing.

Brain-based cycles of suffering, healing, and happiness

As explained elsewhere (Hopper, 2014) and only summarized here, the circuitries of fear, seeking, and embodiment are implicated in suffering of all kinds, including posttraumatic suffering, and healing necessarily involves harnessing those circuitries, especially seeking and embodiment, in positive ways.

All of us experience unwanted memories and feelings, on our own and in interactions with others. For those who have been abused and betrayed, the most unwanted and aversive experiences tend to be associated with feeling vulnerable – e.g., weak, dominated, helpless, sad, ashamed – all of which are antithetical to how boys and men are "supposed" to feel and present themselves to others. Such experiences are greatly feared, and motivations to avoid and escape them are strong. Indeed, the thoughts and behaviors of traumatized people, including men struggling with the impacts of sexual abuse, are often dominated (both consciously and unconsciously) by seeking to avoid and escape from such experiences.

Cycles of suffering. I have described (Hopper, 2014) two basic "suffering cycles," one associated with fear and anxiety and the other with depression, defeat, and demoralization. In the *fear and anxiety* suffering cycle the circuitry of fear is highly active, and the seeking circuitry is not only strongly activated, but focused on – even enslaved to – avoiding and escaping what is feared, including sensations of fear and anxiety that occupy the embodiment circuitry. We see this all the time in fearful and anxious traumatized males who habitually and compulsively seek escape from their suffering with alcohol and drug intoxication, compulsive pornography use, and power trips of all kinds, from angry outbursts to aggressive dominance at home and work. What makes this a *cycle*: the seeking circuitry is focused on avoiding and escaping the fear and anxiety, but what is sought does not bring healing, only temporary relief, and often more problems and suffering.

In the other fundamental cycle of suffering, *depression/defeat*, the circuitries of fear and seeking are both suppressed (Salamone, Koychev, Correa, & McGuire, 2015; Treadway & Zald, 2011). What's feared has already come to pass. The person is overwhelmed, feels defeated, lacks motivation, and is demoralized too – not only because he lacks energy and motivation to pursue anything he truly values, but because he has been "failing" to live up to his own ideals. In this cycle, the embodiment circuitry is occupied by unpleasant sensations that accompany the lethargy and anguish of depression. The seeking circuitry is suppressed, but not completely, otherwise the person would engage in no motivated behavior at all. Its activity tends to be weak, for example, as someone listlessly surfs porn for hours, or sporadic, such as occasionally getting out of bed just long enough to have a few beers or bong hits. Again, we have all encountered this depression/defeat cycle in some of our therapy clients, and perhaps in ourselves. (It is also possible to suffer from "anxious depression," a mixture of these two suffering cycles.)

Consistent with the Buddha's observation that craving (i.e., seeking based on ignorance and confusion) is the single most fundamental source of human suffering, we can see that whenever fear or aversion arise they always and automatically lead to *wanting to avoid or escape* what is feared or aversive. You can't have aversion activated without such wanting and seeking immediately following. An itch arises and we want to scratch it. Shame arises and we try to disappear. A terrible abuse memory is triggered and a man seeks to get high or to feel powerful by flying into a rage. The wanting and craving to avoid or escape are functions of the seeking circuitry, even if they only play out mentally, via imagination or dissociation.

Deliberate versus habitual seeking. As noted above, the seeking circuitry itself has sub-circuitries: one for deliberate and effortful seeking, and another for automatically triggered, habitual, and even compulsive forms of seeking, which can occur outside of awareness (e.g., Everitt & Robbins, 2016). For example, we may exert conscious effort to push a bad memory from awareness; we may automatically start thinking about more pleasant things; or we may habitually dissociate by spacing out. We can go to great lengths over days or weeks to avoid a feared situation, or we can act on a sudden impulsive urge, for example by blurting out something, anything, to derail a conversation that's heading to a scary place. Also, habitual and compulsive seeking behaviors usually develop from initially deliberate and effortful ones. Indeed, this transition literally involves a shift from the sub-circuitry responsible for deliberate and effortful seeking to the sub-circuitry responsible for habitual and stimulus-response based seeking (Balleine & O'Doherty, 2010).

Even if we don't know the underlying brain bases, we all recognize that learning a new skill requires deliberate, effortful, and repeated practice until the skill has become a habitual behavior that can arise automatically when needed. This is true in sports, music, and work; in friendships, intimate relationships, and parenting; and in therapy, e.g., skills for regulating trauma-related emotions and impulses. For those engaged in mindfulness or more intensive Vipassana meditation practice, the skills that require effort but can become habitual include those for observing the moment-to-moment arising and passing away of conditioned and habitual emotions and thoughts, fear and aversion, and wanting, seeking, craving, and clinging.

Cycles of healing and happiness. Again, the fundamental brain-based cycles of healing and happiness are described elsewhere (Hopper, 2014) and summarized here, with some new elaborations.

The healing cycle of *seeking to engage and transform suffering* involves harnessing the seeking circuitry to turning toward suffering, not away from it (as in the suffering cycles), and engaging with suffering in ways that bring healing. This begins with seeking and acquiring support, understanding, and skills that will enable one's engagement with suffering to be healing rather than harmful and re-traumatizing. This cycle includes comforting experiences of embodiment, even in the midst of painful memories and emotions; and activation of the satisfaction circuitry, during experiences of soothing and compassion, even gratitude and joy. This is a healing *cycle* because seeking and acquiring the resources to engage fruitfully with suffering, and experiencing the resulting transformations of suffering into vehicles for healing and opening one's heart, is profoundly satisfying and thereby reinforcing of the effortful and increasingly habitual seeking behaviors of these kinds. Anyone who has benefited from therapy, and witnessed one's therapy clients benefiting from it, has seen this cycle play out.

This healing cycle is also central to humanity's great religious traditions, including those currently less trendy than Buddhism. The redemptive potential of suffering is an essential principle of Christianity. In Judaism the principle of *tikkun olam* requires open-hearted engagement with human suffering and brokenness in order to "repair the world." Rumi, the great Sufi Islamic poet, has written that "through love all that is bitter will be sweet" and "through love all pain will turn to medicine."

For men with histories of childhood abuse, especially sexual abuse that may undermine their sense of being "real men," engaging in this healing cycle of seeking to engage and transform suffering can foster a new and liberating understanding of what it means to be a man who is strong and powerful. They discover that true strength and power are not about suppressing and denying one's vulnerability and suffering, but courageously (with the right support) engaging with them, and thereby transforming them and coming to embody the truly good power and strength of being a compassionate, loving, and more genuinely happy man. (They also discover that the traditional "masculine" power to defend oneself and one's loved ones from attack and harm is not lost but enhanced.)

The other fundamental cycle of healing and happiness is *seeking true goods*. In this cycle the seeking circuitry is harnessed to seeking what is truly good for one's body, mind, and relationships; what is truly satisfying and fulfilling; and what brings human flourishing and genuine happiness, not the fleeting happiness of cheap (or expensive) thrills or quick-fix escapes. Seeking is focused on finding and embracing true goods, including love, wisdom, play, creativity, peace, freedom, and one's highest moral and spiritual ideals. The *seeking true goods* cycle includes experiences of comfort and joy, within oneself and in relationships with others, which involve activation of the opioid satisfaction circuitry and occupation of the embodiment circuitry with pleasant sensations. In the most healthy and optimal functioning of this cycle, the pleasant bodily sensations of experiencing true goods are not craved, grasped, or clung to; they are experienced, with gratitude, as satisfying in and of themselves, even in their transience.

Although nothing impermanent can be ultimately satisfying (a central insight of Buddhist and other contemplative traditions), genuinely satisfying experiences of true goods have the effect of decreasing both aversion and craving, via effects of the mu-opioid satisfaction circuitry on the circuitries of aversion and seeking (Colasanti, Rabiner, Lingford-Hughes, & Nutt, 2011; Love, Stohler, & Zubieta, 2009). The modulated seeking circuitry is then more easily harnessed to seeking true goods, which can bring a self-perpetuating cycle in which seeking true goods brings genuine satisfaction, which facilitates focusing the seeking circuitry on the pursuit of true goods (Hopper, 2014).

A contemporary psychotherapy that fosters seeking of true goods is Acceptance and Commitment Therapy (ACT), in which therapists help clients sort through and discover their values, *commit to seeking and embodying* those values they find most important, and then act on those commitments (Follette & Pistorello, 2007; Harris, 2009). For men with histories of sexual abuse, integrating a critique of traditional masculine gender socialization (Lisak, 1995), and exploring what it truly means to be a good human being (as opposed to a "good man" in the culturally limited sense), can play huge roles in the seeking true goods cycle of healing and happiness. Although religions can reinforce limiting gender stereotypes, they can also promote values and ways of being that are truly good and worthy of seeking (even worshipping) and embodying in our lives; and contemplative and spiritual practices can connect us to supreme moral and spiritual qualities and capacities.

But as sages have always cautioned, when seeking – even for the greatest goods – is colored by craving, grasping, or clinging, it contributes to suffering. To use "spiritual" thinking and practices to avoid engaging with one's suffering, in the naive belief the one can simply "transcend" that suffering (which really means escape it), is to attempt a "spiritual bypass," which never succeeds. And if that's true of potentially transformative spiritual practices, it's certainly true for other true goods: they can be sought in ways that perpetuate suffering. Indeed, it is all too human to seek something genuinely good with an underlying motivation of attempting to escape what we experience as bad; to tell ourselves and perhaps try to impress upon others that our motives are only noble when in fact we are mainly seeking to escape suffering (e.g., "peace" activists driven by outrage). As T. S. Eliot wrote in *Four Quartets* (1968), "The last temptation is the greatest treason: To do the right deed for the wrong reason." Or as Tibetan Buddhist sages continually ask their students, "What is your *motivation*?"

From deliberate to habitual seeking. In both of the healing cycles, there is a progression from deliberate and effortful to habitual seeking. Initially, seeking to engage with one's suffering requires not only support and skillful methods, but also great effort (and courage) to overcome one's fear and aversion. But over time, whether a course of therapy or years of disciplined meditation practice, skills for open-heartedly engaging with and thereby transforming one's suffering can become new habits. Those habits can become second nature, elicited automatically when needed, or accessed with a nudge from the brain's executive circuitry[1] (and some prefrontal executive functions are themselves acquired habits).

Brain circuitries and cycles that we can attend and harness

These brain circuitries and cycles are not just theoretical ideas consistent with neuroscience findings and phenomena we can recognize in our therapy clients. These key brain circuitries' functioning can be directly attended *in our own experience* as they activate and interact in cycles of suffering, healing, and happiness. Indeed, phenomenological inquiry is the essence of contemplative insight into the operations of our minds and brains, but

1 Such habits can also be elicited by a supportive word, look, or touch from a loved one or other trusted and empathic person.

"mindfulness" as typically conceptualized in the West does not fully address the insights that meditation can bring (e.g., Grabovac, Lau, & Willet, 2001; Grossman & van Dam, 2011). It is possible to observe the cycles of suffering, healing, and happiness unfolding moment-to-moment in the stream of mental and brain functioning. We can learn to observe – within fractions of a second of our brain registering external or internal phenomena – the arising of aversion and fear; of wanting and seeking, with or without craving or clinging; of urges, impulses, and other behavioral options; and of intentions and choices to enact a cued-up cognitive or behavioral option, based on a split-second appraisal of those options as "good" or "bad."

Of course, while such direct experiential learning about how our minds and brains function is possible and powerful, the reality is that most of us do not engage in intensive meditation practice, and many of our clients are neither motivated nor ready to do so safely. However, there are other and easier ways to observe, investigate, and work with the fundamental brain circuitries discussed here, and with the cycles of suffering, healing, and happiness in which those circuitries play central roles. One is the Internal Family Systems (IFS) model and its methods for accessing the love, wisdom, and other qualities that enable us to understand and heal our "internal families" (for the most concise and clear introduction to IFS, see Schwartz, 2001). Following are a brief introduction to some key IFS concepts and an integration of my circuitries and cycles framework with the IFS model, which is then applied to understanding men suffering from the consequences of childhood sexual abuse and to helping them heal and find happiness.

Internal Family Systems: "parts" and "self"

Those who embrace the IFS model claim – point out, we could say – that personality and identity are not unitary but entail multiple "parts" that function as more or less complex subpersonalities.[2] For example, we

2 For those familiar with it, the construct of "self-states" in the dissociation literature may seem equivalent to or better than "parts." This is not the case. First, as explained below, in IFS "parts" are not states, but rather relatively autonomous organizations of mental and brain activity that are often activated *simultaneously*, not one-at-a-time as discrete states that arise and pass away. Second, because in IFS the concept of "Self" is central, and has a very different meaning than "self" in various other literatures familiar to clinicians (including the dissociation literature), using the term "self-states" as synonymous with "parts" would be confusing and distracting.

experience a "part" of us that feels one way about a person or situation and another "part" that feels very differently. After doing something inconsistent with our values, we think "I hate that part of me." We have parts of us that we want to be seen and admired, parts skillful at navigating the world of work, and parts that courageously rise to the occasion. We also have parts that we try to keep hidden, that feel pathetic, lash out in rage, or have wants or needs we find shameful. According to IFS, we each have our own "internal family" of parts, which not only play particular roles but also have *relationships with each other*.

According to IFS, these are not just figures of speech, things we sometimes say to ourselves, or metaphors for how the mind works. Nor is it pathological to have parts. It is simply an aspect of how human minds are organized – at least how they self-organize as we develop from infants cycling through basic psychophysiological states with help from caregivers into complex and multifaceted children and adults embedded in families, communities, and cultures. That this is so, we can discover for ourselves, especially with the help of IFS's concepts and tools.

Three extreme roles parts can play. According to IFS, we all have a variety of parts, but there are three types of extreme roles that some parts are forced into playing when we experience overwhelming trauma or other wounding, and so long as we have not healed from those experiences and their impacts. Wounded parts or *exiles* are the parts of us that hold painful memories and emotions associated with wounds and traumas, from loss and neglect to abuse and violence. *Managers* are the most competent parts of us, including personas we present to the world; they are protector parts that work proactively to keep in exile those parts that hold unpleasant, unwanted, frightening, and otherwise potentially overwhelming memories and feelings. Finally, *firefighters* are reactive protector parts that spring into action when managers have failed to keep an exile at bay (e.g., when an abuse memory strongly intrudes, or when intoxication impairs the prefrontal cortex functioning on which managers depend to maintain control). Again, these are extreme roles parts can play, not their essential nature. Indeed, even the most extreme parts are malleable and, when met with curiosity, compassion, courage, and other universal human capacities (called *Self Energy* in IFS, see below), can transform into – or, we might say, reveal themselves as – forces for good.

We can see that managers, firefighters, and exiles manifest in the lives of our clients. Joe, who has a history of childhood sexual abuse, was having a great run at his new job. Then, on the very day he had just received a wonderful three-month review, his boss criticized him in front of a coworker for missing a minor deadline. Joe suddenly "lost it," screamed at his boss, and stormed out of the building. Only days later in therapy did Joe recognize that his outburst was an attempt to squash overwhelming feelings of shame and humiliation, first experienced during sexual abuse by a coach, that were triggered by his boss's comment. A manager part had been handling work really well, but when that comment elicited the exiled part of him that holds the feelings of shame and humiliation, a firefighter came out to douse those flames of emotion. And, like many men, especially traumatized men who struggle with anger and aggression, in the moment before losing it he was not conscious of feeling shame, except perhaps for a fraction of a second in the periphery of his awareness, before the angry part of him popped up to take over the brain circuitries that control speech and movement.

Or consider Mark, who was sexually abused by his mother from ages 5 to 7. For a week or so his wife had been stressed by a conflict with an old friend, and he was proud of how supportive he had been to her. But then he started hearing a voice in his head, in the middle of conversations with her, saying things like, "she's so pathetic," "why can't she just patch things up or toss her 'friend' aside," and "will you just shut up about this!" He then noticed another voice saying things like, "All she does is talk about this fight with her friend. She doesn't even care about me. She's just using me!" Hearing those thoughts, and the feeling of being abandoned and exploited (rooted in the abuse by his mother), in turn triggered feelings of shame and still another voice: "You're a terrible husband, she should have left you a long time ago, and if you don't stop being such a self-centered baby she may leave you yet. And you'll deserve it!"

Relationships among extreme parts in inner families. As noted above, the different parts of our inner families have relationships with each other, just like people in families. In the case of Mark, we can see how some extreme parts of him trigger the activation of other parts, and how parts have feelings and thoughts about other parts. Thus after days of a relatively helpful (manager) part of him genuinely supporting his wife, not only does the (exile) part of him that feels abandoned and exploited get activated, it in turn triggers the (firefighter) part that sees his wife as pathetic and wants to scream "shut up," and then both of those parts in turn activate a self-critical (also firefighter) part that seeks to punish and suppress those parts with cruel thoughts, including how she could leave him if those parts aren't suppressed. On and on, round and round, the parts inside of us and our clients relate to each other in such ways, as we can overhear in the arguments and debates that sometimes dominate our default mode circuitry.

IFS focuses on *polarized* internal family systems of extreme parts characterized by a lot of suffering, especially posttraumatic suffering, in which parts play *extreme* roles, both internally, in their relationships with each other, and externally, especially in relationships with other people (and their parts). As explored further below, all parts have wants and fears, which determine what they seek, including what they seek to avoid and escape – again, in both internal relationships among parts and their impacts on external behaviors and relationships.

The Self. The most important insights and benefits of the IFS model, however, are not about these inner "parts," but rather what IFS refers to as the "Self." As described by Schwartz:

> I find that as people focus on – and, in the process of doing that, separate from – their extreme [parts], they spontaneously manifest qualities that make for good leadership, both internally and externally. It seems that we all have qualities like curiosity, compassion, calmness, confidence, courage, clarity, creativity and connectedness at our core. It's the soul that spiritual traditions talk about but that most psychotherapies don't know about.
>
> (Schwartz, 2001, p. 12)

Critically, in the context of IFS therapy, these universal positive human qualities and capacities typically emerge when the client brings attention to a part of themselves with the curiosity and compassion that can only arise when their awareness is no longer (a) identified with or attached to the thoughts, feelings, and motives of that part, nor (b) identified with yet another part that has *fear or aversion* toward it.

As Buddhist psychology points out and can be discovered by contemplative investigation, it is seeking (for something to cling to) that underlies our identification with certain aspects of experience, especially self-images or self-concepts, which we mistake for our true identity. It is also a central Buddhist insight that only by decreasing the suffering-causing "poisons" of aversion and craving (and ignorance), via concentration, mindfulness, and other disciplined practices, that we can effectively investigate and gain liberating insight into the nature of our minds. Similarly, but more accessible both conceptually and practically, there are simple but powerful IFS methods that enable people to decrease attachment and aversion sufficiently to dis-identify from (or stop clinging to) their inner parts and access "Self."[3]

The most basic method involves the therapist, while embodying a curious and compassionate state of "Self-leadership" (which creates what Winnicott called a "holding environment"), asking the client to explore, "How do you feel toward that part now?" Answers such as "I agree with it" or "I'm angry at it" reveal that the client has not accessed the qualities of "Self" but instead is still identified with that part or identified with another part that is reacting to it with aversion. But when the client can sincerely answer with a statement like, "I'm wondering why it's so angry" or "I feel sad for it," then the client has gained access to "Self" and the "Self-energy" associated with those universal healing and happiness-bringing qualities of curiosity, compassion, etc.

Much of IFS therapy involves helping clients dis-identify from parts, access the Self and Self-energy, and then exercise Self-leadership as a wise and loving parent or therapist to their own inner family of parts. This includes learning about, appreciating, and validating the well-meaning motivations of protector parts, both proactive managers and reactive firefighters; helping exiles parts feel understood, appreciated, and validated for the pain and suffering they hold; and processing or "unburdening" exiles' old traumas and other wounds. (The "burdens" of exiles may be not only from the clients' individual life, but "legacy burdens" from prior generations, e.g., poverty, war, racism, and other persecutions.) Finally, IFS involves the client's Self (or soul) helping extreme protector parts find new, constructive roles to play in the internal family and in their contributions to thinking and behavior (i.e., roles much more focused on seeking goods than avoiding and escaping pain and suffering). In IFS terms, the overriding aim is to help clients develop

3 Buddhist contemplative methods and those of IFS are complementary and enhance each other's efficacy and benefits. Also, the practices of IFS can be quite rigorous and disciplined.

"Self-leadership," with respect to both their own unique inner families of parts and how they engage with other people, their communities, etc.

Parts as apps, running on circuitries, in cycles

With the foundation above, we can see how what IFS calls "parts" can be understood, metaphorically but quite usefully, as software applications or "apps" that are running on the circuitries of our brains and shaping the fundamental brain-based cycles of suffering, healing, and happiness. This apps-running-on-circuitries metaphor does not imply that parts have a software "code" or programming language, nor that parts or apps have been "programmed" by any person, nor that healing and transforming parts involves "reprogramming" in the sense of writing new code. This metaphor simply describes an observable reality: we all experience "parts" of us that reflect psychobiological states and coherent patterns of brain activity, and these patterns of activity play out across a variety of circuitries and can change over time, in ways small or large. Given the pervasiveness of computers and smartphones in our lives, the widespread interest in the brain bases of experience and behavior, and the considerable knowledge of the key circuitries focused upon here, this metaphor is offered as an accessible, intuitive, and scientifically grounded way to understand our inner worlds and what brings suffering, healing, and happiness in our lives.

The metaphor can be explained in terms of (a) general principles; (b) how specific types of apps run on key circuitries; (c) how relationships between apps are based in patterns of seeking and aversion circuitry activity that create cycles of suffering; and, finally, (d) how access to Self, Self-energy, and Self-leadership harnesses key circuitries to transform the apps and foster cycles of healing and happiness. Table 6.1 presents an overview of how parts or apps in polarized internal family systems access, "run on," and compete to dominate the key brain circuitries focused upon here, and how Self utilizes those same circuitries, particularly to lead and heal the internal family.

General principles. With respect to general principles, one is particularly important: *almost all inner parts or brain apps run at least partly on the circuitry of seeking*. (An exception would be an exile part that is so suppressed or "defeated" that it has no access to the seeking circuitry until granted by Self; see below.) Parts have motivations, that is, they are

Table 6.1 Parts/apps, Self/soul, and key brain circuitry activity in (polarized) Internal Family Systems

	Fear/Aversion	*Seeking*	*Executive*	*Embodiment*	*Satisfaction*	*Default*
Managers	Activated but fear often not acknowledged or conscious; more extreme managers entail greater fear circuitry activation	Proactive, focused on (1) adaptation, competence, acceptance, success, etc., and (2) avoidance of feared, unwanted and vulnerable experiences	Dominate this circuitry	Typically little or no focus on contents, especially sensations of vulnerable feelings; may attend deliberately to functional or pleasing sensations	Typically little or no satisfaction; pleasures mostly anticipatory (i.e., mediated by dopaminergic seeking circuitry, not circuitry of satisfaction)	Continual occupation, dominant voices; constantly planning, fantasizing, worrying, ruminating, etc.; debating and vying for dominance with firefighters, sometimes with exiles
Firefighters	Extreme activation; fear and aversion are dominant motivators	Reactive, extreme activation; almost entirely driven by fear and focused on avoidance of and escape from exiled memories, emotions, and sensations	Transient utilization, impaired (neuro-chemically) by hyper- or hypo-arousal	Intense sensations of cravings, urges and impulses; intense sensations of power, control, pleasure; little or none in dissociative and other numb states	Intense but transient satisfactions of (1) relief at having avoided or escaped unwanted feelings and sensations, or (2) power, control, intoxication, sexual pleasure, etc.	When exiles activated, ranging from little voice issuing warnings or suggesting impulsive acts to loud voice demanding action; fleeting to intense intrusive images of impulses and relief

Exiles	Intense activation with fearful/ anxious exiles, minimal with defeated, depressed, etc.	Minimal or no activation until given access by Self and not squeezed out by manager or firefighter apps	Minimal or none unless facilitated by Self and allowed by other apps	Painful and vulnerable sensations, feelings and emotions, unless accepted by Self and other apps	No activation until part is validated, soothed, supported, able to express needs, and/or "unburdened" by sharing pain	Typically excluded from access but appear as voices and memories of hurt, trauma, sadness, depression, shame, guilt, etc.
Self	Only as activated by parts, which may be granted partial and modulated access by Self	Focused on understanding, love, compassion, kindness, and support of parts and other people; allows parts partial and modulated access	Complete and flexible access as needed, but not identified with or clung to	Whole-body experiences of warmth, connection, energy, softness, tenderness, which are context for bodily sensations associated with parts	Strongly activated by soothing and fulfilling embodied experiences of love, compassion, kindness, acceptance, joy, and gratitude	Complete and flexible access as needed to validate and reassure parts and encourage parts' expression via this circuitry; granting exile apps access and supporting their voices

Each type of "part" (or "app") specified by the Internal Family Systems (IFS) model can be understood as "running on" and at times competing to utilize and dominate key brain circuitries, and the "Self" (or soul) as utilizing those circuitries to lead and heal the internal family.

seeking things or experiences. All kinds of things and experiences, including positive memories and fantasized solutions to one's problems, may be craved, pursued, clung to, or longed for. Parts or apps also have things and experiences they fear and find aversive, thus seek to avoid and escape. Furthermore, in most states parts or apps are *competing* to access and dominate the seeking circuitry – that greatest internal biological driver of thinking and behavior, whether deliberate and effortful or automatic and habitual.

Importantly, to attribute seeking, craving and fearing, and other motivations to parts or apps does not imply that they are autonomous "beings" of some kind or that they have independent existence. Rather, the parts we experience internally can be understood as *organized patterns of brain activity* within and across multiple circuitries, including those of seeking; and we can experience those wants and fears belonging to those parts – especially when we give those parts access to the circuitry supporting inner speech.

Another general principle is that *all parts or apps simultaneously run on multiple circuitries*. For example, manager apps run on the seeking, executive, and default mode circuitries. However, no app runs on the entire brain because, as neuroscientists have long recognized, the brain is a "parallel distributed processor" that is always simultaneously running multiple processes across multiple circuitries and timescales (Rummelhart & McClelland, 1987). Indeed, as with IFS, the apps focused upon here do not include every kind of organized process that can run on human brains, only those with emotional and motivational significance that can become objects of introspective awareness.

One more general principle: *different parts typically compete for access to and control of the same circuitries*. Indeed, more than one part may even "run on" the same circuitry at the same time. For example, more than one manager part can compete for use of the executive circuitry. Or manager and firefighter parts may compete for dominance of the default mode circuitry, which we subjectively experience as an argument between rational and impulsive parts of us or "voices in our heads."

Importantly, to avoid confusion about this metaphor of parts as apps running on the brain, it is critical to understand that no type of part, nor individual part, is identified with any particular brain circuitry. Indeed, as specified by two of the general principles above, all parts or apps simultaneously run on multiple circuitries and different parts typically compete for access to and control of the same brain circuitries (especially in polarized internal systems).

Finally, as described next, each of the three types of parts conceptualized by IFS can be understood as apps that access and influence the activities of the key brain circuitries focused upon here.

Manager parts and circuitries.[4] Managers, as proactive protector parts, tend to dominate the functioning of the executive circuitry of the prefrontal cortex. Indeed, manager parts are the most competent at negotiating social and work relationships and responsibilities *because* they are continually employing the executive functions of selective attention, working memory, reasoning, planning, reality testing, monitoring of thinking and behavior, and switching strategies and tactics as needed. However, distress and physiological arousal associated with exile and/or firefighter activation entail neurochemical processes that disrupt the prefrontal executive functioning on which managers depend (Arnsten, 1998, 2009), and some firefighters compete with managers for dominance of whatever executive functioning remains in such states.

Manager parts or apps also tend to dominate the seeking circuitry, with motivations to carry out all their rational, constructive, and adaptive plans. They seek success of various kinds, including approval and recognition in personal and work relationships. But managers' relationships to the seeking circuitry can be complex. First, as with the executive circuitry, managers fully dominate the seeking circuitry only so long as an activated firefighter is not competing for control of it. For example, a manager part may try to remember how the parenting book said to respond to a screaming 4-year-old, but a firefighter part is causing the seeking circuitry to generate (ultimately irresistible) impulses to thrust a threatening finger and scream, "be quiet *right now* or you're not getting any dessert!" Second, the more polarized an internal system, the more the seeking of managers is driven by fear of the "bad" or unwanted than desire for the "good" and wanted (see suffering cycles, above). For example, at first while writing this chapter I was motivated as much by the fear of missing the editor's deadline as I was by the desire to share something beneficial with readers.

4 See Table 6.1 for an overview of how manager parts or apps, as well as firefighters and exiles in polarized internal family systems, access, "run on," and attempt to dominate each of the key brain circuitries.

Third, the more polarized the internal system the less manager thought processes are characterized by awareness of, or honesty about, what is truly motivating them, in particular about how much they are seeking to avoid what is (unconsciously) feared versus seeking to get the goods on which they are consciously focused. For example, a manager part may say to a spouse who has been talking about an upsetting conflict with a coworker, "I'm *only* trying to help," when in reality that manager part is mostly motivated to get their spouse to stop complaining because that's triggering feelings of helplessness and an exile part that holds those feelings. The spouse isn't fooled, of course, but is feeling dismissed and manipulated, yet the manager part insists otherwise, perhaps in a detached hyper-rational tone of voice. Or, a manager part may seek success at work largely to avoid experiences of failure at home but not recognize or admit it. Indeed, such managers are typical of men who, as encouraged by the culture, focus their lives and identities almost exclusively on work success. Other manager parts or apps seek power and control over others to avoid exiled feelings of being dominated, abandoned, and otherwise hurt and vulnerable, but have no recognition of that main underlying motivation. There are so many ways that we (that is, when we identify with our manager apps) do not recognize or acknowledge the fear-based motivations behind otherwise adaptive and successful (manager) behaviors.

Manager parts' relationships with the default mode circuitry are more straightforward. They are almost continually running on that circuitry (often in concert with the executive circuitry) as they internally generate and revise their many plans, fantasies, and ruminations. Much of our inner chatter consists of manager apps' monologues and dialogues about what we could, should, or will think or do about some person, situation, problem, or goal. However, when firefighters are activated, especially by reminders of past hurts or traumas, managers and firefighters vie for dominance of the default mode circuitry and inner conversations can become arguments. For every manager statement like, "let's not overreact," "he's just having a bad day," or "I need to get this conversation back on track," an aggressive firefighter app will say something like, "screw this," "tell him to go to hell," or "punch him!"

With respect to the embodiment circuitry, manager apps are typically less engaged. Indeed, aside from deliberate attention to bodily sensations (e.g., conscious bodily feedback needed to perform an activity), the prefrontal cortex activity that is so central to manager apps tends to be anti-correlated with embodiment circuitry activity (Fransson, 2005, 2006). Certainly managers can seek out experiences that involve positive bodily sensations (e.g., an enjoyable workout and how the body feels afterward), and certainly the experiences of effectiveness, acceptance, and success that managers sometimes achieve may involve positive feelings that manifest in bodily sensations. But managers, especially in polarized and traumatized internal family systems, tend to be focused less on those positive sensations than on all they are *thinking and doing* (to achieve coping and success goals and avoid unwanted sensations associated with the memories and emotions of exiles).

As addressed further below, boys and men are socialized to ignore, suppress, and banish vulnerable feelings, and the manager apps running on male brains tend (consciously or not) to work hard to keep those feelings and associated bodily sensations out of awareness. For males who have been sexually abused, the vulnerable feelings that go with the memories – fear, sadness, shame, etc. – are anathema to their manager apps. Indeed, such feelings and sensations in the embodiment circuitry are what their manager parts most seek to exile from awareness.

Finally, the polarized internal family systems associated with unhealed trauma, including sexual abuse trauma in men, involve little activation of the satisfaction circuitry. While manager parts or apps are certainly seeking satisfactions of various kinds, the more they seek to avoid the suffering associated with exile apps, the less they activate the satisfaction circuitry enough to bring deep or enduring contentment. The pleasure associated with manager apps' functioning – especially in polarized systems – is primarily the appetitive and anticipatory pleasure of the dopaminergic seeking circuitry, not the soothing and fulfilling pleasure of the opioid satisfaction circuitry. Indeed, managers are proactive protector apps that are focused on *seeking* success, approval, recognition, etc. – not on *experiencing* them. The more polarized the system and the more extreme the manager apps, the more any seeking-true-goods motivations are weaker than seeking-to-avoid-suffering motivations, and undermined by them.

Firefighter parts and circuitries. Firefighters engage the seeking circuitry almost exclusively to escape the suffering held by exiles. These parts have very intense fears and aversive reactions to painful and vulnerable feelings, memories, and experiences with other people. These apps are reactive protectors that automatically pop up when unwanted and frightening experiences arise or appear imminent, for example when an abuse memory is triggered but remains outside of awareness. Especially when exiled material has become conscious, firefighter apps can dominate much of the brain, taking over not only the seeking circuitry but the executive circuitry too – although the latter is often impaired by the extreme physiological arousal associated with the desperate seeking to escape that is integral to firefighter apps (Arnsten, 1998, 2009).

Some firefighter apps instantly trigger intense urges and impulses and quickly unleash them as extreme thoughts and behaviors: a nasty comment, a loud angry voice, hitting something or someone. These apps harness the seeking circuitry to rapid and explosive attempts to escape feared and aversive sadness, shame, or anything else that could overwhelm managers and give exiles free reign. Other firefighter apps are like zombie "bots," droning along in dissociative and numb states devoid of emotion or energy: staring into space, mindlessly eating potato chips, mesmerized by a simple game on a screen. These zoned-out firefighters harness the seeking circuitry too, but in relatively low-activation ways and with little recruitment of the executive circuitry, which can be impaired by hypo-arousal in such states (Hains & Arnsten, 2008, esp. Figure 2). In summary, firefighter apps may engage in seeking that is very deliberate and effortful, or very automatic and habitual; but they are always impulsive, compulsive, or both, and the seeking circuitry is always focused almost entirely on escape.

With respect to the embodiment circuitry, firefighters experience and seek some bodily sensations but not others. Many are so devoted to engaging in impulsive or auto-pilot behaviors that they disconnect attention from the embodiment circuitry. To the extent that a firefighter app is running on the embodiment circuitry, that circuitry is occupied by sensations of intense urges and impulses, for example, the sensations of being on the verge of screaming, running, pushing, or hitting, or of doing such things. In the case of a sexually compulsive firefighter, the embodiment circuitry is occupied with sexual sensations (although in pornography use there may be little embodiment circuitry activity relative to visual cortex activity associated with the images). Self-harming firefighter apps involve sensations of pain and its relief. Whatever the sensations a firefighter app brings to the embodiment circuitry, the function is to dominate that circuitry and even completely squeeze out sensations associated with exiles, which firefighters find very frightening and aversive.

Firefighters are often running on the default mode circuitry, including when managers are present or dominant. When exiled material is triggered but not in awareness, or not prominently so, a firefighter app may just be an angry or fearful voice in the background, saying things like, "don't let her get away with that" or "show him who's boss." As a bad memory starts to pop up or the inner conversation seems headed in that direction, a firefighter might say, "don't go there." Firefighter apps may by angry critics of oneself, more specifically of other parts or apps – such as a manager who let out an exile, which is verbally beaten up, or an exile expressing vulnerable feelings, which is shouted down or told, "quit your whining" or "you should just go kill yourself." Firefighters can also occupy the default mode circuitry with planning, ruminating, or worrying that is more intense and desperate than manager-based versions of these. For example, a man may repeatedly relive a recent argument and imagine other things he could have said, now saying them forcefully in his head; he may fantasize about defending himself in the next argument, or rant internally about the revenge he will get. Finally, zombie-like firefighter apps can absorb the default mode circuitry in dissociative and numbed-out escapist reveries, such as winning the lottery.

The experiences and behaviors of firefighter apps can involve brief but intense pleasure and satisfaction. How great it can feel to scream in someone's face, slam a fist on the table, throw a punch, or have an orgasm in loveless sex! But those quick-fix escapes, intensely pleasurable as they are for a few moments, bring no lasting satisfaction or genuine fulfillment. And the inevitable come-down that follows, from a hangover or state of withdrawal from an addictive substance to shame over having acted out in some self-destructive way, is only another link in a cycle of suffering. Indeed, as IFS has helped many to understand, the extreme behavior of firefighters only triggers and creates more exiled bad memories and feelings, and more extreme efforts by managers to keep out both exiles and firefighters – efforts destined to fail so long as the internal system remains polarized.

Exile parts and circuitries. In polarized internal systems, exile parts or apps have little access to the seeking and executive circuitries – until and unless supported by the Self and not blocked by manager or firefighter parts. Indeed, that's what it means to be an exile part or brain app: prevented from accessing the most important circuitries of motivation and control. Some exile apps involve high activation of the fear and anxiety circuitry; others hold memories and feelings of sadness, defeat, depression, and demoralization. When strongly activated, exile apps occupy the embodiment circuitry with very unpleasant sensations. Similarly, although manager and firefighter apps attempt to prevent them from occupying the default mode circuitry, exile apps often manifest as fleeting and barely noticed voices of suffering and images of wounding and hurts. When strongly activated, however, the voices and images are intense, intrusive, and even dominant. And of course exile apps entail little to no activation of the satisfaction circuitry.

For exile apps, more than firefighters and certainly more than managers, open access to the seeking, executive, and default circuitries depends on access to Self. The love, compassion, support, and validation available in Self-led states allow exile apps finally to experience and express their traumas and suffering in safe and healing ways. This occurs when exiles are freely granted access to the embodiment circuitry, as well as the executive circuitry that allows such experiences to be put into words (via Broca's area in the prefrontal cortex). Furthermore, greater access to the default mode circuitry lets exile apps share memories of hurts and hopes for the future while engaging fully in internal conversations with other parts and the Self. These comforting and soothing experiences in turn give rise to feelings of hope and even joy and gratitude, which finally connect (previously) exiled apps with activation of the satisfaction circuitry.

Central roles of fear and seeking in polarized Internal Family Systems

The polarization of an internal family is a function of parts fearing (and even hating) each other, on the one hand, and seeking conflicting experiences and goals, on the other. For example, managers and firefighters fear the unwanted feelings and memories of exiles, and seek to keep those unwanted experiences out of awareness. Exiles fear remaining suppressed, unknown, unheard, and invalidated, and therefore seek for their experiences and suffering to be known, heard, validated, and healed. Managers also fear firefighters and the harmful and shameful things they do, while firefighters fear that managers won't keep the exiles under wraps or will

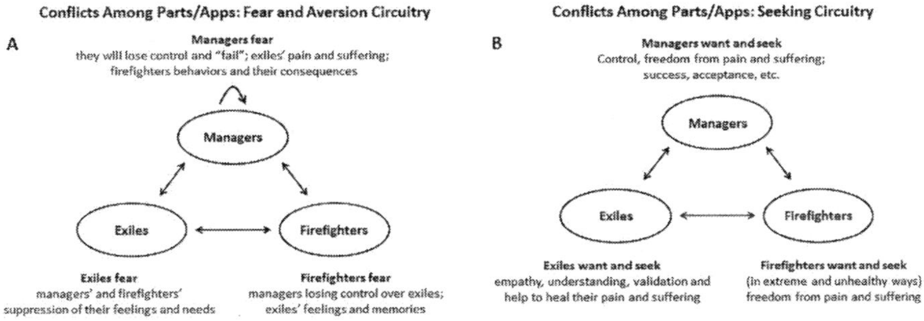

Figure 6.1 Fear circuitry and seeking circuitry involvement in conflicts among parts/apps

Note: (A) Each type of "part" specified by IFS has fears and aversions, including toward other parts or "apps," and these "run on" the brain's fear and aversion circuitry. (B) Each type of part wants and seeks particular experiences and capacities, thus utilizes and competes for the brain's seeking circuitry; all parts want recognition for the valuable roles they're trying to play.

stop the firefighters from taking drastic measures they deem necessary. While these dynamics of fear and seeking among parts are common knowledge among therapists using IFS, that they must be based in the fundamental brain circuitries of fear and seeking is not. Figure 6.1 presents an understanding of how the circuitries of fear and seeking maintain the extreme roles of parts and their polarizations, which perpetuates their continual engagement in cycles of suffering.

If we listen to the conversations in our heads, especially during intense emotional states when firefighter and exile parts or apps are more prominent, we can hear some of these fears and longings in what the voices are saying (or pleading or yelling). Exiles give voice to hurts and fears. Firefighters say things like, "you have to [do something impulsive and extreme] right now, or [something feared will happen]." And managers say things to exiles like, "that doesn't matter," and to firefighters, "Oh yeah, like that's really going to help. That [impulsive/extreme act] worked *great* last time."

However, to truly listen to those fears and longings requires letting go of our identification with the parts and of our identification with the argument itself. It requires accessing the mindfulness, compassion, and curiosity of our Self or soul, and giving all parts or apps the opportunity to articulate their fears, wants, and needs and feel heard and validated – not only by Self, but by other parts too. A lot of inner work (with the help of a therapist) may be needed to bring about such safe, constructive, and healing inner conversations, especially about very traumatic experiences and their impacts. But when we do, and when our clients do, these conversations reveal and render workable those fundamental fears and longings that are often left unsaid, or at least unheard – when managers are on cruise control, arguments are running on the default mode circuitry, or battles are raging for control of the seeking, executive, and other circuitries.

Cultural software shapes the internal family systems of sexually abused males

Every person has a unique internal family system, with its own unique parts or apps, constellations of relationships among them, and ways those parts get triggered and behave in relationships (with other people's parts). Genetics, temperament, social and environmental factors, by sculpting key brain circuitries, also shape parts and the relationships among them. In boys and men, we find common types of parts and ways those parts interact with each other, which are more extreme in traumatized males. This can be understood as resulting from "cultural software," which is running on everyone's brains to some extent and is "installed," via gender socialization, on top of each individual brain's biological "operating system." This cultural software shapes the development and functioning of parts or apps running on key brain circuitries. Trauma, including sexual abuse, further shapes those parts and how they relate to each other, including in ways that are exacerbated by masculine gender socialization.

Masculine gender socialization. As addressed by other chapters in this volume and an extensive literature (e.g., Gilmore, 1990; Pleck, 1981), masculine gender socialization continually impresses upon boys and men – sometimes with harsh sanctions and punishments – that they are supposed to have certain kinds of experiences, but not others; that there are rules governing how they are supposed to feel, think, and act, and *not* supposed to feel, think, and act (e.g., Chodorow, 1978); and that following those rules and embracing those values, or not, has major consequences for their identities, relationships, and status. According to these rules, to be masculine is to embody and enact – not only externally but internally too – strength, power, independence, control, competitiveness, dominance, and aggression (e.g., Connell, 1987). To be masculine is not only to be sexually dominant, but to be heterosexual. And masculinity is defined even more, perhaps, by what it excludes: "weakness" of any kind, homosexuality, and anything that is culturally construed as feminine, especially vulnerability, passivity, and dependence.

At the heart of interpersonal violence, especially child abuse, are experiences of disempowerment and disconnection (Herman, 1992). One person is overpowering and dominating another, and treating him or her not as a person but as an object, to be used for his or her own pleasure (if only the pleasure of feeling, however briefly, powerful and in control rather than vulnerable and dominated). That disempowerment is the antithesis of normative masculinity. Furthermore, to be dominated sexually is to be feminized; and while sexual contact with another male is viewed as homosexual, which precludes being a real male, to be *sexually dominated* by another male is seen as the ultimate destruction of one's masculinity.

If disempowerment is the opposite of masculinity, the emotional and relational *disconnection* central to being abused is, tragically, in some ways *consistent* with masculinity. Boys and men are continually socialized to lack awareness, expression, and empathy for vulnerable and "unmanly" emotions such as fear, sadness, and shame. But suppression of these emotions precludes the full range of experience required for a healthy emotional life and true intimacy. Embracing masculinity's demands for independence, power, and control limits one's capacities for relationships of mutuality and equality. Such disconnection characterizes not only boys' and men's relationships with others, but also their relationships with themselves (in IFS terms, the parts of their internal families).

Masculine gender socialization and parts or apps. The IFS model can help clarify how masculine gender socialization shapes the inner worlds of males, including in combination with the disempowerment and disconnection at the heart of trauma, particularly sexual abuse. Most obviously, experiences of abuse create exile parts or apps that hold the memories of what happened, including sensory and emotional aspects of the abuse itself (e.g., aversive sensations, unwanted sexual arousal, fear, disgust) and associated vulnerable emotions (e.g., sadness, shame). Exiles with such memories and emotions are burdened not only by experiences of profound disempowerment, disconnection, and emotional suffering associated with the abuse, but by experiences deemed utterly "un-masculine," especially the disempowerment and vulnerability.

Manager parts seek to keep such material exiled not only because it is a threat to the relative emotional equilibrium required to achieve their goals, but because it constitutes an existential threat to masculine identity. Manager beliefs, attitudes, motivations, behaviors, and even ways of deploying attention (i.e., away from the vulnerable and "unmanly" within), are all patterns of activity in seeking, executive, and default circuitries that have been shaped by masculine gender socialization. In internal conversations running on the default mode circuitry, manager parts may think and say harsh, judgmental, and rejecting things about and to exile parts (e.g., "you're a wimp," "quit being a pussy"). When we hear from men with sexual abuse histories about their fears of not being "real men" or being exposed as a "fraud," it's often manager parts or apps we're hearing.

Firefighter parts embody the most severe impacts of masculine gender socialization on the inner worlds of males, especially those with histories of sexual abuse. They are driven by fears that become very intense when managers fail to keep exiles from emerging. As reactive protectors, whether impulsively acting out or compulsively engaging in dissociative or other numbed-out ways of thinking and behaving, firefighter parts seek protection from vulnerable and "unmanly" experiences, memories, and feelings. But the seeking circuitry is not just focused on escaping from the vulnerable and un-masculine. Many impulsive firefighter parts or apps harness the seeking and embodiment circuitries (and any executive circuitry functions still available in such extreme states) to achieving and experiencing hyper-masculine states. They seek and grasp at the thoughts, feelings, and sensations of power, control, and domination associated with states of anger, aggression, and violence. These states are disconnected ones too: others are treated as objects for demonstrating one's power and proving one's masculinity.

Compulsive zombie-like firefighter parts more fully manifest the emotional and interpersonal disconnection of masculinity, and their dissociation and numbing can take disconnection to extremes: not only vulnerable emotions are blocked out, but emotions of any kind, even positive ones. Other firefighter apps zone out boys and men on substances or behaviors, such as oxycodone, marijuana, and video games.

Masculine gender socialization and the Self. Most tragically, by pushing boys and men to identify with and embody limited ways of being that revolve around avoiding the un-masculine and proving their manliness, internalizing or installing norms of masculinity disconnects men from universal human potentials for love and compassion, qualities that can heal their wounded parts and bring harmony to their inner worlds (Lisak, 1994). In the language of IFS, cultural norms of masculinity and gender socialization make it harder for men to access Self and bring Self-leadership to their parts.

Self-leadership: harnessing key brain circuitries for healing and happiness

The bottom row of Table 6.1 summarizes how the universal human capacities and qualities that IFS calls *Self* can be understood in terms of activity in key brain circuitries. Most importantly, the Self (or soul) harnesses the seeking circuitry to the motivations to end the suffering and promote the happiness of all beings and all parts (Schwartz & Sparks, 2014) or apps running on our brains. When Self is present, the seeking circuitry is not dominated or even disrupted by craving, grasping, or clinging – whether to experiences, goals, or apps running on the brain. Parts or apps are given access to the seeking circuitry, but only to the extent necessary to express their wants, needs, cravings, and longings *in the context* of the seeking circuitry being focused on love, compassion, kindness, healing, and happiness (and other true goods, including playfulness and creativity).

Self-led states give manager and firefighter parts access to compassionate and kind motivations, which enable them to become less extreme and to channel their seeking in ways that complement healthy motivations of other parts. For example, a work-focused manager can be much less motivated by fear and avoidance, much more motivated by positive aspirations, and compassionate toward previously exiled parts when they get activated. A firefighter part can let go of desperate, fear-based reactive seeking and take on a more constructive role, such as energizing healthy assertive behavior or giving helpful warnings if someone is (attempting to) engage in exploitation or abuse. These transformations – of extreme fear-motivated parts into collaborative and loving parts focused on seeking constructive solutions and true goods – involve harnessing both the deliberate and effortful and the automatic and habitual sub-circuitries of seeking. This enables the discovery and cultivation of new ways of thinking and behaving, and eventually establishes them as new habits. In states of Self-leadership, parts or apps can explore and commit to new ways of thinking and behaving, but healing an internal family system always involves integrating new habits or "subroutines" into old apps in order to replace some of the old ones. This takes some practice and discipline, especially at first.

Similarly, the Self is profoundly embodied. When the Self is present the embodiment circuitry is strongly activated by calm and fulfilling experiences of love, compassion, kindness, acceptance, joy, and gratitude. These experiences can include bodily sensations of warmth, vibratory energy, softness, tenderness, connection, and resonance with others' bodies. The Self gives manager, firefighter, and exile parts access to the embodiment circuitry – so they can experience the bodily sensations associated with their memories, emotions, fears, wants, and needs – to the extent required to foster understanding, acceptance, and support from other parts of the internal family system. Such experiences in turn give those parts access to new and deeply satisfying experiences of embodiment. Previously exiled parts integrate sensations and sensory memories of being loved, comforted, and unburdened of their emotional pain and suffering. Previously disembodied manager parts or apps gain access to sensations of being grounded in the body, and to positive and negative sensations previously excluded from awareness by action- and results-focused attention, thinking, and behavior. Firefighters gain the ability to tolerate impulses and urges, and the unwanted feelings and bodily sensations that trigger them; they experience aversive and craving-related sensations in the context of more comfortable and manageable overall experiences of embodiment.

Much of the healing of the inner family involves loving and collaborative inner conversations among previously battling parts or apps. In states of Self-leadership, a wise, loving, and supportive inner voice can engage with the various parts and help them supportively and collaboratively engage with each other. Among the most remarkable inner work facilitated by the IFS approach are the spontaneous, creative, loving, and healing conversations that one witnesses running on the brain's default mode circuitry. Parts share and learn new things about each other and themselves, come up with ways to collaborate, and make plans and commitments to develop new helpful habits. The nature of inner conversations can be radically transformed in a moment of Self-leadership; and over days, months, and years those conversations – and the remembering, problem-solving, and planning that also run on the default mode circuitry – can be grounded in seeking what is truly good, with integrity, in healthy and constructive ways.

Experiences of Self and Self-leadership of one's internal family are deeply fulfilling and satisfying. In these states the satisfaction circuitry is strongly activated, and even previously exiled parts that had only known suffering can participate in, and incorporate, deeply satisfying experiences of being loved, comforted, and healed. The same is true for fear-driven and emotionally disconnected manager and firefighter parts or apps: with access to the loving and wise Self or soul, they gain access to the circuitry of satisfaction and highly activated states of it.

While Self-leadership certainly involves full access to the executive circuitry and its functions, that is not the most important factor. What are most important and most transformative are, first, access to those universal human capacities that bring healing and happiness, and second, harnessing the brain's seeking, embodiment, default, and satisfaction circuitries to the pursuit of those true goods that are always sought by our Self or soul. Ultimately, it's about surrendering to the deepest love and wisdom that are within us – and ultimately transcend us. In the words of Rumi, "Let yourself be silently drawn by the stronger pull of what you really love."

Finally, all of the transformations described above, of parts or brain apps and their relationships to each other, can be understood in terms of the fundamental cycles of healing and happiness. Access to Self and Self-leadership release the seeking circuitry from clinging to fear-motivated manager and firefighter parts or apps, and bring compassion, comfort, and healing not only to exiles but to managers and firefighters too. All parts or apps are helped to seek the true goods they need and long for, whether that is the acceptance and healing of a wounded exile, or the relaxing of protector parts and the more complete channeling of a manager's driven competence or a firefighter's intense passion into seeking what is truly healing, satisfying, and fulfilling.

Implications for healing and happiness in males with histories of sexual abuse

As shown above, we can understand the inner worlds of men with histories of sexual abuse as apps running on key brain circuitries in cycles of suffering and potentially in cycles of healing and happiness. The extreme parts, the polarized inner worlds, and the cycles of suffering of sexually abused males – all are deeply shaped by the cultural "software" of masculine gender socialization. Experiences of disempowerment and vulnerability are the opposite of how men are supposed to be, and the terrible disconnection involved in sexual abuse can exacerbate the emotional and relational disconnection programmed into boys from before they can walk.

Putting this understanding into action in the treatment of sexually abused males can involve integrating contemplative practices (Hopper, 2014) and, as discussed here, the Internal Family Systems model (Schwartz, 2001). And there is another, even more radical treatment approach for men with histories of sexual abuse, which appears to have great promise and can also be understood using the framework presented here: MDMA-facilitated psychotherapy (Mithoefer, 2013). Therapeutic doses of pure MDMA, also known as "ecstasy," can evoke extremely powerful but safely manageable states of profound wisdom and love, and significantly decrease PTSD symptoms (Mithoefer, Wagner, Mithoefer, Jerome, & Doblin, 2011). With non-directive support from therapists, very traumatized people, including men with severe histories of childhood sexual abuse and war trauma, have been found to spontaneously access Self or soul capacities that enable them to process their most horrible memories, and to compassionately accept, embrace, and transform not only the most wounded and exiled parts of themselves, but their most hyper-masculine and aggressive parts too. Indeed, many men spontaneously disclose working with "parts" in the MDMA-facilitated sessions, despite IFS not being part of the manualized protocol (M. Mithoefer, personal communication, 2013). Initial research has found the treatment gains last many months, even years (Mithoefer et al., 2012), and if the FDA-approved phase 3 clinical trial is successful this treatment may be legal and available as early as 2021.

In closing, if we're deeply committed to understanding and healing traumatized people, including men long-tormented by the wounds of childhood sexual abuse, and to helping them find the happiness they long for and deserve, then I am suggesting that new understandings and new methods – informed by neuroscience, religious and spiritual traditions, and the psychologically and spiritually sophisticated psychotherapy of IFS – hold great promise and are worthy of our consideration.

References

Alcaro, A., & Panksepp, J. (2011). The SEEKING mind: Primal neuro-affective substrates for appetitive incentive states and their pathological dynamics in addictions and depression. *Neuroscience and Biobehavioral Reviews, 35*, 1805–1820.

Arnsten, A. F. T. (1998). The biology of being frazzled. *Science, 5370*, 1711–1712.

Arnsten, A. F. T. (2009). Stress signalling pathways that impair prefrontal cortex structure and function. *Nature Reviews Neuroscience,* 10, 410–422.

Balleine, B. W., & O'Doherty, J. P. (2010). Human and rodent homologies in action control: Corticostriatal determinants of goal-directed and habitual action. *Neuropsychopharmacology, 35*, 48–69.

Buckner, R. L., & Vincent, J. L. (2007). Unrest at rest: Default activity and spontaneous network correlations. *NeuroImage, 37*, 1091–1096.

Chodorow, N. (1978). *The reproduction of mothering: Psychoanalysis and the sociology of gender*. Berkeley, CA: University of California.

Colasanti, A., Rabiner, E. A., Lingford-Hughes, A., & Nutt, D. J. (2011). Opioids and anxiety. *Journal of Psychopharmacology, 25*, 1415–1433.

Connell, R. W. (1987). *Gender and power*. Stanford, CA: Stanford University Press.

Craig, A. D. (2002). How do you feel? Interoception: The sense of the physiological condition of the body. *Nature Reviews Neuroscience, 3*, 655–666.

Eliot, T. S. (1968). *Four Quartets* (1st Ed.). New York, NY: Mariner.

Everitt, B. J., & Robbins, T. W. (2016). Drug addiction: Updating actions to compulsions ten years on. *Annual Review of Psychology, 67*, 23–50.

Follette, V. M., & Pistorello, J. (2007). *Finding life beyond trauma: Using Acceptance and Commitment Therapy to heal from post-traumatic stress and trauma-related problems*. Oakland, CA: New Harbinger.

Fox, K. C., Spreng, R. N., Ellamil, M., Andrews-Hanna, J. R., & Christoff, K. (2015). The wandering brain: Meta-analysis of functional neuroimaging studies of mind-wandering and related spontaneous thought processes. *Neuroimage, 111*, 611–621.

Fransson, P. (2005). Spontaneous low-frequency BOLD signal fluctuations: An fMRI investigation of the resting-state default mode of brain function hypothesis. *Human Brain Mapping, 26*, 15–29.

Fransson, P. (2006). How default is the default mode of brain function? Further evidence from intrinsic BOLD signal fluctuations. *Neuropsychologia, 44*, 2836–2845.

Gilmore, D. D. (1990). *Manhood in the making: Cultural concepts of masculinity*. New Haven, CT: Yale University Press.

Grabovac, A. D., Lau, M. A., & Willet, B. R. (2011). *Mechanisms of mindfulness: A Buddhist psychological model. Mindfulness, 2*, 154–166.

Grossman, P., & van Dam, N. T. (2011). Mindfulness, by any other name . . . : Trial and tribulations of sati in Western psychology. *Contemporary Buddhism, 12*, 219–239.

Gusnard, D. A., & Raichle, M. E. (2001). Searching for a baseline: Functional imaging and the resting human brain. *Nature Reviews Neuroscience, 2*, 685–694.

Hains, A. B., & Arnsten, A. F. T. (2008). Molecular-mechanisms of stress-induced prefrontal cortical impairment: Implications for mental illness. *Learning & Memory, 15*, 551–564.

Harris, R. (2009). *ACT made simple: An easy-to-read primer on Acceptance and Commitment Therapy*. Oakland, CA: New Harbinger.

Herman, J. L. (1992). *Trauma and recovery*. New York, NY: Basic Books.

Hopper, J. W. (2014). Harnessing the seeking, satisfaction and embodiment circuitries in contemplative approaches to healing trauma. In Follette, V. M., Briere, J., Rozelle, D., Hopper, J. W., & Rome, D. I. (Eds.), *Mindfulness-oriented interventions for trauma: Integrating contemplative methods* (pp. 185–209). New York, NY: Guilford.

LeDoux, J. E. (2000). Emotion circuits in the brain. *Annual Review of Neuroscience, 23*, 155–184.

LeDoux, J. E. (2012). Evolution of human emotion: A view through fear. *Progress in Brain Research, 195*, 431–442.

Lisak, D. (1994). The psychological impact of sexual abuse: Content analysis of interviews with male survivors. *Journal of Traumatic Stress, 7*, 525–548.

Lisak, D. (1995). Integrating a critique of gender in the treatment of male survivors of childhood abuse. *Psychotherapy, 32*, 258–269.

Loseth, G. E., Ellingsen, D., & Leknes, S. (2014). State-dependent μ-opioid modulation of social motivation. *Frontiers in Behavioral Neuroscience, 8*, 1–15.

Love, T. M., Stohler, C. S., & Zubieta, J. K. (2009). Positron emission tomography measures of endogenous opioid neurotransmission and impulsiveness traits in humans. *Archives of General Psychiatry, 66*, 1124–1134.

McKiernan, K. A., D'Angelo, B. R., Kaufman, J. N., & Binder, J. R. (2006). Interrupting the "stream of consciousness": An fMRI investigation. *Neuroimage, 29*, 1185–1191.

Mithoefer, M. (2013). MDMA-assisted psychotherapy: How different is it from other psychotherapy? *MAPS Bulletin, 23*, 10–14. Retrieved from www.maps.org/news-letters/v23n1/v23n1_p10-14.pdf.

Mithoefer, M. C., Wagner, M. T., Mithoefer, A. T., Jerome, L., & Doblin, R. (2011). The safety and efficacy of ±3,4-methylenedioxymethamphetamineassisted psychotherapy in subjects with chronic, treatment-resistant posttraumatic stress disorder: The first randomized controlled pilot study. *Journal of Psychopharmacology, 25*, 439–452.

Mithoefer, M. C., Wagner, M. T., Mithoefer, A. T., Jerome, L., Martin, S. F., Yazar-Klosinski, B., Michel, Y., Brewerton, T. D., & Doblin, R. (2012). Durability of improvement in post-traumatic stress disorder symptoms and absence of harmful effects or drug dependency after 3, 4-methylenedioxy-methamphetamine-assisted psychotherapy: A prospective long-term follow-up study. *Journal of Psychopharmacology, 27*, 28–39.

Nelson, E. E., & Panksepp, J. (1998). Brain substrates of infant-mother attachment: Contributions of opioids, oxytocin, and norepinephrine. *Neuroscience and Biobehavioral Reviews, 22*, 437–452.

Pleck, J. H. (1981). *The myth of masculinity*. Cambridge, MA: MIT Press.

Rummelhart, D. E., & McClelland, J. L. (1987). *Parallel distributed processing, Volume 1: Foundations*. Cambridge, MA: MIT Press.

Salamone, J. D., & Correa, M. (2012). The mysterious motivational functions of mesolimbic dopamine. *Neuron, 76*, 470–485.

Salamone, J. D., Koychev, I., Correa, M., & McGuire, P. (2015). Neurobiological basis of motivational deficits in psychopathology. *European Neuropsychopharmacology, 25*, 1225–1238.

Schwartz, R. C. (2001). *Introduction to the Internal Family Systems model*. Oak Park, IL: Trailheads.

Schwartz, R. C., & Sparks, F. (2014). The Internal Family Systems Model in trauma treatment: Parallels with Mahayana Buddhist theory and practice. In Follette, V. M., Briere, J., Rozelle, D., Hopper, J. W., & Rome, D. I. (Eds.), *Mindfulness-oriented interventions for trauma: Integrating contemplative methods* (pp. 125–139). New York, NY: Guilford.

Siegel, D. J. (2010). *Mindsight: The new science of personal transformation*. New York, NY: Bantam.

Singer, T., Critchley, H. D., & Preuschoff, K. (2009). A common role of the insula in feelings, empathy and uncertainty. *Trends in Cognitive Sciences, 13*, 335–340.

Smallwood, J., & Schooler, J. W. (2015). The science of mind wandering: Empirically navigating the stream of consciousness. *Annual Review of Psychology, 66*, 487–518.

Treadway, M. T., & Zald, D. H. (2011). Reconsidering anhedonia in depression: Lessons from translational neuroscience. *Neuroscience and Biobehavioral Reviews, 35*, 537–555.

Part III

Institutional and cultural effects

Chapter 7

Sociocultural considerations in psychotherapy with male survivors of sexual abuse

Ernesto Mujica

The clinical importance of taking into account sociocultural factors in diagnosis and treatment in the area of mental health has been emphasized and well established for over three decades (Akhtar, 1999; McGoldrick, Giordano, & Garcia-Preto, 2006; Altman, 2010). These factors include social class, language, nationality, race, religion, migration, gender identity, and sexual orientation. Of course, family structure, cultural customs, and myths are also integral considerations. We know that socioeconomic and cultural influences affect the symptoms patients present with, how they understand the meaning of their symptoms, and how they view the causal factors and potential effectiveness of treatments or "cures" they may seek.

Sociocultural norms and contexts: our patients' and our own

By acquainting ourselves with the sociocultural background of the patient, we are indeed in a better position to appreciate the impact these factors may have on our patients' development and life experiences, as well as on their presenting problems when seeking psychotherapy. Without a sense of the patient's socioeconomic and cultural background we will be more likely to fall back on our own assumptions about what constitutes appropriate behavior, normality, morality, and psychopathology. Of course, in today's world, this is an increasingly complex task, as many of our patients are multicultural, often living with strong influences from their family's initial culture(s) of origin and then acquiring further layers of acculturation later in their development. When considering the impact of cultural norms in the field of mental health, the focus of "understanding" has placed almost exclusive attention on therapists' knowledge about their patients' cultural norms, often ignoring a thorough consideration of the impact of the therapist's own socioeconomic and cultural background.

Though a broad and more thorough interest in the effect of cultural perspectives on mental health developed during the 1980s, the "managed care" and "for profit" economic goals unleashed in healthcare during the 1990s resulted in a strangulation of humanistic efforts to understand the impact of culture on mental health and psychotherapy (McGoldrick et al., 2006). Gradually, "cultural competence" in mental healthcare became commodified, often allowing only a superficial understanding of the subject. The time previously allotted to clinical supervision in hospitals and clinics is now often consumed by chart-management, as the "productivity" of therapists is mechanized and measured by an ever-increasing requirement of number of sessions per week. With the increased medicalization and commodification of mental health, patients' presenting complaints must increasingly be documented in the language of simplified symptom checklists and severity ratings. This generally excludes any perspective that addresses a sociocultural appreciation or understanding of the individual's more specific, complex, and unique reasons for seeking treatment.

When working intensively with patients from a particular sociocultural subgroup, it is advantageous to have lived alongside that group, or at least to have spent time learning about their main cultural characteristics. Such exposure hopefully provides therapists with a lived experience of some of the key aspects important to patients. Another major approach to learning about the impact of culture is to immerse ourselves in a culture and language unfamiliar to us and note our reactions to the immersion. Such experiences, even for brief periods, can expand awareness and empathic understanding of what our patients may experience when they are immersed in, yet not identified with, the dominant culture. Most patients feel threatened if questioned about significant aspects of their identity during their initial sessions in psychotherapy. For survivors of sexual abuse, especially those who also have suffered as members of a persecuted or oppressed minority, questions about identity may be experienced as a frightening form of objectification. For patients who have experienced persecution (e.g., due to their political or religious beliefs, sexual orientation, gender identity, race, or ethnicity), inquiry about specific aspects of their identity during an initial interview, or even during ongoing psychotherapy, may elicit heightened anxiety accompanied by evasiveness, defensiveness, anger, a wish to flee, or dissociation. Despite the benevolent conscious intentions of the clinician, such patients may feel threatened, targeted, and hurt. It is therefore important to ask patients if they are comfortable discussing sociocultural factors and identity prior to proceeding. The patient should have a choice and the therapist should be respectful of any sense of threat or strong negative reactions emerging from the inquiry. In keeping with mindful attention to the impact of issues of authority, power, and control, an exploratory rather than prescriptive approach to sociocultural factors in psychotherapy is of particular importance with all patients, but perhaps especially those who have suffered significant boundary violations and imposition of another's will.

The initial interview

Nadir, a father of two young children from a Turkish-American Muslim family, came to see me after consulting with three other clinicians and deciding he could not work with any of them. From the time he was approximately 8 to 12 years old he experienced several years of incest from his aunt, and was later sexually abused by a male sports coach in high school. When he decided to seek treatment for recurrent nightmares and sexual dysfunction, he was very concerned about how a therapist might respond to his history of sexual abuse. He had previously told a friend about this abuse and his friend told him it shouldn't be any big deal, that he "should just get over it, forget about it." He feared a therapist might be equally dismissive, given that he is a "grown man, still affected by events that happened more than 20 years ago."

In addition to symptoms related to his history of sexual abuse, Nadir was also very concerned about how a psychotherapist might respond to his being Muslim. He had already had multiple experiences of ostracism and hostility from peers and co-workers due to his religious and ethnic background, especially following the 9/11 attacks. Though he appreciated their concern, he felt the first two psychotherapists he interviewed were too quick to make assumptions about the stress he might be feeling as a Muslim living in New York at this time. He felt these therapists were more interested in exploring his experience of being the object of xenophobia due to his ethnic identity than in his having suffered sexual abuse as a child, the issue that was his primary reason for seeking therapy.

Upon his arrival to his initial interview with the third clinician, the therapist handed him a clipboard in the waiting area with a questionnaire, asking him to fill it out before the interview. From the start, Nadir was put off, subjected to what he felt was a cold survey, having to answer emotionally sensitive questions in a manner that felt devoid of interpersonal contact or empathy. Nadir decided to leave a question about religious affiliation blank. He also wrote nothing about his cultural heritage and simply checked off his racial identity as Caucasian. During the interview, the therapist asked why he omitted responding about religion. Nadir explained he did not feel comfortable answering because he felt religion and ethnicity often elicit complex reactions and assumptions between people who barely know one another. The therapist apparently felt Nadir's answer was suspiciously evasive and pressed further for concrete answers regarding his religion and cultural background. In response, Nadir felt the therapist was now using his reluctance to respond to this question as confirmative diagnostic evidence that Nadir was unreasonably defensive and perhaps clinically paranoid. Nadir explained further that much of his family had experienced ostracism and persecution for being Muslim, and that he was uncomfortable about assumptions others may jump to upon learning about this. According to Nadir, the therapist was unrelenting in his suspicious attitude and remained rather coldly removed in his stance. Nadir felt this experience was a litmus test for whether the therapist would be able to respect the boundaries he set. As the therapist continued to prod beyond Nadir's limits, Nadir became increasingly preoccupied with the feeling that the therapist's responses constituted a form of perpetration. He felt the therapist's relative disregard of his discomfort, and his objectifying insistence on obtaining the information he wanted, constituted a repetition of his own experiences with his childhood abusers. Moreover, he sensed the therapist felt completely justified in these boundary violations and believed they were a perfectly reasonable part of clinical inquiry in his role of psychotherapist. The therapist's use of his own authority to excuse his behavior, despite Nadir's objections and discomfort, triggered memories of his aunt's and coach's rationalizations about their abuse of him. Any compassion and understanding of Nadir's cultural and family history were essentially belied by the therapist's disregard. Nadir was left feeling vulnerable, violated, disrespected, and pathologized; the only safe response he could think of was to not return.

Initial interviews with survivors of sexual abuse and assault are a fragile time in the development of a therapeutic alliance. Hypervigilance is a frequent and long-standing aftermath of trauma; new situations holding a potential for interpersonal confrontation and abuse of power and authority are ripe for triggering a sense of endangerment. Under the stress of an initial interview, any component of sociocultural identity may serve as a sensitive and reflexive trigger of the survivor's defense operations. Sociocultural issues generated between patient and therapist during this initial phase of treatment may be difficult to acknowledge or work through in the absence of an established working alliance. This can quickly lead to feelings of aloneness, alienation, and endangerment for the patient seeking treatment. In addition, juxtapositions of relational power and control, and of similarity and difference, can quickly lead to feelings of aloneness and hopelessness concerning future hopes of being understood and accepted by another.

During this initial phase of therapeutic work, it is therefore crucial to focus on maintaining a sense of interest and concern for the patient's sense of emotional and physical safety. Clinical approaches that pressure therapists and patients to focus on categorical symptom check-lists for differential diagnosis of psychopathology, and further check-lists for severity of symptoms – though diagnostically important – all magnify any sense of objectification and endangerment felt by survivors of sexual abuse. If the clinician pursues inquiry in an authoritarian manner – emotionally detached, factual, and officious – feelings of being targeted, objectified, and potentially harmed are likely to emerge. Such feelings can trigger memories of being carelessly manipulated, fondled unempathically, and victimized by being used for someone else's purposes. An authoritarian approach can unwittingly become a demand that patients tolerate the procedure and that any emotional experience or objections patients have will be minimized or denied. It can therefore be helpful to tell patients they can forego answering any questions that activate marked discomfort and lack of safety.

Sensitizing clinicians to sociocultural considerations

As McGoldrick et al. (2006) emphasize, the most essential aspect of training clinicians about sociocultural issues is helping them understand the presence and influence of their own ethnic and sociocultural backgrounds. Clinicians' socioeconomic and cultural backgrounds orient their attention to particular categories of symptoms, assessment of severity of psychopathology, and consideration of what treatment is best suited for a given individual. For example, in the United Kingdom and the United States, cultural dissimilarities between therapist and patient may lead to more severe assessments of psychopathology by clinicians when treating African American patients (Snowden & Cheung, 1990; Hu, Snowden, Jerrell, & Nguyen, 1991; Lawson et al., 1994), while symptom severity may be under-diagnosed when treating Asian patients (Takeuchi & Uehara, 1996). In diagnosis of major mental illness, primarily psychoses and affective disorders, minorities are more likely than Caucasians to be evaluated as being chronic rather than acute. African Americans in particular are more likely to be labeled as potentially dangerous and are more likely to be overmedicated as well (Adebimpe, 1981; Adebimpe & Cohen, 1989; Good, 1996; Wood, Gar, Lilienfeld, & Nezworski, 2002).

Although current training programs in psychiatry and mental health often include some attention to considerations of culture, we cannot assume a lack of cultural biases on the part of the therapist. Even when a clinician consciously holds opposite beliefs, the biases present in the cultural environment are often unconsciously internalized, enduring as unconscious influences on our responses to others. Current research supports the idea that cultural biases that affect diagnosis and treatment in healthcare stem from such unconscious influences (Littlewood, 1992; Cooper et al., 2012). Evidence of "implicit bias" in our actions is revealed by actions, judgments, and values that contradict those we consciously subscribe to. Hence, though we may consciously believe in equality between gender, race, or ethnic groups, we may at times respond in a non-egalitarian manner consonant with the cultural biases we were raised with and in which we live. Personal analysis of these factors by psychotherapists should be a key component of training and clinical supervision to help them explore culturally based countertransference dispositions. We should attend to these factors not only when we are working with patients with whom we have observable differences, but also with those with whom we have significant similarities.

Context of treatment

In addition to attending to therapists' and patients' socioeconomic and cultural backgrounds, we must also take into account the socioeconomic and cultural context of the therapeutic dyad or group, not only at the start of treatment but also throughout the ongoing psychotherapeutic experience as it unfolds. The very same patient–therapist dyad will often highlight different aspects of their transference–countertransference experiences and enactments (Bromberg, 1991) depending on any changes occurring in their larger cultural context. Accordingly, the context of the treatment can be an important determinant of emerging therapeutic themes.

For example, I once ran a group for male survivors of sexual abuse in a community clinic setting. The existence of this group was known publicly as possibly the only long-term group for male survivors offered through a public clinic in New York City. After I ran this group for two years, it was no longer feasible for me to take the time to travel from my own office to this clinic. Since the clinic was not able to find a suitable therapist to run its men's group, the clinic director and I decided I would offer the group the option of continuing to work with me privately. All six patients in the group decided to continue in my private practice. As I expected, the shift to my private office brought many reactions that we explored, including a sense of greater intimacy and more personal commitment and vulnerability within our therapeutic relationship. In addition, transference themes that previously emerged toward the clinic were now directed at me.

But I was most struck by the fact that several group members were upset the group would no longer exist at a "public" clinic. As we explored this further, group members expressed distress because the public might no longer know a group for male survivors of sexual abuse existed at all!

For the first time, patients expressed grave concern that mental health services for men who suffer from the aftermath of sexual abuse and assault still remain largely neglected in both public and private mental health settings. Group members worried that the transition to my practice contributed to society's ongoing denial that sexual abuse happens to boys and men. The change led them to feel invisible to the world beyond my office. In turn, they expressed feelings of abandonment, neglect, hopelessness, guilt, and anger, all feelings related not only to their own experiences of sexual abuse, but to the persistence of social negation and denial of male victims in the world at large.

This contextual change also led them to fear they were now more vulnerable to my personal influence, since I was no longer being "watched over" by the clinic director, a topic that had never before come to the surface. They feared I had taken them from their larger "family" environment at the clinic, one where they assumed there were parental figures of higher authority looking over my actions and assuring their safety. I had symbolically become their "only parent," with no one to oversee my treatment of them. So, there was nowhere to turn should they feel frightened or mistreated. Though these feelings gradually subsided, feelings of invisibility to the outside world became a recurrent theme. Fortuitously, this change – from public to private – brought with it many strong feelings previously unarticulated, so we could now discuss them. Over time, several group members also decided to become more active in community and national organizations in order to increase awareness of the existence and needs of male survivors.

Cultural influences versus individuals' uniqueness

Our awareness and learning about the sociocultural background of ourselves, our patients, and the context within which we are working with each patient can also facilitate a more profound exploration of the therapeutic relationship as well as an expanded appreciation of mutuality of understanding within the therapeutic relationship. Accordingly, it is essential to keep in mind that each patient is a unique individual who will have processed, absorbed, assimilated, rejected, or denied – consciously and/or unconsciously – the impact of his abuse experience on his life as well as the impact of sociocultural influences on the ways he has processed his abuse and how he has been treated by others. Again, the interactive complexity of sociocultural influences must be attended to in its subjective singularity as it is uniquely experienced by each therapist–patient dyad. Thus, cultural similarities and differences cannot automatically predict the themes or quality of engagement of the therapeutic dyad. Each patient within his own subjective uniqueness may find comfort or fear when he encounters someone he identifies as similar to or different from his own cultural background or identity.

Cultural myths and biases about male sexual victimization

In his book *Betrayed as Boys*, Gartner (1999) discusses the social myths and biases that often lead to false conclusions and hurtful actions against male survivors of sexual abuse and sexual assault. Of the ten myths Gartner identifies, I will highlight eight specifically rooted in gender stereotypes.[1] These myths are:

1 Men cannot be sexually abused.
2 Women do not abuse sexually.
3 Sexual abuse turns a boy gay.
4 Sexually abused boys almost inevitably become sexually abusive men.
5 Male victimizers who molest boys consider themselves homosexual and are sexually interested in other men.
6 If you have allowed abuse, then you are a sissy or a weakling.
7 Children can always say no to abuse if violence is not used. If they don't, they must have wanted the abuse to occur.
8 If a boy becomes sexually aroused, he is an equal participant in the abuse.

Such cultural myths shape the beliefs, judgments, and actions of individuals without their having much reflective awareness about the process of their thoughts and actions. As Gartner points out, none of these myths hold true and "all have been refuted by an expanding body of literature about boyhood sexual victimization" (Gartner, 1999, p. 19). Yet, these myths

1 The other two false myths noted by Gartner are: "Sexual abuse is always overt" and "Victimizers are always conscious of the abuse they are committing" (Gartner, 1999, p. 19).

continue to hold a strong sway in how society judges and treats male survivors of sexual abuse. Several of them hinge on prominent, core cultural beliefs instilled by major falsehoods about maleness and masculinity. These include:

1 The male body is by definition impenetrable and once penetrated is no longer classifiable as male.
2 Males are inherently prone to violence. Once provoked or hurt, their natural response is to become violent and hurtful to others.

Social biases about males and masculinity also exacerbate the harm and destructiveness men and boys are subjected to from their own families, friends, and community, especially once they have been victims of sexual abuse. Because of the widespread nature of these myths and biases, many men – perhaps most – also internalize these false beliefs as negative self-statements. For example, boys and men commonly tell themselves that had they been "man enough" the abuse would not have happened. These myths and cultural biases continue to have a profoundly negative impact on the treatment of male survivors'.

A relevant example of gender bias and its contribution to the denial of sexual victimization of males is the past and current forms of defining rape. The Uniform Crime Reporting (UCR) Program within the Federal Bureau of Investigation (FBI) is the main reference source for law enforcement, media, and the general public for crime within the United States (*CJIS*, 2012). Prior to 2013 its definition of rape excluded all forms of sexual abuse of men and boys. The severity of this denial and neglect is shocking and disgraceful. For 80 years, the UCR definition of rape read:

> The carnal knowledge of a female forcibly and against her will.

As of 2013, the new UCR definition of rape is:

> Penetration, no matter how slight, of the vagina or anus with any body part or object, or oral penetration by a sex organ of another person, without the consent of the victim.

Though the new definition acknowledges men can be victims of rape, it reinforces gender bias against men when considering non-consensual oral sex: it includes women as victims when there is cunnilingus without consent but excludes male victims of fellatio without consent. If written to give equal consideration to female and male victims, the law would have read:

> . . . oral stimulation of a sex organ of another person, without the consent of the victim.

This continued gender bias is, not surprisingly, the product of an "Advisory Policy Board" that included women's, but not men's, victim organizations. Reynolds (2014), reviewing current Center for Disease Control (CDC) figures concerning rape, concluded that with a more egalitarian definition, CDC figures would indicate ". . . men are raped by women at nearly the same rate women are raped by men."[2]

A college student once reported to me he was raped by another male student. At the student mental health offices a female counselor said it was "impossible" for him to have been raped because "men cannot be raped." Feeling disqualified and shamed, he left, not seeking further help until several years later. Only when he learned there are therapists who specialize in working with male sexual abuse survivors did he take the risk of seeking treatment again.

In addition to the negative effects these social biases have on men in general, and on male survivors of sexual abuse in particular, these biases have specific harmful effects on bisexual and homosexual men, as there is still widespread persistence of social biases against bisexual and homosexual behavior and identity.[3] To the extent that a significant proportion of the population continues to view homosexual behavior as "aberrant," homosexuality itself becomes disturbingly confounded with sexual abuse in the minds of many. It is therefore important for clinicians to keep in mind that male victims of sexual abuse who have sex with other men are often considered by others, sometimes including clinicians themselves, to have become homosexual as a consequence of being sexually abused.

This bias of associating sexual abuse with "abnormality" and "homosexuality" results in two ubiquitous but contradictory false sociocultural assumptions: If a homosexual man was sexually molested as a child by a

2 Editor's note: For discussion of the rape of adult men, see Chapter 3 by Barnard and Chapter 4 by Skidmore and Roy in the companion volume to this one, *Healing Sexually Betrayed Men and Boys: Treatment for Sexual Abuse, Assault, and Trauma.*

3 Editor's note: See Chapter 11 by Struve, Fradkin, and Beckstead in this volume for further discussion of gay and bisexual survivors as well as those they term gender and/or sexually diverse.

man, there is often a biased belief that his gayness was caused by his having had a male perpetrator. Yet, if a homosexual man was sexually abused during childhood by a woman, many assume he became homosexual because he repudiated heterosexuality, as a rejection of females as perpetrators. Hence, social myths absurdly predict that boys with male perpetrators are likely to become gay, and, equally, that boys with female perpetrators are also likely to become gay. Within our overwhelmingly heterosexist societies, heterosexuality is considered normative and therefore does not need to be explained (Corbett, 2009; GAP, 2000). Accordingly heterosexual male survivors have no equivalent explanations offered to account for their sexual orientation. Of course, these social constructions and myths often work their way into the treatment relationship through both the therapist's and patient's internalizations as well as through the cultural biases present in their contextual milieu.

The psychological objective of internalization is for the individual to bring into his inner life and identity the predominant relational judgments and values he observes in the cultural environment in which he is immersed (Laplanche & Pontalis, 1973). This process leads to various degrees of identification of the self with the ideals presented in one's cultural environment. Thus, a child surrounded by cultural norms admiring heterosexual relations and denigrating homosexual relations, internalizes these values, making them his own, and thereafter uses these standards to judge the value of same- and opposite-sex attractions in himself or others. If he experiences same-sex attractions, he may be faced with internal conflicts. Experienced clinicians who have worked extensively with male survivors generally agree that the gender of the perpetrator and the fact of abuse itself is not a major determinant of a survivor's sexual orientation (Gartner, 1999; Lew, 2004). However, sexual abuse often does contribute to early self-questioning and confusion around sexuality, which may include increased insecurities about sexual orientation, phobic responses, compulsive sexual behaviors, and concerns about the meaning of intimate relations.

Minority communities' breakdown in communication and self-blame

Virtually all survivors of sexual abuse are likely to question themselves about whether there is something "wrong" with them: whether something is wrong with them because they were "chosen" as victim by the perpetrator, because they were not able to fend off victimization, and/or because the abuse has damaged them irreparably (Gartner, 1999). This common pattern of self-blame for all male survivors of sexual abuse is often exacerbated when the survivor is also part of an oppressed minority. If the survivor's appearance or cultural identity stands out as objectionably different from the dominant cultural environment, self-attribution of causality may also intensify self-denigration and self-blame. As a defense against feelings of culpability and guilt, the dominant culture may also be invested in believing shunned minorities have "deficits" in their abilities and functioning that account for their suffering and perceived limitations. This inclination by the larger society and social elites to justify the shortcomings of oppressed minorities as a product of their inherent inadequacies blocks the capacity for compassion and empathy toward the less fortunate and contributes significantly to blaming the victim (Vaughans, 2014). In short, male survivors from minority groups may be at higher risk for a cycle of self-blame encouraged and supported by the dominant culture.

Writing about "disavowal" of intergenerational trauma, Vaughans (2014) notes the multiple forms of resistance to acknowledging and working through social victimization of minorities. Within society as a whole, shame is perhaps the strongest factor bringing about such resistance, shame on the part of the perpetrator for committing the abuse as well as shame on the part of the victim for not having been able to protect himself from victimization. Those identified as belonging to the perpetrator's cultural group may avoid the topic of sexual abuse for fear of being classified as similar to the perpetrator and therefore barbaric and inhumane. On the other hand, the victimized male of minority status may fear being perceived as having succumbed to the will of those in power. This results in a symbolic confirmation and condemnation from the dominant culture that projects a vision of the minority person as powerless, emasculated, and damaged beyond repair.

Social oppression, dehumanization, and persecution can promote a disturbance of primary developmental communication and attachment that undermines communication between parents and children (McGoldrick et al., 2006; Vaughans, 2014). At times, minority parents may seek to protect their children from understanding the severity of the injustices that may await them. At other times, the dominant culture may intervene to place itself as an authority over the children, over and above the child's parents, thereby undermining parental authority.

This was obviously true for African Americans during slavery, and may also be experienced by immigrant families vis-à-vis fears of family separation or deportation brought on by visits from social service workers or state child protection services. Children may increasingly question parental authority when their parents' customs and cultural views conflict with those of the dominant culture and/or when children become aware of the lower socioeconomic power and "outsider" position of their parents within the dominant host society. These factors contribute to undermining the authority of minority parents and diminishing intra-familial trust.

In summary, language barriers, social isolation, intergenerational trauma, cultural differences between immigrant generations, and the potential negative effects of denigration and oppression by the dominant culture may result in the disruption of communication between minority parents and children. In turn, the disruption of parent–child communication, attachment, and trust can all increase the vulnerability of minority children to being victimized and weaken their ability to inform their caretakers about their victimization.

Religious and ethnic minorities: concerns about reputation and stigmatization

Sexual abuse within a family can stir intense fears of stigmatization by peers within its own subculture. The family may become highly secretive in order to protect itself from shame and disgrace. In very close-knit communities such stigmatization potentially results in social ostracism within the community and in some cases may actually reduce the likelihood that as adults children from the stigmatized family will be able to marry within their own subculture (Sivan, 2011). As noted by Gartner (1999, p. 135): "Generally, the more secretive the boy must be, the more the experience is deviant within his culture, and the more traumatic the sexual experience is likely to be."

This is often compounded not only by intra-familial conflict and denial, but also by conflictual social issues pertaining to the dominant culture surrounding the family. In minority communities that have historically experienced significant oppression and persecution, a family that reports sexual abuse may elicit feelings of betrayal and hostility in those within the community who do not trust the reactions of the dominant host culture toward the community or its individual members.

A central issue is the perceived potential harm to the minority community's reputation within the larger culture. Families filing reports of sexual abuse may consequently be treated as traitors to their communities since they have opened the door for authorities from the larger culture – such as police and child protection services – to come into their homes and community to investigate the crime. Moreover, if there is media coverage about sexual abuse within a minority community, there may be a larger wave of shaming and denigration that follows from the larger culture, thereby increasing the community's sense of vulnerability and shame. Such events are likely to be followed by intensified rejection and accusations of betrayal toward the victim and his family.

A conspicuous example of the difficulties close-knit religious minorities may face when confronting childhood sexual abuse was illustrated by Otterman and Rivera's (2012) *New York Times* report concerning families of child sexual abuse victims within Jewish Orthodox Hassidic communities: "[T]hose who come forward often encounter intense intimidation from their neighbors and from rabbinical authorities, aimed at pressuring them to drop their cases." Otterman and Rivera note that those families who do report sexual abuse to authorities outside their religious community may be seriously harassed, with the intent to cause economic harm to the family. Alternatively, authorities within the community may offer money as a donation for therapeutic treatment of the victim while simultaneously pressuring the family to refrain from judicial prosecution of the case. Reportedly, some children and families have even been expelled from their religious schools and synagogues. At the root of such fervent protection of the insularity of the religious community and its members is an age-old tradition forbidding the denunciation of a fellow member of the community to authorities of the dominant culture:

> [Some rabbis] strictly adhere to an ancient prohibition against *mesirah*, the turning in of a Jew to non-Jewish authorities, and consider publicly airing allegations against fellow Jews to be *chillul Hashem*, a desecration of God's name.
>
> (Otterman & Rivera, 2012)

Thus there is intense culturally sanctioned pressure to protect the community from the impingement of external law authorities or shaming by the dominant surrounding culture. Sexual abuse perpetrators – especially those who are prominent figures within the community – may be intensely supported through community-based denial that also denigrates the reporting family and coerces families to drop their accusations (Sivan, 2011; Rivera, 2012). More recently, following much-needed work by pro-reporting rabbis and pro-victim community-based supporters, there have also been important positive strides within the Jewish ultra-Orthodox communities to encourage judicial actions against perpetrators and provide support for victims and their families. In July, 2011, a Hassidic religious court resolved that the tradition against *mesirah* is not applicable when sexual abuse cases are concerned, emphasizing that in such cases members of the community must not remain silent and must speak out publicly to condemn the abuse (Otterman & Rivera, 2012).

Institutions and the gradual shift from broad social denial to support for victims[4]

Society at large has had major fluctuations in its responses to childhood sexual abuse, ranging from denial, neglect, and even mockery of victims (especially male victims), to recognition and compassionate support. In the United States, the first state mandates for specific classes of citizens to report suspected cases of child abuse took place in 1963, largely spurred on by the landmark publication of "The Battered Child Syndrome" (Kempe, Silverman, Steele, Droegemueller, & Silver, 1962). Kempe's publication, and the media distribution that followed, helped us recognize that it is the duty of those providing care and/or education to children to identify and report suspected abuse to child protection services and law enforcement. Within five years of Kempe's article, all 50 states had some degree of mandated reporting, and by 1974 the Federal Child Abuse Prevention and Treatment Act was enacted (Meyers, 2008). Prior to the 1960s survivors of sexual abuse had virtually no cultural referents to provide a shared language for discussion of their abuse experience. Recognition of child sexual abuse lagged well behind recognition of physical abuse.

4 Editor's note: See Chapter 8 by Burmester in this volume for a discussion of institutional dissociation.

The mandated reporting laws enacted throughout the 1970s played a major role in elevating recognition and public news coverage of child sexual abuse. By 1970, professional and public discourse began to provide an essential social context for survivors, especially for the more culturally marginalized male survivors, to better identify, reflect upon, and communicate about their abuse experiences.

In the early 1980s, weakening of social taboos and political forces that previously prevented reports of childhood sexual abuse from entering public awareness and discourse gave way to allegations of sexual abuse within various organizations. The most dramatic and sensationalized allegations were those concerning reports of extensive and ritualized sexual abuse of children within daycare centers. It has been proposed that conservative social forces contributed to the wildfire spread of abuse allegations regarding daycares during this period (Casey, 2015). Casey also noted additional factors contributing to the frenzy of concern regarding sexual abuse in daycares. These included heightened fear of crime, anti-authoritarianism, homophobia regarding male daycare workers, and anti-feminist concerns about the weakening of the patriarchal family model, alongside the fact that more women than ever had full-time employment (thereby requiring daycare). The media reported for several years that child abuse experts were giving testimony about severe and widespread child abuse, including sexual abuse and "satanic cult abuse" in daycare centers. For male survivors, this "viral" national interest in the uncovering and discussion of child sexual abuse – reported with virtually equal attention to male and female victims – was a long-sought social acknowledgment of their childhood experiences, in contrast to previously prevailing denial and secrecy. Yet for many survivors, these reports also increased distress, eliciting increased traumatic memories, flashbacks, nightmares, and intense preoccupation about children who were insufficiently protected and vulnerable to abuse.

The intense fear spreading through the nation also led to allegations, later described as mass "hysteria," which in turn encouraged prosecutors to proceed with poorly collected evidence, thereby increasing false accusations, incarceration of innocent victims (Dickey, 2012), and perhaps dismissal of valid accusations. The federal government sponsored a study of 270 daycare facilities across the country, including 1,639 children (Leary, 1988). The report eased the concerns of many, as it concluded that risk of sexual abuse in daycare centers was no higher, and perhaps even lower, than risk at home. Fortuitously, this research brought to light new data that clashed against public assumptions regarding the presumed characteristics of perpetrators. Forty percent of perpetrators of daycare sexual abuse were female and 50% were college graduates. The data alerted forensic investigators, child protection advocates, and parents, that perpetrators of CSA often do not support the gender-biased prototype of the "male pedophile."

By the early 1990s a new wave of defense and denial fought back the rising allegations of childhood sexual abuse. Some of the most highly publicized convictions of daycare sexual abuse were overturned, often because evidence from child-victim interviews were judged to be tainted by poorly conducted and biased interview techniques. In tandem, the accusations of ritual abuse of toddlers in daycare centers were now mocked as "daycare hysteria," a "moral panic," a modern-day "witch hunt." Alongside the tightening court restrictions of admissibility of evidence and stricter controls for interviewing techniques pertinent to the investigation of child sexual abuse allegations, there developed a strong backlash with accusations of "false memories" against adult survivors of childhood sexual abuse. The so-called "false memory syndrome" came into vogue for defendants accused of perpetration. It was promoted by Peter and Pamela Freyd (Bickerton, 1997), whose daughter, Jennifer Freyd, accused her father of sexual abuse during her childhood.

Jennifer Freyd (1994), a professor of psychology at the University of Oregon and Editor of the *Journal of Trauma and Dissociation*, has maintained the veracity of her claims of sexual abuse by her father. She has also developed extensive research and publications concerning the traumatic impact of "abuse betrayal" and the effects of abuse on memory (Freyd, 1994). She has emphasized that repression of memories of abuse constitute the victim's psychological defense against the devastating recognition of betrayal by an abuser who has also been a trusted caretaker or other person of authority intimately involved in the child's life. According to Freyd, it is the victim's need to maintain attachment with persons or institutions experienced as essential to their survival and identity that in turn brings about such repression of memory (Freyd, 1994; Gartner, 1999).

Freyd's parents went on to found the "False Memory Syndrome Foundation" in 1992. It supports parents accused by an adult child who has "recovered memories" of sexual abuse, insisting that such memories are more likely to be the product of "cognitive distortions" and "delusions."

Accordingly, a strong objective of this foundation is to provide support to defense attorneys seeking to discard allegations of sexual abuse based on "recovered memories."

Perhaps the greatest impact on social awareness of childhood sexual abuse – especially involving male victims – came from the *Boston Globe*'s exposure of sexual abuse by priests (Paulson & Franklin, 2002; Pfeiffer, Carroll, Rezendes, & Robinson, 2002; Rezendez, Carroll, Pfeiffer, & Robinson, 2002).[5] These detailed reports substantiated the neglect and cover-up by the Catholic Church and its hierarchy. By the early 1990s and increasingly during the following decade, multiple lawsuits against priests and the Catholic Church were made and convictions were obtained. Media coverage revealed that, in many cases, priests previously identified as perpetrators of sexual abuse were negligently transferred to multiple parishes where they were allowed access to potential new victims. Supporters of the Church's denial sought to denigrate and ridicule victim reports as exaggerations that were a product of anti-Catholic politicians and greedy lawyers digging up questionable claims of sexual abuse (Maier, 2006; Nussbaum, 2006). Yet, notwithstanding the many years – if not decades – of denial and cover-up of sexual abuse within the Catholic Church, its report commissioned by the US Conference of Catholic Bishops indicated that between 1950 and 2002 there were well over 10,000 documented allegations of sexual abuse by clergy (Terry, 2004). This report, added to the *Boston Globe*'s coverage, made it increasingly evident to the general public that the Catholic Church's hierarchy systematically minimized and denied the gravity and extent of sexual abuse within its domain, while actively protecting priests who were known perpetrators.

When sexual perpetration occurs within large organizations, and especially by one of its officials, those in power and much of its membership are frequently supportive of their organizations, their leaders, and their peers in their denial of wrongdoing. This defensive reaction of group identity and cohesive self-protection in organizations – whether religious groups, sports teams, schools, etc. – often uses the economic and social status of the organization to disqualify abuse allegations and shun victims. Those with higher status have greater influence over the decision-making

5 See the chapters in this volume by Burmester on institutional dissociation (Chapter 8) and Gartner on abuse by priests (Chapter 9) for further discussions of the Catholic Church scandals.

processes of the organization, and will likely exert influence in favor of accused officials. Leaders of organizations – especially if they are hierarchical and/or authoritarian – are often experienced as parental figures to be obeyed and protected. As noted by Gartner (1999), children raised within authoritarian households and communities will be more likely to succumb to the impositions of an adult perpetrator, and less likely to disclose abuse experiences. I would add that the more authoritarian the organization, the more likely it is that its members will be averse to criticize or question its authority, lest they be identified as heretics and traitors to the group identity.

These larger organizational forms of denial of sexual abuse continue to have widespread influence, and have effectively contributed to an ongoing undermining of the essential role of witnessing and validation that are so central to the process of healing from interpersonal trauma (Laub, 1992; Boulanger, 2007; Abelson, English, Saltzman, & Wallack, 2016). As the legal system and the general public have become more aware of the severity and extent of childhood sexual abuse within a wide range of institutions, the tide of public opinion has shifted from denial to more compassion and support toward victims. Accordingly, it has gradually become more politically disadvantageous for organizations to allow cover-ups than to take sexual abuse allegations seriously by moving forward with investigations and prosecution of perpetrators and their accomplices (Persky, 2013; Hamilton, 2014). For survivors themselves, these changes within the larger social context have been of considerable importance in helping them weather the pain involved in speaking out about their abuse and pursuing their process of healing:

> "It's been a sea change," said Bob Schwiderski, a decades-long victims' advocate who was sexually abused by a priest as a boy. "We're no longer considered ignorant money-grabbers . . . I've gone from being spit on to being applauded."
>
> (Hopfensberger, 2016)

Group therapy and healing male survivors' cultural wounds

Male sexual abuse victims often feel uniquely damaged and stigmatized in relation to others in the world that surrounds them. Group therapy provides a therapeutic experience that often extends well beyond the limits of a dyadic therapeutic relationship. The multiple self–other relations that emerge in groups facilitate survivors working through the social stigma and phobias endemic to their development of isolation, shame, and guilt. Fradkin (2012), Gartner (1999), Lew (2004), and others note these processes, describe the range of groups that may be offered to survivors, and discuss what needs to be considered in forming and running each of them. These groups range from short- and long-term dynamically oriented groups to peer support groups and 12-step programs.[6]

Of greatest relevance to this discussion is that group therapy offers the male sexual abuse survivor a new social environment where he can interact with peers about his abuse and its aftermath. Male survivors of sexual abuse often experience group therapy as a sociocultural environment radically different from their own family and cultural milieu, and this difference is the crux to healing through group therapy. Typically, groups strongly emphasize emotional and physical safety as well as respect and compassion for the experiences shared by each group member.

Common to all these groups is the tremendous healing that occurs when a man walks into a room full of other survivors and comprehends in an emotional rather than intellectualized way that he is not alone. In my experience of over two decades running groups for male survivors, men beginning group therapy are often meeting other male survivors for the first time in their lives. Within a group context, survivors recognize that what they typically assumed to be personal and idiosyncratic problems and deficits are understandable experiences shared by peers. The group may represent a sort of new family where, often for the first time in their lives, they are likely to be listened to with heartfelt compassion. When a survivor is in the presence of peers who are also sharing struggles and successes related to abuse, he may experience a new sense of self. This new self is engaged in a world with mutually supportive and validating interactions that promote trust, strengthen self-esteem, and lessen self-doubt and confusion about himself and others.

Therapeutic peer-group relations often dismantle and disprove the common cultural myths and assumptions about male survivors of sexual abuse listed above. Within group therapy, male survivors are often exposed to

6 Editor's note: See also Chapter 5 by Fradkin and Struve in the companion volume to this one, *Healing Sexually Betrayed Men and Boys: Treatment for Sexual Abuse, Assault, and Trauma.*

ideas about men and boys contrasting with the negative social myths that often marginalize and oppress them with fear, self-doubt, shame, and guilt. As they grow healthier and more self-affirming, they may learn that:

1 "Real" boys and men have a right to be both "masculine" *and* "feminine."
2 They are not irreparably damaged, failures, or "less than" others because they were sexually abused.
3 Males can be sexually victimized by females.
4 Abuse, whether by a male or female perpetrator, does not in and of itself determine sexual orientation, even though they may have experienced great confusion about their sexuality and identity during the abuse and the process of healing and recovery.
5 It is healthy for men and boys to share feelings with peers who can demonstrate caring and support toward one another.

In summary, peer group therapy with other male survivors is likely to diminish or even undo much of the harm that social bias and stigma frequently induce in male survivors of sexual abuse.

Language and bilingualism

Close attention to language use can be a critical factor in the process of psychotherapy with survivors who are bilingual or multilingual. The development of language acquisition is integral to the experience of belonging to one's family and one's community, and is deeply embedded in everyone's cultural environment. In effect, language is the single most important signifier of cultural identity (McGoldrick et al., 2006). Perez-Foster (1998) argues that language provides the template through which we linguistically organize and interpret our experience of the world. It is a cornerstone of our assessment of similarity to and difference from others, and of the "me" and "not me" often tied to other acquired notions of self and other. Breadth of vocabulary, slang, accents, and inflections go even further in emphasizing an individual's belonging or exclusion. They are all key factors denoting community membership and socioeconomic status. Moreover, language plays a key role in the attribution and establishment of social and interpersonal power relations.

These aspects of language use significantly influence the sociocultural milieu of the therapy. They contribute to the playing out of power relations in psychotherapy, often influencing the emotional tone of the therapeutic relationship even as both patient and therapist are unaware of what they are revealing about their respective roles and identities. From the time of the first phone contact, both patient and therapist begin to establish a sense of one another's identity through language. The extent to which we do this is often far greater than we realize in the moment. Accordingly, the attributions we ascribe through our use of language readily shape the nature of the therapeutic relationship – of transference and countertransference – from the moment we exchange our first words with a new patient. As we attend to the particulars of language use within the therapeutic relationship we can open new doors for understanding important aspects of interpersonal influence, especially the enactment of power and submission between therapist and patient, as well as the playing out of themes of inclusion/exclusion, seduction, and rejection.

Dissociation and language use

For those who are bilingual or multilingual, a shift from one language to another – often referred to as "code switching" – may be triggered by changes in the sociocultural environment, and may accordingly trigger shifts in the individual's affect states. For example, a greater range and intensity of affect is generally available in the "native" or dominant language of the speaker, while use of the second language acquired can often lead to a greater sense of emotional detachment and control through intellectualization and isolation of affect (Perez-Foster, 1998). Bilingual sexual abuse survivors' more intense traumatic emotions are often experienced more vividly in their language of origin. This is especially true when sexual abuse occurred during childhood, when a child's first language is closely related to his sense of identity and his emotional connection to his family of origin. For this very reason, bilingual survivors often find it easier in the initial phases of treatment to discuss their history of sexual abuse in their *second* language, as this permits a greater emotional distance from the more visceral experiences of trauma (Perez-Foster, 1998; Cassese & Mujica, 2000).

Dissociation is a common reaction to sexual trauma. Consequently, male survivors are likely to dissociate and therefore compartmentalize emotions when addressing their trauma history. For those who are bi/multicultural and bi/multilingual, dissociation itself is primarily the result of the original traumatic abuse, but we must also consider the compounded effects of immigration and bilingualism on survivors' development and manner of processing their trauma. Psychotherapists able to work in several languages notice that code switching often accompanies changes in the patient's sense of safety, as well as the content and quality of the emotions and memories they recall (Perez-Foster, 1998). When possible, it is best to follow the patient's code switching so the patient is the one who decides which language is used at any given time. This gives patients a greater sense of safety and mastery in titrating the degree of emotional exposure, vulnerability, and intimacy they experience during the therapeutic engagement.

Two experiences with patients illustrate these issues. In both instances, the fact that I am Hispanic and fluent in both Spanish and English was clinically relevant. Moreover, both cases illustrate how a second language – in these cases, English – can be used by patients to engage a less threatened sense of self, allowing themselves to distance from the emotional impact of strong emotions and traumatic memories encoded in the first language (Spanish).

One man was referred to me by a colleague with the following request:

> This patient is from South America and he would like to see an Hispanic therapist who is fluent in Spanish, but would prefer to conduct their sessions primarily in English. The patient would like to know if you would be comfortable in agreeing to this request? The patient is Spanish-dominant but is fairly fluent in English.

I agreed to use the patient's language of preference, as I believe it is best to do in treatment, including during times of switching between languages. I found myself fantasizing: Why would a Spanish-dominant patient want to have his sessions in English? By restricting our communication to English only during our sessions he was able to feel less emotionally vulnerable and better able to stave off the emotional impact of his abuse history. He concurrently enhanced his capacity to intellectualize his experience in therapy (Perez-Foster, 1998). As treatment progressed, this patient was able to gradually use more Spanish during our work together, and explore the impact of doing so.

Upon meeting the patient I quickly observed that, even though we were conducting our initial session in English, he in fact had quite a strong

Spanish accent. I learned he had been living in the United States for only a couple of years prior to our meeting. This confirmed to me that Spanish was not only his first language but also remained very much his dominant language. As I gradually explored the reasons why he preferred to use English in our sessions, the cultural relevance of language was revealed to have very specific meanings involving his history of abuse. From age 12 to 15 he was repeatedly raped by an adult female neighbor, the mother of a close friend. Of course, the entire experience of this abuse had taken place in the monolingual, Spanish-dominant environment of his country of origin in South America. When he was abused he was unable to tell anyone, feeling he was a coward for not being able to stand up to this woman. Furthermore, since she had achieved full control over him, he felt weak and therefore unmanly. He also felt ashamed, worried others would laugh and taunt him if they found out, or that some would tell him he was fortunate for having a woman who wanted to have sex with him despite his young age. He feared his masculinity would be questioned should he complain about his predicament, that peers and older men would expect him to say he was "lucky" to have the sexual attentions of an adult woman. In short, he felt his cultural environment fostered his abuse and was unable to protest or protect himself. He felt abused not only by the woman herself, but also abused and betrayed by the whole culture that sanctioned her using him for her pleasure while forbidding any protestation on his part. Her demands were consonant with the greater social expectation that it was his duty both to satisfy her and to like this experience if he was to be a "real man."

During our sessions, he explained in English that even though he felt securely identified as heterosexual, complaining would mean he was a "sissy, a faggot." He also told me that "sissy" and "faggot" were words used in his culture of origin to remove from boys and men opportunities to complain, to have feelings, or to state they are hurting. He pointedly added that he did not ever want to hear himself or me say these words in Spanish (referring to *marica* and *maricón*, but not saying the words in Spanish). There was therefore a potential for enactment: if I did say these words in Spanish I would be violating the boundaries he had set.

At one juncture, I asked him why then did he not want to see a monolingual, English-speaking therapist, someone who did not have a language or cultural overlap with being Hispanic? He explained that for him to feel deeply understood, it was very important for him to know I had a lived experience of his cultural background. He explained that he'd grown to trust me, and that through our relationship we could both stand between our Latin American and North American cultures, not having to totally disconnect or deny one in order to exist in the other. He felt I understood the language that encoded his traumas and respected the boundaries that secured his sense of identity while being mindful of the culturally loaded experiences that had threatened and hurt him. He longed for a sense of cultural kinship between us, of familiarity, of cultural knowing from the inside out. Yet he also feared the humiliations he experienced prior to immigrating and wanted to stay connected to the sense of refuge and safety he achieved in his new environment, most of which felt more tangible when speaking English. He wished to be supported by my accompanying him on the new path he was choosing, no longer plagued by fear and submissiveness, along a more consciously self-affirmative path tied to his new language, new culture, and new aspects of himself. Thus, we observed that his second and less dominant language (English) had become the vehicle for an opportunity to exercise new and previously hidden and demoralized aspects of himself.

In a similar manner, another patient with whom I usually held sessions in Spanish periodically switched to English. He could become deeply immersed in his discussion of dreams and childhood memories or feelings in Spanish. Yet I noticed his switching to English often occurred when he was pointedly talking about his future, especially his personal aspirations and goals. When I inquired if he too noticed this, he replied, "English is the language of my recovery." He noted that having moved to the United States at 16 went hand in hand with his steps to gain greater autonomy from familial and social oppressions. His breaking away had been supported what he read in English once he immigrated to the United States, readings essential to his maturing identity, including his sexual orientation as a gay man and his learning about other men who experienced homophobic bullying and sexual abuse in childhood. English had become the container of the strength and autonomy he yearned for and wanted to accomplish. It was the language of affirmation of him as a gay man and a survivor of sexual abuse who was determined to succeed in both his personal and professional life.

Thus, for both men, immigration and acquisition of fluency in English paralleled their efforts to exercise a greater sense of autonomy, identity, and self-assertion. Yet, they also wanted to have the freedom to speak

Spanish with me when moved to do so, thereby not denying either of the main cultural roots of their current identifications. Language code switching allowed us to explore a wider range of affects, memories, and relational dynamics.

Conclusions

Recognition and acceptance of the multiplicity of sociocultural identifications of both patient and therapist allow for greater self-awareness and interpersonal intimacy, as they promote a dismantling of rigid defenses. A thorough exploration of these themes facilitates the analysis of defenses relying on avoidance, denial, splitting, projective identification, and dissociation, thereby leading to a fuller appreciation of the complexities of self and other. By attending with our patients to the impact of sociocultural influences throughout the therapeutic process, both within their developmental history and in relation to the cultural context in which the treatment takes place, we help uncover the culturally embedded relational patterns that are the substrate of the analysis of transference and countertransference dynamics. By turning our attention to the patient's struggles to adapt, reject, and/or assimilate aspects of likeness and otherness, we promote development and strengthening of a more flexible sense of self. In this process we also help ourselves and our patients gain greater awareness of the pressures for sociocultural assimilation that often lead to internalized self-blame, self-punishment, self-neglect, and isolation. Moreover, by attending to the many ways that gender-bias continues to deny recognition of sexual abuse – including rape – of boys and men, we can bring much-needed awareness to the responsibility of society and government to provide protection and care for their suffering.

When aspects of sociocultural difference and similarity are attended to within the therapeutic relationship, opportunities for the resurrection and healing of disowned aspects of self and other are renewed. These aspects often touch directly upon the central issues of sexual abuse: domination and submission, love and hate, trust and betrayal, knowing and denial, repression, projection, and dissociation. Enactments of traumatic events can thereby be more readily addressed within the immediacy of the therapeutic relationship. In this broadened therapeutic context, disowned and shamed aspects of self can then be more safely re-examined and reclaimed, so recovery from past trauma can take place more steadily and fully.

References

Abelson, J., English, B., Saltzman, J., & Wallack, T. (2016, October 1). Educators accused of sexual misconduct often find new posts. *Boston Globe*. Retrieved from www.bostonglobe.com/metro/2016/10/01/how-educators-find-new-jobs-after-alleged-sexual-misconduct/TpwwzQkFmRNbrENTmzfluJ/story.html.

Adebimpe, V. (1981). Overview: White norms and psychiatric diagnosis of black patients. *American Journal of Psychiatry, 138*(3), 279–285.

Adebimpe, V., & Cohen, E. (1989). Schizophrenia and affective disorder in black and white patients: A methodologic note. *Journal of the National Medical Association, 81*(7), 761–765.

Akhtar, S. (1999). *Immigration and identity: Turmoil, treatment, and transformation*. Northvale, NJ: Jason Aronson.

Altman, N. (2010). *The analyst in the inner city*. New York, NY: Routledge.

Bickerton, D. (1997, January 26). Memory's secret places: Victims of childhood sex abuse have good reasons to forget it. *New York Times*. Retrieved from www.nytimes.com/books/97/01/26/reviews/970126.26bickert.html.

Boulanger, G. (2007). *Wounded by reality: Understanding and treating adult onset trauma*. Mahwah, NJ: Analytic Press.

Bromberg, P. M. (1991). *Standing in the spaces: Essays on clinical process, trauma, and dissociation*. Hillsdale, NJ: Analytic Press.

Casey, M. (2015, July 31). How the daycare child abuse hysteria of the 1980's became a witch hunt. *Washington Post*. Retrieved from www.washingtonpost.com/opinions/a-modern-witch-hunt/2015/07/31/057effd8-2f1a-11e5-8353-1215475949f4_story.html?utm_term=.281d638dffad.

Cassese, J., & Mujica, E. (2000). Cross cultural perspectives in treating the gay male trauma survivor. In J. Cassese (Ed.), *Gay men and childhood sexual trauma: Integrating the shattered self* (pp. 153–182). New York, NY: Hayworth.

Cooper, L. A., Roter, D. L., Carson, K. A., Beach, M. C., Sabin J. A., Greenwald, A. G., & Inui, T. S. (2012). The associations of clinicians' implicit attitudes about race with medical visit communication and patient ratings of interpersonal care. *American Journal of Public Health, 102*(5), 979–987.

Corbett, K. (2009). *Boyhoods: Rethinking masculinities*. New Haven, CT: Yale University Press.

Criminal Justice Information Services (*CJIS*) (2012, March 19). UCR program changes definition of rape: Includes all victims and omits requirement of physical force. *CJIS, 14*(1). Retrieved from www.fbi.gov/services/cjis/cjis-link/ucr-program-changes-definition-of-rape.

Dickey, F. (2012, May 9). Dale Akiki reflects on historic trial. *The San Diego Union-Tribune*. Retrieved from www.sandiegouniontribune.com/sdut-dale-akiki-reflects-historic-molestation-trial-2012may09-story.html.

Fradkin, H. (2012). *Joining forces: Empowering male survivors to thrive*. New York, NY: Hay House.

Freyd, J. (1994). Betrayal trauma: Traumatic amnesia as an adaptive response to childhood abuse. *Ethics & Behavior, 4*(4), 307–329.

GAP, Committee on Human Sexuality (2000). *Homosexuality and the mental health professions: The impact of bias*. Hillsdale, NJ: Analytic Press.

Gartner, R. B. (1999). *Betrayed as boys: Psychodynamic treatment of sexually abused men*. New York, NY: Guilford.

Good, B. J. (1996). Culture and DSM-IV: Diagnosis, knowledge and power. *Culture, Medicine and Psychiatry, 20*, 127–132.

Hamilton, M. A. (2014, January 9). 2013: The year in review for child sex abuse victims' access to justice. *Justia: Verdict*. Retrieved from https://verdict.justia.com/2014/01/09/2013-year-review-child-sex-abuse-victims-access-justice.

Hopfensberger, J. (2016, May 23). More than 800 sex abuse claims filed under Minnesota law: Law that lanced victims' pain and roiled Catholic Church hits deadline. *Star Tribune*. Retrieved from www.startribune.com/more-than-800-sex-abuse-claims-filed-under-minnesota-law/380524441/.

Hu, T. W., Snowden, L. R., Jerrell, J. M., & Nguyen, T. D. (1991). Ethnic populations in public mental health: Services choice and level of use. *American Journal of Public Health, 81*(11), 1429–1434.

Kempe, C. H., Silverman, F. N., Steele, B. F., Droegemueller, W., & Silver, H. K. (1962). The battered child syndrome. *J. American Medical Association,* 181, 17–24.

Laplanche, J., & Pontalis, J. B. (1973). *The language of psychoanalysis*. New York: W. W. Norton.

Laub, D. (1992). Bearing witness, or the vicissitudes of listening. In S. Felman & D. Laub (Eds.), *Testimony: Crises of witnessing in literature, psychoanalysis, and history* (pp. 57–74). New York, NY: Routledge.

Lawson, W. B., Hepler, N., Holladay, J., & Cuffel, B. (1994). Race as a factor in inpatient and outpatient admissions and diagnosis. *Hospital and Community Psychiatry, 45*(1), 72–74.

Leary, W. E. (1988, March 22). Risk of sex abuse in day care seen as lower than at home. *New York Times*. Retrieved from www.nytimes.com/1988/03/22/us/risk-of-sex-abuse-in-day-care-seen-as-lower-than-at-home.html.

Lew, M. (2004). *Victims no longer: The classic guide for men recovering from sexual child abuse* (2nd Ed.). New York, NY: HarperCollins.

Littlewood, R. (1992). Psychiatric diagnosis and racial bias: Empirical and interpretive approaches. *Social Science and Medicine, 34*(2), 141–149.

Maier, F. X. (2006, May). Shakedown: How Catholics are getting ripped off in the name of justice. *Catholic Education Resource Center*. Retrieved from www.catholiceducation.org/en/religion-and-philosophy/social-justice/shakedown-how-catholics-are-getting-ripped-off-in-the-name-of-justice.html.

McGoldrick, M., Giordano, J., & Garcia-Preto, N. (Eds.). (2006). *Ethnicity and family therapy* (3rd Ed.). New York, NY: Guilford.

Meyers, J. E. (2008). A short history of child protection in America. *Family Law Quarterly, 42*(3), 449–463.

Nussbaum, L. (2006, May 15). Changing the rules. *America: The National Catholic Review*. Retrieved from http://americamagazine.org/issue/572/article/changing-rules.

Otterman, S., & Rivera, R. (2012, May 9). Ultra-Orthodox shun their own for reporting child sexual abuse. *New York Times*. Retrieved from www.nytimes.com/2012/05/10/nyregion/ultra-orthodox-jews-shun-their-own-for-reporting-child-sexual-abuse.html.

Paulson, M., & Franklin, J. (2002, April 8). World doesn't share U.S. view of scandal: Clergy sexual abuse reaches far, receives an uneven focus. *Boston Globe*. Retrieved from http://archive.boston.com/globe/spotlight/abuse/stories/040802_world.htm.

Perez-Foster, R. M. (1998). *The power of language in the clinical process*. Northvale, NJ: Jason Aronson.

Persky, A. S. (2013). Prosecutors battle the wall of silence around sex assault in religious communities. *ABA Journal, 99*(12), 46–51.

Pfeiffer, S., Carroll, M., Rezendes, M., & Robinson, W. V. (2002, January 7). Geoghan preferred preying on poorer children: Children to therapist, priest cited sexual revolution. *Boston Globe*. Retrieved from www.bostonglobe.com/news/special-reports/2002/01/07/geoghan-preferred-preying-poorer-children/69DE1kOuETjphwmIBcgzCM/story.html.

Reynolds, G. H. (2014, September 22). A rape epidemic – by women? USA Today. Retrieved from https://www.usatoday.com/story/opinion/2014/09/22/rape-cdc-numbers-misleading-definition-date-forced-sexual-assault-column/16007089/.

Rezendez, M., Carroll, M., Pfeiffer, S., & Robinson, W. V. (2002, January 6). Church allowed abuse by priest for years: Aware of Geoghan record, Archdiocese still shuttled him from parish to parish. *Boston Globe*. Retrieved from www.bostonglobe.com/news/special-reports/2002/01/06/church-allowed-abuse-priest-for-years/cSHfGkTIrAT25qKGvBuDNM/story.html.

Rivera, R. (2012, June 28). Brooklyn prosecutor's role in abuse case is examined. *New York Times*. Retrieved from www.nytimes.com/2012/06/29/nyregion/hyness-claims-on-extradition-of-abuse-suspect-are-challenged.html.

Sivan, Y. (2011, May 26). Rabbis finally break silence on sex abuse. *The Jewish Chronicle Online*. Retrieved from www.thejc.com/news/world-news/49538/rabbis-%EF%AC%81nally-break-silence-sex-abuse.

Snowden, L., & Cheung, F. (1990). Use of inpatient mental health services by members of ethnic minority groups. *American Psychologist, 45*, 347–355.

Takeuchi, D. T., & Uehara, E. S. (1996). Ethnic minority mental health services: Current research and future conceptual directions. In B. L. Levin & J. Petrila (Eds.), *Mental health services: A public health perspective* (pp. 63–79). New York: Oxford University Press.

Terry, K. (2004). The nature and scope of the problem of sexual abuse of minors by Catholic priests and deacons in the United States, 1950–2002. *U.S. Conference of Catholic Bishops*. Washington, DC: USCCB. Retrieved from www.bishop-accountability.org/reports/2004_02_27_JohnJay_revised/2004_02_27_John_Jay_Main_Report_Optimized.pdf.

Vaughans, K. D. (2014). Disavowed fragments of the intergenerational transmission of trauma from slavery among African Americans. In K. D. Vaughans & W. Spielberg (Eds.), *The psychology of black boys and adolescents* (pp. 563–575). Santa Barbara, CA: Praeger.

Wood, J. M., Gar, H. N., Lilienfeld, S. O., & Nezworski, M. T. (2002). Clinical assessment of personality. *Annual Review of Psychology, 53*, 519–543.

Chapter 8

Interpersonal and institutional dissociation in the sexual abuse of boys

William Burmester

Introduction

In June, 2012, former Penn State Assistant Football Coach Jerry Sandusky was convicted of sexually abusing ten boys from The Second Mile, the youth charity organization for underprivileged children he founded in 1977. On the same day, clergy secretary Monsignor William Lynn of Philadelphia became the first U.S. Church official to be convicted of child endangerment for covering up sexual abuses committed by priests he was charged with disciplining (Hurdle & Eckholm, 2012).

The following week, the *New York Times* published a brief article documenting a consistent 20-year decline in reported cases of sexual abuse (Goode, 2012; see Finkelhor & Jones, 2001). Even as disclosure and reporting became more common and the sexual abuse of boys more broadly acknowledged, the prevalence of sexual abuse was apparently declining. A drop of over 60% in substantiated cases between 1992 and 2010 (Goode, 2012) offers grounds for cautious optimism regarding public awareness and the success of prevention efforts. However, most male survivors abused in institutional settings, often decades ago, are still struggling to break through the silence and isolation sexual abuse imposes on males in particular, because of how betrayed, emasculated, and shamed they feel (Gartner, 1999).

How have serial sexual abusers of boys in institutional settings operated, not only covertly and unchecked, but often idealized and celebrated for decades as beloved and respected teachers, coaches, mentors, and leaders? Their Jekyll–Hyde duplicity, or multiplicity, and the persistent pattern of institutional blindness and collusion that so often enables them to abuse children undetected and undeterred offends our comfortable beliefs about who they are and how vigilant we are. We prefer something less complex and disturbing than iconic abusers like Sandusky who convince us they are God's gift to children until their victims – often very belatedly – force us to realize otherwise.

Many recent sexual abuse scandals involving boys, beyond those within the Catholic Church, have occurred in schools and youth organizations that explicitly or implicitly celebrate ideals of male mentorship originating with the ancient Greeks (Füller, 2015). They include Horace Mann School in New York City, the Odenwaldschule in Germany, and many others. But variations of Greek pederasty also play a role in abusive cultural practices from *bacha bazi* in Afghanistan to international sex trafficking rings in the contemporary West using sports, for instance, as cover. The ancient Greeks, however, seem to have struggled far more with these practices than their contemporary emulators: they at least openly debated how dangerously their pedagogical ideals suspended male youth between honor and disaster (Foucault, 1990).

Bacha bazi

Many in the West were first exposed to *bacha bazi* ("boy play") through *The Kite Runner*, both the 2003 novel by Khaled Hosseini (Hosseini, 2003) and the 2007 film of the same name (Forster & Yeldham, 2007). In it, a boy from the persecuted Afghan Hazara minority is raped by a Pashtun-German teen when the Hazara stands up to him for threatening his best friend. Years later, as a Taliban warlord, the rapist purchases his victim's son from an orphanage and exploits him as a "dancing boy." In contemporary *bacha bazi*, wealthy and influential Pashtun men, many of whom served as military commanders in armed conflict against their Soviet occupiers, acquire, groom, and train boys – typically from poor families – to dance in women's attire for the entertainment of male audiences. Afterwards, the boys are sold or traded for sex to the highest bidder. Although this practice is illegal and condemned as well under Sharia law, its leaders often practice with impunity, wielding sufficient wealth and power to ensure police compliance, protection, and even participation. A 2010 PBS Frontline documentary, *The Dancing Boys of Afghanistan* (Doran, 2010) exposes *bacha bazi* through an Afghan reporter who'd been beaten almost to death a decade earlier while investigating a massacre of prisoners. The boy dancers likewise risk being murdered if they attempt escape, and several such cases are featured in the documentary.

The United States has also played a role in perpetuating *bacha bazi* on at least one occasion, through the private U.S. security contractor DynCorp. Charged with training Afghan police, DynCorp bankrolled at least one *bacha bazi* party for police recruits, paid for with American tax dollars, after the claim of liberating Afghanistan from the practice had been used to justify the U.S. war effort.[1] The DynCorp Vice President of Communications first denied these allegations, then wrote them off as "extremely poor judgement" (Lomax, J., 2010).

Bacha bazi challenges our automatic assumption that shame and secrecy shroud child sex abusers everywhere. Instead, these Afghan men proudly compete with each other for status over the boys they "own." Former Special Forces Captain Dan Quinn, who beat up an American-backed Afghan militia commander for keeping a boy chained to his bed as a sex slave, explained, "We were putting people in power who would do things that were worse than the Taliban did – that was something village elders voiced to me" (Goldstein, 2015). Yet Quinn was quickly relieved of his command by his U.S. superiors.

Rape warfare

Even *bacha bazi*, however, pales beside the rape of boys and men as an institutionalized weapon of warfare in genocidal conflicts, most recently in Africa, but documented in many other countries as well. In 2011, Will Storr published an article in the *Guardian* that describes in difficult detail the pervasive and brutal rape of boys and men in civil conflicts. He cites a 2010 survey from the *Journal of the American Medical Association* placing the number of victims in Eastern Congo at 22% of men (compared with 30% of women), while noting that a doctor with the

1 This was by far not the first sexual abuse scandal for DynCorp, the largest private American military contractor abroad, whose legal immunity contributed to numerous crimes committed by its employees. In 1999, whistleblower Kathryn Bolkovac, a former DynCorp police employee, exposed its involvement in sex trafficking in Bosnia before she was fired for speaking out. See *The Whistleblower* (book: Bolkovac & Lynn, 2011; film: Nola, Plovesan, Rattray, & Kondracki, 2010) and Isenberg (2010).

Refugee Law Project in Uganda claimed *all* the men she saw had been sexually violated. Storr reports further that a survey of political prisoners in El Salvador put the toll of those sexually tortured at 76%, and that of 6,000 male concentration-camp inmates in Sarajevo during the war in Bosnia, 80% reported having been raped.

In the United States

Some of these more extreme practices resurface in U.S.-based sex trafficking rings,[2] as Richard Gartner describes in the case of his patient "Duncan," who was inducted into sexual slavery by the coach who mentored him in sports (Gartner, 2014, 2017). A Nebraska senator reports in "The Franklin Cover-up" (DeCamp, 1996) that "recruits" from Boy's Town were used for sex by men in positions of power. And the former director of a non-profit serving trafficked boys in Denver attested: "There's a big demand for boys . . . We just don't talk about it as a community. We just don't want to talk about it" (Paul, 2015).

Also on the domestic front, press reports and legal convictions have drawn attention to the widespread downloading and viewing of child pornography at the Pentagon and other branches of government (MacAskill, 2010). Of 5,200 Pentagon employees suspected of downloading child pornography, 3,500 were investigated, 300 found guilty and prosecuted, and 1,700 cases were dropped, at least until challenged by Congressman Grassley of Iowa (Bender, 2011), who considered the lapse in investigation a national security risk. In August, 2014, the Acting Director of Cyber Security at the U.S. Department of Health and Human Services was convicted on multiple charges involving online activity at a child porn site (United States Department of Justice, 2014).

In 2015, former Republican Speaker of the House Dennis Hastert was convicted of fraud in relation to molesting a male student early in his career as a successful high school wrestling coach, and was suspected of abusing at least four more. Because the statute of limitations had run out, he was tried not on charges of sexual abuse but on the basis of illegal financial transactions intended to keep his victim silent (Davey, 2016).

2 Editor's note: See Chapter 10 by Procopio in this volume for discussion of trafficking of boys.

As I write, Hastert has just been sentenced to 15 months in prison. The judge commented, "Nothing is more stunning than having 'serial child molester' and 'Speaker of the House' in the same sentence" (Bellware, 2016). Hastert is neither the only nor the first Congressman to face sexual abuse related charges involving boys[3] but his sentencing may reflect a rising challenge to antiquated statute of limitations laws in the United States.

Scouts scandals

Coinciding with the Sandusky revelations in 2012, Boy Scouts organizations in the United States, Canada, and Australia were exposed for decades-long cover-ups of sexual abuse designed to preserve the reputation of Scouting as an institution. Boy Scouts of America (BSA) kept what it called "perversion files," a database of sexual abusers for inner policing, while reporting only a minority of suspected offenses to police.[4] This lapse placed boys at increased risk when the abusers crossed state and national lines. After lengthy court cases, the BSA was forced to release its records, and today a list of almost 1,300 names is available online.[5]

Prison rape

Shortly before his 17th birthday, Rodney Hulin was arrested for starting a fire in a dumpster near his Texas home. His brother described it as a prank. He was held for nine months and tried as an adult. In November, 1995, he was sent to the Clemens unit for younger offenders in Brazoria County, where he was beaten and raped. A prison doctor confirmed the rape, but Rodney's repeated appeals for protection following further rapes were denied as not meeting "emergency grievance criteria." According to his father, Rodney, at 5'2" and 125 lbs, was probably the smallest inmate on

3 Mark Foley, Republican Congressman from Florida, resigned when sexually explicit instant messages from him to underage male pages were released to the media in September 2006. Zack Stanton, one of those pages, reports on his role in the online article, "The Page Who Took Down the GOP" (Stanton, 2015), where he also notes previous cases of congressional sex scandals involving boys, and the fact that the House ultimately responded to the Hastert scandal by eliminating the page program in the House of Representatives.

4 See *Los Angeles Times* (2015, January 13) for documentation of the Boy Scouts Perversion Files scandal.

5 See Crew Janci LLP (n.d.) for a version of the offender list.

the unit. After two-and-a-half more months of ongoing rape and repeated denials of his written appeals for help, Rodney hung himself. He lingered in a coma for four months before dying.[6]

Estimates of prevalence rates for sexual abuse in prisons vary widely, from as little as 2% to as much as 23% (Prison rape in the United States, n.d.). As with the general population, incarcerated men are reluctant to report rape and assault due to shame, fear of disbelief and rejection, and, perhaps most of all, fear of retaliation. Being branded a "snitch" risks revenge even worse than rape. Prison staff have regularly abetted or ignored such retaliation, since potentially disruptive offenders are beholden to staff who tacitly condone the rapes. Therefore, staff may look the other way as a means of controlling the perpetrators' other behavior (Harris, 2016). Lesser offenders – those with shorter sentences – have much to lose by fighting and resisting: to do so may incur disciplinary action that jeopardizes their chances for early or planned release. Despite these factors discouraging the report of rape in prison, Bureau of Justice statistics place the prevalence rate – probably an under-estimate for the reasons stated above – at about 200,000 victims per year (Singer, 2013), a devastating number. These include inmates abused by prison officers and staff, for instance the unanticipated 90% of juvenile male victims abused by female staff (Rojas, 2015).[7]

Rodney Hulin's case fueled a movement to keep younger inmates out of adult prison, where they are five times more likely to be sexually assaulted than in such juvenile facilities as training schools (Forst, Fagan, & Vivona, 1989). These efforts were codified in the Prisoner Rape Elimination Act (PREA) of 2003, which was not finalized until 2012. PREA was voted into law by both houses of Congress without a single dissenting voice. It mandated further study and periodic surveys

6 Rodney Hulin's story is told on the Human Rights Watch website (No Escape: Male Rape in U.S. Prison: Case History of Rodney Hulin, 2010). Video interviews with his family and friends are also available online (No Escape: Prison Rape in America – The Rodney Hulin Story, 2010).

7 According to the U.S. Department of Justice, "The number of allegations of criminal sexual abuse and sexual misconduct against BOP [Bureau of Prisons] staff more than doubled since 2001. From FY 2001 through FY 2008, BOP institutions reported a total of 1,585 allegations of staff sexual abuse (1,028) and sexual misconduct (557) with federal inmates. Allegations of staff sexual abuse and sexual misconduct were reported in all but 1 of the 93 BOP-managed prison sites" (Department of Justice, 2009, p. 19).

of inmates and imposed a policy of "zero tolerance" for sexual assault in prisons. But it is a largely voluntary directive that has been unevenly applied and enforced. As Mike Farrell commented in *The Huffington Post* (2008, 2011), "the National Prison Rape Elimination Commission meets periodically to 'study the impact of prisoner rape.' While they study, rape continues." And in March of 2014, Gov. Rick Perry of Texas – where Rodney Hulin was incarcerated – declared that the Texas Department of Criminal Justice would not adopt PREA, dismissing it as a "counterproductive and unnecessarily cumbersome and costly regulatory mess" (Law, 2014).

Turned Out: Sexual Assault Behind Bars (Schwartz, 2004) is a powerful in-depth documentary film about the dynamics of prison sexual assault and servitude among men. Rodney Hulin's story involves violent sexual assault, as prison rape is often depicted in the popular imagination. But the film depicts a generational shift from the arbitrary violent assaults widespread in the past to a grooming process more common in the present day.[8] Such grooming is based on deceit, manipulation, and betrayal, as is common in child sexual abuse.[9] This suggests to me a re-enactment of abuse suffered by the perpetrators themselves as younger men and children, which then became institutionalized through the power dynamics of prison life.

The non-profit organization Just Detention (originally, Stop Prisoner Rape) is the strongest voice currently advocating legal reform to eliminate prison rape while also addressing the needs of incarcerated victims (see https://justdetention.org). Also hopeful is that among those who do survive and leave prison more resilient than broken, some have gone on to advocate for reform on their own. For example, T. J. Parsell, imprisoned at 17 for robbing a Fotomat with a toy gun and raped while incarcerated, went on to write *Fish: A Boy in a Man's Prison* (2006) decades after his release and following success as a computer executive.[10]

8 Editor's note: See Chapter 13 by Clemente and Hakes in the companion volume to this one, *Healing Sexually Betrayed Men and Boys: Treatment for Sexual Abuse, Assault, and Trauma*, for further discussion of grooming behavior.

9 For prisoners' own statements about prison rape, see: http://pantheon.hrw.org/reports/2001/prison/voices.html.

10 Parsell also undertook a film version of his story (see http://tjparsell.com/Page_2.php for its trailer; also www.youtube.com/watch?v=avZdCDjsu9w).

Educational institutions

The scope of sexual abuse of boys in institutions is distressingly broad. The clergy abuse that initiated broad media coverage of abused boys in 2002 is covered elsewhere in this book (Chapter 9, this volume; see also Frawley-O'Dea, 2007). In sexually abusive school settings, a persistent pattern of blindness and collusion emerges in the relationship between institutional leaders and influential coaches, teachers, and even school directors,[11] who appear to mentor and champion their male students, while profoundly harming a number of them, sometimes fatally when the victims commit suicide. At times, the abuser and the founder or director of an institution are the same person, as were Jerry Sandusky (as founder of The Second Mile), Inslee Clark, Jr. (as director at Horace Mann), and Gerold Becker (as director for 13 years at the Odenwaldschule). But the dissociative split between the benign and the malignant sides of high-profile serial child abusers is perpetuated by the disengagement of others in positions of institutional leadership who, while not abusing boys directly, prioritize institutional reputation over student safety and fail to identify and hold predators accountable, even when the evidence of risk is obvious and based on prior allegations.

Although I will focus on the Penn State University scandal and the court transcripts of the Sandusky trial for the verbatim documentation of dissociation they provide, Robert Berman at Horace Mann in New York City (Fisher, 2013; see also Kamil & Elder, 2015) and Gerold Becker at the Odenwaldschule (Dehmers, 2011; Füller, 2011) may more typically exemplify the institutional dynamics of the sexual abuse of boys in schools.

As we first consider a few key theories and case studies relevant to male sexual abuse and dissociation in the clinical literature, I offer three questions as points of departure and reference:

1 Why do most boys abused in institutional settings "go back for more"?
2 Why do some go on to abuse others while most do not?
3 Why are most institutional victims of sexual abuse boys?

11 See for instance the German documentary on the Odenwald School scandal, *Und wir sind nicht die Einzigen (And We're Not the Only Ones)*, directed by Christoph Röhl (2011), with English subtitles. For trailer see: www.imdb.com/title/tt1854590/?ref_=fn_al_tt_1.

Ferenczi: the confusion of tongues

The most incisive attempt after early Freud to understand the psychodynamics of child sexual abuse was made by Sandor Ferenczi, Freud's last intimate collaborator in the development of psychoanalysis. Toward the end of his life, Ferenczi began to disagree openly with Freud about the role played by childhood sexual trauma in the origin of psychological disturbances. Freud initially believed neuroses like hysteria were the result of the "seduction" of children by adults, typically fathers, and he counted male victims among "hysterics" alongside females. There was much evidence for the sexual abuse of children in Freud's studies with Charcot and others in Paris in 1896 and in his own early clinical cases (Masson, 1992, p. 15).

After 1897, however, when the list of suspects became too large and he might have had to implicate his own father, Freud abandoned his seduction theory (Masson, 1985, p. 264). Ferenczi, as both a psychoanalyst and a survivor (Rachman, 1997, pp. 241–242), knew from clinical practice and personal experience that adults sexually violate children and what happens to children when they do. He risked his considerable standing in the growing psychoanalytic community to present his most famous paper, "The Confusion of Tongues between Adults and the Child," at the 12th International Psychoanalytic Congress in 1932. In it he sought to revive Freud's seduction theory, increase attention to the etiological significance of childhood sexual trauma, and challenge what he called the "hypocrisy" of the analytic situation. When the analyst is reserved, cool, and hides his true feelings (often a dislike of the patient, Ferenczi claimed), he recreates the family context of secrecy, duplicity, neglect, and abandonment in which most sexual abuse of children takes place.

Ferenczi presented his paper over the strong objections of Freud, who was not present to hear it. The paper was negatively received (Rachman, 1997), just as Freud claimed his own early paper on male hysteria had been (Gay, 1998). Ferenczi was even deemed mentally unstable by Freud's orthodox followers (e.g., Jones, 1957), effectively excommunicated from the psychoanalytic community, and died of pernicious anemia within the year. An English translation of the paper was not published for another 16 years. It has since become one of the cornerstones of the relational movement in psychoanalysis (Aron & Harris, 1993) and of the psycho analytic treatment of trauma.

In "Confusion of Tongues," Ferenczi posits that the mental states of adults and children are so radically different, given the nature and extent of the child's vulnerable dependency upon his caregivers, that adults lose emotional touch with this vulnerability and confuse the child's need for "tenderness" – what today we might call secure attachment – with adult sexual desire, which Ferenczi calls the "language of passion." Here, in his own words, is the core of Ferenczi's understanding of what happens in the unconscious "confusion of tongues" between adults and children in sexual abuse:

> It is difficult to imagine the behavior and the emotions of children after such violence. One would expect their first impulse to be rejection, hatred, disgust, and energetic refusal. "No, no, I don't want this; it is too intense for me; it hurts. Leave me alone." This or something similar would be the immediate reaction if it were not paralyzed by overwhelming anxiety. These children feel physically and morally helpless; their personalities are not sufficiently consolidated to be able to protest, even if only in thought, for the overwhelming force and authority of the adult mutes them and often robs them of their senses. *In fact, this anxiety, when it reaches a maximum, automatically forces them to subordinate themselves to the will of the aggressor, to guess and to gratify each of his desires, and, fully forgetting themselves, to identify completely with the aggressor.*
>
> (Author's translation from Ferenczi, 1933/2004, p. 308, italics in the original, based on the 1949 translation by Balint)

This concept of "identifying with the aggressor" deserves further scrutiny. It does not mean the abused child is destined to violate other children in imitation of his abuser, an erroneous and stigmatizing myth about adult male survivors. Although a minority of victims does go on to abuse other children, most imitate and incorporate the abuser by hurting themselves instead. I propose that:

1. the sexually abused boy typically identifies with a dissociated and victimized childhood self-state in the abuser which the abuser disavows and unconsciously pressures the child to embody; and
2. the child *feels* what the abuser *should* feel, namely, at fault and guilty for the violations the abuser commits. The child victim "empathically" absorbs and even relieves his abuser of the distress of bearing unbearable emotions alone.

Ferenczi continues, "The most important change produced in the mind of the child by the anxiety-fear-ridden identification with the adult, is *the introjection of the guilt feelings of the adult*" (Ferenczi, 1949, p. 228, italics in the original).

The child appropriates his abuser's disavowed guilt, whose healthy function is to protect others from potential harm at one's own hands. Because guilt may feel persecutory to the abuser and too distressing to tolerate, he ends up projecting it onto the child victim with such accusations as "You wanted it" (especially if sexual contact has physiologically and involuntarily aroused the boy victim), "You made me do it," and "It's your fault." As psychoanalyst Sue Grand put it almost 70 years after Ferenczi, "The perpetrator lives in possession of the victim's innocence while the victim lives in possession of the perpetrator's guilt" (Grand, 2000, p. 64).

In 1989, psychoanalyst Leonard Shengold published *Soul Murder* (Shengold, 1989), one of the first psychoanalytic books to revive Ferenczi's cause. He opens by explaining: "Psychologically, seduction [of children] can produce the same effect as outright rape . . . The frightening overstimulation inevitably leads to rage and an overwhelming mixture of sexual and aggressive feelings" (p. 1).

Bollas: the structure of evil

Christopher Bollas's 1995 psychological study of serial murderers, "The Structure of Evil," has, I believe, special bearing on the unconscious psychodynamics of childhood sexual abuse as "soul murder." With some debt to Winnicott, Bollas posits a model for the psychological stages of deceptive, deadly assault in the serial murderer, which I offer here in somewhat abbreviated form and pick up later in my analysis of institutional cases of boyhood sexual abuse:

1 "*Presentation of good to the other.* The evil one searches for someone who is in need and presents himself as good."
2 "*Creation of a false potential space.* The arrival of the apparently good one . . . evokes hope (or greed, or the urge for power) and the recipient views him as a potential resolution to circumstance [such as deprivation and loss]."

3 "*Malignant dependence.* When the victim takes up the offer of assistance, he becomes dependent on the provider. We may regard this dependence as malignant since the nurturer feeds in order to destroy, since the initiator of the structure will turn this need into a dire fate."
4 "*Shocking betrayal* . . . the perpetrator . . . suddenly and violently changes his presentation, and the victim is catastrophically shocked by this reversal of fortune . . . by the change in reality itself, which he had assumed to be relatively benign."
5 "*Radical infantilization.* With the total collapse of trust . . . the victim experiences an annihilation of adult personality structures, and is time-warped into a certain kind of infantile position."
6 "*Psychic Death.* The victim experiences the murder of being. The self that was in need, that trusted the world, that felt the arrival of a potential space, that became dependent, and that believed in a good fate, is suddenly killed" (pp. 211–212, italics in original).

Jennifer Freyd: betrayal trauma and Ross Cheit

We turn next to look at this terrain of evil from an institutional perspective. Jennifer Freyd has spent her career developing and researching theories of "betrayal trauma" and "betrayal blindness," especially in relation to the sexual abuse of children. Introducing these concepts, she writes:

> To know is to put oneself in danger. Not to know is to align oneself with the caregiver and ensure survival . . . Memory repression will be shown to arise not because it reduces suffering, but because not knowing about abuse by a caregiver is often necessary for survival.
>
> (Freyd, 1997, p. 4)

Freyd here presents a version of dissociative response to attachment trauma, to which I add the notion of "empathic self-sacrifice" that helps preserve the victim's childhood capacity for concern and empathy into the future.

The first case Freyd presents is that of Ross Cheit. In 1992, Cheit, then Associate Professor of Political Science at Brown University, awoke one summer morning while on vacation with his wife to recollections of a man he'd admired deeply as a child but hadn't thought about in 24 years.

"[S]omething akin to a bad taste in my mouth" accompanied these thoughts (Freyd, 1997, p. 7). His emerging memories of daily sexual abuse by this man, a student minister who ran the summer camp of the San Francisco Boy's Chorus Cheit attended between the ages of 10 and 13, did not arrive full blown. At first the recollections were sensory and nostalgic, not something Cheit encoded as trauma or abuse:

> It was like he was in the room with me. I could picture him. I could hear his voice . . . there was a combination of real affection and fondness for this man and something very unsettling. What I remember I would describe as "those things he used to do to me," but it was in no terms any clearer than that and I didn't dwell on "those things he used to do to me."
>
> (Freyd, 1997, p. 7)

Like many male survivors, Cheit blamed himself for letting "those things" happen. But the conviction that he should have stopped them is that of an older person who *would* resist being abused but who has forgotten what it feels like to be dependent, overwhelmed, and helpless as a child. For that child, the preservation of core relationships is more important than securing immediate physical, emotional, or sexual safety through fight or flight, because children seek safety above all in trusting relationships. This need for attachment places the child in a double bind, a fact not lost on acquaintance abusers. In fact, they cover themselves, as Bollas notes, by assiduously cultivating their victims' dependency, presenting themselves as attentive, kind, generous, and loving to the child and to his caretakers long before their attention turns toxic. Most child victims of acquaintance and serial sexual abuse are groomed in this way.[12]

Against this backdrop of manipulated trust, the betrayal trauma of sexual violation is often dissociated before it ever registers in narrative memory. The abusive events are stored in implicit memory as body sensation, fragmentary imagery, and emotional states rather than cognitive, narrative content, and the abused boy often grows up distancing himself from his affective memory and tender emotions altogether,

12 Editor's note: See Chapter 13 by Clemente and Hakes in the companion volume, *Healing Sexually Betrayed Men and Boys: Treatment for Sexual Abuse, Assault, and Trauma*, for further discussion of acquaintance abuse and grooming.

abetted by a culture that trains him to be rational, objective, strong, and invulnerable at all times.

In the face of internally stimulated arousal and rage, the abused child cannot preserve his needed dependence upon a caretaking abuser without dissociating the bad parts of the relationship, especially any rage that threatens to destroy the good parts. Cheit explained to Freyd that the concept of "sexual trauma" did not fit his experience well:

> I use the word "injury" advisedly. The concept of trauma never seemed right to me. It didn't fit my story. There were no threats. I never sensed danger. I didn't fear him. He was nice to me. Something didn't add up – and it slowly started bothering me more and more.
>
> (Freyd, 1997, p. 11)

The emotional impact set in only when Cheit retrieved and reread the letters he'd sent home from the choir camp as a boy, thereby reconnecting with his voice and state of mind as a child. In the words of his wife:

> He broke down and cried with his whole body, as if he would never stop . . . He came into the bedroom where I was half asleep saying over and over, "but he was such a great guy." He was so hurt that someone he loved did this to him.
>
> (Freyd, 1997, p. 158)

Cheit explains, "These were not just perverse sexual acts, but the most profound betrayal possible for a kid" (Horn, 1993, p. 55). The intensely emotional recollection Cheit experienced in adulthood in the company of a caring wife reminds us how catastrophic full awareness of the betrayal would be for a boy with nowhere to turn. He survives and preserves his world by dissociating the abuse, and that protection becomes a habit. Dissociation in childhood is not a decision. It just happens instinctively, in order to allow the child to continue pursuing some kind of normal, benign life while sequestering an inner core of true selfhood against destruction.

Having later released himself from blame for his abuse, Cheit's attention turned to the institution that knew but did not act (Smith & Freyd, 2014). Initially, Cheit did not know others had lodged complaints about his abuser, William Farmer, with the Founder and Director of the San Francisco Boy's Choir, Madi Bacon (Freyd, 1997, p. 159). Someone caught Farmer in bed with another boy and reported it to her. With the help of a detective, Cheit found five other victims and even recorded a confession by the perpetrator.

When he eventually took legal action as a middle-aged man, Cheit was even angrier at the institution under whose negligent and/or dissociated watch these abuses occurred than at his abuser, whose good side he had been too attached to as a child to simply reject and lose. Being groomed for exploitation left a confusing split, evident in Cheit's recollections of Farmer: "The abuse I remembered occurred on a nightly basis – but never during the day. That's when I did fun things with Bill Farmer . . . How could I act during the day as if nothing happened at night?" (Freyd, 1997, p. 160; cf. Freyd & Birrell, 2013).

But an understanding of betrayal trauma begs the question: how could he afford *not* to dissociate? Because "children need secure and trusting relationships to grow and thrive" (Freyd, 1997, p. 11), they are even more taken in by the abuser's benevolent self-presentation than most adults, and need protective parents and social institutions to notice and intervene. These are functions for which the adult abuser has made himself useless. Since the development of PTSD from a childhood traumatic experience is as much (if not more) determined by whether the child victim has someone safe and reassuring to turn to than it is by the traumatic event itself, Cheit turned his sense of betrayal from Farmer to Farmer's boss, with whom he had a far less personal and ambivalent relationship. Explaining his adult sense of betrayal and outrage, he says, "The rage at Madi is better understood, I think, in a less literal way. Madi stands for the institution. She founded it. She ran it. And the institution betrayed me beyond Bill Farmer. It tolerated the whole thing" (Freyd, 1997, p. 160).

In order to preserve the sense of good in the relationship to the person who appears to love him (while also abusing him), the victim tends to direct his anger instead toward the institution under whose authority he was abused. This parallels what frequently happens in families when the child victim is angrier at the parent who seemed not to notice and/or did not protect him than at the one who sexually exploited his affection. The non-offending parent or caretaker is then the safer target for the anger evoked by the abuser's betrayal. But when leaders or representatives of an implicated institution are targeted this way, they feel unjustly accused of something they did not do. They appropriate the victim's sense of betrayal from having been accused by him, and turn it back upon him by neglecting his plight rather than accepting how they have contributed to his injury by lack of awareness and omission of care. For them, too, it becomes safer to target the child victim as the less threatening one than an adult they may still depend on or fear retaliation from.

Extending Freyd's theory of betrayal trauma in another direction, I propose that, far from simply being oppressed by his abuser, the victim rescues him from his guilt and other bad feelings by bearing them for him. He does so in order to be needed in the absence of feeling valued, and thereby preserves some effective sense of the attachment crucial to his survival. Abusers often pick children with nowhere else to turn, and most child victims who know their abusers offer them the coerced generosity of their vulnerability to being used.

Stout case: an introduction to dissociation in Sandusky

Although this case is familial rather than institutional, it highlights how something crucial about the dissociative interaction between abuser and victim spreads to bystanders and institutions. The case appears in Martha Stout's 2001 book on dissociative disorders, *The Myth of Sanity*.

Dr. Stout had been working with a young adult male survivor of sexual abuse whose symptoms included chronic anxiety and a Valium addiction. In the course of their treatment, the survivor received an unsolicited nine-page letter from his abuser, a paternal aunt,

> confessing to and apologizing for the very abuse he had been discussing in our sessions. Both the patient and I were astounded by the letter; child abusers seldom admit their acts, and for her to do so spontaneously in this way was something on the order of a miracle.
>
> (Stout, 2001, p. 204)

In response, the nephew invited his aunt to a therapy session, hoping to repair and resume their damaged relationship. He wanted her to hear what her sexually abusive behavior had cost him. On the telephone, she confirmed that naturally she would do anything she could to help.

On the day of their conjoint meeting, after struggling with whether to even shake this woman's hand, Dr. Stout did, and they started in. The aunt "said she had come because she loved her nephew deeply, that she felt like a second mother to him, and wanted to end their estrangement" (p. 205). The nephew simply handed his aunt her letter to review; she took it without comment and read for about 10 minutes. After five minutes, the nephew "sighed shakily" and left to get a drink of water. He returned just as she was finishing.

> [She] refolded the letter, placed it in the envelope, and returned it to him.
>
> "This is really awful," she said. "Why did you show it to me?"
>
> "I thought we could discuss it here," he answered expectantly. "I guess . . . I guess first of all I'd like to find out why you chose now to write it. I mean why you waited so long."
>
> "Write it? I don't understand. I didn't write that letter . . ."
>
> "Of course you wrote the letter. You sent it to me. You signed it. Look here."
>
> He took the letter out of its envelope again and held up the last page for her to see.
>
> (p. 206)

More denial. An argument ensued. The nephew was now desperate, almost pleading, but to no avail. The abuser had radically altered her self-presentation, leaving her victim to "regress" into confusion and anger. Dr. Stout cut the meeting short. At the door the aunt repeated that she loved and missed her nephew and "had, she said gently, taken no offense at all from his accusations" (p. 207).

Imagine what the experience of abuse must have been like for the nephew if she dissociated like this while abusing him: one version of her during the abuse and another for the times in between. Could any of it have seemed real to him if it didn't register as real to *her*? He might not have noted her switching then any better than she remembered the abuse during their therapy session. But what falsely accused person takes no offense at being considered a child abuser? Here are Dr. Stout's concluding remarks:

> To switch and commit child abuse and then not to remember: a more horrifying destiny is difficult to imagine. But . . . there are other, even more far-reaching possibilities. For example, what if a luminary or a

> leader – someone in a position of power not in the context of one family only, but in the context of a whole community or a trusted institution or a nation – were to be, in addition, a switcher. The potential for the abuse and subversion of an entire society is stupefying.
>
> (p. 208)

Sandusky's sentencing statement

Just prior to his sentencing hearing on October 9, 2012, Sandusky had this audio statement delivered to a local radio station:

> I'm responding to the worst loss of my life. First I looked at myself. Over and over I asked, "Why?" Why didn't we have a fair opportunity to prepare for trial? Why have so many people suffered as a result of false allegations? What's the purpose? Maybe it will help others. Some vulnerable children who could be abused might not be as a result of all the publicity. That would be nice, but I'm not sure about it.
>
> I would cherish the opportunity to become a candle for others, as they have been a light for me. They could make me out as a monster, they could treat me as a monster, but they can't take away my heart. In my heart, I know I did not do any of these alleged disgusting acts . . .
>
> The accusers were products of many more people and experiences than me. Look at their confidantes and their honesty. *Think about how easy it was for them to turn on me, given the information, attention and potential perks.*
>
> (Edmonds, 2012, emphasis added)

Ever self-referential, if not effectively self-reflective, Sandusky's statement describes how *he* abused his victims, using the authority and protection of his position as football icon at Penn State to shower attention and perks on his disenfranchised but longing and hopeful wards. He projects his own acts of exploitation onto those who came to the rescue of his victims.

In the light of the court testimony of his victims, it is hard not to be incredulous of Sandusky's denials. But imagine what it might be like for someone so dissociated – like the aunt in Stout's story – that the part of him protesting his innocence and preoccupied with a dedication to children in need is never around to witness his crimes, while the part committing sexual acts with boys only experiences them as playful and well-intentioned and reads the dissociation he evokes in his victims as negligible discomfort and unharmed acquiescence. The urge not to know affects abusers under stress no less than children struggling to survive, in no small part because the culpability and consequences of their actions are so dire and reprehensible under current laws.

Brett

Brett H., victim #4, and the first to testify at Sandusky's trial, was referred as a 13-year-old by his school guidance counselor to Sandusky's charitable organization because of trouble he was having at home. He described the ritual Sandusky used to test how seducible a boy would be: well into the grooming process, with both of them naked in the locker room showers, Sandusky would pump handfuls of soap from the dispensers and sling them playfully at Brett, as if he were the boy's age-mate. This devolved into silently lathering Brett up, hugging, caressing, and then wanting the boy to wash his adult body (*Commonwealth* v. *Gerald A. Sandusky*, 2012, Day 1, p. 54). In Bollas's terms, the boy's need for attention becomes his dire fate.

In this way, Sandusky apparently induced a dissociative state in Brett – and possibly also within himself – common to all his abuses. The sexual contact was executed in a zone of speechless action, dissociated from a sense of reality. Because the speech centers in the brain shut down under this kind of assault, it becomes verbally uncommunicable to others, as many survivors have struggled to explain. It's all dissociated action, like a football game gone surreal. With intense stimuli going neurologically unmediated, derealization[13] sets in. Nothing seems real.

Brett has linguistic trouble[14] trying to explain his experience in court: "He wouldn't say just it. He would just kind of like take his hand, you

13 In the most recent version of the DSM (DSM-5), derealization has been ensconced as a core form of dissociation.

14 This kind of intrusion into the grammatical and logical structure of speech is what serves to identify disorganized attachment in the Adult Attachment Interview (AAI) for adults with severe developmental trauma and DID, according to Main, Hesse, and Siegel (2016). While it is possible that Brett's wording is just a coincidental slip in an otherwise coherent narrative, this is exactly how histories of trauma show up in the AAI.

know, wash his body thing. He would do the same to me" (*Commonwealth* v. *Gerald A. Sandusky*, 2012, Day 1, p. 54: lines 10–12). As he does frequently during the trial, prosecuting State Attorney Joe McGettigan asks Brett whether he ever objected or expressed discomfort about showering with Sandusky, giving voice to the false adult expectation, described by Ferenczi, that child victims experiencing revulsion would protest. Brett replies he did not. But he did take strong exception when Sandusky put a hand on his leg while they were driving, as if declaring with that gesture that Brett was his "girlfriend":

> It freaked me out like extremely bad. I could not stand it. That would happen almost every time that I was in the car. I would brush that off. *I never would say anything* . . . But after a little while with me not paying attention, it would be right back. That just drove me nuts.
>
> (p. 57: 4–14, emphasis added)

Significantly, Brett is far less dissociated from healthy feelings of disgust and protest here than during the sexual assaults in the showers. The sexual attacks occurred in that speechless zone that just doesn't seem real, whereas being feminized closer to the traffic of public scrutiny felt far more immediate, threatening, and objectionable to him. When Sandusky overrides Brett's physical cues to stop touching him in the car, he does so with just another silent grooming gesture.

In public, Sandusky inundated Brett with the perks and privileges of his status as assistant coach at Penn State, treatment guaranteed to make the boy feel extremely special and place a lot at stake for him should he protest. Sandusky took him onto the football field during Penn State games in the presence of 100,000 spectators. When McGettigan asks Brett whether he liked that, he replies, "Oh I loved it" (p. 58: 4–7). Sandusky even got Brett's picture published in *Sports Illustrated* (p. 72: 234).

But back in the silent showers, "He wouldn't be so forthright about it. You know, it would be more of a glancing over or brushing thing for me" (p. 59: 5–12). It's unclear who's who in this statement, as though the boundary between self and other blurs in Brett's mind. He may also have dissociated while submitting to Sandusky's wishes in the locker room. Recall Ferenczi describing what happens when the intensity of the child's anxiety forces him to subordinate himself to the will of the abuser. McGettigan seems to pick up on this fusion or ambiguity of identity in the following exchange when he asks, "himself then?":

Q. Was he putting your hand on him—
A. Yes.
Q. –himself then?
A. Yes.
Q. And did you say anything to him when he did this?
A. No.
Q. Did you tell anyone else?
A. No.

(p. 59: 18–25)

McGettigan refuses to accept Brett's silence or passivity at face value (or else goes out of his way to establish it), and keeps pressing the point:

Q. Did it occur to you to tell your grandmother or somebody else?
A. No, no way. Not ever. I was too scared to.
Q. Okay.
A. And I didn't want to lose what, you know – I mean, this was – other than that, the other things were, you know, nice. I didn't want to lose that.
Q. Was the defendant being nice to you other than that?
A. Yes. Yes.

(p. 60: 5–16)

Brett's linguistic hesitations suggest that, even more than a decade after the fact, he feels implicated in or guilty about the abuse, because he enjoyed the good things preceding and following it. Like Stout, McGettigan reminds us of the serial abuser's dual self-states: nice guy and sexual predator. Once the boy's sexual boundaries have been violated and his personal integrity betrayed, the outer signs of being special carry disproportionate weight because they may be all he has left of feeling cared about. Imagine Brett's confusion: the glaring contradiction between the devoted and generous public Sandusky everyone else witnesses and the terrifyingly playful private one, the first full of powerful action, speech, and sports glamour, the second intruding on his body in silence as if under water. Again:

Q. Did he ever discuss what was going on in there?
A. It was never talked about, ever.
Q. Did he ever ask you not to say anything to anybody?
A. No, no. *It was basically, like whatever happened there never really happened.* And as soon as we – before the shower, nothing, you know. After the shower, it was like nothing ever happened.

(p. 63: 23, p. 64: 1–7, emphasis added)

In the very telling of it, Brett enacts the dissociative process he describes, a communication in action parallel to the abuse itself. As his narrative approaches mention of some abusive sex act in the words "As soon as we . . . ," he abruptly breaks off, encapsulating the abusive acts out of sight, and focuses only on a before and an after, from which vantage point there is nothing in between. A dissociative gap. He also implicates himself as complicit and guilty by saying "as soon as *we* . . ." instead of "as soon as *he* . . . ." The structure of his speech shows us how the dissociation works. The collapse and fusion of identity makes Brett a co-agent of the abuse. Consciously, he may also be trying to protect his privacy in court by blanking out details, but, ultimately, Brett is able to trace the dissociation back to the adult Sandusky:

Q. Did he ever say anything in his home or any place else about the things he was doing?
A. No.
Q. *Did he act like it was even happening?*
A. No.
Q. Okay.
A. I told you it would be literally like night and day[15] when you go in the shower and get out of it.

(p. 84: 16–25, italics added)

By the end of McGettigan's questioning, Brett confirms about 40 incidents of oral sex, along with attempts at anal penetration by Sandusky, which Brett claims to have walked out on. Of course we all hope that's what happened, and other boys claimed the same, but, given the dissociative nature of the abuse, who knows?

15 Note the parallel here with Ross Cheit's description, noted earlier, of his experience of his abuser being split into contradictory day and night versions.

Zachary

In 1998, victim #6, Zachary, casually mentioned to his mother upon returning home from an outing with Coach Sandusky that they'd showered together. At the trial 14 years later he explained to the prosecutor that he'd alluded to the experience without telling her what happened:

> I walked into the room and said just a few things of what he showed me about the players, and then I said to my mom, "And by the way, if you're wondering why my hair is wet, it's because we took a shower," and then I took off.
>
> (Day 4, p. 18: 11–16)

She had the intuitive good sense to follow up. Even after questioning him further and eliciting no details of abuse, she reported the incident to Alycia Chambers, a psychologist at Children and Youth Services (CYS) who had worked with Zachary. At her urging, Zachary's mother contacted university police. A detective interviewed Zachary the following day. As Freyd leads us to anticipate, Zachary did not want to get Sandusky in trouble and said his actions probably didn't mean anything. As with Brett, silence was already staking a claim on him for the sake of preserving his connection to the big man who had taken such an interest in him.

Compared to other assaults by Sandusky, Zachary's experience almost doesn't seem abusive, in part because it apparently happened only once. After the usual grooming of acquaintanceship over two to three years via Zachary's involvement with The Second Mile, invitations to football games to which the Coach transported him personally, the hand-on-the-thigh maneuver while driving, a brief workout and wrestling lesson, Sandusky moved him on to the showers. Zachary tried to maintain his distance but was distracted by trying not to displease or anger him:

> [H]e, you know, grabbed me from behind, gave me a big bear hug and, you know, kind of lifted me up and just said, "I'm going to squeeze your guts out," like in a playful manner and just, you know, squeezed and made a growling sound.
>
> (Day 4, p. 15: 6–10)

Sandusky kept joking while Zachary's discomfort escalated:

> I just remember going into the showerhead and having to close my eyes so the soap wouldn't get in my eyes. And that's the last thing I remember about being in the shower. It's just kind of black.
>
> (p. 16: 1–14)

The episode reminds me of an attachment video I once saw in which a dissociative mother is playing on the floor with her baby. Happy play takes a sudden turn when she "playfully" growls at her infant like a wild animal. What she appears to do in jest paralyzes the infant, sending him into a dissociative state, all caught on film and scrutinized later in slow motion by the attachment researchers. Recall the similar moment in Bollas's stages of serial murder when the perpetrator suddenly and violently changes his self-presentation: "With the total collapse of trust . . . the victim experiences an annihilation of adult personality structures, and is time-warped into a certain kind of infantile position" (Bollas, 1995, p. 211). Sandusky's jocular image of murder-by-crushing, delivered to a prospective new victim anxiously swinging between hypervigilance and disorientation, closely presages the moment at which Zachary's memory ends: "I don't even remember being put down. I got home somehow and everything else is just blackout. I just don't remember it" (p. 17: 20, p. 18: 4).

This is Ferenczi's moment of maximal anxiety, when self vanishes and the will of the abuser fills the vacuum. Again, we hope nothing more happened to Zachary in the showers, but one wonders whether a sudden switch in the offender evoked something similar but more dire in his victim, as I speculated in the cases of Stout's young client and the infant with his growling mother.

Without even knowing the missing details, Zachary's mother arranged for detectives to listen secretly to two separate conversations she set up with Sandusky in her home. With them in hiding, she grilled Sandusky on whether the encounter with her son was sexual, including whose body parts ended up where. When Sandusky refused her eventual request to stop showering with boys – one wonders why he didn't just lie to her – and she in turn refused his request to speak with her son, she told the coach he could no longer see him. This is when Sandusky uttered words close to a confession: "I understand. I was wrong. I wish I could get forgiveness. I know I won't get it from you. I wish I were dead" (Grand Jury Presentment, 2011, p. 20).

Meanwhile, Zachary's therapist conferred with colleagues who determined Sandusky's actions met criteria for pedophilic grooming behavior. Another evaluator, who allowed himself to be called a psychologist but wasn't (Dawson, 2012), had been hired to avoid a potential conflict of interest. Freeh reports one of the detectives quoting this counselor, John Seasock, as saying he had never heard of a 52-year-old man "becoming a pedophile." Seasock naively and deferentially recommended someone educate Sandusky: "The intent of the conversation with Mr. Sandusky is not to cast dispersion [*sic*] upon his actions but to help him stay out of such gray area situations in the future" (Freeh, 2012, pp. 44–45). And so Seasock declared in writing that Sandusky "didn't fit the profile of a pedophile" (Freeh, 2012, p. 45), and thereby guaranteed that attention to the risk Sandusky posed *did* get "dispersed." "Somehow," his report was the only one sent on to the District Attorney. Consequently, by the time Sandusky himself was interviewed by the detectives, the DA had already declined to prosecute. At his interview, Sandusky admitted to hugging Zachary in the shower but claimed "honest to God, nothing happened" (Freeh, 2012, p. 46). When they too told him to stop showering with boys, Sandusky assured them he would stop, and they closed their case. It is distressing to think this man continued abusing boys for another decade because he could now assume even his own confession would be officially overlooked, a fateful example of institutional dissociation at work.

But in his particular state of mind, was Sandusky lying – even consciously to himself – when he claimed "nothing happened"? Is it conceivable that he dissociated so completely that in his own mind nothing *had* happened? Similarly, why would the aunt who abused Dr. Stout's client have absurdly continued reaching out for reconciliation and a return to the past if she were aware of her actual guilt?

Sandusky expressed concern to the detectives about how their interrogations might affect Zachary. This can be variously interpreted as concern or dissimulation. At the very least his magnanimity suspiciously recalls the aunt's equanimity at being reminded of the sexual abuse she had already admitted to and apologized for in the letter she later claimed not to have written. The institutional "bystanders" at Penn State, regardless of how empowered and responsible they were as detectives and senior university administrators, were far readier to exonerate the suspected coach on "humane" grounds for lack of evidence than to suspect he could both *be* guilty and convincingly *appear* innocent.

Much hangs on popular ignorance of the nature of multiplicity and dissociation. But those who accuse Sandusky of deliberate and manipulative duplicity equally overlook the role dissociation may have played in his behavior. If I am right, Sandusky did not and may still not believe he was guilty of anything abusive or criminal. Thus his self-presentation would be even more likely to cue his victims and others to assume the same about him over the course of so many years.

Institutional dissociation

A decade after Sandusky's brief and abortive encounter with the law, Special Investigator Louis Freeh uncovered confidential notes PSU Senior Vice President Schultz concealed from the Grand Jury regarding the shower incident with Zachary, ending with the question, "Is this opening Pandora's box? Other children?" (Freeh, 2012, p. 48). Yet, having briefed Athletic Director Curley and University President Spanier on the detectives' meeting with Sandusky, Schultz concluded by writing, "I think the matter has been appropriately investigated and hope it is now behind us" (p. 50). Maintaining institutional distance made it increasingly expedient and tempting to disavow the persistent danger Sandusky posed.

Head football coach Joe Paterno, in his handwritten notes regarding Sandusky's proposal for retirement shortly after the latter's 1998 interview with detectives and in reference to Sandusky's request for ongoing access to Penn State's athletic facilities, wondered: "Is this for personal use or 2nd Mile kids? No to 2nd Mile. Liability problems" (Freeh, 2012, p. 55). The concern is real but once again gets displaced from the boys' welfare onto that of the institution. According to Freeh, when they testified before the Grand Jury a decade later in 2011, Schulz, Spanier, Curley, and Paterno all denied knowledge of details they themselves had documented regarding the investigation of Sandusky showering with Zachary in 1998.

The farther up the ladder of mostly male authority and power these allegations of sexual misconduct went, the more they evaporated, reminiscent of both Brett's and Zachary's obliterated shower memories but without even the immediate stressor of sexual intrusion. While the women directly involved with Zachary intuitively and professionally knew something was seriously amiss, others in positions to do something about it appear to have *wanted NOT to know*, even preventively for the sake of protecting children in the future. This need to protect their institution had dire consequences for another decade of victims and ultimately for the institution itself.

The survival pressure "not to know," of which Freyd writes, does not end with childhood. At the trial, Zachary claimed he pursued a grateful, non-sexual relationship with Sandusky for several years. His mother may have succeeded in protecting him – but only him – while the institutions of higher learning and law enforcement forgot. It took one of Sandusky's later victims, Aaron Fisher, again with the support of his mother and therapist, to file the charges that eventually brought Sandusky to justice in 2012 (Fisher & Gillum, 2012).

There is much more to be said not only about dissociation during episodes of sexual abuse but about minimization – dissociation's more conscious cousin – when these episodes come to light within the institutions harboring them. In 2001, for instance, Penn State Assistant Football Coach Mike McQueary accidentally witnessed another PSU shower incident involving an apparent sexual assault by Sandusky upon another prepubescent boy. McQueary was shaken speechless in his moment of exposure, but did report to Paterno that he'd fleetingly heard and seen something very sexual in the showers, although he could never bring himself to call it rape. Paterno, in turn, passed the news up the chain of command ending with University President Spanier, assuming others would know better than he how to deal with it. As a result of Louis Freeh's investigation, published soon after the trial, Schultz, Curley, Spanier, and Paterno were all fired, but not until a decade after Zachary's and McQueary's initial reports of Sandusky's extreme behavior. How sexual abuse persists for so long in places as public as schools – and in this case, a major university – remains the silent hallmark of dissociation's power to dispel the distress of sexual abuse – for all involved – by making the real appear unreal or just making it disappear. When the institution housing the abuse abets it by failing to notice and intervene, the young victim in his isolation and threatened loss of community typically identifies with the neglecter: he remains silent and protects the comfort of those refusing to engage on his behalf. Institutional betrayal acts as a cue to the victim to subordinate himself once more to the will of a more powerful force and reinforces his identity as a victim with no power.[16]

Deconstructing predators' sexual abuse of power

How can we understand the psychology driving publicly benevolent serial child molesters and the psychological consequences for their victims? Most abusers have complex histories of abuse and neglect, including early attachment trauma (Marshall, Serran, & Cortoni, 2000). It is easy and common to dismiss or downplay the role this early childhood trauma plays in abusers' crimes, because abusers may exploit their childhood victimization to excuse unpardonable behavior. But no matter how much psychodynamic sense any of us makes of childhood sexual abuse, it no more indemnifies abusers than it does those who abused them. Explanation is not exoneration.[17]

By attending carefully to origins of childhood sexual abuse in abusers' own childhoods, both victims and abusers may learn to see themselves more clearly embedded in a dissociative logic and lineage of exploitation,[18] from which many may extricate themselves with the right balance of empathic support, effective therapy, and accountability.[19] Only half of child sex abusers claim to have been sexually abused as children themselves (Thomas et al., 2012). However, percentages vary dramatically depending upon *how* abusers are asked about their history, how abuse is defined, and even whether their behavior is labeled "abuse," since one of the key myths of male sexual abuse is that boys and men cannot be abused

16 As this book went to press it was reported that, in addition to fines against the university and penalties levied against the football team, ex-president Spanier was found guilty of child endangerment in a jury trial while Schultz and Curley both pled guilty and were offered deals (Hobson, 2017). In addition, word came of McQueary's jury award of $7.3 million in a defamation suit he brought against Penn State when the administration denied that those he informed about Sandusky perjured themselves in claiming they didn't know (Tracy, 2016). Thus, bystanders with power and authority have been held accountable alongside Sandusky.

17 Editor's note: See Chapter 15 by MacDonell and Bolton on treating survivors with histories of offending in the companion volume to this one, Healing Sexually Betrayed Men and Boys: Treatment for Sexual Abuse, Assault, and Trauma.

18 See Mark Wolynn's *It Didn't Start With You* (2016) for a current discussion of the intergenerational transmission of trauma.

19 Germany's health ministry has just decided to extend and increase funding for the therapeutic treatment of pedophiles in Germany through the Dunkelfeld Project (Scholz, 2016).

without forfeiting their masculinity (Briggs, 1995; Mendel, 1995). Lack of reported sexual abuse history or even lack of conscious recall does not mean a man wasn't victimized, sexually or otherwise, in ways that later contribute to him sexually offending against children. In fact, the less conscious the abuse, the more likely it is to be re-enacted; shame and the public scapegoating of abusers guarantees sexual abuse is the most likely abuse to be minimized, overlooked, and forgotten.

I believe serial sexual abuse is an unconscious – even addictive – strategy the abuser uses to dissociate his own childhood victimization. The abuser enacts his abuse with roles reversed instead of remembering it as his own, in one of many acts of identification with those who abused him. The power exercised in victimizing someone perceived as more vulnerable than themselves banishes abusers' felt powerlessness of being victims. This helps explain why pedophilic attractions age out. As they grow up, boy victims cease to embody the vulnerability, powerlessness, and presumed weakness their abusers projectively demand of them, however unconsciously.

Meanwhile, the child's capacity to offer himself up is rarely appreciated for the emotional survival strength and stamina it demands, let alone for the empathy and generosity it often involves. Few notice these strengths except perhaps the abuser him- or herself. Awareness of the victim's strengths is likely to be unconscious (sensed rather than known), in keeping with the truism in family systems that the child elected to be the defective one (the system's "identified patient") is typically the one most capable of tolerating and surviving that role, so other family members can relieve themselves of it by continuing to scapegoat him or her.

When we are shocked by the serial abuser's criminal failures of empathy we fail to realize that for him the goal of abusing is to *avoid* feeling empathy for suffering that is already too close to home. The abuser is loath to have any *internal* contact with the injured vulnerability of having been an abused child and therefore recreates that child *outside* himself by staging experiences of loss and betrayal through acts of sexual assault on children. The abuser weakly and dependently gets someone who *appears* weaker and more dependent than himself to suffer for him, even if the pain transferred to the victim is apparent only briefly between his shock at being betrayed and his own defensive dissociation. Grooming may be less about getting access to a child for sexual release and more about getting the child to trust from a position of vulnerability that was violated for the offender when he was a child, so the child mirrors him in that experience of betrayal. Ultimately, abuse is both release and betrayal, but typically only the sexual assault is seen so we in turn can more easily distance ourselves from the abused abuser as victim.

The abuser's dissociation is like that of the child who, while being sexually traumatized, spontaneously floats up to witness somebody doing something bad to "another" child beneath him, but without feeling much about it.[20] The abuser repeats this extreme spontaneous form of childhood dissociation, except that for him the "other" child – himself as a child – now lives in the body of his current child victim, without the abuser suffering that child's emotional crisis. The abuser psychologically – and often sexually – repeats what was done to him. Abuse dissociates feeling from action and the new child victim learns soon enough from his abuser how to dissociate as well, if he hasn't done so instinctively. Once the child victim protects himself by dissociating, whether spontaneously or by imitating his abuser's dissociative state, the abuser perceives an *absence* of feeling rather than pain in his victim and can more readily convince himself he causes no harm, while also readily moving on to his next victim.

Bollas sums up this lethal progression as follows:

> The serial killer – a killed self – seems to go on living by transforming other selves into similarly killed ones, establishing a companionship of the dead . . . In place of a once-live self, a new being emerges, identified with the killing of what is good, the destruction of trust, love, and reparation.
>
> (Bollas, 1995, p. 189)

This passage helps explain why it is such a challenge for survivors of sexual abuse – male survivors especially – to establish trust in the course of healing. Distrust has been their protection.

Interpersonal dissociation in the victim–victimizer dyad

In contrast to literal murder, the "soul murder" of sexual abuse is a parts-driven dissociative process. Other parts of the victim typically survive it, and may even master it, for instance by developing a caretaker identity or

20 This process is profoundly captured and communicated by one of Gerold Becker's victims at the Odenwaldschule, Andreas Hückele, in the German documentary, *Gescholssene Gesellschaft* (Schmidt & Schilling, 2012), as of this writing not yet released with English subtitles.

other compensatory and sometimes highly successful adult capability. Even in the victim who goes on to abuse others, dissociation may facilitate the abuser not only expressing but genuinely *experiencing* a benevolent desire to nurture children. Both the aunt of Stout's young client and Sandusky presented themselves as this kind of person in public. This benign but malignant "both-and" of dissociation is particularly difficult for "normally" non-dissociative people to accept because it wreaks havoc on assumptions we have about guilt, accountability, and justice.

At some point, however, the abuser's benign self is short-circuited by the threat of emotional contagion from early attachment trauma. Exposure to vulnerable children starts evoking whatever sexual, physical, and/or emotional trauma the abused abuser suffered. The more vulnerable and infantilized the unsuspecting victim becomes in his state of mounting, trauma-induced dependency, the more he reminds the abuser of himself as a dependent and therefore victimizable, emasculated child. As this felt memory intensifies, remains un-assuaged, and threatens to become completely unbearable (as when it threatened to collapse the abuser's developing ego in childhood), the abuser gets rid of it by becoming sexual with his victim. Adult sexuality distances him from childhood vulnerability. The abuser's "confusion of tongues" is neither accidental nor coincidental, but motivated, even if unconsciously so.

For abusers who do not simply take sadistic pleasure in causing children's pain, the pleasure and preoccupation of erotic stimulation effectively distracts them from perceiving whatever emotional distress their victims are suffering. The abuser tolerates only so much internal contact with his "murdered" younger self before fully recreating, externalizing, and distancing from it in his victim. The more sadistic abuser need not deceive himself that the child he victimizes "likes it too," but equally feeds off the child's pain and confusion as not his own.

From another point of view, however, the sexually abused abuser can be seen to re-enact his early experiences of betrayal not just in defensive identification with his own lineage of abusers but in pursuing children in order to re-contact, revive, and reintegrate the vital child self he lost to trauma. In the end, however, *losing* this vital self defines him more compellingly as an adult than the innocence lost and any serious desire to restore it. That innocence is too close to the vulnerability that got him catastrophically hurt in the first place. The abuser may find his abused self in the child he sexually stimulates (especially if this was done to him), but he then goes on to dis-identify with the child whose need for love endangers him. He may relish his future victim's love of his nurturing persona but denies or reframes having been such a child himself because he knows what it leads to.

What is missing is the intervention of a protective, rescuing other who is capable of empathy. Given that the healthful "drive" to reintegrate a lost part of himself stays unconscious as it evokes increasing distress, the abuser repeats rather than suffers and resolves past injury.[21] The role of rescuer gets displaced not only into his benign but superficial public persona – the dedicated teacher, coach, or mentor – but also into the child victim, insofar as he "parents" the abuser by tolerating his assaults without retaliating. The victim "comes back for more," much like Winnicott's "good-enough mother" faced with an aggressive 2-year-old in need of holding and soothing. What gets repeated from abuser to child victim is the shocking betrayal of the child's belief and trust that he matters for who *he* is and for what *he* needs as a child (Bollas's stage 4). By turning sexual, the abuser simultaneously (1) evokes in his victim his own history of trauma, betrayal, and disorientation, (2) abandons him to its unmanageable intensities, and (3) distracts himself from the child's actual distress by "getting off" on it as a vulnerability belonging to someone else.[22] He trivializes and denatures suffering by sexualizing it. In short, the abuser repeats what was done to him as something for someone else to feel the pain of. This mechanism may be a traumatic remnant of the inherently healthy pre-verbal projective identification an infant naturally engages in with his mother when his cries induce in her the states of distress he needs for help surviving, resolving, and repairing (Schore, 2003).

The tragic irony is that child victims often play out the mirroring and ministering role of the "good-enough mother" so well that abusers become dependent on the relief they provide, and come back for more. In this way, the abuser does again become the child he was, a child frustrated in search

21 A particularly tragic outcome of this search for a childhood self lost to sexual abuse occurs when a survivor uses child pornography in an attempt to reconnect to himself as a child victim and is detected by law enforcement: arrested, prosecuted, and imprisoned without receiving therapeutic help. While consumption of child pornography should be illegal, no one drawn into it this way should suffer the fate of Jesse Loskarn, the 35-year-old chief of staff to Sen. Lamar Alexander, who described his ordeal in a suicide note posted online posthumously by his family (Loskarn, n.d.; Bresnahan, 2014)

22 A similar and deeply provocative version of this dissociative process is explored in the Venezuelan film, *From Afar (Desde allá)*, directed by Lorenzo Vigas (2015) and winner of the 2015 Venice Film Festival Golden Lion. It is available online at: www.amazon.com/dp/B01LG8JVFY?ref_=imdbref_tt_wbr_aiv&tag=imdbtag_tt_wbr_aiv-20.

of emotional nurture, while the child victim protects and rescues him by containing his frustration and worse, like a good parent. The missing mothering function appropriated by the attached child victim is at the core of what Ferenczi calls the child's "precocious maturity."

> When subjected to a sexual attack, under the pressure of such traumatic urgency, the child can develop instantaneously all the emotions of [the] mature adult and all the potential qualities dormant in him that normally belong to marriage, maternity and fatherhood.
>
> (Ferenczi, 1949, p. 229)

Help from the outside: the *Boston Globe* story

It often takes an attuned outsider to inspire survivors to confront their traumatic pasts in order to heal. We saw Zachary's mother assume this role in a private capacity. On a public, institutional level the role of outsider was played most dramatically by the *Boston Globe* in its 2002 exposé of the extensive history of sexual abuse and institutional collusion within the Catholic Church. It was the newspaper's newly hired and transplanted Jewish editor who directed and encouraged the *Globe*'s Catholic Spotlight staff to take on their Church.

The film *Spotlight*, winner of the 2016 Academy Awards for Best Picture and Original Screenplay, tells their story. It portrays the Spotlight team coming to terms with its own institutional forgetting before going public; the staff gradually realizes its own newspaper had published a previous exposé of priest abuse in 1992 – a full decade earlier – that no one pursued through the ensuing years, while clergy abuses continued. The lead investigator of the team, Walter Robinson, functions as its conscience by gradually remembering.

But actual events seem to have played out more dissociatively than the film's account of soul-searching implies. Robinson revealed in an online interview after the release of the film (Robinson, 2016) that no one on the Spotlight team even remembered this reportorial past until it was re-discovered by the filmmakers. In fact, the *Globe* published not one but 54 articles about an accused priest, James Porter, in 1992 and another nine in 1993. The last was published a few days after Porter's sentencing in December, 1993. Ceasing to report on clergy abuse thereafter might have made sense if Porter were the only offending party, but in that last article, the victims' lawyer, Roderick MacLeish, is quoted as accusing 20 more priests of abusing children and condemning Massachusetts law for failing to provide justice for the victims. Also reported was that all officially accused priests had retired or been put on indefinite leave, and that the statute of limitations had run out on all but one. However, until shortly before Porter's parole hearing six years later, Father John Geoghan and other priests continued to abuse boys with full knowledge of the Church; hence MacLeish's 1993 warning.[23]

Currently, by contrast, the issue of institutional sexual abuse of children and youths, largely boys, increasingly enters public discourse, through investigative journalism, films, and fiction. Amy Berg, for instance, has produced and directed several feature-length documentaries on child sexual abuse, including *Deliver Us From Evil* (2006), about priests who sexually abuse; *An Open Secret* (2014), about the sexual abuse of mostly boy actors in the Hollywood film industry; and *Prophet's Prey* (2015) about Warren Jeffs, a fundamentalist Mormon leader currently serving a 20-year sentence for child sexual assault. Germany's equivalent of the Sandusky scandal, decades-long sexual abuse at the Odenwald School, Germany's most progressive boarding school, became the subject of many articles, two full-length documentaries (Schmidt, 2012; Röhl, 2011), and a few books (Füller, 2011; Dehmers, 2011).

The *Boston Globe*'s Spotlight team recently published a further institutional investigation into widespread sexual abuse of students in private schools across New England, involving 200 cases in 67 schools. They presented their findings in both traditional print and powerful YouTube testimonials by mostly male survivors (Abelson et al., 2016a). Even more recently, the Spotlight team has followed up on this story to reveal the ways the schools themselves "passed the trash" by writing letters of recommendation for faculty fired for sexual violations when the accused sought teaching positions elsewhere, or they simply remained silent to protect their own reputations (Abelson et al., 2016b). In addition, a decades-long pattern of sexual abuse of new cadets at Australian military schools has recently come to light (Lim, 2016).

In the world of fiction, Hanya Yanagihara's critically acclaimed 2015 novel, *A Little Life*, chronicles in unvarnished and moving detail one male victim's lifelong and ultimately losing battle with speaking out rather than

23 This parallels the institutional dissociation at Penn State University (described above) a decade before Sandusky's conviction, when Vice President Schultz, having privately asked himself whether there were "other children," then wrote that Sandusky's assault on Zachary had been adequately investigated.

repeating his extreme history of sexual abuse and betrayal.[24] And male survivors themselves have increasingly published their own stories of abuse and survival (see DeMilly, 1999; Rosenthal, 2004; Moran, 2006; Oxnam, 2006; Fisher & Gillum, 2012; Harty, 2015).

Our original questions

1 *Why do abused children go back for more?*
Children are absolutely dependent and deeply loyal to those they depend upon, dedicated to keeping their caretakers attached to them and as functional as possible. This often involves reversing roles to become the emotional parent to the adults who violate them sexually. Rightly or wrongly, they believe their survival depends on such loyalty. If not already inherently empathic, these children typically become highly sensitized, attuned, and responsive to those who hurt and betray them. The child victim knows instinctively that if he cannot be loved and protected, making sure he is "needed" as a proxy victim is better than not mattering at all. Those child victims who survive somehow find the strength to serve their abusers by enduring the burdens of victimization, badness, and guilt transferred onto them, in exchange for physical and social survival and the hope or illusion that they have been born into a basically benign world where they are the only real problem.[25] Blinded by the idealized personas predators offer up publicly, we overlook their private exercise of power and cruelty, and the fact that these abusers are as emotionally dependent on the children they exploit as their child victims are on them.

2 *Why do some survivors go on to abuse others while most do not?*
Many survivors experience just enough "good-enough" caretaking themselves – being seen, loved, and affirmed by someone along the way for who they are and what they need. In this way, they may contact or

24 Yanagihara's prior, debut novel, *The People in the Trees* (2014), deals even more directly with a publicly benevolent, Nobel-prize-winning abused abuser, based upon the true story of Carleton Gujdusek.

25 This survival strategy was formulated by Fairbairn as the child's "moral defense": "[T]he child would rather be bad himself than have bad objects . . ." (Fairbairn, 1952, p. 64). Daniel Shaw extends our understanding of this dynamic when he adds the child is "coercively driven to adopt the moral defense" (Shaw, 2014, p. 29). But to my knowledge no one has suggested this coercion may be the act of a child state in the adult who suffered it, repeating what was done to him or her when no longer hostage to the childhood state of exploited dependency.

develop enough core Self to tolerate the emotional distress imposed on them by sexual abuse without inflicting it on others. Those who survive without mimicking the aggressor's violations often sacrifice themselves by appropriating badness that does not belong to them while not perpetrating on others as if it did. Their capacity for empathy is strong enough early on in life to prematurely support the golden rule. Perhaps ironically, these survivors often target themselves later in self-destructive ways – through addictions, self-harm, recklessness, and failures to prosper – that simulate and give voice to the abuses they suffered. Thus they are more likely to evoke the empathy and concern they need from the healthier people in their lives in order to begin healing and to develop the sense that they *deserve* to heal now that survival does not depend on servicing those who hurt them.

3 *Why are most sexual abuse victims in institutional settings boys?*
I propose that male serial sexual abusers of boys have a core narcissistic character structure, drained of vitality by the soul murders they themselves suffered as children. Further, they are drawn to sustaining themselves by amassing power and prestige in institutions that provide them access to boy victims who will serve them as psychic doubles and emotional caretakers. Boy victims initially embody for them the innocent self they lost and – at an unconscious, un-mourned level – may still long to reunite with. Since these institutionally enabled abusers are overwhelmingly male, so are their mirroring victims. Through sexually traumatizing their victims they force them to share in and reflect back primal moments of loss and betrayal, then also coerce them to embody the damaged victim-identity that replaced the innocent child they once were. Bollas (1995, p. 189) calls the consequence a "companionship of the dead." I consider it a primitive and perverse act of attachment. Male serial abusers unconsciously seek boys for subjugation who can be relied upon to mirror their own dissociated victim identities, in compensation for the primal, developmentally crucial, benign mirroring they typically failed to experience and internalize as infants and children. This failure may predispose some survivors to abuse in turn. But their victims are not fated to remain in sacrificial, parentified roles forever.

Conclusion: institutional dissociation and healing in community

Increasingly, male survivors have emerged from abused states of self-sacrifice and self-condemnation to heal by going public with the truth of what they have suffered. Still, dissociation is often so pervasive in child sexual abuse that evidence and memory of the perpetrator's abusive sexuality often dematerialize in the traumatizing sexual act for both victim and abuser, as it seems to have for Sandusky and many of his victims. Institutional bystanders under the sway of this dissociative field likewise fail to register what is happening, often *don't want to*, and typically don't have the survivor's imperative or resources to be willing to.

This dissociative contagion makes the role of vigilant others even more crucial to the safety of potential child victims. But our adult mandate to witness and protect is chronically eroded by the public status and seductive power of narcissistic high-profile serial abusers. These priests, coaches, admired teachers, celebrities, and other deceptively admirable figures typically threaten and coerce victims only in private and often in dissociative silence. In spite of his publicized retrospective hope that he might act as a candle for others, Sandusky neither stopped himself nor was he stopped initially by his superiors and their institutions. Only when his victims accepted the support of those who cared enough to believe and witness them and persistently doubt their denials, and only when they spoke loudly and long enough on behalf of themselves and other children at risk, did those in power begin to listen, act, adjudicate, and make institutional changes at Penn State University. The same is true for many other educational institutions that harbored and abetted sexual abuse and were eventually forced to become accountable for it, like the Horace Mann School and the Odenwaldschule.

Just as boyhood victims, driven by attachment need, venture back repeatedly to rescue their abusers from narcissistic implosion, they also become capable of exercising empathy on their own behalf when they reframe the vulnerability their childhood demanded of them as a survival strategy and reclaim their emotional sensitivity – once a source of "unmanly" shame and guilt – by viewing it instead as a fund of relational strength, moral maturity, and self-respect instead. This kind of strength reaches deeper than the individualistic, unempathic missile masculinity boys are socially conditioned to aspire to in a narcissistic culture. Already endowed with a deep capacity for empathy – which gets coercively honed in service to their abusers – survivors, once in contact with one another through therapy and/or advocacy, empathically open up to one another and ultimately to themselves. The rage instilled through sexual coercion then shifts from implosive self-sabotage and the assaultiveness modeled by their abusers to a self-affirming awareness of their own innocence, and then to advocacy, and prevention. But this is neither easy nor a guaranteed outcome. As survivors break silence and speak openly about what was done to them to the right people in the right settings at the right time, it becomes safe enough for them to relinquish and exchange their sacrificial roles for those of empowerment and self-affirmation. Survivors like Cheit and the original whistleblowers at Horace Mann and the Odenwaldschule all acted when they realized another generation of children was at risk.

Trauma therapy and in particular trauma-focused group and community therapy[26] can provide safe-enough social access to survivors' enduring desire and capacity for relationship and intimacy, however exploited these have been by their abusers.[27] With each other's support, male survivors live and grow as men and fathers who provide the children in their lives – their internal as well as their external children – with the secure attachment, self-awareness, and self-worth needed to protect the next generation of children from abuse.

References

Abelson, J., English, B., Saltzman, J., & Wallack, T. (2016a, May 6). Private schools, painful secrets. *Boston Globe*. Retrieved from www.bostonglobe.com/metro/2016/05/06/private-schools-painful-secrets/OaRI9PFpRnCTJxCzko5hkN/story.html.

Abelson, J., English, B., Saltzman, J., & Wallack, T. (2016b, October 1). Educators accused of sexual misconduct often find new posts. *Boston Globe*. Retrieved from www.bostonglobe.com/metro/2016/10/01/how-educators-find-new-jobs-after-alleged-sexual-misconduct/TpwwzQkFmRNbrENTmzfluJ/story.html.

Aron, L., & Harris, A. (Eds.). (1993). *The legacy of Sandor Ferenczi*. Hillsdale, NJ: Analytic Press.

Bellware, K. (2016, April 14). Dennis Hastert: Facing "The worst of both worlds" ahead of sentencing. *Hufffington Post*. Retrieved from http://www.huffington-post.com/entry/dennis-hastert-sentencing-lies_us_570ec219e4b03d8b7b9f6775

Bender, Bryan (2011, January 5). Pentagon lagged on pursuing porn cases. *Boston Globe*. Retrieved from http://archive.boston.com/news/nation/washington/articles/2011/01/05/pentagon_lagged_on_pursuing_porn_cases/

Bolkovac, K., & Lynn, C. (2011). *The Whistleblower: Sex Trafficking, Military Contractors, and One Woman's Fight for Justice*. New York: Palgrave MacMillan.

26 Editor's note: See Chapter 5 by Fradkin and Struve on MaleSurvivor Weekends of Recovery in the companion volume to this one, *Healing Sexually Betrayed Men and Boys: Treatment for Sexual Abuse, Assault, and Trauma* and Chapter 6 by Goodwin in the same book for discussion of community-based treatment.

27 The abused abuser is as yet rarely treated as a survivor. For exceptions, see Scholz (2016) and Chapter 15 by MacDonell & Bolton on dual history groups in the companion volume to this one, *Healing Sexually Betrayed Boys and Men: Treatment for Sexual Abuse, Assault, and Trauma*.

Bollas, C. (1995). The structure of evil. In *Cracking up: The work of unconscious experience* (Chapter 7). New York, NY: Hill & Wang.

Bresnahan, J. (2014, January 28). Jesse Loskarn leaves letter. *Polito*. Retrieved from www.politico.com/story/2014/01/ryan-loskarn-letter-102716.

Briggs, F. (1995). *From victim to offender*. Crows Nest, New South Wales, AU: Allen & Unwin.

Commonwealth v. *Gerald A. Sandusky*, Jury Trial, Day 1 (2012, June 11). Court of Common Pleas Center County, Pennsylvania Criminal Division. Transcript of Proceedings.

Crew Janci LLP. (n.d.). Boy Scout Perversion Files. Retrieved from http://crewjanci.com/resources/boy-scout-perversion-files/.

Davey, M., & Smith, M. (2016, April 8). Hastert molested at least four boys, prosecutors say. *New York Times*. Retrieved from https://www.nytimes.com/2016/04/09/us/dennis-hastert-molested-at-least-four-boys-prosecutors-say.html?_r=0

Dawson, M. (2012, March 28). Sandusky case: Man who evaluated alleged victim was not psychologist. *Centre Daily Times* (State College, PA). Retrieved from www.centredaily.com/news/local/education/penn-state/jerry-sandusky/article42808443.html.

DeCamp, J.W. (1996). *The Franklin cover-up*. Lincoln, NE: AWT.

Dehmers, J. (2011). *Wie laut soll ich denn noch schreien? Die Odenwaldschule und der sexuelle Missbrauch*. Reinbeck bei Hamburg, Germany: Rowohlt Verlag.

DeMilly, W. (1999). *In my father's arms*. Madison, WI: University of Wisconsin Press.

Department of Justice's Efforts to Prevent Staff Sexual Abuse of Federal Inmates. (2009, September Retrieved from https://oig.justice.gov/reports/plus/e0904.pdf.

Doran, J. (Producer). (2010). *The dancing boys of Afghanistan*. *Frontline* segment. PBS. Retrieved from www.pbs.org/wgbh/frontline/film/dancingboys/.

Edmonds, J. (2012, October 8). Jerry Sandusky releases statement to Penn State radio station night before sentencing. *NBC25News*. Retrieved from http://nbc25news.com/sports/content/jerry-sandusky-releases-statement-to-penn-state-radio-station-night-before-sentencing?id=810629#.UHOhPvl26aF.

Fairbairn, R. (1952). *Psychoanalytic studies of the personality*. London, England: Tavistock.

Farrell, M. (2008, 2011). Ending the hidden, savage routine of prison rape. *The Huffington Post*. Retrieved from www.huffingtonpost.com/mike-farrell/ending-the-hidden-savage-_b_91867.html.

Ferenczi, S. (1933/2004). *Schriften zur Psychoanalyse II: Sprachverwirrung zwischen den Erwachsenen und dem Kind*. Gießen, Germany: Psychosozial Verlag.

Ferenczi, S., trans. Michael Balint. (1949). Confusion of the tongues between the adults and the child. *International Journal of Psychoanalysis, 30*, 225–230.

Finkelhor, D., & Jones, L. (2001). The decline in child sexual abuse cases. *Juvenile Justice Bulletin*. Washington, DC: U.S. Department of Justice, Office of Justice Programs, Office of Juvenile Justice and Delinquency Prevention. Retrieved from www.ncjrs.gov/PDFfiles1/ojjdp/199298.PDF.

Fisher, A., & Gillum, M. (2012). *Silent no more*. New York, NY: Ballantine Books.

Fisher, M. (2013, April 1). The master. *New Yorker*. Retrieved from www.newyorker.com/magazine/2013/04/01/the-master-2.

Forst, M., Fagan, J., & Vivona, T. S. (1989). Youth in prisons and training schools: Perceptions and consequences of the treatment-custody dichotomy. *Juvenile and Family Court Journal, 40*, 1–14. doi: 10.1111/j.1755-6988.1989.tb00634.x

Forster, M., & Yeldham, R. (Directors). (2007). *The Kite Runner* (Motion picture). USA: Dreamworks.

Foucault, M. (1990). A boy's honor. In *The history of sexuality, Vol. 2: The use of pleasure* (pp. 204–214). New York, NY: Vintage Books.

Frawley-O'Dea, M. G. (2007). *Perversion of power: Sexual abuse in the Catholic Church*. Nashville, TN: Vanderbilt University Press.

Freeh, L. (2012). *Report of the special investigative counsel regarding the actions of the Pennsylvania State University related to the child sexual abuse committed by Gerald A. Sandusky*. Retrieved from www.documentcloud.org/documents/396512-report-final-071212.html.

Freyd, J. J. (1997). *Betrayal trauma: The logic of forgetting childhood abuse*. Cambridge, MA: Harvard University Press.

Freyd, J. J., & Birrell, P. (2013). *Blind to betrayal: Why we fool ourselves we aren't being fooled*. Hoboken, NJ: Wiley.

Füller, C. (2011). *Sündenfall: Wie die Reformschule ihre Ideale missbrauchte*. Cologne, Germany: DuMont Buchverlag.

Füller, C. (2015). *Die Revolution missbraucht ihre Kinder: Sexuelle Gewalt in deutschen Protestantbewegungen*. Munich, Germany: Carl Hanser Verlag.

Gartner, R. B. (1999). *Betrayed as boys: Psychodynamic treatment of sexually abused men*. New York, NY: Guilford.

Gartner, R. B. (2014). Trauma and countertrauma, resilience and counterresilience. *Contemporary Psychoanalysis, 50*(4), 609–626.

Gartner, R. B. (2017). Trauma and countertrauma, resilience and counterresilience. In R. B. Gartner (Ed.), *Trauma and countertrauma, resilience and counterresilience: Insights from psychoanalysts and trauma experts* (pp. 13–26). New York, NY: Routledge.

Gay, P. (1988). *Freud: A life for our time*. New York, NY: Norton.

Goldstein, J. (2015, September 28). U.S. soldiers told to ignore sexual abuse of boys by Afghan allies. *New York Times*. Retrieved from www.nytimes.com/2015/09/21/world/asia/us-soldiers-told-to-ignore-afghan-allies-abuse-of-boys.html.

Goode, E. (2012, June 28). Researchers see decline in child sexual abuse rate. *New York Times*. Retrieved from www.nytimes.com/2012/06/29/us/rate-of-child-sexual-abuse-on-the-decline.html.

Grand Jury Presentment: Gerald A. Sandusky. (2011, November 4). Retrieved from https://assets.documentcloud.org/documents/264894/sandusky-grand-jury-presentment.pdf

Grand, S. (2000). *The reproduction of evil: A clinical & cultural perspective*. New York, NY: Routledge.

Harris, D. (2016, April 16). Prison rape widely ignored by authorities. *World News Tonight*, ABCNews.Go.com. Retrieved from http://abcnews.go.com/WNT/story?id=131113&page=1.

Harty, C. (2015). *Empty playground*. Amazon Digital Services LLC: Create Space Independent Publishing Platform.

Hobson, W. (2017, March 24). Former Penn State president Graham Spanier convicted of child endangerment. *Washington Post*. Retrieved from https://www.washingtonpost.com/sports/colleges/former-penn-state-president-graham-spanier-convicted-of-child-endangerment/2017/03/24/d1936e34-109a-11e7-9b0d-d27c98455440_story.html?utm_term=.f79d2300bb64.

Horn, M. (1993, November 29). Memories lost and found. *U.S. News & World Report, 115*, 62.

Hosseini, K. (2003). *The kite runner*. New York, NY: Riverhead.

Hurdle, J., & Eckholm, E. (2012, June 22). Cardinal's aide is found guilty in abuse case. *New York Times*. Retrieved from www.nytimes.com/2012/06/23/us/philadelphias-msgr-william-j-lynn-is-convicted-of-allowing-abuse.html.

Isenberg, D. (2010, December 6). It's déjà vu for DynCorp all over again. *Huffpost Business*. Retrieved from www.huffingtonpost.com/david-isenberg/its-dj-vu-for-dyncorp-all_b_792394.html.

Jones, E. (1957). *The life and work of Sigmund Freud, Volume 3: The last phase, 1919–1939*. New York, NY: Basic Books.

Kamil, A., & Elder, S. (2015). *Great is the truth: Secrecy, scandal, and the quest for justice at the Horace Mann School*. New York, NY: Farrar, Straus & Giroux.

Law, V. (2014). What does Rick Perry's refusal to adopt prison rape elimination act mean for Texans behind bars? *Truth-out.org*. Retrieved from www.truth-out.org/news/item/23008-what-does-texas-governors-announcement-that-state-wont-adopt-prison-rape-elimination-act-mean-for-texans-behind-bars.

Lim, Louisa (2016, June 30). In Australia, decades of abuse against military recruits comes to light. NPR. Retrieved from www.npr.org/sections/parallels/2016/06/30/484193073/in-australia-decades-of-abuse-against-military-recruits-comes-to-light.

Lomax, J. (2010, December 9). WikiLeaks: DynCorp responds to dancing boys scandal. *Houston Press*. Retrieved from http://www.houstonpress.com/news/wikileaks-dyncorp-responds-to-dancing-boys-scandal-6751320.

Loskarn, J. (n.d.). Website: www.jesseryanloskarnslastmessage.com/333880300.

Los Angeles Times (2015, January 13). Watchdog: Inside the Boy Scouts' "Perversion files." Retrieved from http://www.latimes.com/la-me-boy-scouts-perversion-files-full-coverage-storygallery.html.

MacAskill, E. (2010) Pentagon workers found to have downloaded child pornography. *The Guardian.* Retrieved from https://www.theguardian.com/world/2010/jul/24/pentagon-us-staff-downloaded-child-pornography

Main, M., Hesse, E., & Siegel, D. (2016, April 2). Disorganized Attachment, the Mind, and Psychotherapy. ISSTD Conference Plenary Session, San Francisco, CA.

Marshall, W., Serran, G., & Cortoni, F. (2000). Childhood attachments, sexual abuse, and their relationship to adult coping in child molesters. *Sex Abuse, 12*(1), 17–26.

Masson, J. (1985). *The complete letters of Sigmund Freud to Wilhelm Fliess 1887–1904.* Cambridge, MA: Harvard University Press.

Masson, J. (1992). Freud at the Paris Morgue. In *The assault on truth* (Chapter 2). New York, NY: Harper Perennial

Mendel, M. (1995). *The male survivor.* Thousand Oaks, CA: Sage.

Moran, M. (2006). *The tricky part.* New York, NY: Anchor Books.

No Escape: Male Rape in U.S. Prison – Case History of Rodney Hulin (2010). *Human Rights Watch.* Retrieved from www.hrw.org/reports/2001/prison/rodney_hulin.html.

No Escape: Prison Rape in America – The Rodney Hulin Story (2010). Retrieved from www.youtube.com/watch?v=R3j3Wk711zY.

Nola, I., Plovesan, C., & Rattray, C. (Producers). Kondracki, L. (Director). (2010). *The Whistleblower* (Motion picture). Canada-Germany-U.S.A.: Goldwyn.

Oxnam, R. (2006). *A fractured mind.* New York, NY: Hyperion.

Parsell, T. J. (2006). *Fish: A boy in a man's prison.* Cambridge, MA: Da Capo Press.

Paul, J. (2015, October 4). Officials say sex trafficking cases with male victims highlight issue. *Denver Post.* Retrieved from www.denverpost.com/2015/10/04/officials-say-sex-trafficking-cases-with-male-victims-highlight-issue/.

Prison rape in the United States (n.d.). Wikipedia entry. Retrieved from https://en.wikipedia.org/wiki/Prison_rape_in_the_United_States.

Rachman, A. W. (1997). *Sandor Ferenczi: The psychotherapist of tenderness and passion.* Northvale, NJ: Jason Aronson.

Robinson, W. (2016, April 8). Getting the word out about trauma: Spotlight's investigation of child sexual abuse in the Catholic Church. APA Division 56 (Trauma Psychology) Webinar. Retrieved from www.youtube.com/watch?v=P4X3bGewYQo&feature=youtu.be and www.apatraumadivision.org/81/webinar-series.html.

Röhl, Christoph. (Director/Writer). (2011). *Und Wir Sind Nicht die Einzigen.* Germany. Production Company: Herbstfilm GmbH.

Rojas, N. (2015). Female prison offenders commit 90% of assaults on male teens in U.S. juvenile detentions centers. *International Business Times.* Retrieved from www.ibtimes.co.uk/us-idaho-lawsuit-reveals-sexual-assault-by-staff-male-teens-juvenile-detention-centers-1494582.

Rosenthal, C. (2004). *Never let me go*. Pasadena, CA: Red Hen Press.

Schmidt, L., & Schilling, R. (Directors/Writers). (2012). *Geschlossene Gesellschaft: Missbrauch an der Odenwaldschule.* Germany.

Scholz, K.-A. (2016, October 25). Model project for pedophiles saved. *Deutche Welle*. Retrieved from www.dw.com/en/model-project-for-pedophiles-saved/a-36154362.

Schore, A. (2003). Clinical implications of a psychoneurobiological model of projective identification. In *Affect regulation and the repair of the self* (Chapter 3). New York, NY: Norton.

Schwartz, J. (Director) (2004). *Turned Out: Sexual Assault Behind Bars* (Motion picture). New York, NY: Films Media Group.

Shaw, D. (2014). *Traumatic narcissism: Relational systems of subjugation*. London: Routledge.

Shengold, L. (1989). *Soul murder*. New Haven, CT: Yale University Press.

Singer, M. (2013). *Prison rape: An American institution?* Santa Barbara, CA: Praeger.

Smith, C. P., & Freyd, J. (2014). Institutional betrayal. *American Psychologist, 69*(6), 575–587.

Stanton, Z. (2015). The page who took down the GOP. *Politico*. Retrieved from: www.politico.com/magazine/story/2015/11/the-page-who-took-down-the-gop-mark-foley-dennis-hastert-213378?o=0.

Stout, M. (2001). *The myth of sanity*. New York, NY: Penguin Books.

Thomas, S., Phillips, K., Carlson, K., Shieh, E., Kirkwook, E., Cabage, L., & Worley, J. (2013). Childhood experiences of perpetrators of child sexual abuse. *Perspectives in Psychiatric Care, 49*, 187–201.

Tracy, M. (2016, October 27). Mike McQueary is awarded $7.3 million in Penn State defamation case. *New York Times*. Retrieved from www.nytimes.com/2016/10/28/sports/ncaafootball/mike-mcqueary-penn-state-verdict.html.

United States Department of Justice (2014, August 26). Former Acting HHS Cyber Security Director convicted for engaging in child pornography enterprise. *Justice News*. Department of Justice Office of Public Affairs. Retrieved from https://www.justice.gov/opa/pr/former-acting-hhs-cyber-security-director-convicted-engaging-child-pornography-enterprise

Vigas, L. (Director) (2015). *From Afar (Desde allá)*. Venezuela/Mexico: Factor RH Producciones, Malandro Films, Lucia Films.

Wolynn, M. (2016). *It didn't start with you*. New York, NY: Viking.

Yanagihara, H. (2014). *The people in the trees*. New York, NY: Anchor.

Yanagihara, H. (2015). *A little life*. New York, NY: Doubleday.

Chapter 9

When predatory priests become sexually abusing "Fathers"

Richard B. Gartner

The controversy surrounding the scandalous abuse of children by priests has churned throughout our culture and boiled over into bitterness and vindictiveness. Many men and women have sought acknowledgment and redress for grievous harm done to them as children. Numerous priests have been accused, a few disciplined, many fewer prosecuted. Occasionally some were sent for "treatment" of their pedophilia, pronounced "cured," and sent back to work within the Church, often with access to children again. Bishops and other higher-ups in the Catholic Church have been found sorely deficient in tending their flocks, but not in protecting their institution: Methodical cover-ups of priests' crimes by those in authority have been revealed, with accused and even admitted pedophile priests often being switched from one parish to another, with no warning given to those in the new parish about who has been sent their way.

The Church kept tight control over any possible publicity related to these events. For example, the fine exposé docudrama *The Boys of St. Vincent*, based on true events at an orphanage in Newfoundland, was made for television in Canada in 1992. It is a harrowing, somber, but not sensationalist film. Yet because of pressure from the Church it was not shown on Canadian television at that time.[1]

This is an expanded form of a paper published in *Studies in Gender and Psychoanalysis* (Gartner, 2004) and is reprinted by permission of Taylor & Francis, LLC. Portions of the chapter have also appeared in other forms elsewhere (Gartner, 1999a, 1999b, 2002, 2007).

1 The film was finally released in the United States in 1994. For a fuller discussion of its psychological meaning, see Gartner (1999b).

While the outrages perpetrated by both priests and the Church were known to some observers prior to 2002, few understood their extent, and little credence was given to anyone who tried to speak up about them. That changed when the *Boston Globe* published a series of articles that led to scandal after scandal, first in Boston, and eventually throughout the United States and the world. The investigation by the *Boston Globe* eventually became the basis for the movie *Spotlight*, winner of the 2016 Academy Award for Best Picture of the Year.[2]

Scrutiny of these crimes meant they could no longer be ignored. Yet, the media, like the Church itself, paid far more attention to the effects of the scandals on the Church than to the effects of the abuse on its victims. In Chapter 1 in this volume, I discussed the general consequences for boys of sexual trauma.[3] Here I will focus on the meaning to male victims of sexual betrayal by Catholic clergy.

Sexual abuse by priests

Priests certainly have no monopoly on being sexual predators. I have known sexual victims who were abused by family members of all kinds: teachers, coaches, scoutmasters, babysitters, neighbors, or doctors, not to mention non-Catholic clergy.[4]

Yet abuse by priests has specific meanings for victims. In many Catholic families, there is a concerted effort – usually benign – to include Catholic clergy as part of a parishioner's "family." Catholic children are told to call clergy Father, Mother, Sister, Brother. Children can be quite literal in understanding such adult concepts.

The more victims accept the familial implications of calling someone Father, Mother, Sister, or Brother, the more the sexual abuse has incestuous connotations. So, many victims of priests are psychologically dealing

2 For more thorough examinations of the history of the sexual abuse of children by priests and the role the Catholic Church played in its cover-up, see Doyle, Sipe, and Wall (2005), Frawley-O'Dea (2007), and Plante and McChesney (2011). See also Chapter 8 by Burmester in this volume.

3 See also Gartner (1996, 1997a, 1997b, 1999a, 1999c, 1999d, 2005).

4 Priests are certainly not the only clergy who abuse boys. Much of this chapter applies to abuse by any clergy or spiritual leader. I have written elsewhere (Gartner, 1999a) about a man I called Yale who was abused by a nun, and have treated men abused by ministers, rabbis, gurus, and other religious leaders.

with a form of incest. And, a priest is not simply "a" father. He is a direct representative of "The" Father, a living representation of Christ.

Having been encouraged to consider clergy as special family members with immediate links to God, how are children to understand when Father, Mother, Sister, or Brother makes sexual overtures? A sacrosanct family member has betrayed them in a fundamental way. The more they believe in a link to God through a priest, the more horrific the betrayal.

Priests' words are understood as God's words. If a child is abused by a priest, he may not simply have a crisis of faith. He may literally feel he is betraying God. One priest/abuser told a child that to resist molestation would be a direct defiance of God's wishes.

Additionally, the child knows his abuser has taken a vow of chastity. Even if he is sure he never desired the priest sexually, he may still feel he somehow instigated the abuse, tempting the priest to break those vows. He is particularly likely to think so if he is told they are doing this because he is special or beautiful. The boy may well conclude the abuse was his own fault.

As a man discerns he was exploited by someone he considered a direct link to God, his whole spiritual world begins to crumble. Boys most easily preyed upon by priests are likely to come from families with deep religious convictions. They may be altar boys or choir boys who feel engaged in their religious lives and have idealized views of their spiritual mentors. Also, they may come from troubled families, looking for parental figures in the Church to act as role models and provide the structure that they lack.

Lorenzo and Julian: two men abused by priests as boys

I have elsewhere (Gartner, 1999a) discussed two men who were sexually abused as boys by priests. (Their treatments began in the 1990s, before the reality of abuse by priests was thrust into the public eye.) The circumstances of their abuse were different: Julian was abused by a priest/mentor from age 12 to 15. Lorenzo was abused by multiple men before a sexual encounter with a priest at age 15.

Both Lorenzo and Julian came from large families in which tenderness was almost unknown and violence was the norm. Starved of affection and guidance, they looked to the Church for help. This made them easy prey for the priests they idealized.

Following their abuse, they both became sexually compulsive, and each had vast reserves of rage and problems with older authorities. Lorenzo, a gay man, had never had a relationship of any depth. Julian, a married straight man, found ongoing intimacy with his wife nearly impossible to achieve. Both had crises of faith superimposed on the other sequelae of boyhood sexual abuse.

By age 15, Lorenzo had numerous exploitative and callous sexual encounters where he sexually serviced men, all of them publicly identified as heterosexual, many of them married. Confused about the meaning of his own behavior and only vaguely knowledgeable about sexual orientation, he began to wonder if he were gay. He had no one to talk to about this in the working-class mill town where he grew up. One of ten children in a lower middle-class family with rampant physical abuse, he knew better than to discuss gay sex at home. Feeling desperate about his sexual feelings, Lorenzo contacted a priest he considered "cool" and told him about his abuse experiences and his concern that he was gay.

> He looked at me and said, "I knew you were gay the minute I laid eyes on you!" At first he was good about it – he invited me to visit him, and when I did he took me around the city and showed me gay neighborhoods, gay bars, gay shops. But then we went back to the house he lived in with other priests, and I wanted to get high – I was a crazy kid in those days – and I asked him where to get grass. He said, "No problem, just go upstairs and ask Father Donald." So I went upstairs, and there was nice Father Donald, and we got high together, and then he made a pass at me.

Lorenzo laughed.

> It was the first time anyone serviced *me*, and I really liked it. When I went downstairs and told the first priest about it, he said, "Oh, sure, Father Donald does that with everyone." Can you believe this? He *knew* what was going to happen when he sent me up there!

Lorenzo was talking faster and faster. I asked him how he felt about all this. "I thought it was funny. And exciting. But, you know, I'm 35 now, about the age Father Donald was then. I have no interest in 15-year-olds! My nephews are that age! I'd *never* go near them for sex." For the first time, he became reflective. "It was a terrible thing to do. They knew how fucked up I was about sex with all those men and how unsure I was about being gay. I went to them for sanctuary! And they just helped me party." Lorenzo looked sad. "In those days I really believed in the Catholic Church." He sighed. "No more."

Julian, a straight man, was deeply ambivalent about the priest who simultaneously mentored, loved, and abused him. From age 12, Julian was abused for three years by Father Scott, a parish priest who required that he come for special counseling sessions in order to get confirmed. Father Scott made Julian his "special" altar boy, invited him to visit him in his rooms, and undertook to educate him in classical texts, languages, and music.

Julian came from a psychologically and physically invasive large family in which emotions and boundaries were ignored. Although he flunked out of school after Father Scott began to abuse him, once the abuse stopped he became an A student, largely, he believes, because of the earlier influence of the priest. He entered seminary himself but as we shall see he fell apart after two years and dropped out. He eventually went on to get an advanced degree in another field.

Father Scott taught Julian to idealize the male relationships described in ancient Greek texts. These idyllic relationships included intellectual mentoring, deep commitment, and interpersonal intimacy, as well as physical sexuality, which began a few months after Father Scott started counseling Julian. Father Scott groomed[5] Julian for "seduction" by asking him about the pain he felt about his physically abusive but otherwise unresponsive family. Then the priest would hug Julian. These hugs were precious to the boy, who was starved of physical affection and, indeed, any kind of positive regard from an adult.

With time, the hugs got longer, and then one day Father Scott kissed Julian, putting his tongue in the boy's mouth. Julian was startled and confused. After the kiss, Father Scott said, "*I know you want more*, but that's all for now." As a man, Julian said, "So, right from the beginning he made the abuse my idea. I felt guilty even though I had no concept of men kissing at the time, and certainly no interest in it." Shortly thereafter, the priest

5 See Chapter 13 by Clemente and Hakes in the companion volume to this one, *Healing Sexually Betrayed Men and Boys: Treatment for Sexual Abuse, Assault, and Trauma*, for discussion of grooming boys for abuse.

introduced Julian to anal sex, and for two years they had regular sexual encounters that included anal sex and mutual masturbation.

The priest said their relationship existed on the highest plane possible for two human beings, that they had attained the ideal glorified by the greatest poets of the ancient world. He reiterated that they experienced all forms of love together: love of beauty, love of thought, love of logic, love of art, and love of one another that was intellectual, sensual, and emotional.

Julian did love Father Scott and craved the priest's companionship and deep interest in him. Still, he was confused and conflicted about the sex that accompanied that interest. "He did so much for me! Anyone would think he was the best mentor a boy could ever have, and, except for the sex, he was."

Julian put a stop to the sex when he was 15. Eventually, he excelled in school and entered a seminary to become a priest, but dropped out when he realized this path was somehow an outgrowth of his relationship with Father Scott. He married, but remained ashamed, conflicted, and secretive about his abuse. He continued to be grateful for the intellectual and emotional expansion the relationship with Father Scott had afforded him. At the same time, however, he was covertly furious about the exploitation and mystification involved in their sexual activity. As an adult, he was a compulsive masturbator driven furtively to view peep shows and consumed by female pornography when he was anxious. When he began treatment, he felt out of control, in the grip of the sexual impulses that flooded him at these times.

Painful ambivalence about priest/predators

In their treatments, both Julian and Lorenzo became increasingly aware of the extent of their rage at their priest/abusers. But they also realized, sadly, how much they still hoped for from these inadequate men. Lorenzo phoned the priest who sent him to the abusing priest to try to speak about what happened. He found him receptive until he realized that Lorenzo wanted to talk to him about how hurt he was. The priest then abruptly terminated the conversation. He never returned other phone calls. Nor did he respond to a letter in which Lorenzo told him he wanted to understand what happened, not to hurt the priest.

At age 30, already an accomplished professional, Julian saw Father Scott at a funeral. He felt furious but paralyzed, wanting to shame and hurt the priest but barely able to speak to him. The priest drew him into a corner and whispered, "You may feel better than the rest of us now, but you and I know that all I have to do is rub your belly and you'll squeal like a puppy!" Feeling helpless and shamed once again, Julian finally got in touch with the full extent of his rage at his former mentor. Yet he was never able to confront Father Scott and maintained a fantasy of reconciling with him. Then he got word that Father Scott had died, ending all hope of coming to some peace with him in actual dialogue. But Father Scott remembered Julian in his will, causing a host of nearly inchoate ambivalent feelings. Julian eventually decided to donate that money to a victims' cause.

Both Lorenzo and Julian entertained thoughts of legal redress long before the Church scandals became public. Many suits against the Church are brought by men who initially sought some kind of healing pastoral experience. Met with silence or denial, they choose legal means to get acknowledgment of the wrong done to them.

Lorenzo considered writing the diocese where the priests were now serving to warn of the danger the men might still pose. But he reasoned the Church was unlikely to do anything about the situation. This conclusion was, of course, later confirmed by the many stories made public about abusive priests who were transferred by Church authorities from one parish to another. Eventually, Lorenzo decided that writing to Church authorities would only give new life to the devastating conflicts that had been largely worked through in his lengthy analysis.

At one point, Julian considered suing to have his analysis paid for by either the Church or the estate of his now-deceased abuser. He felt that such a demand would be justified but decided that entering into a lengthy legal battle would do him more harm than good, keeping him stuck in his anger and in his memories for at least the five or six years it would take to pursue such a court case. He also recognized that a legal battle would risk his having to re-experience the psychological fragmentation he had felt before he began treatment and that there was no guarantee he would gain anything at all from the process.

Both Lorenzo and Julian, then, recognized that the Church would not offer either justice or solace. This surmise, of course, has turned out to be largely substantiated by the Church's responses to victims who have come to the Church for either pastoral or legal redress. Therefore, Julian and Lorenzo seem to have been correct in assessing that their most fruitful path would be to mourn their childhood and innocence, and that this was better accomplished in the consulting room than the court room.

When the Church scandal broke in 2002, Julian and Lorenzo experienced a liberating sense of having their torment validated. They were very glad the Church was being forced to acknowledge the extent of abuse by priests. Yet, they simultaneously felt a recurrence of shame, Furthermore, they were conflicted about not having come forward as other victims had, a conflict constantly triggered by news reports about the Church. Lorenzo said he had to monitor tightly what he allowed himself to read or hear in the media in order to keep himself from being overwhelmed by anxiety. And Julian noted sadly that he was a religious man without a church:

> I went to seminary because Catholicism means something to me. But now I can't go into a church without feeling I will vomit. My wife says, "Let's go to an Episcopalian Church – it's almost the same!" But it's not the same. I'm not an Episcopalian, I'm a *Catholic*. And there's nowhere I can go to be one.

Dr. X: alone with fury

The theme of religious betrayal overlaying betrayal by a trusted adult is underlined by a third man who spoke to me about his abuse by a priest. Dr. X[6] is a mental health professional, married and in his 50s when we met, who had had personal therapy for over 20 years and who had treated numerous male victims of sexual abuse. He has in many ways successfully dealt with his boyhood trauma. But he is left with a cold fury at the Church and all it stands for, as well as a bleak contempt for organized religion.

Dr. X was raised in a rural area of the American heartland, the son of a devout Catholic mother and a less religious father who nevertheless "went along with the program." A pious child who always wanted to please his mother, Dr. X was a very literal believer in Church doctrine. He absolutely believed that priests were God's representatives on earth.

Of his mother, he says, "To her dying day she was a praying, God-fearing woman. She was the ultimate Catholic, and she wanted me to be one, too." He paints a mixed picture of his father: unpredictable, a workaholic, sometimes dangerous, demeaning, and physically abusive, at other

6 I am indebted to Dr. X for his willingness to speak so frankly to me about his painful history and permit me to write about him.

times strong, capable, and "centering." Dr. X says his sense of self-esteem and goodness came not from his parents but from two men close to his family. One was a friend of his father's who seems to have been a near-ideal role model. The other was the family's parish priest.

The priest came from New York and was viewed by Dr. X and his parents as worldly and wise. He visited the family frequently and often stayed the night, even though he lived only three blocks away. He slept on a couch outside Dr. X's room. Starting when Dr. X was 5 years old, the priest would take the boy out of his bed and bring him onto his couch, placing the boy on top of himself. Dr. X could feel the priest's erection through the sheet that separated them. The priest moved under him, pressing the boy's moving body against his erection until the priest reached orgasm. He would also fondle Dr. X's genitals, sometimes with an ice cube. As far as Dr. X can recall, there was never any oral or anal contact. He notes, however, his numerous memory gaps about the priest.

When the priest later moved to a distant parish, he visited the family every few months and took Dr. X away for the weekend. At these times they went to a suburban house that Dr. X believed at the time was where the priest lived with other priests. He now believes it was a house the priests kept for their encounters with young boys, since all the other priests also brought boys with them on these weekends. There were many incidents that Dr. X remembers only vaguely, but he recalls one clearly from within his dissociated state at the time. Watching himself from above, he sees himself step out of the shower while the priest squats down and rubs shaving cream all over his genitals, then "lovingly" wipes it off. Dr. X's younger brother came on at least one of these weekend trips, and the brother still recalls clinging to a maid when the other priests tried to get him to accompany them as they took their own boys into the bathroom to watch Dr. X being fondled.

These incidents continued until Dr. X was 15.

> As I grew older, the guilt intensified. I sensed that things were off, but I felt it was only me, that I was not able to exercise self-control. I didn't want him to take me with him any more and grew increasingly wary of his visits. I dreaded them but felt obliged to be "good" – a good Catholic, a good, compliant boy in both his eyes and my parents'. I could not disappoint him.

When he was in his late teens, Dr. X's mother told him there were rumors about the priest being sexually involved with children.

> I became enraged. I'd thought I was special to him. I told her what he'd done to me, but, amazingly, she stayed in touch with him, and *so did I!* I didn't truly realize that I'd been abused. It was just something that happened.

When Dr. X moved to New York as a young adult, the priest lived there, having left the priesthood. For a while, Dr. X stayed with him. The priest tried to seduce him again "for old times sake," but Dr. X fended him off. A year later, he began therapy and started to identify his experience as abusive. He decided to confront the priest, and, taking a "huge friend" along for protection, went to see him. "I told him, 'You abused me,' but he said, 'What I did was just love. It was good for you.' He never acknowledged any wrongdoing."

Trying to gauge the extent of his trauma, Dr. X exclaimed, "I felt so betrayed! It went on for ten years, a person who seemed to love me and whom I loved. That reduces the trauma, I suppose, but 10 years adds up to a lot of trauma in itself." He noted that only after 20-odd years of therapy was he aware of how enraged he has been all his life. He had always known about his anger toward his father, and even his mother, a seemingly more passive figure. "My rage was always under the surface, and I knew that. But there was more, and I knew that, too. Only now do I affix it to him as well."

At the time, Dr. X never considered telling anyone about his abuse. The priest had said, "This is between you and me. *God thinks it's OK.* You don't have to tell your mommy and daddy." In retrospect, Dr. X believes his mother was in love with the priest, albeit from a worshipful distance. In any case, he felt sure that all hell would break loose if he disclosed the abuse, and that he, not the priest, would be the loser. "He was awesome. He would not be blamed. He was God-like."

As a boy, Dr. X was ambivalent about what the priest was doing. While he had an underlying sense of disgust, he now feels he was somehow seduced into thinking that participating in these acts was good and noble. "I remember once, at age 6 or so, laying there, expecting him to come in. I lay there in the form of a crucifix. I thought he'd see me as Jesus.

I'd please him. I *so* wanted his attention!" His self-esteem depended on the priest's coming in and making him feel special. "I had a love affair with him in my heart, even at age 5."

In addition, Dr. X felt, as Julian had, that his priest held out the promise of helping the boy become like himself, worldly and well read.

> I somehow thought he would show me how to be intelligent and sophisticated, how to live in a better way, not like my redneck family. I don't know how much of that was my fantasy, but certainly his manner reinforced the idea – he was on a pedestal, aloof, someone to be in awe of.

Differentiating between the physical and psychological abuse by his father and the sexual abuse by the priest, Dr. X said,

> I had no power in either situation, but somehow my connection to my father remained. I could actively hate him as a counterpart to my love. He was a man. A sick, scary, fucked-up, angry, mean, heartless man at times, but loving, strong, safe, and capable of protecting me, too. The priest was lascivious, stomach sickening, confusing, obligatory, awesome, and desirable. My relationship with him did not carry the attachment, dependency, and love that I felt with my father. Yet I was more powerless with him in a way, given his religious status.

Noting how vulnerable he was, Dr. X at first said his trauma would have been of an equal magnitude had his abuser been someone other than a priest.

> Perhaps if my dad had sex with me I would feel the same way about him, but it was the priest, in his God-like position and his misuse of it, that soured me to ultimate authority. Although today I think that is a good thing, at that time it left me hopeless, angry, rebellious, hostile, and running in circles. I survived. I did not live.

While he says he is now glad his eyes were opened to the "hypocrisy" of religion through his trauma, there was clearly a painful crisis of faith because of the specific nature of his relationship to his abuser: "I felt it was God's representative on earth that opened my eyes to God's failing. I don't believe in God today at all any more." Reconsidering, he went on:

> I am angry at God. To the degree God exists for me I am angry at Him. The idea of a Supreme Being was shattered for me by this man. He introduced evidence to me that God failed, that God won't protect you or prevent bad things from happening to you. The fact that it was a priest was cataclysmic. It taught me that there is a lie in the world. I developed a slowly evolving cynicism. As I got older and gave up on my piety, I grew to hate the smells, sounds, feelings of the Church – the incense, the collars, the robes. My spirituality and ability to believe in a higher power were destroyed.

Wrestling with whether and how priest abuse is different from abuse by others, Dr. X said, "What is unique is that one's connection to religious belief, trust in God, belief in a higher power, all becomes skewed, confused, shaken, questioned, tainted. And that might be a good thing, ultimately. I think it was for me." Yet, he went on to say,

> The fact of his "priestness" had little real specific contribution. It was more the betrayal, the stigmatization, the powerlessness, the frustration. His priestness just gave him the right-of-way. Being a priest was his ticket to taking advantage. His tool. Like anyone who abuses a child. They all have some tool.

Conclusion

Why did the media focus more on the effect of the scandals on the Catholic Church than on the effect on young children of sexual betrayal by priests? Perhaps we all would like to have faith in the basic goodness of the Church; focusing on how the Church is affected by scandal somehow forces us to consider how to make the Church regain its exalted state. Such concerns are legitimate, and it is crucial that Church practices about predatory priests be reformed and that protections be put in place to stop abuse by priests wherever it occurs, from the parish level to the Vatican.[7]

7 As of this writing, two Popes have met with victims of abuse by priests, promising accountability (Goodstein, 2015). Little changed after Pope Benedict's meetings. Pope Francis has called clergy sex abuse "a leprosy" (Pullella, 2014), demanding zero tolerance of it. Subsequently more cases have been given hearings, with consequences for the priests involved (Faiola, 2015). Nevertheless, his vigilance has been questioned because of actions ignoring revelations of abuse, such as installing Bishop Juan Barros in Chile despite outcries because of his complicity in a notorious case of clerical sexual abuse there (Bonnefoy, 2015).

But I think a more important cause of this relative neglect of victims by the media is the fundamental taboo many of us continue to have about boys being sexual victims. The media were faced with hundreds of hurting male victims of sexual abuse by priests. Yet, like many of us, they seemed unable to consider for long the effects of these betrayals. I have personally found this to be true when being interviewed by some reporters about the sexual abuse of boys, whether by priests or someone else. The reporters, of course, want to know about numbers and facts. But when I talk about the specific outrageous acts that sexual abuse inflicts on boys, or the long-term negative effects of these acts, the reporters frequently gasp in horror and disbelief, then move on to another aspect of the story. None of us wants to hear these stories, yet they must be heard.

If a parent betrays a child in a fundamental way, the child's resulting wounds are profound. To the extent that a priest is experienced as a father, he will likewise be the object of conflicting, complex feelings. Therefore, if a priest is a child's Father, his betrayal affects the child to his core.

Each of the men I have described was in a vulnerable psychological state in boyhood. Indeed, their vulnerability made them easy targets for priest/predators. As boys, they looked to their abusers for solace and support, and were betrayed. The trauma for each was shattering.

Overlaying their betrayal was the specific effect on the child's spiritual life following abuse by a trusted "representative of God." Each man had a terrible crisis of faith. When that faith was destroyed they were thereby further alienated from their religiously observant families. The boys survived, and yet they were truly victims of what Shengold (1989) has aptly called "soul murder."

References

Bonnefoy, P. (2015, March 21). Angry protest over new bishop in Chile. *New York Times*. Retrieved from www.nytimes.com/2015/03/22/world/americas/angry-protest-over-bishop-juan-barros-in-chile.html?_r=0.

Doyle, T. P., Sipe, A. W. R., & Wall, P. J. (2005). *Sex, priests, and secret codes: The Catholic Church's 2,000 year paper trail of sexual abuse*. Los Angeles, CA: Volt Press.

Faiola, A. (2015, March 15). When the pope speaks, priest abuse cases get heard. *Washington Post*. Retrieved from www.washingtonpost.com/world/europe/when-the-pope-speaks-priest-abuse-cases-get-heard/2015/03/15/257c0b66-bd35-11e4-9dfb-03366e719af8_story.html.

Frawley-O'Dea, M. G. (2007). *Perversion of power: Sexual abuse in the Catholic Church*. Nashville, TN: Vanderbilt University Press.

Gartner, R. B. (1996). Incestuous boundary violations in families of borderline patients. *Contemporary Psychoanalysis, 32*, 73–80.

Gartner, R. B. (1997a). Considerations in the psychoanalytic treatment of men who were sexually abused as children. *Psychoanalytic Psychology, 14*, 13–41.

Gartner, R. B. (1997b). An analytic group for sexually abused men. *International Journal of Group Psychotherapy, 47*, 373–383.

Gartner, R. B. (1999a). *Betrayed as boys: Psychodynamic treatment of sexually abused men*. New York, NY: Guilford.

Gartner, R. B. (1999b). Cinematic depictions of boyhood sexual victimization. *Gender and Psychoanalysis, 4*, 253–289.

Gartner, R. B. (1999c). Relational aftereffects in manhood of boyhood sexual abuse. *Journal of Contemporary Psychotherapy, 29*, 319–353.

Gartner, R. B. (1999d). Sexual victimization of boys by men: Meanings and consequences. *Journal of Gay and Lesbian Psychotherapy, 3*, 1–33.

Gartner, R. B. (2002). Effects on boys of priest abuse. *Psychologist-Psychoanalyst, 22*, 15–17.

Gartner, R. B. (2004). Predatory priests: Sexually abusing Fathers. *Studies in Gender and Sexuality, 5*, 31–56.

Gartner, R. B. (2005). *Beyond betrayal: Taking charge of your life after boyhood sexual abuse*. New York, NY: Wiley.

Gartner, R. B. (2007). Failed "Fathers," boys betrayed. In M.G. Frawley-O'Dea & V. Goldner (Eds.), *Predatory priests, silenced victims* (pp. 85–100). Hillsdale, NJ: Analytic Press.

Goodstein, L. (2015, September 27). After criticism, Pope Francis confronts priestly sexual abuse. *New York Times*. Retrieved from www.nytimes.com/2015/09/28/us/pope-francis-philadelphia-sexual-abuse.html?_r=0.

Plante, T. G., & McChesney, K. L. (Eds.). (2011). *Sexual abuse in the Catholic Church: A decade of crisis, 2002–2012*. Santa Barbara, CA: Praeger.

Pullella, P. (2014, July 13). Pope Francis calls clergy sex abuse "a leprosy," says 2 percent of priests are pedophiles in Eugenio Scalfari interview. *Huffington Post*. Retrieved from www.huffingtonpost.com/2014/07/13/pope-francis-priests-pedophiles-two-percent_n_5582157.html.

Shengold, L. (1989). *Soul murder*. New York: Fawcett Columbine.

Part IV

Exploitation and sexuality

Chapter 10

Commercial sexual exploitation of boys and adolescent males

Steven L. Procopio

In recent years, the phenomenon of the commercial sexual exploitation[1] of children (CSEC) has primarily centered on the victimization of girls and young women. The research has focused on gender-specific victims. But sexual victimization is universal and not gender specific, affecting both girls and boys.

This chapter reviews what we know about sexual exploitation of boys and young men. The paths to victimization will be described; the argument will be made that it is underreported and undertreated.

Male victims

A commonly cited figure is that 10% of men in the United States have experienced trauma as a result of sexual victimization, with the average age of victims being 17 (National Center for PTSD, 2016).[2] The CDC National Intimate Partner and Sexual Violence Survey in 2011 studied lifetime and 12-month prevalence in the United States of sexual violence victimization, surveyed by sex of victim (Finkelhor, Turner,

1 While all sexually victimized children are exploited in one way or another, for the purposes of this discussion "exploitation" refers to "the sexual abuse of children and youth through the exchange of sex or sexual acts for drugs, food, shelter, protection, other basics of life, and/or money. Sexual exploitation includes involving children and youth in creating pornography and sexually explicit websites" (Sexual Exploitation Toolkit, 2008).

2 Editor's note: See Chapter 4 by Easton in this volume for a comprehensive account of the research on sexually abused males, including the ACE study and polyvictimization (discussed in this section).

Ormrod, Hamby, & Kracke, 2009). It found that the number of male rape victims numbered 1,971,000, with completed forced penetration numbering 834,000. Other sexual violence included forms of coercion and unwanted contact and/or non-contact sexual acts. Male victims totaled 26,590,000.

Reported sexual exploitation of children in the United States increased substantially with the passage of the Trafficking Victims Protection Act (TVPA) and subsequent reauthorizations. This law defines any person under the age of 18 years of age who is "induced to perform a commercial sexual act" as a victim of human trafficking, not as a criminal. Unfortunately, most law enforcement, media, policy makers, researchers, funders, and government agents have focused their attention on CSEC girls. This is arguably based on such factors as homophobia, sexism, stigma, shame, lack of screening tools, lack of outreach, fear, gender bias, and a marked perception in our culture of males as perpetrators. These all lead to an indifference toward researching and providing services to male victims of human sex trafficking.

Multiple victimization experiences

Many kinds of childhood trauma are considered adverse childhood experiences,[3] Many young people can recover from a traumatic experience by reorganizing their defenses and adapting a new reality, but others develop severe and chronic symptoms that impact them for life (Levine & Kline, 2007).

At high risk are children with multiple victimization experiences, also called polyvictimizations (Finkelhor, Ormrod, & Turner, 2007). These are victimizations of diverse kinds intersecting in the life of a single child. Such experiences are most likely to result in long-term effects on a child's cognitive and emotional development.

Repeated adverse victimizations are regarded in the literature as multiple forms of maltreatment or violence (Ford, Wasser, & Connor, 2011). According to the National Survey of Children's Exposure to Violence (NatSCEV), children exposed to even one type of victimization trauma were at greater risk for other types of victimization (Finkelhor, Turner, Hamby, & Ormrod, 2011). Polyvictimization can be

3 For discussion of the Adverse Childhood Experience (ACE) study that gave rise to this term, see Felitti et al., 1998; Anda et al., 2006.

studied as a continuous or categorical variable, allowing clinicians and researchers to identify important relationships rather than just rates of exposure to certain types of adverse experiences.

Multiple victimization of children is pervasive in the United States. In a national representative sample of over 2,000 children, Finkelhor et al. (2007) studied trauma symptoms exhibited during a year. Of the children studied, 22% were victims of four or more types victimization in the previous year. Indeed, in a later study, Finkelhor et al. (2011) reported that some children had rates as high as seven or more exposures to the 51 types of victimization identified. The study suggested four routes to multiple victimizations:

1 Living in a family where violence and conflict are pervasive.
2 Family disruption leading to poor parenting skills with an inability to support emotional needs of children.
3 Residing in a community plagued by violence.
4 Having existing emotional and behavioral problems that lead to risky behavior.

Finkelhor et al. (2011) report that 54% of victims of multiple victimizations were boys; it was most common in the 14–17 age group. They suggest that dangerous neighborhoods can lead directly to sexual assault, while family disruption and emotional problems may lead to sexual assault indirectly. Sexual assault can lead to further sexual exploitation such as trafficking and prostitution, which in turn leads to further multiple victimization experiences.

In a study commissioned by Covenant House New York, Bigelsen and Vuotto (2013) interviewed 51 male, 130 female, and 4 transgender homeless youth aged between 18 and 23. They found that 78% of respondents reported a history of sexual abuse and/or other extreme traumas. They detailed trading sex for daily living needs such as food, shelter, clothing, and drugs in addition to money to support younger siblings or children. A majority reported multiple risk factors in their developing years, including neglect, lack of adult guidance, lack of a caring adult, and lack of opportunities for education and employment.

Children like these who have experienced numerous episodes of polyvictimization are at greater risk of developing complex trauma in childhood (see Cook et al., 2005; Spinazzola et al., 2005; Ford, Connor, & Hawke, 2009; NCTSN, n.d.). Additional exposures contributing to polyvictimization

(Felitti et al., 1998; Anda et al., 2006) include emotional abuse and neglect, physical or sexual abuse, witnessing domestic violence, having been bullied, gang violence within a community, terrorism, being witness to murder, loss of loved ones, and custodial interference. There are also long-term health consequences for people impacted by numerous adverse childhood experiences, including increase in heart disease, diabetes, depression/anxiety, suicidal behaviors, decrease in longevity, and so on.[4]

Research about trafficking and exploitation

The intersection of childhood trauma, sexual abuse of boys, and entry into commercial sexual exploitation has been long been recognized but rarely studied. Although sexual exploitation of boys is common, Lillywhite and Skidmore (2006) reported that researchers for the most part focus on girls and young women and that the literature on prostitution remains silent about male sex workers. So, while in recent years there have been studies of trafficking and sexual exploitation as a form of multi-victimization, we have learned little specifically about exploited boys and young men.

One report, however, included both male and female victims among the 111 they studied. Conducted by Ric Curtis and his colleagues at the John Jay College of Criminal Justice in New York and the Center for Court Innovation, *The Commercial Sexual Exploitation of Children in New York City* (Curtis, Terry, Dank, Dombrowski, & Khan, 2008) was not originally looking for gender differences. They had not expected to focus on boys as a significant segment of the market, or on their unique sets of problems, since they anticipated their respondents would be primarily female. Yet unexpectedly large numbers of boys were interviewed and they concluded that high percentages of CSEC victims were in fact male. They determined that despite arguments on the relative proportion of girls to boys in the "sex market," boys are far more numerous than is commonly acknowledged. They found that boys enter the cycle of sexual exploitation at the same age as girls or perhaps even younger (11–13 years).

Dennis (2008, p.11) studied "the invisibility of men and boys in scholarly discussions of the global sex trade" by analyzing 166 articles in social science journals. He found that

4 Editor's note: See Chapter 3 by Spinelli in this volume for discussion of the medical implications of boyhood sexual abuse.

> Most failed to acknowledge the existence of male sex workers at all. When male sex workers were discussed, they were assigned considerably more agency than female sex workers, the chief danger ascribed to them was HIV rather than violence, and the question of their sexual orientation was always addressed, whereas female sex workers were always assumed heterosexual.

The results were discussed in the context of "world system theory, orientalism, and heteronormativity."

McIntyre (2005) found that 70% of male sex workers in Canada experienced a history of sexual abuse prior to entering into sex work, and approximately 75% were polyvictimized, for example, having been physically abused and/or witnessing aggression in childhood. As cited in Lillywhite and Skidmore (2006), Scott and Skidmore reported in a small sample study that in the histories of seven exploited young men, five had been sexually abused prior to their sexual exploitation. Co-risk factors for these youth included parents with alcohol problems and a period in their lives when parental units neglected them.

Struggles of exploited and trafficked boys and young men

The sexual abuse of boys has been shown to impact self-concept, the development of gender identity, and self-esteem (Gartner, 1999). Sexually exploited and trafficked boys have much higher rates of anxiety, depression, HIV/AIDS, PTSD, STIs, and increased rates of suicide attempts. They also suffered a high degree of injury due to their exploiters' violence, and commonly exhibited acts of self-mutilation, sleep disturbance, eating disorder, and fire setting (cf. Estes, 2001; Estes & Weiner, 2001; Valente, 2005; Finkelhor et al., 2009). And, like other sexually abused boys, they encounter difficulties maintaining intimate partner relationships and are more likely to have episodes of increased risk-taking behavior (Valente, 2005).

In the John Jay College project of adolescent prostitution (Curtis et al., 2008), the majority of exploited youth were homeless. This varied by gender: 44% of boys but only 24% of girls in their sample were homeless. More than half the boys reported living alone, as opposed to one quarter of the girls. The authors reported that "In general, based upon how the youth described their living arrangements, boys seemed much more solitary and disconnected from others, including family members" (p. 43). They suggest there are different paths of entry into commercial sexual exploitation: recruitment by friends was reported by 68% of transgender youth, compared to 46% of girls and 44% of boys. On the other hand, boys reported that 32% of the time they entered into "the life" after "customers approached them" for the first time; the corresponding figures were 10.5% for transgender youth and 16% for girls (Curtis et al., 2008 p.46).

The study suggested that *upwards* of 50% of exploited children in the United States are boys. Therefore, of the approximately 100,000–300,000 homeless/runaway youth on the street on any given day the majority are male. And we now know that homelessness and runaway behaviors are the leading factors in sexual exploitation (Bigelson & Vuotto, 2013).

The commercial sexual exploitation of boys is not a gender or sexual orientation issue. It is about power and control, and all at-risk male youth need to be equally and appropriately identified and supported through the various systems charged with protecting them. Nevertheless, according to the Young Men's Project (Lillywhite & Skidmore, 2006), LGBT youth are generally uneducated about their sexual feelings and thoughts. Living in an unaccepting environment where those thoughts are neither welcome nor tolerated may lead to increased risk of sexual exploitation, since boys may engage in risky behavior out of curiosity, ignorance, or desperation. Or, as boys commonly report, they may be thrown out of their house because of their sexual orientation, and thus placed at high risk for sexual exploitation as they attempt to meet their basic needs.

Identifying and serving this population

Trafficked and exploited boys are woefully underserved by social and governmental agencies. In a British study of social agencies (Hudson & Rivers, 2002), 74% of the interviewees reported their organizations did not have specific policies for working with trafficked young men as opposed to young women. Willis, Robert, and Friedman (2013) concluded that law enforcement officers do not refer exploited boys for services, as they are conditioned to look for the "stereotypical female" victim. Boys are therefore rarely screened for sexual exploitation.

The various public and private systems that work with male youth need to be informed about the factors leading to sexual exploitation and the behavioral indicators that can identify males at risk for or actively exploited in our culture (cf. Estes, 2001; Estes & Weiner, 2001). Adverse childhood experiences including sexual abuse, homes with domestic violence, family histories of substance abuse, gang related activities in neighborhoods, homelessness/runaway behavior, war-torn communities, poverty, and multiple foster placements, to name a few, lead to victimizing experiences for children, which in turn contribute to multi-victimization experiences as the children develop. For youth with multiple adverse experiences, possible indicators of victimization include depression, anxiety, oppositional behavior disorder, self-mutilation, suicidal episodes, and truancy. These patterns often lead youth to the criminal justice system (cf. Gartner, 1999; Estes, 2001; Estes & Weiner, 2001; Whealin & Barnett, n.d.).

According to a report by ECPAT-USA entitled *And Boys Too* (Willis, Robert, & Friedman, 2013), these are the major contributing factors for sexually exploited boys and young men not being identified or served:

1 Unwillingness of boys to self-identify due to shame and stigma about their sexual orientation or perception of sexual orientation by family/ community.
2 Lack of appropriate screening and intake by law enforcement and social service organizations based on the belief that boys are not victims.
3 Limited outreach by anti-trafficking organizations to areas or venues known for male "prostitution."
4 The misperception that boys are rarely pimped.

Studies of the commercial exploitation of boys have usually focused on homeless and runaway youth. The literature (e.g., Estes & Weiner, 2001) finds that boys enter into the commercial sexual exploitation in order to meet their basic need for money, food, shelter, drugs, clothing, and transportation. Like young women in these circumstances, these young men commonly have histories of physical and sexual abuse. However, whether sexually victimized or not, these youth are seldom tracked or asked probing questions about victimization at intake into the social service system.

An additional area of concern for male victims of commercial sexual exploitation is the high incidence of boys' involvement with the criminal justice system. Lillywhite and Skidmore (2006) report that some authorities view sexually exploited boys as victims and others as offenders, often leading to problems identifying appropriate services for them. As a result, they are either channeled into child protective service or criminal justice systems, often the latter. Many professionals target male victims as likely future offenders and neglect to treat them with a trauma-informed focus or an appreciation of how males may manifest their victimization.

Studies of sexually exploited boys (cf. Elifson, Boles, & Sweat, 1993; Degraaf, Vanwesenbeeck, van Zessen, Straver, & Visser, 1995; Estes & Weiner, 2001; Clawson, Dutch, Salomon, & Goldblatt Grace, 2009; see also Gartner, 1999; Lew, 2004; Fradkin, 2011) found that:

1 Male victims are difficult to identify or engage and are often not recognized by health, social service, or criminal justice programs.
2 Life on the streets for these youth brings high levels of risk for HIV/AIDS, STIs, substance abuse, violence, and other compromising physical and health challenges.
3 Boys and young men at risk for or actively being sexually exploited can be engaged and supported through outreach interventions designed to reflect the realities of their circumstances, needs, and desires.

Robbie: gangs and "oppositional defiance"

Gangs are at the heart of the "prostitution industry" across the United States. Both boys and girls are victimized by gangs, with drastic long-term psychosocial implications. Boys on either end of the behavioral spectrum are likely victims of commercial sexual exploitation.

A case reluctantly referred to me by the child welfare system involved Robbie, a 14-year-old who demonstrated "criminal" behaviors and had a "child requiring assistance" claim filed with the state by his mother. The state social worker characterized him as "oppositional defiant," and did not recognize that Robbie's behavior was a response to sexual victimization. It emerged in a case conference I requested that Robbie was a victim of a neighborhood gang involved in the commercial sex industry, exploiting both girls and boys. Comprehensive case management services were provided to Robbie to mitigate his victimization.

It is critical for providers from all disciplines to be aware of the underlying issues related to oppositional defiant behaviors, which can signify a child's call for help rather than a boy prone to adversity for its own sake. The social worker in this case was unaware of the behavioral dynamics that might indicate risk for exploitation.

Young men describe "the life"

In 2012, I was a consultant at a Boston non-profit agency that worked with marginalized, homeless, and runaway youth – many with histories of commercial sexual exploitation. I held two focus groups for participants who were at-risk youth and/or actively being sexually exploited. The two groups, consisting of young men between 15 and 22 years of age, were designed to collect data on CSEC boys and life on the streets. Participants were recruited by staff, with incentives provided. (See Box 10.1 for definitions of key terms related to "the life.")

Box 10.1 Key terms and definitions for youth victimized by sex trafficking

Sex trafficking: a form of modern slavery that exists throughout the United States and globally. Sex traffickers use violence, threats, lies, debt bondage, and other forms of coercion to compel adults and children to engage in commercial sex acts against their will. (See National Human Trafficking Resource Center, n.d.)

Branding: a tattoo or carving on a victim indicating "ownership" of a youth by a trafficker/pimp/gang.

Caught a case: a term used to denote that a pimp or victim has been arrested and charged with a crime.

Choosing up: the process by which a different pimp takes "ownership" of a victim.

Circuit: series of cities among which commercially sexually exploited people are moved.

(continued)

(continued)

Daddy/Mommy:	a term pimps often require victims to call them.
Date:	the meeting when prostitution is scheduled.
Escort service:	an organization operating chiefly by cell phone or internet that sends a victim to a buyer's location (an "out-call") or arranges for the buyer to come to a house or apartment (an "in-call").
John/Buyer/Trick:	an individual who pays for or trades something of value for sexual acts.
Seasoning:	a combination of coercive acts, perhaps including psychological manipulation; intimidation; gang rape; sodomy; beatings; deprivation of food and sleep; isolation from friends, family, and other sources of support; and threatening or holding a victim's family hostage. Seasoning is designed to break down a victim's resistance and ensure compliance.
The game/the life:	the subculture of prostitution, complete with rules, hierarchy of authority, and language.
Trade up/trade down:	to move a victim like merchandise between pimps. A pimp may trade one victim for another or trade with an exchange of money.
Trauma bonding:	a term developed by Patrick Carnes, trauma bonding is the misuse of fear, excitement, sexual feelings, and sexual physiology to entangle another person. Many primary aggressors tend toward extreme behavior and risk taking, and trauma bonding is a factor in their relationships.

Source: Adapted from National Human Trafficking Hotline, operated by Polaris. Accessed April 10, 2016 from https://polarisproject.org/national-human-trafficking-hotline. Used with permission from Polaris.

Before each group, I told participants about my work developing services for exploited males and said I was seeking their counsel and expertise on life on the street as they knew it and how males came to the commercial sex industry. We explained confidentiality would be protected and furthermore that they should respond to questions based on their knowledge of the topic rather than their personal experience(s). This was to make clear they were not implicating themselves in a crime. Additionally, I explained that information from the interviews would be used to develop services for males impacted by sexual exploitation.

The participants were not familiar with the term "commercial sexual exploitation" and did not connect their experiences to it. The terms they used for prostitution/exploitation included: "survival sex," "hustling," "sex work," "tricking," "stepping out," and "making coins."

These are the questions I developed and the participants' summarized responses:

1 How do young men identify sexual exploitation?
  Participants identified five forms:

  a *Escort services*: Young men, usually aged 16–22, have a set number of clients to whom they provide services, usually on an on-call basis. The "hookup" is made either via cell phone or the Internet. The youth uses his credit card to reserve a hotel room; the buyer refrains from making the arrangement so there is no paper trail to him/her. The young man gets the key cards to the room, gives the buyer a card outside the hotel, and they enter the hotel separately, meeting in the reserved room where "business" is exchanged. Interestingly, the young man and buyer often develop a long-term "relationship" wherein the young man has intimate knowledge of the buyer: his name, profession, place of employment, marital status, and number of children. The young man can then gain and retain control of the "relationship" – up to a point – by threatening to disclose information to the buyer's employer and/or wife should he feel abused in one way or another by the buyer. As one young man said: "If he tries to screw me up in any way or gyp me out, he knows I'll be on the phone to the wife!"
  b *Street work*: Street work is still a viable way to connect with a buyer, depending on geography. In the South and Southwest of the United

States, and in southern California and up the California coast, for example, street work remains feasible. Young men "hook up" in strategic locations where buyers drive by, select a young man, enter into negotiations to define terms of service, drive to a secluded area, engage in sexual contact, and complete the transaction. This type of sexual exploitation is usually anonymous.

c *Internet sites*: Participants identified this as a growing and prevalent way of hooking up with buyers. There are various Internet sites where they can connect with a potential buyer. Negotiations for services are completed via the Internet and then a hookup location is selected. The venues can be hotels, cars, apartments, and so on.

d *Telecommunication*: In addition to Internet sites, connections can be made via Skype or another telecommunication connection. Potential buyers connect with young men through Internet surfing on the various hookup sites. Once contact is made, the buyer and youth join one another on Skype. The buyer pays his negotiated fee by swiping his credit card into the young man's account and sexual acts are then performed online. From a harm reduction perspective, this protects the young man from any possibility of contracting STIs or facing any danger that might arise with person-to-person contact.

e *Clubs*: Traditional men's clubs and strip clubs have exploited girls and women for many years. The participants of the focus groups reported that sexual activity for a fee is also common in gay clubs. With the knowledge of the club owner(s), young men hook up with club patrons for sex in exchange for money. Boys hired as dancers in these clubs are also expected to provide sexual services to patrons. Club owner(s) demand a cut of the money involved. Focus group participants also noted that many club owners have winter homes in Florida and transport young men there to work for them.

2 What are the reasons why boys and young men enter into "the life" of sex work/exploitation?

These young men said they rely on sex work to secure food, shelter, clothing, and daily living needs. The "work" is done out of necessity, based on limited options for survival, and not embraced as a lifestyle. Note that any male youth regardless of race or ethnicity is at high risk for sexual exploitation if he is impacted by any of the following risk factors:

a Many young men identified an earlier history of sexual abuse and/or neglect, confirming our expectation that this contributes to sexual exploitation.

b Boys and young men whose home life includes domestic violence, substance abuse, sexual abuse, or conflicts about house rules and limit setting may run away from home. They then run a great risk of being sexually exploited and brought into the commercial sex industry.

c A boy or young man with a single mother head of household often becomes parentified (i.e., becomes a surrogate spouse for his mother). If conflict ensues resulting in negative behaviors on his part, he may run away or be forced to leave home, running into the same risks of exploitation.

d Many youth are "throwaways," pushed out of their homes because of sexual orientation and/or gender identification.

e In further discussion, group participants were asked how the "client community" is identified and what they understood about the buyers. They defined the client community as frequently white males, 35 years of age or older, and married with children. Although clients cross socio-economic lines, the majority were identified as professional, including doctors, bank presidents, politicians, law enforcement personnel, and company CEOs. They are generally men with flexible work schedules, making hookups easy to manage. Participants commented that buyers commonly say they "can do things to them that they cannot do to their wives." They also remarked that many men had a preference for youth of color and wanted to fulfill fantasies of "being with a black man."

3 If outreach workers were to provide services to exploited youth, where would they find these youth?
Most participants agreed that common venues be included (but were not limited to) clubs, hookup Internet sites, public transportation centers, notorious cruising areas, hotel lobbies, and community areas where youth congregate.

4 What services do males need to help support them in not having to rely on sex work?

The participants listed five key services needed:

a Adequate and safe long-term supported housing with case management services.
b Educational programs to help them obtain the necessary credentials for gainful employment.
c Job training/apprenticeship and/or vocational training programs (see Strauser & Lustig, 2001).
d Compassionate health care from providers who do not make judgments about their lifestyle.
e Long-term mental health treatment by providers trained about this population's unique issues.

5 What can service providers do to help support youth involved in sexual exploitation?
The need for long-term supported housing was called the most critical issue for helping youth stay off the streets. They emphasized this is their number one need in order to avoid sexual exploitation. Beyond that, all the other services listed under question 4 were also named.
6 What other information can you offer that would enable a provider to understand young men involved in sex work?
The participants referred to themselves as "streetwise" people. Early life experiences with socially challenged families, disengaged or absent parents, limited socio-economic opportunities, and other adverse childhood experiences made them feel "older than their years." Participants concluded they had experienced more adversity in life than people three times their age. Having no childhood and enduring daily struggles about survival had given them very bleak prospects. They were aware that their buyers were using them, and they felt exploited, but they were in need of survival money. They believed the system supports their exploitation, especially since many clients have powerful professional positions. But they "do what they have to do and that's it."

Keith: needing stabilization

The outreach team I supervised engaged with at-risk boys and those being actively exploited by providing basic services to them. In doing so we aimed to establish trust and build relationships with the boys. Our ultimate goal was to provide long-term supportive services to help youth out of "the life."

Keith was an 18-year-old youth with a long history of homelessness and substance use. His need to feed his habit resulted in his having multiple criminal charges for petty crimes and frequent experiences with the court system. As a first step, it was essential that we stabilize him by finding him housing; this was critical in stopping his ongoing and future sexual exploitation. Once Keith was housed, services for his substance use were provided. We then worked with his probation officer to get his criminal charges dropped so the underlying issue, his sexual exploitation, could be treated. The key factor here was having workers who understand the impact of sexual exploitation and were willing to provide the intensive mentorship and case management needed for Keith to recover his life.

Pimps

Participants in the focus groups asserted that pimps were not usually part of the scenario. They did, however, say that some people, for example club managers, used intimidating techniques to coerce boys to engage in sex work in order to keep their jobs. Older men who had transitioned out of "the life" were also described as using coercive techniques to lure boys into "the life." But even though they defined these men as coercive the youth minimized or were not in touch with their impact. They insisted these were not pimps; yet coercion is integral to a pimp building a relationship with a victim. Whatever they called these men, it seems clear that pimps are commonly part of their "working life."

Based on the findings from these focus groups and subsequent work by this author, we can identify five principal ways boys become involved with pimps:

1 For many boys the initial entry into sexual exploitation is through family members. This usually occurs because the parental figures need money to feed their addictions. In chronically dysfunctional families, pimping out children brings the quick financial returns needed to feed the parents' habits. Additionally, prostitution may be the "family business"; exploited male youth frequently come from families where multi-generational prostitution is the norm. In such cases interventions are extremely challenging, since it takes generations of healing to break the cycle of this "family business."
2 In recent years, pimps have diversified their "workforce" (i.e., the kinds of boys they pimp out). In order to maximize their ability to meet the demands of the marketplace, pimps seek youth representing various demographics: girls, boys, trans youth, youth of color, etc.

They are thus able to bring greater financial returns for their business.
3 Communities can essentially become pimps when youth are sexually exploited in order for them to survive (this is known as "survival sex"). People in their immediate network introduce new youth into the homeless/runaway culture, teaching them what they need to do to subsist on the street.
4 Older men or women establish relationships with vulnerable at-risk/homeless/runaway male youth, grooming them with gifts of money, clothing, nice hotel rooms to stay in for the weekend, "bling" (ostentatious jewelry or other finery), technology, and so on. Over time, they gradually pimp them out to get a return for this economic support. In such situations, pimps often house the youth at their home or in hotels.
5 Fee-for-service pimps connect with youth indiscriminately on the street, asking if they are interested in making money that evening. If the youth agrees, the pimp drives them to nearby cruising areas and arranges for them to perform sex services for clients. At the end of a night's work, the pimp drops the youth off. That particular youth may not necessarily see that specific pimp again, but there is an abundant supply of fee-for-service pimps.

Service providers representing law enforcement, social services, medical services, courts, probation, youth shelters, outreach workers, and others need to be aware of these kinds of victimization and support the development of intervention systems to work with these young men, not solely as perpetrators, but as victims to be freed from their exploiters.

Todd: dangerous games

Todd, an 18-year-old male, was reported by his outreach worker to be spending his weekends in a local hotel. An adult woman "befriended" him and paid for his weekend expenses, "getting him off the streets" and providing him with food and other basic needs. He returned to the local youth drop-in center on Monday mornings. One day a staff member noticed Todd exiting a shower stall with welts on his body. The worker inquired and Todd admitted the woman gave them to him as part of "game playing." He said he did not like this but at least he was off the streets, was well fed, and had a warm bed to sleep in. Things began to escalate when the woman wanted to transport him to other states each weekend to play "the game." It turned out this woman was a dominatrix who was grooming Todd so she could exploit him with others. As a result of various interventions by Todd's support systems, he was able to end the "relationship" with her and begin receiving intensive mentorship and case management services to support his stabilization and work toward self-sufficiency.

International trafficking/commercial sexual exploitation

Although my work with the commercial sexual exploitation of male youth is specific to domestic cases in the United States, trafficking and sexual exploitation is universal (cf. Leon & Raws, 2016). Boys are exploited and trafficked to pedophiles throughout the world, through personal contact, the pornographic industry, the Internet, and other venues.

Poverty, regardless of the country, is commonly a gateway into the commercial sex industry. In countries such as the United Kingdom and other Western European countries, sexual exploitation resembles what happens in the United States. In Asian countries, it develops differently (see Davis & Miles, 2006; Miles & Blanch, 2011; Blanch & Miles, 2012; Miles, Blanch, & Thakur, 2012). In Thailand and Cambodia, for example, boys are often exploited out of massage parlors. In Afghanistan, boys bought from their abjectly poverty-stricken families with promises to educate them and provide them with employment, are instead subject to the sex slave industry. Afghan military personnel have been known to keep young male sex slaves while on military assignments. This is a practice known as *bacha bazi* (Goldstein, 2015).

Conclusions

The sexual exploitation and trafficking of boys and young men is a pervasive – though often invisible – problem worldwide, including in the United States. It affects its victims' health and ability to thrive, and leads to a host of psychosocial, medical, and environmental problems. It nevertheless continues to be largely ignored and denied by social and governmental agencies.

Nevertheless, research has begun to untangle the multiple factors that lead to sex trafficking of boys, from polyvictimization (including sexual victimization), to homelessness, to multi-generational participation in prostitution, to lack of screening by appropriate agencies due to the false belief that the boys are not victimized. The recognition of male victims of trafficking and commercial sexual exploitation is only now emerging in the public consciousness. In all its abusive forms it begs for further research, identification, and publicity.

References

Anda, R. F., Felitti, V. J., Bremner, J. D., Walker, J. D., Whitfield, C., Perry, B. D., . . . Giles, W. H. (2006). The enduring effects of abuse and related adverse experiences in childhood. *European Archives of Psychiatry and Clinical Neuroscience, 256*, 174–186.

Bigelsen, J., & Vuotto, S. (2013). *Homeless, survival sex and human trafficking: As experienced by the youth of Covenant House New York*. Retrieved from www.endhomelessness.org/page/-/files/Covenant%20House%20Fordham%20University%20Trafficking%20Report.pdf.

Blanch, H., & Miles, G. M. (2012). An initial exploration of young males in the male-to-male massage industry in Phnom Penh, Cambodia. *Social Work & Christianity, 39*(4), 407–434.

Clawson, H. J., Dutch, N. M., Salomon, A., & Goldblatt Grace, L. (2009). *Study of HHS Programs Serving Human Trafficking Victims – Final Report.* Retrieved from https://aspe.hhs.gov/basic-report/study-hhs-programs-serving-human-trafficking-victims-final-report.

Cook, A., Spinazzola, J., Ford, J. D., Lanktree, C., Blaustein, M., Cloitre, M., . . . van der Kolk, B. (2005). Complex trauma in children and adolescents. *Psychiatric Annals, 35*(5), 390–398. Retrieved from www.traumacenter.org/products/Complex%20Trauma%20White%20Paper.pdf.

Curtis, R., Terry, K., Dank, M., Dombrowski, K., & Khan, B. (2008). *The commercial sexual exploitation of children in New York City, Volume One: The CSEC population in New York City: Size, characteristics, and needs*. Retrieved from www.ncjrs.gov/pdffiles1/nij/grants/225083.pdf.

Davis, J., and Miles, G. M. (2006). The lingha boys of Siem Reap: A baseline study of sexually exploited young men in Siem Reap, Cambodia. *Fourth Annual Interdisciplinary Conference on Human Trafficking, 2012*. Paper 12. Retrieved from http://digitalcommons.unl.edu/cgi/viewcontent.cgi?article=1013&context=humtrafconf4.

Degraaf, R., Vanwesenbeeck, I., van Zessen, G., Straver, C. J., & Visser, J. H. (1995). Alcohol and drug use in heterosexual and homosexual prostitution, and its relation to protection behaviour. *AIDS Care, 7*(1), 35–47.

Dennis, J. P. (2008). Women are victims, men make choices: The invisibility of men and boys and young men in the global sex trade. *Gender Issues, 25*(1), 11–25. doi: 10.1007/s12147-008-9051-y

Elifson, K. W., Boles, J., & Sweat, M. (1993). Risk factors associated with HIV infection among male prostitutes. *American Journal of Public Health, 83*(1), 79–83.

Estes, R. J. (2001). *Commercial sexual exploitation of children: A working guide to the empirical literature.* University of Pennsylvania School of Social Work, Philadelphia, PA. Retrieved from www.researchgate.net/publication/237780283_THE_SEXUAL_EXPLOITATION_OF_CHILDREN_A_Working_Guide_to_the_Empirical_Literature.

Estes, R. J., & Weiner, N. A. (2001). *The commercial sexual exploitation of children in the U. S., Canada and Mexico.* University of Pennsylvania School of Social Work, Philadelphia, PA. Retrieved from www.thenightministry.org/070_facts_figures/030_research_links/060_homeless_youth/CommercialSexualExploitationofChildren.pdf.

Felitti, V. J., Anda, R. F., Nordenberg, D., Williamson, D. F., Spitz, A. M., Edwards, V., Koss, M. P., & Marks, J. S. (1998). The relationship of adult health status to childhood abuse and household dysfunction. *American Journal of Preventive Medicine, 14*, 245–258.

Finkelhor, D., Ormrod, R., & Turner, H. (2007). Polyvictimization: A neglected component of child victimization. *Child Abuse and Neglect, 31*, 7–26.

Finkelhor, D., Turner, H., Hamby, S., & Ormrod, R. (2011, October). *Polyvictimization: Children's exposure to multiple types of violence, crime and abuse. Juvenile Justice Bulletin.* OJJDP: National Survey of Children's Exposure to Violence. Retrieved from www.ncjrs.gov/pdffiles1/ojjdp/235504.pdf.

Finkelhor, D., Turner, H., Ormrod, R., Hamby, S., & Kracke, K. (2009). *Children's exposure to violence: A comprehensive national survey.* OJJDP: National Survey of Children's Exposure to Violence. Retrieved from www.ncjrs.gov/pdffiles1/ojjdp/227744.pdf.

Ford, J. D., Connor, D., & Hawke, J. (2009). Complex trauma among psychiatrically impaired children. *Journal of Clinical Psychiatry, 70*, 1155–1163.

Ford, J. D., Wasser, T., & Connor, D. F. (2011). Identifying and determining the symptom severity associated with polyvictimization among psychiatrically impaired children in the outpatient setting. *Child Maltreatment, 16*(3), 216–226. Retrieved from www.traumacenter.org/initiatives/FordWasserConnorCM2011_11_216-226.pdf.

Fradkin, H. (2011). Invisible survivors: The legacy of male sexual trauma. Presentation at Fenway Community Health Center, Boston, MA.

Gartner, R. B. (1999). *Betrayed as boys: Psychodynamic treatment of sexually abused men.* New York, NY: Guilford.

Goldstein, J. (2015, September 20). U.S. soldiers told to ignore sexual abuse of boys by Afghan allies. *New York Times.* Retrieved from www.nytimes.com/2015/09/21/world/asia/us-soldiers-told-to-ignore-afghan-allies-abuse-of-boys.html.

Hudson, P., & Rivers, I. (2002). Men and boys: Selling sex in the Bradford district. *Social Inclusion and Diversity Paper Number 1.* Retrieved from http://bura.brunel.ac.uk/bitstream/2438/2706/1/MEN%20AND%20BOYS%20BOOK.pdf.

Leon, L., & Raws, P. (2016). Boys don't cry: Improving identification and disclosure of sexual exploitation of boys and young men trafficked to the UK. The Children's Society. doi: 10.13140/RG.2.1.4933.4167

Levine, P. A., & Kline, M. (2007). *Trauma through a child's eyes: Infancy through adolescence.* Berkeley, CA: North Atlantic Books.

Lew, M. (2004). *Victims no longer: The classic guide for men recovering from sexual child abuse* (2nd Ed.). New York, NY: Harper Perennial.

Lillywhite, R., & Skidmore, P. (2006). Boys are not sexually exploited: A challenge to practitioners. *Child Abuse Review, 15*(5), 351–361. doi: 10.1002/car.952

McIntyre, S. (2005). *Under the radar: The sexual exploitation of young men – Western Canadian Edition.* Retrieved from www.humanservices.alberta.ca/documents/child-sexual-exploitation-under-the-radar-western-canada.pd.

Miles, G. M., & Blanch, H. (2011). *What about boys? An initial exploration of sexually exploited boys in Cambodia.* Third Annual Interdisciplinary Conference on Human Trafficking, Paper 20. Retrieved from http://digitalcommons.unl.edu/cgi/viewcontent.cgi?article=1019&context=humtraffconf3.

Miles, G. M., Blanch, H., & Thakur, J. (2011). *"What about boys?": The sexual exploitation of boys and young men in Asia.* Presentation for 2011 Interdisciplinary Conference on Human Trafficking, September 29 - October 1, 2011, Lincoln, Nebraska. Retrieved from http://digitalcommons.unl.edu/cgi/viewcontent.cgi?article=1020&context=humtraffconf3.

National Center for PTSD. (2016). *Men and sexual trauma.* PTSD: National Center for PTSD, US Department of Veterans Affairs. Retrieved from www.ptsd.va.gov/public/types/violence/men-sexual-trauma.asp.

National Human Trafficking Resource Center (n.d.). *Sex trafficking.* Polaris: Freedom Happens Now. Retrieved from http://polarisproject.org/sex-trafficking.

NCTSN (National Child Traumatic Stress Network) (n.d.). *Effects of complex trauma.* Retrieved from www.nctsn.org/trauma-types/complex-trauma/effects-of-complex-trauma.

Sexual Exploitation Toolkit (2008). What is sexual exploitation? Justice Institute of British Columbia, Centre for Counselling and Community Safety. Retrieved from http://host.jibc.ca/seytoolkit/what.htm.

Spinazzola, J., Ford, J. D., Zucker, M., van der Kolk, B., Silva, S., Smith, S., & Blaustein, M. (2005). Survey evaluates complex trauma exposure, outcome and intervention among children and adolescents. *Psychiatric Annals, 35*(5), 433–439.

Strauser, D., & Lustig, D. (2001). The implications of posttraumatic stress disorder on vocational behavior and rehabilitation planning. *Journal of Rehabilitation, 67*(4), 26–30.

Valente, S. (2005). Sexual abuse of boys. *Journal of Child and Adolescent Psychiatric Nursing, 18*, 10–16. Retrieved from http://onlinelibrary.wiley.com/doi/10.1111/j.1744-6171.2005.00005.x/abstract?deniedAccessCustomisedMessage=&userIsAuthenticated=false.

Whealin, J., & Barnett, E. (n.d.). *Child sexual abuse*. PTSD: National Center for PTSD, US Department of Veterans Affairs. Retrieved from www.ptsd.va.gov/professional/trauma/other/child_sexual_abuse.asp.

Willis, B., Robert, N., & Friedman, S. A. (2013). *And boys too: Needed: A spotlight on commercial sexual exploitation of boys. An ECPAT-USA discussion paper about the lack of recognition of the commercial sexual exploitation of boys in the United States*. Retrieved from https://traffickingresourcecenter.org/sites/default/files/And%20Boys%20Too%20-%20ECPAT%20USA.pdf.

Chapter 11

Beyond the gay/straight binary

Gender and/or sexually diverse male survivors

Jim Struve, Howard Fradkin, and Lee Beckstead

Writing this chapter began as an effort to elaborate on the effects of sexual trauma for gay and bisexual males. But we were immediately captured by the inherent limitations of writing about this subject within the binary rules for sexuality and gender. Approaching this topic from a strict dualistic perspective (e.g., gay and bisexual male survivors as opposed to heterosexual male survivors) repeatedly constrained, blocked, or distorted the observations we wished to communicate. Sexual trauma furthermore introduces confusion and distress about matters of gender and sexuality. Therefore, we will begin with a discussion of terms and how they may be used to understand a range of experiences but also can be problematic in perpetuating marginalization. We hope this discussion will reduce stigma and expand options for healing.

Defining a framework for sexuality and gender

One initial challenge in working with this population is determining appropriate definitions and labels. For instance, describing this population as "non-heterosexual" distinguishes individuals who experience some degree of same-sex sexual attractions from those who experience exclusively heterosexual attractions. However, the binary term "non-heterosexual" leaves this population defined against who they are not rather than describing who they are.[1] It also positions this population

1 This section was informed by a discussion on the American Psychological Association's Division 44 (Society for the Psychological Study of Lesbian, Gay, Bisexual and Transgender Issues) email Listserv in March, 2016. We appreciate those who shared their views on these diversity issues.

against the majority and reinforces a heterocentric privilege. This is similar to referring to everyone who is a person of color as non-White. It combines and reduces a diverse group of individuals and cultures into a "non" category by comparing them to the majority. It can be oppressive to be defined as a "not" and even more difficult to try and develop an identity based on being a "not."

Yet, minority identity development often includes periods of defining oneself as separate from the majority so the individual can examine experiences of stigmatization and find personal ways to adapt positively to a minority status. This type of separation and differentiation can help individuals develop self-acceptance and stop efforts to try to be who they are not (i.e., the majority).

All survivors of sexual trauma in general hold a minority status. They may feel ashamed of being different from the norm until they are able to meet peers with similar victimization experiences, which can help them feel less stigmatized and more empowered about their own life experiences.

The term "sexual and/or gender minority" is an inclusive term denoting the spectrum of sexual and gender identities. It recognizes that not everyone who experiences same-sex sexual attractions will identify as lesbian, gay, or bisexual (LGB). This inclusiveness is important because recent population statistics suggest that there are more individuals who experience same-sex attractions who do not identify as LGB than there are who identify as LGB (Bailey et al., 2016). In addition, someone may have an asexual sexual orientation, experiencing little or no sexual desire but no erotic aversion. This does not represent a pathological condition, such as being afraid and avoidant of being sexual, but is another variant of human sexuality.

"Gender non-conforming" and "non-traditional gender" have been used to refer to transgender individuals; however, the first term applies only to gender expression and the second could apply to identity or to a person's biological sex (e.g., intersex), each with a comparison to the norm. These terms can be misleading because someone who is transsexual (referring to those who change their body to look more male or female, matching how they feel inside) may express their[2] gender in traditionally

2 The third-person plural pronouns "they," "them," and "their" are sometimes used in this document as third-person singular pronouns to avoid the use of gendered pronouns and include individuals who are gender non-binary.

normative ways. Also, a person may be cisgender (referring to individuals whose gender identity is congruent with the sex they were assigned at birth), but have manners of dress and behavior that do not fit cultural norms of masculinity and femininity. Furthermore, transgender and transsexual individuals often identify as heterosexual.

Some individuals report experiencing erotic aversion, not just disinterest or social aversion, to being sexual with individuals of their non-preferred sex (Beckstead, 2012). Erotic aversion has not been extensively studied, but this physiological, emotional limit may distinguish those who are exclusively same-sex attracted or exclusive other-sex attracted from those who experience some capacity for erotic satisfaction with both women and men. Trauma may be intensified when violations occur between a person's erotic-aversion limit and their abuse-relational dynamic (e.g., exclusively same-sex attracted male victim and female offender, exclusively other-sex attracted male victim and male offender).

Many still adopt the LGB labels because they imply belonging to a group with specific norms, values, and behaviors. Historically, however, bisexual people have been left out of – or been invisible within – this LGB group membership, even though LGB includes bisexuality. Reasons some who experience same-sex attractions do not adopt the LGB label include that they do not pursue same-sex sexual relationships, may experience stronger other-sex attractions, may hold negative biases about being LGB, and/or do not see themselves reflected in that sociopolitical identity (Beckstead & Morrow, 2004; Savin-Williams & Vrangalova, 2013; Yarhouse, Tan, & Pawlowski, 2005). Therefore, their sexual orientation, behaviors, and public and personal identities may not always match. This is because the process of identity development depends upon cultural definitions and opportunities and how a person makes decisions about sexuality and behaviors.[3]

We recommend that readers make a conscious choice to avoid the use of "homosexual" or "homosexuality" to limit the historical pathological meaning attributed to these terms. They can be too simplistic, not encompassing the totality of someone's affectional, romantic, behavioral, relational, and cultural experience. Similarly, "heterosexual" can be misleading because it can refer to a person's orientation, behavior, and identity. However, this can

3 Editor's note: See Chapter 12 by Kort in this volume for discussion of sexual identity/orientation confusion.

lead to ambiguous assumptions; for example, not all heterosexually married individuals are heterosexual in orientation (Corley & Kort, 2006). "Gay," for some, simply means "being attracted to the same sex"; however, for others, it implies specific social norms of how a person lives out their orientation (e.g., "I have same-sex attractions, but I am not gay"). "Same-sex attracted" is descriptive but may also offend some as reducing their identity to only their attractions. Some may not adopt a bisexual identity because of bi-negative beliefs that bisexuals are promiscuous, can't make up their minds, or are too afraid to come out as gay, all of which do not match how they see their sexuality.

Each of these terms also implies that sexual and gender identities are fixed, ignoring how identity development can be fluid or in flux throughout life. Because of this potential for misunderstanding and bias, it is important to help survivors clarify the best terms to describe their sexuality and to understand how they came to label themselves this way. For these reasons, we encourage clinicians to prioritize two principles of ethical mental-health services: "Do no harm" and "Facilitate individual self-determination." This ensures that interventions are respectful and compassionate to the lived realities from all points on the spectrum, without dismissing any (Reconciliation and Growth Project, 2017).

Likewise, biological sex is not binary. In reality, research reveals that between 1.7% and 4% of the world's population is intersex (Haas, 2004). "Intersex" refers to a medical condition for a person born with a reproductive or sexual anatomy not fitting typical definitions of female or male (Intersex Society of North America, 2016). It is the contemporary term that replaces the historically stigmatizing term "hermaphrodite." The existence of individuals who are intersex presents a conundrum for those subscribing to a binary view of gender (e.g., is it a heterosexual or same-sex marriage between a man and someone with an intersex condition?). In addition, the term "same-sex attractions" leaves out individuals not identifying with a binary gender.

Clearly, our language is evolving, finding terms that are more inclusive and accurate. We decided to use the term "gender and/or sexually diverse" (GSD) to refer to those who experience same-sex attractions and/or a gender expression that does not fit with cultural norms. However, we recognize there is also a spectrum of sexuality and gender expression for cisgender, exclusively heterosexual individuals. That population of male survivors is beyond the scope of our attention here.

We also acknowledge the monumental changes rapidly impacting social justice for GSD individuals and allies. In many parts of the world, new freedoms for expressing sexuality and gender are emerging while historical sanctions based on discrimination and inequality are being lifted. The psychological effects of these changes on current and future generations are still unknown. We hope for more positive outcomes in the future, as people's lived experiences reflect the dynamics of lesser degrees of oppression of healthy sexual and gender expression.

Overall, clinicians who strive for cultural competence should consider the explosion of language among vast numbers of people whose lived realities reflect a spectrum of sexual and gender identities instead of binary identifications (van Anders, 2015). Even Facebook now acknowledges this spectrum by offering users 50 options for gender identification. Given the above complexities, we challenge three core concepts of the binary paradigm:

1 Limiting sexuality and gender to the dual choices of male or female, masculine or feminine, "straight" or "gay," is unnatural and contrived. Sexuality and gender more realistically exist as spectrums of possibilities.
2 Categorizing sexuality, gender, and culture as distinctly separate and independent features of human identity ignores the reality that these characteristics often overlap, intersect, and therefore affect each other.
3 Prioritizing cisgender heterosexual masculinity as the gold standard by which all expressions of sexuality and gender are judged potentially causes mental-health distress.

How viewing male sexual trauma through a binary lens causes harm

Within a binary paradigm, options for sexuality and gender are either right or wrong, normal or pathological. Tolerance for expressions of diversity is narrow within families and cultures that adhere to binary perspectives about sexuality and gender. In these settings, victims in their healing process may struggle to feel normal, desiring to fit in with the majority. Viewing sexual trauma within a binary template may impose unnecessary expectations, perpetuate blind spots, neglect to challenge false beliefs, and therefore blur understanding of the trauma's complexity. These stereotypes and biases may contribute to the gross underreporting and the disproportionate muting of the effects of male sexual trauma as well as the unfortunate isolation of so many male survivors.

We can see how binary views impact our interpretations of sexual trauma through the different observations emerging when victims are female versus male. We know that a high proportion of sexual offenders are male, whether the victim is male or female. In situations of female victimization by a male, there is usually minimal or no suspicion about sexual orientation or gender identity. It is unlikely that the female survivor will fear she became heterosexual because of her male perpetrator. In contrast, for male survivors with a male offender, sexual orientation and gender are almost universally analyzed, with a disproportionate level of scrutiny.

Consider the example of a boy sexually assaulted by an older male. The assault represents an act of same-sex sexual aggression that both victim and society often interpret as "gay behavior." Often the perpetrator is believed to be gay rather than more attracted to underage males, whether pre-pubescent or adolescent (pedophilic or hebephilic), than to adult males (androphilic). Although the sexual orientation of the victim cannot be assumed, usually this traumatic episode is infused with considerations about whether he is – or will become – gay. This fear, however, has no scientific basis; no scientific evidence exists that sexual abuse can change or create a person's orientation (LeVay, 2016; Stevenson, 2000; Xu & Zheng, 2015). If sexual trauma were to cause sexual orientation, then a higher percentage of the population would be LGB, given the rates of sexual abuse reported (Andersen & Blosnich, 2013).

Yet, a survivor is often left with residual struggles of untangling confusions and prejudice from sexual identity. Others may scrutinize him to assess his orientation and identity or otherwise explain whether his sexuality was tainted by his sexual trauma. In contrast, female victims (almost always) or male victims abused by a female (most often) do not face the same level of societal pressure to prove they are heterosexual.

Males sexually abused by males may come to feel negatively about same-sex sexuality and their own maleness/masculinity because of the association of same-sex trauma with being gay and male. False conceptions about same-sex sexuality and gender (e.g., equating victimization and passivity with being gay or transgender; equating same-sex sexual reenactments as signs of being gay) may interfere with survivors' ability to accept their sexual orientation and gender identity and deal effectively with the abuse (Gartner, 1999a). This is particularly problematic when bias leads to the survivor's sexual orientation or gender identity being pathologized, thereby diverting attention from traumatic aspects of sexual assault(s). Social bias may cause some survivors to invest in changing their attractions to prove they are not "weak" or shameful.

Sometimes, when the offender is female, the male survivor may reject being sexual with women due to a posttraumatic response and is left with only a gay or asexual identity, although this does not represent their core sexual orientation. But a binary paradigm sets up heterosexual survivors to be assumed to be gay when they do not initiate or are averse to heterosexual sexual activity due to a posttraumatic response.

Living in a world that operates by the rules of binary classifications, a male survivor may struggle to "pick a team" (i.e., straight or gay, masculine or feminine) in describing past, present, or future aspects of his sense of self. When treatment focuses on trying to change survivors' sexual orientation or gender identity to fit heterosexual norms, rather than providing them a safe space to discover their own sexuality and gender, it becomes a harmful re-enactment of a victim submitting to a powerful other (cf. Brady, 2008; Morris & Balsam, 2003; Russell, Jones, Barclay, & Anderson, 2008).

For most people, racial and gender identity (e.g. being Black or female) is apparent to oneself and visible to the external world. However, sexual and gender identity are often unformed, disguised, or intentionally hidden. It is not unusual for GSD individuals to be deeply inculcated with sexual or gender prejudice before they realize their own GSD identity. Also, childhood sexual abuse occurs for many well before the average age of awareness of sexual feelings. Traumatic impact in such situations may be complicated if survivors are struggling to hide or deny their identity from themselves or the external world. This concealment can prevent a GSD survivor from developing necessary aspects of self.

Given the harm that sexual abuse can inflict on identity development, conducting a comprehensive assessment of developmental dynamics for sexuality and gender is a prerequisite to clinician competency in working with GSD male survivors. Clinicians must understand that the internal realities of the GSD male survivor may or may not be congruent with external presentation. More precisely, self-awareness, self-acceptance, identity, and expressions of sexuality and gender may not be synonymous. Perceptions, cognitions, behaviors, and emotional experiences may be vastly different depending on where in the developmental process of sexuality and gender a survivor was at the time of victimization as well as when he seeks help for healing.

Consider the spectrum of developmental variation (i.e., age, stage of developmental awareness, and context) within which sexual trauma may have occurred and the differing implications for how the GSD male victim might process his experience:

1. A male assigned at birth who is the victim of sexual trauma before he understands he is GSD.
2. A male assigned at birth who is the victim of sexual trauma who understands at the time of the trauma that he is GSD.
3. A male assigned at birth who was confused about his sexual orientation at the time he was the victim of sexual trauma and who later considers himself neither gay nor straight.
4. A male assigned at birth who experiences same-sex attractions but does not identify as gay, bisexual, or a sexual/gender minority, perhaps due to cultural, religious, or ideological reasons.
5. A male assigned at birth who identifies as heterosexually male but is targeted as a victim of sexual trauma because he displays "feminine" or "unmasculine" gender traits.
6. A female assigned at birth who identifies as male (or closer to male than female), who may be attracted to men, women, or both, and who is a victim of sexual trauma(s) in which the perpetrator(s) perceived the individual as female and/or whose assault targeted the individual's gender expression and perceived sexual orientation.

In any of these scenarios, who decides whether or when a male survivor is gay, bisexual, traditionally masculine, or somewhere else on the GSD spectrum? Clinicians must exercise care to avoid making assumptions and interpretations about developmental stages of awareness and identity.

Box 11.1 Five guiding principles for clinical work with a male survivor who is gender and/or sexually diverse

- Sexuality and gender are represented by a spectrum of identities versus being limited to the binary choices of straight–gay, male–female, masculine–feminine.
- Sexuality and gender sometimes overlap or intersect; therefore, they are not necessarily bifurcated and exclusionary.
- Awareness, identity, and expression about sexuality and gender are distinct stages of development, perhaps evolving at different rates.
- The impact of sexual trauma may be vastly different depending upon the victim's stage of development regarding awareness, identity, and expression about sexuality and gender.
- There may be a dual layering of trauma when sexual assault occurs within the context of sexual/gender minority distress.

Understanding the impact of sexual and gender prejudice

GSD men have much in common with male sexual trauma survivors; many GSD men experience common concerns, whether or not they are sexual abuse survivors. Also, numerous factors exist for most male sexual abuse survivors, whatever their sexual orientation. Ironically, many of these factors are the same for survivors and GSD men. For example, both survivors and GSD individuals may struggle with telling others about their stigmatized identity. Survivors who are GSD, therefore, may struggle with a "double layered" impact of these factors. Many of these factors and their influence may be culture-based, so their specific impact is not inherently universal in nature. Table 11.1 represents some similarities between male sexual trauma survivors and GSD males.

GSD male survivors are commonly alert to threats of rejection and violence. Repercussions of sexual and gender prejudice/violence are one plausible explanation for why GSD males face higher risks for sexual trauma (Xu & Zheng, 2015). Data from the past 20 years indicate that LGB individuals report higher rates of childhood sexual abuse than heterosexuals (Roberts, Rosario, Koenen, & Austin, 2012), with gay men reporting rates close to levels reported by heterosexual women (Rothman, Exner, & Baughman, 2011). A 2001 nonclinical study (Tomeo, Templer, Anderson, & Kotler, 2001) revealed that whereas only 7% of heterosexual men in their sample reported same-sex molestation during childhood, 46% of gay men acknowledged childhood sexual trauma. Data from the 2010 National Intimate Partner & Sexual Violence Survey (Center for Disease Control & Prevention, 2013) revealed that 26% of gay men and 37% of bisexual men experienced rape, physical violence, and/or stalking by an intimate partner at some point in their lifetime. That same survey reported that 40% of gay men and nearly 50% of bisexual men had experienced sexual violence other than rape in their lifetime, compared to 21% of heterosexual men. It is important to note a caution in how we interpret data comparing risk factors for males who identify as GSD versus heterosexual, as it is possible that heterosexual males are less likely than GSD males to acknowledge having been victims of sexual trauma. More research is needed to clarify how sexual and gender prejudice affects heterosexual male survivors.

Unfortunately, sexual, gender, and racial prejudice is woven into many of the primary institutions that govern society (e.g., laws and traditionally religious doctrines). This creates a context for the sanctioned marginalization and abuse of minorities: Vives (2002) found that 75% of a sample of 445 gay and bisexual males had experienced verbal harassment and 33% confirmed physical violence related to sexual orientation. Data from another survey found that nearly 50% of gay and bisexual adults experienced verbal abuse and 20% experienced physical violence or property crimes because of their sexual orientation (Herek, 2009). A study of Latino men who have sex with men revealed they had a higher incident rate of childhood sexual abuse compared to Caucasian men who have sex with men (Arreola, Neilands, & Diaz, 2009). Grant et al. (2011) interviewed 6450 transgender or gender non-conforming adults. Results indicated that 15% of respondents reported being sexually assaulted while in prison and 22% of respondents reported being sexually assaulted by residents or staff while in homeless shelters.

The character of sexual trauma that results from discrimination is quite different from incestuous abuse because of the added dimension of revulsion and prejudice against the minority identity itself (Gartner, 1999a, 1999b). Hate crimes are frequently perpetrated with the intent to disgrace or obliterate the personal and cultural identity of the victim(s).

Table 11.1 Similarities between sexual abuse survivors and GSD males

	Sexual abuse survivor	*GSD male*
Isolation	Abusers are masterful in enrolling their victim in a web of secrecy, often leading the victim to isolate himself from critical members of his support system.	GSD men commonly separate themselves from the dominant heterosexual culture, constructing a lifestyle dominated by secrecy and isolation.
Secrecy	Abused individuals learn that secrecy is linked to loyalty; violating the ground rules of secrecy may result in abandonment or further abuse.	Oppressive cultural norms create a context in which GSD men who are open and non-secretive are frequently judged as "flaunting" their sexual orientation; therefore, many GSD men choose secrecy rather than risking judgment, rejection, or loss.
Disclosure	Victims of abuse frequently become targets of blame or are ostracized after accidental or intentional disclosure.	Accidental or intentional disclosure of stigmatized minority sexuality may precipitate a "big explosion" and/or result in negative repercussions in a GSD man's life.
Hypervigilance	Abused men are normally intensely hypervigilant about others' behavioral and mood changes, always watchful for potential abusers.	GSD men often rely on a finely tuned "gaydar" as a guide in searching for friends and foes as they negotiate life in a less-than-safe world.
Control	Many survivors feel insecure or fearful when they do not or cannot exercise control.	Feeling powerless to affect the larger world, GSD men often seek to control people and situations within their inner circle of relationships.

Shame	Most survivors feel shame about being victimized; shame is devastating to self-esteem and results in highly negative self-images for most survivors.	GSD men often learn to hate their sexuality before discovering their own membership in this sexual minority; self-hatred is a fertile breeding ground for shame.
Vulnerability	Children are inherently dependent on adult guardians to provide for safety and protection. Innocence and dependency sometimes create circumstances where children become the vulnerable prey of adult sexual offenders.	Because transphobia, bi-phobia, and homophobia are generally accepted as the normal, acceptable social order, GSD men usually normalize their vulnerability to myriad aspects of life in a precarious world.
Intimacy	Intimacy may trigger survivors' responses that are defensive or undermine relationship; closeness may be perceived as a dangerous precursor of abuse.	Culturally, GSD men need to learn about relationships under cover of secrecy; a lack of familial or community support often creates stressors that interfere with GSD men's efforts to achieve intimacy in primary relationships.
Dissociation	By "tuning out," "numbing out," or "diverting attention from reality," victims of abuse are able to tolerate what might otherwise be intolerable life circumstances.	Dissociation is a predictable survival strategy for GSD men who consciously acknowledge they live in a dominant culture that unapologetically rejects them.
Sexuality	Many abuse survivors struggle to disentangle sexual feelings and behaviors natural to their core personality from learned or conditioned responses to abuse.	Heterosexuality is the cultural norm for "healthy" sexuality; a GSD man frequently struggles to gain acceptance of his sexuality without the filter of oppressive judgments.

The resulting impact of "identity trauma" may utterly overshadow the sexual components of the attack (Kira et al., 2011). Victims of this kind of sexual violence characteristically exhibit features of complex trauma resulting from being the target of hate intermixed with sexual violation (Courtois & Ford, 2013).

Research shows higher rates of posttraumatic stress disorder for sexual abuse survivors who were gender non-conforming compared to survivors who were gender conforming (Roberts, et al., 2012). Brooks (2001) asserted that violence is a customary tool used against gender atypical males and that acts of aggression may be used to reprimand "misbehavior" and to instill the "rules" for socially acceptable male behavior. As one GSD male survivor described:

> *In college the sexual assault that I experienced at 18 was definitely associated with being not masculine enough. My abuser wanted to prove that I was gay to his friends by having me perform oral sex on him while they watched and then by anally penetrating me to prove to them I liked it as he had me masturbate while he penetrated me. So the "proof" that I liked it and that I was gay was the fact that I came while he was anally penetrating me.* (Jason)[4]

Sexual and gender prejudice is also carefully intertwined within hazing rituals, a phenomenon that seems to be more characteristic of masculinized environments (e.g., fraternal organizations, sports teams, the military, social clubs, etc.). Within these rituals, sexuality and gender are routinely manipulated, distorted, or completely denied for some overarching purpose (e.g., gaining entry into a group, enforcing compliance and loyalty, testing someone's personal fortitude). The environments within which these hazing rituals occur and the long-standing traditions that may encase their implementation often sanction, disguise, or dismiss any responsibility for the effects of sexual trauma that belong to the offenders, yet may

4 Jim Struve and Howard Fradkin are co-chairs for the MaleSurvivor Weekends of Recovery (WOR) program, which provides three-day experiential workshops for male survivors. We have included throughout the remainder of this chapter selected quotes from a survey of WOR alumni, which Jim and Howard conducted in 2015. Real names are not used in any of these quotes.

be internalized by the recipient. One complication in addressing sexual trauma that occurs under the guise of this socially sanctioned discrimination is that the victim may not recognize the experience as being a sexual violation. Furthermore, institutional tradition may lead victims to accept trauma as the price they agreed to pay by submitting to the hazing, or may stifle bystanders from intervening to stop such harmful behavior.

Unfortunately, investigators of hate crimes and subsequent treatment providers often miss uncovering dynamics of this complex trauma. A contributing factor is that GSD survivors will frequently not disclose sexual details of their assault. There are a variety of reasons this may occur, including that they (a) may have internalized the assault as expected discrimination or customary punishment, (b) may not identify as a sexual or gender minority and thereby do not perceive the assault as a hate crime, (c) may have dissociated the sexual aspects of the assault for fear of harmful repercussions – internal or external – that might result if they acknowledged or disclosed them, and/or (d) may fear disclosure that they have a body that does not look entirely male if they are someone with intersex anatomy or if they were assigned a female sex at birth and have transitioned to express a male identity and appearance. To complicate treatment further, professionals helping the victim may not inquire about any of these aspects of the assault.

GSD male survivors who experience sexual trauma before they are fully aware of their sexual or gender identity or during a period when they are questioning or confused about their identity may be averse to disclosing their victim status due to fears that doing so will imply they are other than heterosexual masculine males (Cassese, 2000). This can be especially complex for the transgender male survivor who may have been sexually assaulted while identifying and living as a male but targeted because of his female anatomy:

> *I didn't think anybody would believe me. I thought, "Who's going to believe that a guy would rape a 'woman' who looks like a prepubescent boy? I'm hideous!" In addition, I was worried what the implications would be on my gender identity. I feared that if I let a man overpower me, if I was raped vaginally, I could never become the man I knew I was.* (Gerald)

In some cases – for instance, male survivors living in a country with harsh laws against sexual non-conformity or in an isolated cult – being assumed to be a GSD male can result in monstrous physical harm or even death. For them, remaining silent about sexual trauma is an appropriately wise and protective strategy to avoid harsh punishment reflecting judgment about a GSD identity.

Although not a hate crime, some offenders use aspects of sanctioned social bias to manipulate or control GSD male victims. For example, a male victim may internalize his offender's blaming messages of "If you didn't like the sex, why did you get an erection?" and/or "If you didn't like the sex, why didn't you stop it?" For the survivor who knows they are or suspects they may be GSD males, those messages can be very destabilizing and can interfere with the processing of their trauma. Not understanding the physiology whereby sexual responsiveness may occur even during traumatic encounters, GSD male victims may internalize their body response as proof of consent – a factor that many manipulative offenders will maliciously use to control their victim. The following quote is an example of how sexual messages and trauma dynamics can interfere with processing confusion about body physiology and identity.

> *I feel like a straight man trapped in a gay man's body. I feel I was born to be a straight man but that the abuse conditioned my body and arousal template to understand sex as being submissive to an aggressive . . . man, which is still the primary interest of my body's sexuality even as my primary self is disgusted by what my body compels me to do.* (Jamaal)

This can be particularly tricky when GSD male survivors and/or their allies subscribe to deeply held convictions that any degree of GSD identity or expression is pathological, religiously apostate, or otherwise rejected. There may be faith-based or ideological prohibitions that prevent GSD male survivors from honest disclosure or engagement in unrestricted discussions of same-sex aspects of their sexual trauma. The GSD male survivor may be overwhelmed by the dissonance between the norms of their support environments (e.g., family, faith, peers) and their internal aspirations for identity and expression. GSD male survivors who are caught in these real-life cultural dilemmas commonly develop highly refined skills for dissociating sexual aspects of whatever trauma they experienced.

This application of dissociation may provide a necessary degree of protective refuge, whereby others in the survivor's life may exhibit greater acceptance when the survivor remains shrouded in silent conformity or an identity of confusion. For many GSD male survivors, identity dissociation and trauma dissociation may become intertwined in complex ways. The task for the clinician is to provide safety that allows the survivor to bring those considerations back into consciousness.

Risky sexual behavior

Sexual trauma can interrupt sexual identity development and therefore a survivor's chance for sexual health. As previously mentioned, GSD male survivors may exhibit a number of health and behavior issues whose origin can be linked to the residual impact of sexual minority stress. An important issue to explore is the prevalence of risky sexual behaviors among GSD male survivors. There are two viewpoints to this issue: First, many GSD males are at greater risk for sexual trauma prior to any assault. Second, many GSD male survivors engage in intensified risky sexual behavior after being assaulted. Regardless of sexual identity, men who are abused are more likely to report engaging in high-risk sexual behavior compared to their non-abused counterparts (Jinich et al., 1998; Kalichman, Gore-Felton, Benotsch, Cage, & Rompa, 2004).

A first pathway to risky sexual behavior originates in real or perceived obstacles to equal and open access to other GSD male peers. Sexual and gender prejudice is again a pre-existing factor in this discussion. For instance, GSD children may isolate themselves for fear of being different or may be isolated due to not fitting in. This seclusion may leave them vulnerable to predators, especially if the youth displays gender traits setting them apart from the norm (Roberts et al., 2012; Sandfort, Melendez, & Diaz, 2007).

Identification as GSD has historically been shrouded in secrecy and marginalization. Expressions of identity that do not conform to the expectations of non-traditional heterosexual masculinity are often viewed with suspicion and may even be subject to punitive repercussions that are grounded in legal or faith-based prohibitions. For this reason, GSD or questioning youth tend to be restricted in opportunities and locations where they can explore their sexuality safely.

Lacking permissible access to male peers who share their sensibilities, prepubescent and adolescent GSD males may search for like-minded others and put themselves in situations (e.g., public sex environments, internet chatrooms) where there is an increased risk of being sexually abused (Balsam, Rothblum, & Beauchaine, 2005) or seek inclusion in all-male environments such as sporting activities, Scouting, extracurricular youth groups, etc. Close physical contact in these settings with older males may be particularly comforting. However, inexperienced GSD males are therefore more vulnerable to influences of older males who may invite, manipulate, or coerce them into sexual contact(s) before they learn the rules and skills of consent. The context of this sexual contact may be further complicated if the young male was secretly desiring an opportunity for same-sex sexual expression and connection of a non-exploitative nature.

Recognition of the inappropriateness of this kind of sexual contact may be muted by internalized self-blame when GSD males believe they were complicit in instigating the sexual contact or if the experience was justified as "sexual initiation." A GSD male who has this historical scenario may need input from an outside observer – clinician or ally – to help them decipher how a lack of opportunities to express their attractions safely created a vulnerable pathway to victimization.

> *I had experienced same-sex attraction and wanted to seek out others who identified as gay. For this reason, I had gone online to speak with what I hoped would be older gay role models and a community but instead found men who wanted to sexually exploit me. My family was highly homophobic and I was scared to come forward about the abuse because I was more afraid of getting in trouble with them than with preventing what was happening.* (Ben)

The second pathway to risky sexual behavior is an outgrowth of having been subjected to traumatic sexual experiences. Depending upon the vulnerability of the survivor, the perpetrator's abusive behaviors may become internalized and create an unsafe template for how to express sexual feelings (see Ben's comments above). "Risky" behaviors include but are not limited to having unprotected sex with one or more anonymous partners; exchanging sex for drugs or money; having unprotected sex with an intravenous drug user; and engaging in non-consensual bondage, dominance/discipline, sadism/submission, and masochism (BDSM).

A 1994 study of 1001 men in three American cities (Chicago, Denver, and San Francisco) reported that men who also disclosed a history of sexual trauma were more likely to have participated at least once in unprotected anal intercourse during the four-month pre-study period (Cassese, 2000). Another study (Kalichman et al., 2004) reported a higher risk for HIV/AIDS among gay men – especially gay men of color – who also acknowledged a history of childhood trauma (including sexual trauma). Gay and bisexual Latino men who perceived their sexual assault to be coerced reported more consumption of alcohol, a greater number of sexual partners, and a greater frequency of unprotected anal sex (Dolezal, 2002).

In our clinical experience, many GSD survivors' risky sexual conduct reflects either reenactment behaviors or repetition compulsion patterns, as one GSD male survivor described:

> *I have come to realize that the past and current type of pornography that I watch resembles to a great degree the behaviors, positions, and language that was used as part of my sexual victimization. I see a clear pattern of repeating my sexual trauma.* (Kaleem)

We observe three factors that may exacerbate the interaction of sexual trauma and risky sexual behaviors for GSD male survivors:

1 Premature imprinting of "learned homoerotic response patterns" may be a powerful residue for GSD males who are sexually victimized at a young age by an older male (Brady, 2008; Gartner, 1999a; Gilgun & Reiser, 1990; King, 2000). The offender's sexual dynamics may eclipse the victim's ability to experience his own, leaving the victim developmentally frozen, bonded to the sexual practices of his trauma, and repetitively engaging in sexual behaviors that are familiar. The GSD survivor may believe his only value is in being a good sex

object. Lacking self-awareness, education about healthy sex, appropriate outlets, and assertiveness skills, these GSD male survivors may habitually seek out partners in ways that cross the boundaries into risky and unfulfilling sexual encounters. This may reflect chronic sexual behaviors that are essentially reenactments of their sexual trauma, as this GSD survivor surmised:

> *The history of risky sexual behaviors IS the sexual trauma.* (Jose)

2 Some males who engage in sex with other males struggle with intense denial of their non-heterosexual feelings. These survivors may feel compelled to avoid any associations with their authentic sexual self, no matter where they reside on the spectrum of sexuality. They may manage real or anticipated triggering by avoidance, and struggle with guilt and shame if they "surrender" to their desires for same-sex intimacy. Therefore, if they succumb to same-sex desires, their denial may put them at risk of engaging in unsafe sexual practices (Rosario, Schrimshaw, & Hunter, 2006). Often, such a same-sex sexual encounter will occur impulsively, with a greater risk that their sexual behavior is re-enacting an abuse scenario. Taking steps to be safe may require them to acknowledge the reality of their behavior, thereby making the sexual encounter(s) too real. The dissociative dimensions of denial and minimization create the perfect context for avoiding considerations of safety. One GSD male survivor described it this way:

> *My sexuality is compartmentalized. On one side, I have a loving heterosexual relationship with my wife. On the other is this part of me that wants a man to hurt and abuse me for his sexual pleasure. I do not classify myself as bisexual.* (Henri)

3 Shame is an overriding emotional dynamic for many GSD male survivors. Therefore, resulting issues of self-hatred and low self-esteem often contribute to avoiding safe sexual practices. Engaging in

risky sexual encounters may be a way to inflict self-punishment, treat themselves as they were treated, and/or reinforce internalized beliefs that they are unworthy of safety and protection. If the GSD male survivor is struggling to accept non-heterosexual emotions and behaviors, intense shame may further reinforce the tendency to avoid considerations of risk management and safety. Sadly, sometimes GSD male survivors seek out exposure to HIV as a way to validate feelings of negative self-worth.

> *I normally have unprotected sex every time unless my partner asks for it. Very, very, very few do. I probably currently average 2–3 casual sexual encounters per month. If I'm honest with myself I realize that this self-destructive behavior just feeds my self-hatred and feelings of worthlessness.* (Alejandro)

While any one of these factors may fuel risky sexual behavior for the GSD male survivor, there may also be a cascading process whereby multiple levels of these factors interplay with each other. Wright (2001) refers to this dynamic as a "spiral of risk," wherein GSD male survivors seek high-risk behavior in their quest to belong or to avoid abandonment. As one GSD male survivor related:

> *In my case, I think the connection is clear. Violent abuse that my body responded to strongly correlates with the yearning for violent sexual contact with men as an adult.* (Steven)

Promoting healthy sexual and gender identities

It is essential to co-create sufficient safety with GSD male survivors to allow them to access and reveal their authentic self, in their own words and at their self-determined pace of disclosure. There is, predictably, a natural fluidity about exploration, awareness, examination, acceptance, identity, and expression; however, the clinician must avoid a priori assumptions based on judgments of linear progress between these developmental stages. Maintaining safety can nurture a GSD male survivor's ability to be accurate and authentic in his communications about his trauma experience(s) and define what he needs for his healing journey.

The risk for disconnection is always possible when survivor, ally, and/or clinician do not share the same assumptions about sexual and gender diversity. To some degree, almost everyone in our culture is vulnerable to false notions of sexuality and gender and the cultural myths that sometimes overshadow substantiated truths about diversity issues and sexual trauma. The following are some common myth–truth distortions that may impact GSD male survivors, allies, and professional caregivers alike:

1 Being gay is contagious; a male is at risk for becoming gay, bisexual, or some other presentation of GSD if he is sexually assaulted.
2 A male victim must be gay if they did not stop their sexual assault; any degree of genital arousal confirms they must not be fully heterosexual.
3 GSD males are known to be promiscuous, so the victim was probably somehow complicit in seeking out the sexual encounter.
4 The survivor's same-sex sexual reenactment behavior constitutes "gay" behavior. Thus, prejudice gets reinforced by pairing a gay or bisexual identity only to reenacting their sexual trauma. When the client and clinician are misled by this prejudice, then assessment and treatment options are limited.
5 "Man up" is a common adage that differentiates "real men" (who can simply dismiss sexual trauma and move on with life) from GSD males (who are perceived to be lower on the hierarchy of manhood, thereby stigmatized as weak and unable to get over negative reactions from whatever sexual contact occurred). Unfortunately, heterosexual males who do not display the norms of "manning up" are frequently assumed to be GSD, thereby being similarly stigmatized.

The presence of myth–truth and bias is like having a window blind that shutters out truth or reinforces patterns of dissociation that block realities of sexual trauma. For the GSD male survivor who experiences overt or covert prejudice or myth–truth dilemmas, this additional dimension of the assault(s) may overshadow or intensify the experience of the sexual trauma(s) and complicate the process of healing (King, 2000).

Helping GSD male survivors free themselves of the effects of sexual trauma may require support from the clinician about ways to challenge these myth–truth dilemmas and examine biases that interfere with the GSD male survivor's authenticity (Martell, Safren, & Prince, 2004). For many, it is critical to find a peaceful resolution to perplexing questions about sexuality and gender, including:

> "Was I targeted for sexual assault because of my GSD traits?"
>
> "Did my sexual trauma make me a GSD male?"
>
> "How do I know what is my authentic sexual and gender identity?"
>
> "If I wanted sexual contact with another man, does that mean the sexual assault was my fault?"

Therapeutic safety provides the opportunity for GSD male survivors to identify and examine vulnerabilities, questions, shame, and confusion about sexuality and gender. Empowering GSD male survivors with skills to challenge these myth–truth distortions if they exist in their support systems may be another essential task of successful healing. Within this environment of safety and freedom to make choices, the GSD survivor may more authentically articulate a fluidity or blending of distinctly different aspects of identity. None of this work can be accomplished, however, if clinicians working with this population have not deconstructed these myth–truth dilemmas and biases for themselves.

Providing therapeutic guidance to help GSD male survivors develop authentic identity and healthy self-expression is core to congruent healing. Identity and expression are subjective. Therefore, the clinician must carefully balance when to validate the survivor's alternative values and behavioral choices and when and how to challenge decisions that seem unhealthy. This clinical task can be very complicated when the choices being made by the GSD male survivor stir biases about life choice options within the clinician.

Just as we earlier challenged the binary paradigm as it pertains to discovery and assessment, we also approach healing from the perspective of spectrum. Reminding GSD male survivors of the continuum of options for sexual and gender identity and expression can relieve many aspects of distress. The clinician needs to honor the possibility that the GSD male survivor is not now – nor perhaps ever was – a member of either the straight or the gay "team." A first order task may be to educate the survivor – and perhaps his allies – about the validity of spectrum.

The following questions may help GSD survivors articulate their own gender and sexual diversity:

1 How do you define your sexual and gender identity currently?
2 Were you aware of your sexual feelings and identity prior to the trauma?
3 Did you have any concerns about your gender expression or sexual attractions prior to the sexual trauma?
4 Did the offender assign or imply a sexual identity to you during your sexual victimization?
5 How did you define your sexual and gender identity after the victimization?
6 Were there specific ways the offender used your gender expression or sexuality as a feature of your sexual victimization? Do you feel any specific aspects of your gender or sexuality contributed to being targeted?
7 Do you currently feel unsettled or conflicted about your gender expression or sexuality in any way that relates to your sexual trauma?
8 Do you have a history of engaging in risky sexual behaviors? If so, how are they similar and different from your original sexual trauma?
9 How do cultural values, bias, minority stress, and social privilege affect your sexual and gender identity development?

A second order task may be helping survivors differentiate the perpetrator(s)' dynamics from their own sexual orientation, values, and needs. One way to do this is inviting survivors to draw two overlapping circles and identify in one circle what represents for them healthy sexuality and indicate in the other circle what represents traumatic sexuality. This differentiation is important for self-direction and de-linking the survivor's physical and emotional desires from his sexual trauma. This process may also help acknowledge the benign overlaps between healthy and traumatic sexuality (e.g., smells, sounds, body parts, power dynamics, gender). As the survivor can learn to tolerate and accept the naturalness of sexual desires that are not linked to trauma, he acquires the capacity to know more about his inner self, discover possibilities for healthy intimacy, and thereby access his authentic sexual orientation.

Other overlapping circles can be added to this Venn diagram to indicate other characteristics (e.g., racial/ethnic, religious, LGBT identities) so the survivor can decide which of those communities' norms and values indicate healthy sexuality and which do not apply to the survivor personally. This process may help them accept and attend to what promotes safety, health, and connection, and therefore correct damage done by the abuse and societal discrimination.

It is complicated for the GSD male survivor to decipher – through the residual overlays from sexual trauma – which aspects of their sexuality and gender are core to their identity. Either attractions or aversions can possibly be symptomatic of unresolved trauma. Transgender survivors may have the most difficulty differentiating between the gender dysphoria they feel about their genitals from the posttraumatic stress responses they feel about being sexual. As with a compass that has been juggled, careful and patient observation allows the needle to eventually find its way back to pointing north. This metaphor, when applied as a real clinical intervention, can assist GSD male survivors to find their authentic orientation. Careful excavation of residual eroticized debris, pursued with patience over time, can be successful in discovering features of attraction and/or aversion that seem genuine.

External values or prohibitions may frequently be sources of disturbance. If so, therapeutic interventions that reduce shame and anxiety associated with same-sex desires and/or a diverse gender expression may calm any compulsivity in pursuing those interests. With this therapy outcome, the GSD survivor becomes more empowered and capable of making informed decisions about sexuality, gender, and other related social circumstances.

As with most therapeutic endeavors, the goal is not to achieve a definitive ending. Rather, successful healing allows the GSD male survivor to realize an ongoing process of homeostasis, a stable balance in which the survivor can continue to grow and thrive. Developing healthy sexuality and a positive sense of gender are key components to a life of equilibrium. Clinicians working with GSD male survivors on developing this equilibrium will need to enhance their own capacity to address social justice issues so they can counter the trauma done by sexual and gender prejudice.

References

Andersen, J. P., & Blosnich, J. (2013). Disparities in adverse childhood experiences among sexual minority and heterosexual adults: Results from a multi-state probability-based sample. *PLoS ONE, 8*, e54691.

Arreola, S. G., Neilands, T. B., & Dıaz, R. (2009). Childhood sexual abuse and the sociocultural context of sexual risk among adult Latino gay and bisexual men. *American Journal of Public Health, 99*, 432–438.

Bailey, J. M., Vasey, P. L., Diamond, L. M., Breedlove, S. M., Vilain, E., & Epprecht, M. (2016). Sexual orientation, controversy, and science. *Psychological Science in the Public Interest, 17*(2), 45–101.

Balsam, K. F., Rothblum, E. D., & Beauchaine, T. P. (2005). Victimization over the life span: A comparison of lesbian, gay, bisexual, and heterosexual siblings. *Journal of Consulting and Clinical Psychology, 73*, 477–487.

Beckstead, A. L. (2012). Can we change sexual orientation? *Archives of Sexual Behavior, 41*, 121–134.

Beckstead, A. L., & Morrow, S. L. (2004). Mormon clients' experiences of conversion therapy: The need for a new treatment approach. *The Counseling Psychologist, 32*, 651–690.

Brady, S. (2008). The impact of sexual abuse on sexual identity formation in gay men. *Journal of Child Sexual Abuse, 17*(3–4), 359–376.

Brooks, F. (2001). Beneath contempt: The mistreatment of non-traditional/gender atypical boys. In J. Cassese (Ed.), *Gay men and childhood sexual trauma: Integrating the shattered self* (pp. 1–17). Binghamton, NY: Haworth.

Cassese, J. (Ed.). (2000). *Gay men & childhood sexual trauma: Integrating the shattered self.* Binghamton, NY: Haworth.

Center for Disease Control & Prevention. (2013). *The National Intimate Partner and Sexual Violence Survey: 2010 findings on victimization by sexual orientation.* Atlanta, GA: National Center for Injury Prevention and Control.

Corley, M. D., & Kort, J. (2006). The sex addicted mixed-orientation marriage: Examining attachment styles, internalized homophobia and viability of marriage after disclosure. *Sexual Addiction & Compulsivity, 13*(2–3), 167–193.

Courtois, C. A., & Ford, J. (Eds.). (2013). *Treatment of complex trauma: A sequenced, relationship-based approach.* New York: Guilford.

Dolezal, C. (2002). Childhood sexual experiences and the perception of abuse among Latino men who have sex with men. *Journal of Sex Research, 39*, 165–173.

Gartner, R. B. (1999a). *Betrayed as boys: Psychodynamic treatment of sexually abused men.* New York, NY: Guilford.

Gartner, R. B. (1999b). Sexual victimization of boys by men. *Journal of Gay & Lesbian Psychotherapy, 3*(2), 1–33.

Gilgun, J. F., & Reiser, E. (1990). The development of sexual identity among men sexually abused as children. *Families in Society, 71*(9), 515–523.

Grant, J. M., Mottet, L. A., Tanis, J., Harrison, J., Herman, J. L., & Keisling, M. (2011). *Injustice at every turn: A report of the national transgender discrimination survey*. Washington, DC: National Center for Transgender Equality and National Gay and Lesbian Task Force. Retrieved from www.thetaskforce.org/static_html/downloads/reports/reports/ntds_full.pdf.

Haas, K. (2004). Who will make room for the intersexed? *American Journal of Law & Medicine, 30*(1), 41–68.

Herek, G. M. (2009). Hate crimes and stigma-related experiences among sexual minority adults in the United States: Prevalence estimates from a national probability sample. *Journal of Interpersonal Violence, 24*(1), 54–74.

Intersex Society of North America. (2016). What is intersex? Retrieved from www.isna.org/faq/what_is_intersex.

Jinich, S., Paul, J., Stall, R., Acree, M., Kegeles, S., Hoff, C., & Coates, T. (1998). Childhood sexual abuse in HIV risk taking behavior among gay and bisexual men. *AIDS and Behavior, 2*(1), 41–51.

Kalichman, S., Gore-Felton, C., Benotsch, E., Cage, M., & Rompa, D. (2004). Trauma symptoms, sexual behaviors and substance abuse: Correlates of childhood sexual abuse and HIV risk among men who have sex with men. *Journal of Child Sexual Abuse, 13*(1), 1–15.

King, N. (2000). Childhood sexual trauma in gay men: Social context and the imprinted arousal pattern. In J. Cassese (Ed.), *Gay men and childhood sexual trauma: Integrating the shattered self* (pp. 19–36). New York, NY: Routledge.

Kira, I. A., Templin, T., Lewandowski, L., Ramaswamy, V., Ozcan, B., Abou-Mediane, S., et al. (2011). Cumulative tertiary appraisal of traumatic events across cultures: Two studies. *Journal of Loss and Trauma: International Perspectives on Stress and Coping, 16*, 43–66.

LeVay, S. (2016). *Gay, straight, and the reason why: The science of sexual orientation* (2nd Ed.). New York, NY: Oxford University Press.

Martell, C. R., Safren, S. A., & Prince, S. E. (2004). *Cognitive-behavioral therapies with lesbian, gay, and bisexual clients*. New York, NY: Guilford.

Morris, J. F., & Balsam, K. F. (2003). Lesbian and bisexual women's experiences of victimization: Mental health, revictimization, and sexual identity development. *Journal of Lesbian Studies, 7*, 67–85.

Reconciliation and Growth Project. (2017). Resolving distress between faith-based values and sexual and gender diversity. Retrieved May 26, 2017 from http://reconciliationandgrowth.org/wp-content/uploads/2017/04/RGP-Guide-Abbreviated-4-26.pd.

Roberts, A. L., Rosario, M., Koenen, K. C., & Austin, S. B. (2012). Elevated risk of posttraumatic stress in sexual minority youths: Mediation by childhood abuse and gender nonconformity. *American Journal of Public Health, 102*(8), 1587–1593.

Rosario, M., Schrimshaw, E. W., & Hunter, J. (2006). A model of sexual risk behaviors among young gay and bisexual men: Longitudinal associations of mental health, substance abuse, sexual abuse, and the coming-out process. *AIDS Education and Prevention, 18*(5), 444–460.

Rothman, E. F., Exner, D., & Baughman, A. L. (2011). The prevalence of sexual assault against people who identify as gay, lesbian, or bisexual in the United States: A systematic review. *Trauma, Violence, & Abuse, 12*(2), 55–66.

Russell, J. D., Jones, R. A., Barclay, K., & Anderson, M. (2008). Managing transference and countertransference in the treatment of gay, lesbian and bisexual survivors of childhood sexual abuse. *Journal of Gay & Lesbian Mental Health, 12*(3), 227–243.

Sandfort, T. G., Melendez, R. M., & Diaz, R. M. (2007). Gender nonconformity, homophobia, and mental distress in Latino gay and bisexual men. *Journal of Sex Research, 44*, 181–189.

Savin-Williams, R. C., & Vrangalova, Z. (2013). Mostly heterosexual as a distinct sexual orientation group: A systematic review of the empirical evidence. *Developmental Review, 33*(1), 58–88.

Stevenson, M. R. (2000). Public policy, homosexuality, and the sexual coercion of children. *Journal of Psychology & Human Sexuality, 12*(4), 1–19.

Struve, J., & Fradkin, H. R. (2015). *Survey of GBT MaleSurvivor Weekend of Recovery Alumni*. Unpublished raw data.

Tomeo, M., Templer, D., Anderson, S., & Kotler, D. (2001). Comparative data of childhood and adolescence molestation in heterosexual and homosexual persons. *Archives of Sexual Behavior, 30*, 535–541.

van Anders, S. M. (2015). Beyond sexual orientation: Integrating gender/sex and diverse sexualities via sexual configurations theory. *Archives of Sexual Behavior, 44*(5), 1177–1213.

Vives, A. (2002). The psychological sequelae of victimization based on sexual orientation: A structural equation model of predicting suicidality among lesbian and gay young adults. *Dissertation Abstracts International,* 62(12-B), 5983B (UMI No. 95012210).

Wright, D. (2001). Illusions of intimacy. In J. Cassese (Ed.), *Gay men and childhood sexual trauma: Integrating the shattered self* (pp. 117–126). Binghamton, NY: Haworth.

Xu, Y., & Zheng, Y. (2015). Prevalence of childhood sexual abuse among lesbian, gay, and bisexual people: A meta-analysis. *Journal of Child Sexual Abuse, 24*(3), 315–331.

Yarhouse, M. A, Tan, E. S. N., & Pawlowski, L. M. (2005). Sexual identity development and synthesis among LGB-identified and LGB dis-identified persons. *Journal of Psychology and Theology, 33*(1), 3–16.

Chapter 12

Sexual aftereffects in male survivors of childhood sexual abuse

Orientation confusion, compulsions, kinky sexual interests, and dysfunctions

Joe Kort

Childhood sexual abuse (CSA) can color an adult's sexual interests and behaviors. More importantly, CSA can lead to considerable trouble and grief, and as a therapist I work to reduce the trouble and the grief and help my clients lead happier, more functional lives. At the same time, many childhood events (positive and negative) can affect an adult's sexual interests, and my focus is not to try to change what turns a person on (usually an impossible task, even if what turns them on is the result of CSA). Instead, I try to help clients be less troubled by their sexuality.

In this chapter we will consider four possible consequences of CSA: sexual disorientation, sexual compulsions, kinky sexual interests, and sexual dysfunctions. The focus will be on male survivors. We start with four brief discussions defining these four main topic areas, then two considerations of supplemental topics, leading into the four main sections of the chapter. The chapter ends with a summary of the process and goals of psychotherapy and some finals thoughts.

Disorientation

Some men are confused about their sexual orientation. There can be many causes and many types of confusion. However, men who have been sexually abused as children by a male perpetrator are often subject to confusion about their sexual orientation. If they are straight, they may seek sex with men. If they are gay or bisexual, they may find that while they want sex with men, they don't see it as part of their sexual identity. The labels "gay" or "bisexual" don't feel "right." For both straight and gay men, the abuse is getting in the way of the man's connection to, and awareness of, his basic sexual identity.

Let me be clear. I've never had a gay man come in to see me saying, "I have this compulsion to have sex with women." That doesn't happen. However, a man might come to see me saying he has a compulsion to have sex with men, but it doesn't feel right for him. And sometimes it doesn't feel right, even though he's gay, because his gayness has been confused by CSA, and sometimes it doesn't feel right because he really is straight.

Some men seem to be sexually fluid without having any psychopathology. They identify as primarily gay or straight but occasionally choose partners of the other gender. As we learn more about variations on orientation, we no doubt will come to understand various forms of flexibility. In this chapter, for simplicity, I generally assume a man is gay, straight, or bi.

Compulsions

A man may come to me and tell me he's a "sex addict," meaning he engages in sexual behaviors even when he doesn't want to. Although this is sometimes labeled "sexual addiction" or "compulsive sexual behaviors," I've come to favor the more generic term "out-of-control sexual behaviors" (OCSB). OCSB in some form is a common male response to CSA, although "sexual dysfunction" is another less common result. There is some evidence that men with early CSA tend toward OCSB, while dysfunction is more common for men abused as older children or adolescents (Aaron, 2012).

Kinks

Some OCSB is linked to nonstandard sexual fantasies, and when CSA is present it is common for the fantasy in some sense to reflect the abuse. Although it is not always possible to attribute specific fantasies to specific childhood experiences, we will look at the common situation in which OCSB is "trauma reenactment," that is, replaying the abuse in some eroticized form.

I use the term "kink" to refer to any sexual interest that is nonstandard or not heteronormative. A kink becomes a *paraphilia* if it is "necessary." This generally means the person with the paraphilia cannot become sexually aroused without it, for example, a man who cannot get an erection unless he is spanked (or imagines himself being spanked). A paraphilia generally does not require a therapeutic intervention unless it is causing somebody grief or is trouble in some other way, e.g., it is illegal (DSM-5, 2013).

Kinky sexual fantasies are commonly the core of a compulsion. The man who cannot stop watching obese girl-on-girl porn to the point that he loses his job and his marriage, may have a problem with a compulsion linked to a kink. Kinks are discussed in more detail in the section on kinks below.

Sexual dysfunction

Although less common for men than women (Aaron, 2012, pp. 203–204), CSA can lead to sexual dysfunction. A man who suffered CSA may lose sexual interest or the ability to function sexually when he is an adult. Pharmaceutical interventions are fairly common, but the psychological issues leading to male dysfunction are still not well understood.

What makes the consequences of CSA more or less severe?

Although this chapter focuses on male survivors, we should note at least in passing that gender seems to be an important factor in the severity of the consequences of CSA. Aaron's (2012) survey paper notes a number of differences between men and women and presents some theoretical arguments to explain these differences.

Other factors (besides gender) significant in the consequences of CSA are the relationship of the perpetrator to the child (a trusted perpetrator – parent, uncle, teacher, coach, priest – is much more damaging than an abusive stranger), the severity and duration of the abuse, and the age of the child being abused. A final extremely significant factor is the reaction of parents or caretakers if the child discloses the abuse to them. Being listened to and believed can greatly moderate the severity of the consequences.

One of the most confusing aspects of the consequences of CSA is that sometimes it leads to problematic sexual behavior (OCSB, compulsive unsafe or risky sex, criminal sexual behavior), yet on the other hand, it can lead to sexual dysfunctions that tend to "shut down" sexual behavior (lack of interest in sex, difficulty getting or keeping an erection, difficulty reaching orgasm). Men dealing with this consequence of CSA often come to me married but losing interest in their wives, turning to porn and masturbation for sexual release but avoiding human sexual contact.

When clients present either issues with excessive sexual behavior (especially when it feels unsatisfying and/or involves compulsive unsafe sex) or issues involving losing interest or ability to function sexually with their partners, then I am alerted to the possibility of CSA. Therapy starts with a detailed sexual history as well as specifics of the behavior and the feelings associated with the behavior. The treatment plan is then customized to what we find.

Sexual abuse: overt, covert, and hazing

When people say "sexual abuse," they often have in mind specific overt physical acts in which genital contact is involved: genital stimulation (perhaps to orgasm), oral sex, anal penetration, male–female sexual intercourse. Many other sexual acts, involving the genitals but not touching, such as exhibitionism and voyeurism, are frequently included. The line between overt and covert sexual abuse is not necessarily clear. Aggressive verbal acts, such as sexual teasing, baiting, mocking, and threatening, are explicitly sexual and essentially "overt abuse" but do not involve touching. However, the damage done to children by overt abuse has been well documented and makes common sense to most people.

Covert abuse has been invisible in our culture until recently, but the damage done to children can often be the same or similar to the damage done by overt abuse. By definition, covert abuse does not explicitly involve the genitals. It can include words, pornography, touching, kissing, spousification, exposure, looking, suggestive games, and others. The feeling is "icky." The intent is often sexual domination or humiliation. The child is left feeling dirty, used, and dehumanized, but the adult has perfect deniability: "Nothing happened." The varieties of covert abuse, like overt abuse, are wide-ranging, and it is difficult to explicitly define every act of covert abuse. Books about covert abuse, such as *When He's Married to Mom* (Adams with Morgan, 2007),[1] include many examples but do not attempt exhaustive cataloging. The bottom line for covert sexual abuse of children by adults is that the child perceives the adult's "sexual intent," and the effect can be extremely destructive and long lasting.

1 Editor's note: See Chapter 11 by Adams in the companion volume to this one, *Healing Sexually Betrayed Men and Boys: Treatment for Sexual Abuse, Assault, and Trauma.*

I have a Google alert about "hazing," and such assaults happen every day all over the country. It's not big news for some reason; the media hardly ever pick it up. Our society has a strange insensitivity to sexual hazing and other forms of "schoolyard rape." Acts of sexual violence that would be clearly condemned in any other context are acceptable in a locker room or fraternity house, and the victims are often silenced by fear of social ostracization or lack of sympathy by the authorities. (This is documented in Jane Ward's 2015 book *Not Gay: Sex Between Straight White Men*.) Sheer terror or humiliation can silence victims who do not feel they will be protected from more violence if they tell. Further complicating the situation, especially for adolescents and young adults, is a strange confusion about whether oral or anal sex is "sex," and whether violent oral or anal rape is really "rape." We might consider this a sex education issue, although the compliance of supposedly responsible adults – parents, teachers, coaches, religious leaders, journalists, citizens of the community – is almost too bizarre to categorize.

Orientation confusion

When a man comes to see me seeking therapy because he isn't sure whether he is gay, straight, or bi, I say he is "sexually disoriented."[2]

Helping clients with their sexual problems is never a simple matter. We cannot be formulaic and say, "If you're concerned about *this* set of issues, then *this* from your past caused your problems and you will get better if we carry out *this program* of therapy." When a client comes to see me, I must always consider a number of possible issues and interpretations and courses of therapy. Having said that, often when a client comes to see me confused about his sexual orientation, I am likely to find certain backgrounds and issues, quite often CSA. And if the client has been the victim of CSA, then we must lift the cloud of confusion CSA generates before we can begin to address the client's questions about his orientation.

I say, "CSA disorients a man, it does not orient him." In other words, sexual abuse will not shape a man's sexual orientation. It might impact his erotic *interests*, but this is not the same as *orientation*. Sexual orientation

2 While, of course, there are more complicated permutations of sexual orientation and sexual fluidity (see Chapter 11 by Struve, Fradkin, and Beckstead in this volume), for the purpose of simplicity I will mainly consider here only the general categories of straight, bisexual, and gay.

determines who a man is attracted to whether it be a man, a woman, both, or even exotic combinations of gender characteristics. Erotic interest is different: it captures the sexual fantasies and erotic situations one is turned on by; gender may be less important here. For example, there are men sexually turned on by "muscles," whether on a female or male bodybuilder. The attraction is to muscle, not gender. More about unusual erotic interests later in the chapter.

And, yes, a straight man with certain kinds of CSA in his background will seek sex with men even though he is not gay.

Ron's story

Ron started his first session with, "I think I must be gay, because I want sex with men, but it just doesn't feel right. I just don't feel like I'm gay."

"What would you like us to work on in therapy?" I asked him. "When we're finished, what would you like the outcome to be?"

"I want to know who and what I am. If I am gay or bisexual, then fine. That's what I am. If I'm straight, that's okay, too," Ron told me. "I came out to my friends and family. I was that sure I was gay. I've made lots of friends at the gay community center. They're nice guys. I've had sex with them, which was okay – some better than others – but I don't want to hang out with them. I don't feel a connection to them or the gay culture. Is that crazy or what?"

"What do you think?"

"Just tell me if I'm gay or not. If I'm gay, okay, I'll live with it. I just need to know."

After Ron and I talked a bit more, I moved on to taking his family history and asking him about his childhood.

Here's what I'm thinking when a client like Ron first comes to see me. He might be suppressing his identity because of cultural reasons, religious reasons, and/or psychological reasons having nothing to do with sexual abuse. But I also want to consider the possibility of CSA.

When a straight man is sexually abused as a child, particularly by a male perpetrator, one of several possible consequences is "disorientation." He is drawn to sex with men, sometimes compulsively, but instead of feeling great about it, he feels confused and unhappy. The CSA is clouding the issue. He needs therapy to lift the confusion of the abuse, so that he can then discover his basic orientation.

Gay and bisexual men who suffered CSA often report enjoying adult sex but not some aspects of it: Perhaps they feel a general compulsivity to have sex, or perhaps they feel compelled to specific sex acts that they don't actually enjoy. Sometimes, they feel enormous shame thinking about what they want or what they have done. So, they interpret these various negative feelings as meaning they might not be gay or bisexual.

One notable difference between straight and non-straight adult men who have sex with men: Some gay and bisexual men report enjoying parts of their CSA so much that they refer to it as their first experience of gay sex, whereas straight men rarely report enjoyment. Straight men who do report pleasure say they had an erection and an orgasm against their psychological will, later questioning why their body felt pleasure and wondering if they are gay or bisexual. They might also have enjoyed the contact and connection with the male perpetrator not because of sexual interest but because of a felt closeness during the abuse, which would also make them question themselves.

The process of psychotherapy can take time, and the client doesn't suddenly achieve clarity. Therapy is a "slowly stopping train," where the compulsive behavior becomes less and less compelling and more natural feelings and reactions emerge. "Stations" in this train journey may include family history, uncovering the history and working with whatever trauma is uncovered; grief work; sometimes Eye Movement Desensitization Reprocessing (EMDR, a form of therapy working directly with the brain to alleviate painful reactions to trauma); group therapy, especially all-male groups of survivors; psychopharmacology; 12-step programs; meditation or other forms of stress management; and sometimes couples therapy, as partners are brought in to help. In time, successful therapy lifts the confusion and pain and shame of the unconsciously embedded consequences of the abuse, and the client can discover his true sexual orientation.

Ron, it turns out, was straight. His draw to gay sex was "trauma reenactment," the attempt of the unconscious mind to draw attention to the hidden story of the abuse by acting it out. It went against his basic state of being heterosexual.

Ron had been sexually abused by his father. The abuse began when he was 4 years old and continued until he was 11, when he began to complain and raise questions, first with his father and then with his mother. His father was always easy-going in the sex with his son, starting with mutual masturbation, then oral, and finally anal penetration. Still, despite the extent of the sexual activity, the father always maintained an aura of playfulness and praise around it, saying things to Ron like "no big deal" or "do this for me" or "you know you like it, too," and Ron did like the praise and attention. His father even told Ron this was good practice for when he would be with a girl when he got older. As Ron began to question the logic of this, his father tried to jolly him along, but after Ron told his mother, everything changed. While denying to his wife any wrongdoing, Ron's father clearly let Ron know he had betrayed his father, and from then on he would have nothing to do with him. Ron's mother accepted that "nothing had happened" and would not listen to her son that something bad really had happened. Ron was left to deal with the abuse, losing his father, and living without the support of his mother, all as he was entering middle-school age, that most vulnerable time for a child.

As Ron got older, he "forgot" what had happened with his father. In psychological terms, he repressed and compartmentalized it to prevent him from feeling the pain and trauma associated with it. He was attracted to girls, dated them, and was even engaged, but "suddenly" at the age of 22, he discovered he wanted, needed, to have sex with men. Ron found gay men welcoming and sympathetic to his uncertainty, and he broke off his engagement by telling his fiancée that he was gay. He drifted into a gay life with the thought that his doubts were merely the "coming out pains" of a gay man. Yet, he knew he was attracted to women, and he didn't actually feel attracted to men. He just wanted to have sex with them.

In therapy, as we lifted the cloud of confusion caused by the abuse, Ron became less and less compulsively drawn to sex with men. For Ron, wanting sex with men was entirely trauma reenactment. With his new clarity, he was able to seek out women, which he'd been afraid to do. He was still drawn to gay sex but that erotic interest was separate from his basic sexual orientation. His attraction to sex with men was part of the erotic template created by the CSA. This didn't make him gay any more than a gay man sleeping with women makes him straight. A person's sexual behavior is not always consistent with his or her sexual orientation.

Some people (therapists and others) think that if a client like Ron continues to have gay sexual fantasies, then he has not really properly addressed his trauma and abuse. This is not necessarily true. In childhood, erotica and sexual interests become intertwined with our developing selves, becoming permanent imprints determining who and how we love and how we behave sexually. A CSA survivor who has not sought treatment will often engage in compulsive sexual trauma reenactment, engaging in unwanted sexual behaviors and putting himself in harm's way. With successful treatment, his compulsivity will diminish, and he will have more of a choice in terms of what he does and does not do. On the other hand, his sexual desires and arousal patterns don't necessarily change. I tell my clients who have used therapy to successfully control their compulsivity, "Even though some of your turn-ons come from trauma and abuse, they are yours now, yours to play with and use in whatever way you want without shame."

It's okay that some of a person's erotic interests have their origins in CSA. Part of therapy is to help clients live with themselves without shame. They learn to go from *trauma reenactment* to *trauma play*.

When last I heard from Ron, he had married and was no longer confused or distressed by the controllable residue of his old trauma-driven compulsion to have sex with men. He still thought about gay sex from time to time and masturbated to gay porn when he wanted to without any shame or bad feelings. He understood this was now a part of him, and he accepted it. He knew it was related to his CSA, but that was no longer important. It was just part of what turned him on.

As a gay therapist who works with gay, bisexual, straight, and sexually fluid individuals and couples, I have had many disoriented men come to see me. Many are straight, some are gay, a few bi or fluid, but whatever their fundamental sexual orientation, a history of childhood abuse always adds an overlay of confusion that must be dealt with before the client can come to understand who he is sexually.

Sexual compulsions

Many men come to see me troubled by their OCSB. Often, but not always, we discover CSA in the man's past that seems to provide the original pattern for the client's current problems. Often, we decide the current compulsion is what we've already called "trauma reenactment," a tendency of the unconscious mind to "tell its story" by forcing the man to repeatedly and compulsively "act out" his abuse as an erotic fantasy. In such a case, I begin therapy by offering the client a way to more directly tell in a therapeutic setting the painful story of his CSA. As the force of his compulsions diminishes, the client regains control over when and how to express his sexuality. Therapy is a complicated process. The client's journey begins with identifying and talking about his CSA; it continues by doing various therapies to heal the old damage that doesn't just disappear as soon as it is acknowledged.

Andrew's story

Let's consider the case of Andrew, who did in fact have CSA in his background, to see how a person experiences his sexual compulsions without understanding them, how shame can control his reactions, and how he was finally able to resolve his difficulties with himself and in his marriage. Andrew's story also illustrates the fact that compulsions and kinks can go together, which will be discussed in the next section.

Andrew was obsessed by a particular kinky scene: He was turned on by the fantasy of having a woman ridicule him for having a small penis. Andrew discovered in college that porn featuring women making fun of men turned him on. He particularly liked "small penis humiliation." He never tried to enact this fantasy with any of his girlfriends because he was too ashamed. He didn't connect his sexual kink with his past "real life." He got married, had kids, and had good sex with his wife, all while maintaining a "secret life" of being turned on by fantasies (and porn) featuring this particular kind of sexual humiliation.

Andrew was ashamed of his favorite fantasy and never talked about it, but he also didn't like the way it separated him from his wife. One day, he suggested that they play out his fantasy in the bedroom: He would be naked, she clothed, she would make fun of his minimal endowment. His wife, Ann, wasn't particularly turned on by this fantasy, but she was curious and tried it with him. Andrew was very turned on and appreciative.

Ann didn't mind playing the fantasy occasionally, but after a while Andrew didn't want to have sex with her unless they began with this prelude, and Ann began to be worried that he wasn't turned on by her, only by what was going on in his head. She became more and more upset. What was wrong with her? How come Andrew couldn't be turned on by her and had to have something else going on?

Andrew didn't know. He promised her he would stop, but actually he didn't think he could stop. For as long as he could remember, he had always used this fantasy when he masturbated and when he made love. He didn't talk about it any more with her, but now she was alerted. She called him on being distant or silent or inattentive when they made love, and he would dutifully focus on her and lose his erection. They both found it frustrating.

Secretly, he turned to the Internet more and more for sex, first just porn on "small penis humiliation" sites, then on cam sites, where he would stand naked in front of his computer and "real women" would make fun of his penis in real time, using his name so he'd know they were really seeing him.

One night, after they had an aborted attempt to make love, Ann discovered her naked masturbating husband standing in front of his computer. She was shocked, sad, and exasperated.

"Get help," she demanded, "or get out."

He came to see me. "I've got to give this up," he told me. "Just help me get it out of my head."

After some preliminaries, where Andrew told me about what was going on at home and the persistence of his fantasy, I began (as my practice always is in such cases) to ask him about his childhood, to develop a family history, and to explore whether there seemed to be any sort of significant trauma or CSA in his past. In my experience, certain kinds of persistent sexual fantasies reflect childhood trauma fairly directly, although no hard-and-fast rules are possible for what causes these kinds of kinks. For Andrew, the pieces of the puzzle fit together fairly easily.

His mother had never liked him. In fact, she didn't like boys or men at all. Not even her husband. She was sweet and supportive to Andrew's sisters, but she had nothing for him but scorn and snubbing. Besides the burden of a misandrist mother, Andrew had a passive father. The man didn't know what to do with his son at all. When Andrew began to complain at home of being picked on at school, his mother was contemptuous. "Well, fight back," she told him. "Don't be a sissy!" His father was more theoretical but just as unhelpful. "If I get involved, you won't learn how to take care of yourself," he told Andrew when Andrew complained of being held down on the playground in third grade and being spit on and made fun of.

Andrew was one of those children predators recognize as their natural victims. Often, children who are abused or neglected in their homes become easy targets for school bullies and perpetrators. By middle school, the gym locker room had become a torture chamber for Andrew. He was mocked for his weakness and his small penis. The bullies would call him names and laugh at him. The boys who did this told their girlfriends, who then told other girls in his class, who in turn continued the humiliation whenever they saw him around school. He told his father and mother that he hated middle school, but by now they were used to ignoring his complaints, and he was too ashamed to tell them the details. He was horrified at what was being done to him, but, fearing worse abuse, he dared not complain at school. He didn't just fear the bullies. He knew that boys who reported bullying were often not treated with sympathy. "How did you make this happen?" he imagined being asked. "Are you gay? You must have done something to provoke it."

One day in the eighth grade, he did finally try to fight back. In the locker room, he shouted at his tormenters to stop teasing him. However, this merely incited them. They told him he would never know what it was like to hold a "normal" penis while peeing. Together, they forced him to hold the penises of a few guys while they urinated. Then, they urinated on him and into his mouth, and finally they forced their penises into his mouth. He tried to fight back, but there were too many of them. They left him on the floor of the locker room, crying uncontrollably. The bullies told others at the school what they had done to him, and both boys and girls teased him mercilessly about it. He never told any adult what happened. His parents had done nothing before; he had no faith in them now.

After that, Andrew began cutting classes and not going to the boys' rooms or locker room at all. He attempted suicide by taking a whole bottle of his mother's Valium. Finally, after the ensuing ambulance trip to the emergency room, he got his parents' attention. They let him drop out of eighth grade and change the following school year to a high school in a different district. They made sure he understood they were going to a lot of cost and trouble because he was too weak and lazy to solve his own problems. In the new high school, he was not so actively abused, but by then the imprint of his past humiliation was permanent.

When Andrew came to see me, he had "forgotten" all about this abuse at school. He remembered he hadn't felt particularly connected to his parents or sisters, but he had forgotten all the details of his seeking help and not getting it. He didn't particularly resent his sisters. It just seemed natural to him that his mother would be more involved with them than with him. His father was a nobody at home, and Andrew seemed surprised that I even asked about him. The way real-life events patterned his kink hadn't occurred to him either, but he remembered fairly quickly when I began asking him to think of humiliating or embarrassing things that might have happened to him as a child.

Andrew was humiliated by both girls and boys at his school, but he eroticized the abuse by the girls, perhaps because his sexual orientation was heterosexual. This was an entirely unconscious process. He forgot about the real abuse, despite being terrified and devastated by it at the time, but his unconscious mind encoded it as a sexual fantasy, both to remember it and to soften it. This "trauma reenactment" process is sometimes described as "turning pain into orgasm" or, in more professional language, the "eroticization of trauma." The unconscious mind is forcing the "reenactment," so that the little boy's pain will (finally) be acknowledged.

The bad consequences of CSA are more significant, as noted above, when support is not offered at the time of the trauma. The moderating effect of the eroticization is not powerful enough to heal the wound, so the person will repeat and repeat the behavior as a compulsion until it is dealt with more effectively through therapy.

I worked with Andrew to reduce the compulsivity of his fantasy. We talked about what had happened. He cried in my office as he remembered the contempt his mother had unleashed on him and how unhelpful his father had been. He found his anger at the boys who had tortured and abused him and the girls who had joined in. As well as being angry and hurt, he found himself surprised they could be so mean to him. He hadn't done anything to them. I had to remind him that perpetrators are all around us all the time, looking for people they can hurt. It is a sad commentary on humanity, but it is the truth.

Although I could help Andrew with the grief and despair of his CSA and diminish the compulsive force of the fantasy, I could not take away the fact that it turned him on. No therapy can do such a thing. I could not perform a kink-ectomy on him. "Small penis humiliation" fantasies had become a part of his erotic template, and they always would be. I told him he had the option of playing with the fantasy, now that it was less compulsive, but he still needed to make peace with his wife. It was time to invite her to join Andrew in my office.

We started doing couples therapy. Andrew let her know what the fantasy was connected to from his past, and she let him know what issues it raised for her. He told her how he had been brutally humiliated and sexually abused in middle school and how this had been made worse because his parents offered no support or understanding. Ann was sympathetic that he had been so hurt, but she still wanted him to give up his fantasy.

Here, I had to be firm and clear. Andrew's CSA experience, eroticized, was imprinted in him. It was part of his hardwiring. It was part of his erotic orientation, even though it had its origin in abuse. It was not going away. I told her she had three choices:

1 She could allow Andrew to incorporate his fantasy into their mutual sex life.
2 Andrew could keep this part of his sex life private, and she could accept the fact that he would have his porn and his masturbation without shaming him about it.
3 Andrew and Ann could get divorced.

Ann was not happy with any of these options, but when she clearly understood that "getting rid of his kink" was not possible, she agreed to option 2. I then helped them develop some forms of mutual sexual expression that made her feel less lonely. They could, for example, work on his being more "present" when they were making love together. I also mentioned some options for them to focus on her pleasure when they were in bed together, relieving him of the pressure of needing to have a particular physical response during lovemaking. With these various compromises they were able to continue as husband and wife.

Kinks: unusual sexual interests, trauma, shame, and play

Kinks and paraphilias

Like Andrew, many people are turned on by kinky sexual fantasies and interests, called kinks in this chapter. When a kink is in some way "necessary" for the person to become aroused, clinicians call them paraphilias.[3]

3 The term "fetish" is sometimes informally used to mean the same thing as "paraphilia," but a fetish is more specialized. It refers to needing a particular *object* to be turned on (say, a shoe). Thus, a fetish is a paraphilia but not all paraphilias are fetishes.

If a person is turned on by spanking, then he has a kink for spanking. If he also needs to be spanked to be turned on, then for him the kink is a paraphilia. (Making a distinction between *necessary* as opposed to *desired* can be difficult except in the extreme cases.) Clinicians have cataloged literally thousands of paraphilias. Paraphilias can focus on objects (for example, underwear, clothing, food), or particular kinds of living beings (children, animals) or scenes (acts, actions) such as those depicting humiliation, dominance, submission, pain, and so on. An individual's kink is often very specific and unchanging. Some kinksters write out scripts for their scenes so that each word and action is exactly right. It misses the point to say a kinkster is "into pain," when more likely he wants a very particular scene, say, for example, involving a man spanking a woman in a schoolroom setting.

Paraphilias (or kinks) are generally not a problem unless they cause grief to the person with the paraphilia or to other people. Men are more likely to be attached to a paraphilia than women. In any population, for every woman with a paraphilia, there are 20 men (Beidel, Frueh, & Hersen, 2014, p. 573). I never support the futile and frustrating attempt to "eliminate" a person's core erotic fantasies, even if they are kinks. Fighting a core fantasy can cause more problems than playing with it. What I advocate is taking away the compulsivity, especially if it is trauma reenactment, and then soothing the kinky need by playing with it. This is one reason I avoid the terminology of "sexual addiction." I believe the addiction mindset, with its emphasis on abstinence, can cause more grief than alleviate it.[4]

Because kinks and paraphilias are much more common for men than women, my work often includes educating women on the "normalcy" of their men's sexual interests. Women often tell their men to "get rid of their kinks." Many male clients come to me saying, essentially, if you can't help me get rid of my kink, I'll lose my marriage. Almost always, I must tell the client that he cannot get rid of a core sexual interest. In fact, if a person fights his own sexual nature, then that may cause problems far worse than merely having a nonstandard turn-on. In particular, compulsivity is sometimes made much worse by fighting. Jack Morin (1996, as cited

4 Editor's note: See Chapter 8 by Courtois and Weiss in the companion volume to this one, *Healing Sexually Betrayed Men and Boys: Treatment for Sexual Abuse, Assault, and Trauma*, for a focused look at sexual compulsivity/addiction treatment.

in Ley, 2012) says, "If you go to war with your sexuality, you will lose, and end up in more trouble than before you started. I have never seen a single exception to this principle."

Where do kinks come from?

In his book, *Ties That Bind*, psychotherapist and author Guy Baldwin writes, "While presenting seminars to leather folks, I have often asked how many in the room were subjected to child abuse as children, and I am still shocked when usually more than half the hands in the room go up" (1993, p. 127). He goes on to say that bottoms (who are submissives in the BDSM world) "unconsciously try to recreate their abusive experiences in the hopes that they can somehow un-do the traumas of their past and find love" (1993, p. 128). Thus, BDSM kinks often do derive from early child sexual abuse, but trying to heal the abuse through BDSM play alone doesn't work. That is just trauma reenactment; in other words, the unconscious mind "tells its story" by forcing the man to repeatedly "act out" his abuse as an erotic fantasy. Because a person in the grip of these compulsions often lacks normal cognitive restraints, he often places himself at emotional risk and/or in physical jeopardy. This is obviously unhealthy and dangerous, and we therapists need to work with our clients to help them stop engaging in compulsive behaviors that put them in harm's way.

Although in many individual cases CSA seems to lead to kinks, no one really knows where kinks come from. In fact, no one knows where any erotic interests come from. We presume early childhood experiences, good and bad, are often eroticized and become a part of an adult's erotic turn-ons. Therapists often see clients whose early childhood trauma seems to be connected to their (disturbing and intrusive) adult sexual compulsions. Yet we cannot say categorically that sexual kinks always come from CSA.

Some kinks just seem to be a part of an individual's basic erotic makeup. A person might like to be spanked because it feels good. They're oriented that way, and there's no detectable abuse in their lives. If a client comes in liking spanking (or whatever else is their kink) and they do not seem to have been abused, I don't strain to attribute their penchant to abuse. On the other hand, the client may still be suffering from consequences of the kink, so we move on to deal with whatever shame or conflicts with others may be causing the client grief.

The good news is we don't need to have all the answers on what causes kinks. We can use education and shame reduction to help channel sexual interests into playful and nondestructive channels. We can use psychotherapeutic tools to diminish the impact of early trauma, including CSA, and reduce the force of compulsions.

Shame

One of the most important drivers of sexual compulsions is shame. A man, call him Sam, may feel shame about his sexual interests or behaviors. Perhaps his religious or moral perspectives cause him to feel he shouldn't have such interests or act on them. Perhaps Sam is worried about what other people will think of him. Perhaps his wife, or his neighbor, or his boss. There was a time when gay people felt shame for being gay (for having-same sex feelings) and also feared the opinions of others. In many places, gay people still do. Or perhaps Sam has a harmless kink; let's say that the idea – only the idea – of surprising a woman by exposing his genitals to her is exciting to him. Sam's shame about his kink may, in fact, make him feel a stronger compulsion to act it out. His ability to channel or play with his kink (say, by exposing himself to a knowing woman who has agreed to enact the fantasy) is diminished by his shame, and because of the shame he is more likely to have less ability to control his behavior. It becomes more and more compulsive. Therefore, when a client comes to me troubled by a sexual compulsion, I always consider shame reduction therapy, whatever we discover the cause of the compulsion to be. When the person with the kink feels less shame, he is in a better position to negotiate about it with other people (like his partner) or avoid acting on it if it would be distressing to others or against the law, which of course I never support.

In the end, I believe in the benefits of shame reduction and education about kinks. I find myself saying over and over again to my clients: "This is your fantasy. This is what you get off on. Almost everybody is turned on by something kinky. We don't know where it comes from, but you shouldn't have to feel ashamed of it."

Compulsions versus strong personal interests

Here, I'd like to make a distinction. A true compulsion is often trouble for a client and requires therapeutic relief. On the other hand, if you really like something, it may not be a compulsion. You just like it. And you may have trouble giving it up. Of course, if it's dangerous, then you may have to find ways to avoid or control it. But trying to give up something essential to your nature can feel like you're fighting a compulsion when you're only fighting yourself. If you don't need to give it up for reasons of safety or health, you may be able to enjoy it in a safe way without "starving" yourself of something you need.

Sam might get his wife to let him expose himself to her as a game. Or perhaps he could find another willing woman, say, in the city's kinkster community, or perhaps he could just write erotic stories about men exposing themselves, thereby satisfying his need and acknowledging it, without causing any harm. Here, you can see why shame reduction is so important. Sam cannot play with his kink if he's all balled up in his shame over it. In my experience playing with a strong sexual interest does not lead to acting on it in a more public way after therapy has been completed.

Trauma play

The term "trauma play" denotes what can happen after therapy has given a client more control and his behavior is no longer compulsive. He can then learn how to "play" with the kinks generated by his childhood traumas without putting himself in danger or stunting his emotional growth. He learns to transcend his past rather than having it inflicted upon him. Using the example of the man who was physically beaten as a child, he may be sexually turned on by being spanked or whipped. Thus, he has a kink that reflects his abuse. (It's not particularly important here if the kink is a paraphilia or not.) No longer controlled by compulsivity and shame, he can act out his kink with consenting adult partners. Just as artists may use past trauma to express themselves in their work, a person may use past trauma to express him- or herself in the bedroom. Nobody tries to get an artist to stop expressing past traumas!

The term "trauma reenactment" is used only in cases where the adult returns in some form to the scene of the crime to unconsciously seek to correct it, thereby remaining emotionally trapped and stunted. In cases of BDSM play or other play with kinks, however, the return is consciously manipulated or played with to enhance a sexual experience. Period. There need be no angst or shaming involved. And no need for years of therapy to correct.

Some people worry because erotic fantasies are so often not politically correct or moral or reasonable. Esther Perel (2013) conveys the paradox this way: "Most of us will get turned on at night by the very same things that we will demonstrate against during the day." This realization goes along with the paradox of trauma reenactment versus trauma play: It's horrible when it's happening, but it's erotic later after it has been assimiliated. "This was a horrible thing that happened to me, but you know what? Now, I kind of like it." There's not much to be done about either paradox. They are part of human erotic nature.

Sexual disinterest and dysfunction

As a child, Ron was actively and overtly abused by his father over many years. In middle school, Andrew was the object of sadistic sexual torture and taunting by his peers. But Bill's story is different.

Bill's story

Bill came to see me, sad and ashamed because he was no longer interested in his wife. Nothing bad had happened. Over several years he had just become less and less interested. He admitted to me in his first appointment that his wife had told him she felt neglected. He had tried to please her, but sometimes he couldn't get an erection and when he did, he couldn't keep it. Once, he had entered her and then come at once. It was almost as if he didn't want to please her. But he assured me he did. He just couldn't.

Check for physical causes

I asked Bill to get checked out by a physician. However, his medical evaluation didn't suggest any physical cause for his sexual problems.

I should note that many MDs don't think of psychological causes for erectile dysfunction or other forms of sexual dysfunction. CSA might be a factor, but an MD usually won't ask about it.[5] They typically offer Viagra or other medications. If you first consulted with a physician about your dysfunction, you might have to look into consulting with a sexologist or psychologist for yourself whether or not your physician mentions it.

5 Editor's note: See Chapter 3 by Spinelli in this volume for discussion of survivors' relationships with physicians.

The subtleties of covert sexual abuse

I asked Bill if he'd been abused at home, and he assured me he hadn't been. Not physically. Not sexually. Not by scorn or meanness. We talked about school. We talked about relatives. Nothing sadistic or overtly sexual came out of his history. I asked about fear, about humiliation, about embarrassment. Finally, on embarrassment, Bill hesitated, then admitted something.

"I don't know if this is important," he said, my cue that something important is coming up. "Boys get self-conscious around their mothers."

"Yes," I agreed. "What in particular made you self-conscious around your mother?"

Bill's hesitation suggested he was still embarrassed. "She didn't mean anything by it. I'm still not sure why she did it, but while we were watching TV on the couch together, she would sometimes put her hand down the back of my pants."

"And leave it there?"

"Yeah," he agreed, "I guess so. I didn't really mind, at least not until I was older. Then I asked her to stop and she did. The same with the penis thing."

I asked the obvious question.

"While I was growing up, she wanted to make sure I was developing okay," he told me, "so every so often she asked me to show her my penis."

"How often was that?"

"I don't know. A few times a year. Maybe once a month. When I told her it was embarrassing me, she laughed and said it wasn't important. But finally I had to just refuse, because she kept asking me about it. Up until I was 12, maybe 13."

"It made you uncomfortable?"

"I guess so, I mean, it felt weird to always be showing her my penis, although she didn't touch it."

"But she touched your ass."

"Yes, that, but she didn't do anything else, you know, reach around."

Covert sexual abuse is often so subtle it's very difficult to describe. What Bill was telling me amounted to covert abuse by his mother. She was too interested in his penis. Her hand down the back of his pants was inappropriate touch, even though she wasn't touching his genitals. Asking to see his penis, touching his bottom, were "boundary violations," and boundary violations of any kind can be encoded by the unconscious as sexual. These violations were overtly sexual, even though the actions were not what is called overt sexual abuse.

Over a period of months, Bill and I discussed his mother's excessive interest in his "development," her touch that felt just a bit too intimate. The moments of inappropriate touch and interest by his mother multiplied as he remembered more and more. It turned out that Bill had been significantly "intruded upon" by his mother, and this had embedded in his unconscious in a way that now was affecting his ability to be intimate with his wife.

Bill's sexual disinterest and dysfunction with his wife were being caused by his unconscious mind, which wanted to get away from his mother, his wife being his adult stand-in for her. Although childhood abuse is often encoded by the unconscious in unexpected ways – we don't expect abuse to be literally transcribed into problematic adult behaviors – the connection here wasn't too difficult to make, once Bill had remembered his mother's "weird" behaviors.

Bill's therapy work required not just that he acknowledge the historical facts but that he "admit" that his mother's attention had caused him significant grief over a long period of his childhood. He needed to feel the hurt, fear, and confusion of an unprotected little boy. He needed to feel the shame of being forced to expose himself to an adult woman. Over time, the therapy helped reduce his symptoms, and he was once again able to function sexually with his wife.

The process of psychotherapy

We therapists have a process called "play therapy" to help very little children who have been abused. The child goes with the therapist into a room with some toys, and he takes two dolls and has them sexually abuse each other. Then the therapist can intervene right away. "Okay, is this what happened to you? This is the way mommy put her mouth on your penis?" The child is reenacting what happened to him through the doll play.

When an adult client takes part in a kinky sexual scene based on the same childhood trauma, he is reenacting with humans instead of dolls what happened to him as a child. So, his "play therapy" is finding women to do this to him. If a therapist were actually in the room, she'd be watching and could intervene just as therapists do for children. "See what this woman's about to do to you? That's exactly what your mother did." As therapists, we are not actually present when the client is sexually acting out, but the client tells us about it, so then we make that connection for him in our office. The client might be "acting out" with porn, but when he tells us that, we can use it in the therapy in the same way.

For example, a number of my clients have paid women to abuse them. (Sometimes, the clients just use porn and masturbation.) In any case, when a client tells me he's troubled by his sexual thoughts or behaviors, I say, "Let's talk about why you're troubled. Does it feel obligatory, compulsive? Does it feel like you want to get rid of these feelings? Do you feel ashamed of them?"

A client may tell me he asks women to slap him around and humiliate him. There are several possible ways to understand this: First, it was cathartic. He might have been abused as a child and the sexual acting out was a way of expressing the residual bad feelings in a controlled way. Second, he might act out but feel really bad about it because it's evoking bad feelings, but it's not cathartic. And, third, he could feel bad about it because it just seems wrong to him.

After the client tells me what he's doing and how he feels about it, I will do a family history. I ask about abuse and humiliation from his childhood and especially about sexual abuse, both covert and overt. Sometimes, I discover that his kinky behavior now imitates what happened to him in childhood.

Whether the current behavior reflects the past or not, when I discover the past contains significant trauma, I induce the client to do standard therapy "trauma work." I ask the client to talk about what it felt like for him as a 5-year-old or a 10-year-old. I want him to talk about it, feel it. I help him connect himself to that little boy who was abused.

In eroticizing the abuse and acting it out sexually, the client achieves a certain level of mastery and relief, but usually the relief is temporary, leading to the need to repeat the acting out, which creates a cycle of compulsive sexual behavior. Therapy allows the client to revisit the past in a nonsexual way. In particular, by giving up the sexual anesthesia, he can discover what happened and feel the bad feelings from the past, how it felt when he was little to be treated the way he was. This can lead to real healing and long-term mastery of the sexual behavior. It can become less compulsive.

We start the therapy to reduce the force of the client's compulsions by offering him a way to more directly tell in a therapeutic setting the painful story of his CSA. Therapy is a complicated process. The client's journey begins with identifying and talking about his CSA; it continues by doing various therapies to heal the old damage, which doesn't just disappear as soon as it is acknowledged. But as the force of the compulsions diminishes, the client regains control over when and how to express his sexuality.

The client still might choose to play with the erotic scenes embedded in him by his abuse, but now his behavior is no longer obligatory and compulsive. Or, the eroticism of the abuse may completely vanish and no longer be exciting to reenact. We never know until we do the healing work. There is no formula for whether someone will or won't continue to have sexual fantasies and desires about what occurred during their abuse.

Final thoughts about CSA and sexual behaviors

For men, a very common result of CSA in early childhood is some version of out-of-control sexual behavior. A man will come into my office unhappy about his excessive or unsafe sexual behaviors, and we are often led back through his history to early CSA. (The man might also be brought into my office by his unhappy wife or sent to me by an unhappy judge. OCSB often gets men into trouble with their partners or the law.)

According to Aaron (2012), sexual dysfunction is less common in men (but common in women) as a result of CSA. Some data supports the hypothesis that sexual abuse in later childhood or adolescence is more likely to lead to sexual dysfunction in men than early CSA. The data (and my clinical experience) seems to be too incomplete to convincingly support this conclusion. As with all matters of psychological cause and effect, it is difficult to isolate causes from effects without carefully controlled experiments that often are too expensive (or unethical) to conduct.

I can say from my practice, however, that I often see confusion about sexual orientation in clients to who turn out to have significant CSA. However, first let me be clear: bisexual orientation and sexually fluid orientations exist independent of CSA, as of course do gay and straight orientations. While it is true that CSA may cause a straight man to appear to be acting bisexual, bisexuality exists independent of any psychopathology.

The "disorientation" caused by CSA clouds all forms of true orientation. As only one example among several, a straight man may appear to be bisexual because he is sexually attracted to women but has sex with men, when a closer look reveals that his attraction to women is a result of his "true" sexual orientation while his draw to sex with men is trauma reenactment.

At one time "experts" insisted that a man who has sex with men must be gay. Now that bisexuality is more acknowledged, men who have sexual connections to both men and women are often assumed to be bisexual. Of course, many men are truly bisexual, but the phenomenon of trauma reenactment must be considered as an alternative, especially when a client comes to a therapist expressing conflicts related to his choice of sexual partners. Going beyond our old practice of assuming a "fixed" sexual orientation, therapists have only recently come to understand that some men seem to have a fundamental "sexual fluidity." They occasionally choose partners different from those expected from any inherent sexual orientation. I discuss this further in my book *Is My Husband Gay, Straight, or Bi?* (Kort with Morgan, 2014).

As we all learn to be more flexible in our understanding of sexual behavior, pragmatic clinicians will focus on behaviors that cause trouble and grief with less concern for categories of orientation or nonstandard sexual practices. The goal for therapy is to reduce compulsivity, enable shame reduction, and help individuals embrace their erotic turn-ons as a positive part of themselves. In other words, victim turns to victor, trauma turns into triumph.

References

Aaron, M. (2012). The pathways of problematic sexual behavior: A literature review of factors affecting adult sexual behavior in survivors of childhood sexual abuse. *Sexual Addiction & Compulsivity: The Journal of Treatment & Prevention, 19*(3), 199–218.

Adams, K., with Morgan, A. (2007). *When he's married to mom: How to help mother-enmeshed men open their hearts to true love and commitment*. New York, NY: Touchstone.

Baldwin, G. (1993). *Ties that bind: The SM/leather/fetish erotic style: Issues, commentaries and advice* (2nd Ed.). Los Angeles, CA: Daedalus.

Beidel, D. C., Frueh, B. C., & Hersen, M. (2014). *Adult psychopathology and diagnosis* (7th Ed.). New York, NY: Wiley.

DSM-5 (2013). *Diagnostic and statistical manual of mental disorders*. Arlington, VA: American Psychiatric Association.

Kort, J., with Morgan, A. (2014). *Is my husband gay, straight, or bi? A guide for women concerned about their men.* Lanham, MD: Rowman & Littlefield.

Ley, David J. (2012). *The myth of sex addiction.* Lanham, MD: Rowman & Littlefield.

Morin, J. (1996). *The erotic mind: Unlocking the inner sources of sexual passion and fulfillment.* New York, NY: Harper Perennial.

Perel, E. (2013). The secret to desire in a long-term relationship. TED talk. Retrieved May 7, 2016 from www.ted.com/talks/esther_perel_the_secret_to_desire_in_a_long_term_relationship/transcript?language=en.

Ward, J. (2015). *Not gay: Sex between straight white men.* New York, NY: New York University Press.

Index